Jules Arthur Harder

The Physiology of Taste

Harder's book of practical American cookery

Jules Arthur Harder

The Physiology of Taste
Harder's book of practical American cookery

ISBN/EAN: 9783744785358

Printed in Europe, USA, Canada, Australia, Japan

Cover: Foto ©Lupo / pixelio.de

More available books at **www.hansebooks.com**

THE PHYSIOLOGY OF TASTE

HARDER'S BOOK

OF

PRACTICAL AMERICAN COOKERY

(IN SIX VOLUMES)

VOLUME I

Treating of American Vegetables, and all Alimentary Plants, Roots and Seeds.

Containing a Description of the Best Varieties, Mode of Cultivation, and the Art of Preparing them for the Table

Designed for the Use of Families, Hotels and Restaurants

By JULES ARTHUR HARDER
Chef de Cuisine, Palace Hotel

SAN FRANCISCO
1885

Dedication.

A friendship of many years' duration, and an appreciation of his kindly and generous disposition, as well as of his cultivated taste, impel me to dedicate

THESE VOLUMES

TO

ALEXANDER DUMAS SHARON, Esquire

Notable among the whole-souled Californians who have kept step with the spirit and progress of the age.

PREFACE.

"What!"—the reader may exclaim—"Another book on cookery! Have we not Carême and Francatelli, Vatel and Soyer, Ude and Gouffé, Miss Acton and Mrs. Beeton, Meg Dodds and Mrs. Hale, and scores of other authorities on the same subject? Must every cook be an author, and we be asked to read his book, as well as to eat of the dishes he prepares?" Gentle reader, it is to anticipate this possible state of mind, and to answer these probable questions, that this explanatory preface is submitted. Many a dish is cooked that is not worth the time and trouble, even by an ordinarily educated palate, given to its discussion, and many a book written—especially on the subject of Cookery—the reading of which is worse than time wasted. There have been innumerable Cook Books for popular use published, I grant you; but if you ask nine out of ten persons who consult them, they will tell you they become more and more perplexed as they attempt to follow their guidance. The housekeeper will confess she has been led into errors by their vague recipes, injurious to the family health, and, at the same time, expensive to the family purse. It is to dissipate this fog enveloping the literature of the kitchen that the publication of the BOOK OF AMERICAN PRACTICAL COOKERY is undertaken. The author claims that the work is the result of a lifetime of study, constant observation, and practical experience in the best culinary establishments of both Continents. He, therefore, brings to his task a thorough knowledge of the subject, and asserts, fearless of successful contradiction, that the result of his labors will be the only competent treatise—applying culinary science especially to the material conditions of this country—ever written. He intends it for a trustworthy guide to all what to eat and drink, and what to avoid.

In pursuance of the plan laid down, he proposes to embrace the whole list of food articles, their selection, treatment, and best method of preparing them for the table, showing how the utmost value can be obtained from every edible designed by the Almighty for the comfort and nourishment of mankind. It is due to the intelligence of the present age that there should no longer be room for the old sneer of the dyspeptic cynic: "God sends the material, but the Devil sends cooks."

To accomplish this important object will require at least six volumes. Marie Antoine Carême, the great French cook, who lived between the years 1784 and 1833, and who was called the "regenerator of cookery," took twelve volumes to give Europe of his day the information which the author of the present series proposes to give America of the present, in six. Each volume of the AMERICAN PRACTICAL COOKERY series will be devoted to a leading food staple. This, the first volume, deals with vegetables and all alimentary plants, roots, and seeds grown on the American continent, with full remarks of the best varieties, their mode of cultivation, cooking, dishing, and other matters of interest connected with this branch of the culinary art—one, by the way, of no small importance, but to which generally scant attention is paid by the household, and even by the club and hotel, cook.

It comes quite in place here to give a few cursory hints on the subject-matter more definitely and precisely stated in the body of this volume. In preparing all alimentary plants for the table, the best, freshest, and those in season, should always be chosen. Stale or decayed vegetables, or those that have been overheated in packing, or bruised in transportation, are unwholesome. Avoid them if you value your health. Preserved vegetables should not be used for the table, if they can be possibly declined. Where their use cannot be avoided, be careful to select those put up at creditable establishments, with the name of the proprietor or company, and the quality of the goods marked plainly on the package. Often flashy and picturesque labels conceal germs of disease, in the shape of imperfectly preserved vegetables, sufficient to cause an epidemic. Vegetables should only be freely eaten in the spring, because most kinds are then seasonable, and consequently wholesome and nutritious. Some of the few fall varieties are improved by light frosts.

Vegetables forced in hot-houses are not as good as those grown in the open air, and subjected to ordinary natural conditions. The variety of climate with which the United States is blessed, promotes the growth of every variety of fruit and vegetable known in the world, and the facilities for transportation put nearly every section of our country on the same footing, so far as the enjoyment at their best of the products of each is concerned.

In cooking vegetables, good pure water is essential. To cook green vegetables properly, they should be put into a vessel while the water is boiling—the pot remaining uncovered. By this means they will retain their natural color. Vegetables can be served with each course, or alone, before or after the roast. It is better that they precede the roast, as the appetite is thereby improved for the course that follows. Too many vegetables should not be served with a dinner. They ought to be selected with care according to the course they accompany. These hints, although general, will serve a good purpose in awakening attention.

In conclusion, the author may, without egotism, again state, that he feels confident in his ability to make this series on AMERICAN PRACTICAL COOKERY a standard work, because he is practically acquainted with the details of every branch on which he writes, and, at the same time, familiar with the broader requirements of the culinary profession. A chief cook, besides being versed in the technique of the kitchen, should also be a good judge of the kinds, qualities and uses of every dietetic article. As the old Greek comic poet Dionysius, says:

> "To roast some beef, to carve with neatness,
> To blow up sauces, and to blow the fire,
> Is anybody's task; he who does this
> Is but a seasoner and a broth-maker.
> A cook is quite another thing. His mind
> Must comprehend all facts and circumstances,
> Where is the place, and what the time of supper,
> Who are the guests, and who the entertainer,
> What fish he ought to buy, and where he ought to buy it," etc.

The author does not expect to realize a fortune by this publication. The work is, in a degree, a labor of love, prompted as much by a desire to benefit the culinary art, as by any other feeling. But though his reward may not reach the munificent one of Antony's cook, who received a city for his skill in arranging a Cleopatra banquet, he feels assured at least of the gratitude of all those who wish to intelligently enjoy the pleasures of the table, and of the hearty appreciation of his fellow-workers in the important field of culinary science.

J. A. H.

NOTE.

☞ The entire work on "AMERICAN PRACTICAL COOKERY," now in course of preparation by Mr. Harder, will consist of six volumes, each devoted to a particular article of food—soups, fish, flesh, fowl, farinacé, sauces, conserves, liqueurs, &c.—and each treated in the same thoroughly exhaustive manner exemplified in this, the first of the series. Prefixed, is a glossary of such technical terms and phrases as occur in the text of this volume, and which the general reader may have need to consult. A copious index will also facilitate reference to the different details of the subjects treated. Due notice will be given of the appearance of Volume II of the series.

INDEX TO ARTICLES.

ENGLISH.

	PAGE		PAGE
Alecost	134	Burnet	59
Alexanders	1	Cabbage	60
Alkekengi	345	Calabash	75
Allspice	5	Calamint	75
Ambrosia	1	Cantaloupe	75
Angelica	2	Capers	78
Anise	3	Capillary	78
Aromatic Herbs	4	Caraway	79
Aromatic Nigelle	5	Cardoon	79
Arrow-Root Plant	193	Carrot	83
Artichoke	6	Caterpillar	89
Asparagus	18	Catnip	89
Asparagus Bean	26	Catsup	89
Balm	26	Cauliflower	90
Balm-mint	27	Celeriac	94
Barley	27	Celery	97
Basil, Sweet	29	Centaury	105
Bay Leaves (Common)	30	Cepes	208
Bay Leaves (Larustine)	30	Chamomile	105
Beans	30	Chervil	106
Beets	47	Chestnut	106
Bene	51	Chick Pea	108
Black Salsify	321	Chickling Wetch	109
Boletus (Esculent)	52	Chicoree	157
Borage	53	Chiccory	109
Borecole	176	Chinese Spinach	109
Briar Leaves	53	Chinese Yam, or Potato	110
Brocoli	53	Chives	110
Brookline	55	Chives (Common)	111
Brussels Sprouts	55	Chufa	111
Buck's-horn	57	Cicely, Sweet	112
Buckwheat	57	Cinnamon	112
Bugloss	59	Clary	112

	PAGE		PAGE
Clavaria	113	Gherkin	167
Cloves	113	Ginger	167
Cocks-head, Plantain	57	Globe Cucumber	168
Cocoa	113	Goose-foot	168
Coffee	116	Graham Flour	169
Colt's-foot (Common)	119	Green Peppers	253
Common Gourds	75	Gumbo	223
Coquelicot	120	Herbs	169
Coriander	120	Hoarhound	173
Corn	122	Hollyhock	171
Corn Poppy	120	Hoosung	171
Corn Salad	121	Hops	171
Cos Lettuce	133	Horse-Radish	173
Costmary	134	Hyssop	175
Couch Grass	133	Indian Star Anise-seed	175
Cranberry	134	Iris Root	239
Cress (Garden)	136	Japan Pea	175
Cress (Pepper)	135	Jasmine	176
Cress, (Water)	136	Jerusalem Artichokes	17
Cuckoo-flower Cress	145	Juniper	176
Cucumber	137	Kale	176
Cumin	145	Kohl-Rabi	380
Curcuma	373	Lamb Lettuce	121
Curry	145	Laurel Leaves (Common)	30
Dandelion	146	Laurel Leaves (Larustine)	30
Diet Drinks	147	Lavender	178
Dill	147	Leek	178
Earth Nut	111	Lens	180
Egg Plant	151	Lentil	180
Egyptian Cucumber	156	Lettuce	182
Egyptian Pea	108	Licorice	189
Elderberries	156	Lima Beans	189
Elecampane	157	Lime Tree	191
Endive	157	Linden Tree	191
Eschalot	326	Lovage	191
Essences	165	Lupine	191
Extracts	165	Mace	192
Farina	160	Madras Radish	192
Fecula	163	Mallow (Curled leaved)	193
Fennel (Sweet)	164	Manioca	351
Flavors	165	Maranta	193
Flour	165	Marjoram	194
Garbure	166	Marsh Mallow	195
Garlic	166	Medical Herbs	4

INDEX TO ARTICLES.

	PAGE		PAGE
Mellilot	196	Pumpkin	281
Mint	196	Purslain	283
Morel	197	Radish	283
Mountain Spinach	237	Rampion	288
Mullein	199	Rampion or Primrose	289
Mullen	199	Rape	289
Mushrooms	199	Red Cabbage	290
Muskmelon	211	Rhubarb	290
Mustard	215	Rice	293
Nasturtium	217	Rocambole	308
Nettle	218	Rocket	308
New Zealand Spinach	219	Romaine	133
Nutmeg,	219	Rose Mallow	171
Oak (common wall Germander)	220	Rosemary	309
Oats	221	Rue	310
Okra	223	Russian Turnip	310
Onions	225	Ruta Baga	310
Oosung	171	Rye	311
Orach	237	Saffron	312
Orris	239	Sage	313
Oxalis	239	Sago	314
Oyster Plant	316	Salad Garnitures	316
Pak-choi	240	Salep	318
Palmate leaved Rhubarb	240	Salsify	316
Palm Cabbage	240	Salt	319
Parsley	241	Saltpeter	319
Parsnips	242	Samphire	319
Patience	244	Savory	320
Peanuts	245	Savoy Cabbage	321
Peas	246	Scorzonara	321
Pennyroyal	253	Scurvy Grass	322
Pepper	253	Sea Beet	322
Pepper Grass	135	Sea Fennel	319
Peppermint	258	Sea Kale	323
Persian Melons	75	Sea Kale Beet	350
Pickles	259	Semoule	324
Picridium	260	Shallot	326
Pigeon Berry	260	Shepherd's Purse	327
Pi-Tsai	259	Sieva	328
Poke	260	Skirret	328
Poppy	261	Small Lima Bean	328
Portugal Cabbage	261	Snake Cucumber	329
Potatoes	262	Sorrel	329
Pot Herbs	4	Southernwood	332

	PAGE		PAGE
Spanish Lentil	109	Tonka Bean	368
Spanish Oyster Plant	333	Truffles	368
Spearmint	333	Tuberous Rooted Chickling	
Speedwell	55	Wetch, or Pea	372
Spices	334	Tuberous Rooted Wood Sorrel	239
Spinach	336	Turmeric	373
Spinach (Chinese)	109	Turnip	373
Spinnage	336	Turnip Cabbage	380
Squash	339	Turnip Rooted Celery	94
Strawberry Tomato	345	Turnip Rooted Chervil	382
Succory	109	Unicorn Root	382
Swedish Turnip	310	Valerian	383
Sweet Cicely	112	Vanilla	383
Sweet Fennel	164	Vegetables,	384
Sweet Potatoes	346	Venus Hair	78
Sweet Scented Chervil	112	Vetch	401
Swiss Chard	350	Water Cress	136
Tansy	350	Watermelon	401
Tapioca	351	Welsh Onion	110
Tare	401	Wheat	404
Tarragon	352	White Quinoa	168
Tea	352	Winged Pea	407
Thyme	355	Wit Loef	407
Tisanes	147	Wood Sorrel	407
Tomato	355	Wormwood	408

FRENCH.

	PAGE		PAGE
Absinthe	408	Armoise	408
Achars	167	Arroche	237
Ail	166	Arrowroot	193
Alisandre	1	Artichaut	6
Amarante	109	Asperge	18
Ambrosie	1	Aubergine	151
Aneth	147	Aunée	157
Angelique	2	Aurone Citronnelle	332
Angelique a feuille d'ache	191	Avoine (Farine 'd)	221
Anis	3	Badiane	175
Anis Etoilé	175	Basilic	29
Anserine	168	Baume	26
Arachis	245	Ben	51

	PAGE		PAGE
Berle Chervi	328	Choux Pi Tsai	259
Bette	322	Choux Pommé	60
Betterave	47	Choux Portugais	261
Blé noir	57	Choux Rouge	290
Bouillon Blanc	199	Choux Vert	176
Bourrache	53	Ciboulette	111
Buglose	59	Citrouille	75
Café	116	Citrouille	281
Calament	75	Cive	110
Calamus	75	Civette	110
Camomille	105	Cochlearia	322
Canneberge	134	Cocoa ou Coco	113
Cannelle	112	Colza	289
Cantaloup	75	Concombre	137
Capillaire	78	Concombre des Prophêtes	168
Câpre	78	Concombre Egyptien	156
Capselle	327	Concombre Serpentine	329
Capucine	217	Coquelicot	120
Carde Poirée	350	Coriandre	120
Cardon	79	Corn de serf	57
Carrotte	83	Cornichon	167
Carvi	79	Cornichon	259
Catsup	89	Courge	339
Celeri	97	Crambe Maritime	323
Celeri Rave	94	Cresson	135
Centaurée	105	Cresson Alenois de Jardin	136
Cépes	52	Cresson de Fontaine	136
Cerfeuil	106	Cresson élégant des prés	145
Cerfeuil Odorant	112	Cressonnée Veronique	55
Cerfeuil enraciné	382	Crête Marine	319
Champignon	199	Cumin	145
Champignon (Clavaria)	113	Curcuma	373
Chataigne	106	Echalote	326
Chiche	108	Épice	334
Chiccorée	109	Epinard	336
Chicorée	157	Epinard belle dame	219
Chiendent	133	Essence	165
Choufleur	90	Estragon	352
Chou Rave	380	Farina	160
Chou Savoy	321	Farine	165
Choux Brocoli	53	Farine Graham	169
Choux de Bruxelles	55	Fécule	163
Choux Marins	323	Fenouil	164
Choux Palmiste	240	Feuille de Ronce	53

Féve.................... 189	Menthe Poivré............. 258
Féve (Petite)............. 328	Menthe Verte............. 333
Fleur de Lis............. 239	Moléne................. 199
Fourniture de Salade....... 316	Morille................. 197
Froment................. 404	Mousseron............... 199
Garbure................. 166	Moutarde............... 215
Genièvre................ 176	Muscade (noix de)......... 219
Gerofle (clou de)........... 113	Navet.................. 373
Gesse.................. 109	Navet Rave............. 310
Gesse.................. 372	Nepeta................. 89
Gingembre.............. 167	Oignon................ 225
Glan de terre............ 111	Oosung................ 171
Gourge................. 339	Orge.................. 27
Graine de Surreau......... 156	Ortie.................. 218
Guimauve............... 195	Oseille................. 329
Gumbo................. 223	Oseille Oxalide........... 407
Haricot................. 30	Oxalis................. 239
Haricot Asperge.......... 26	Pak-choi............... 240
Herbe.................. 169	Panais................. 242
Houplon................ 171	Patate................. 346
Hysope................. 175	Patience............... 244
Igname................. 110	Pavot.................. 261
Iris.................... 239	Persil.................. 241
Jasmin................. 176	Petits Chéne............ 220
Kari................... 145	Picridium............... 260
Laitue.................. 182	Piment................. 5
Laurier Amande.......... 30	Piment Vert............. 253
Laurier Franc ou d'Appolon.. 30	Pimprenelle............. 59
Lavande................ 178	Pisse en lit.............. 146
Legume Variée........... 384	Plantain................ 57
Lentilles............... 180	Plante et Herbes, Aromatic
Lupin.................. 191	et Médicinal.......... 4
Mâche................. 121	Poireau................ 178
Macis.................. 192	Pois................... 246
Maïs................... 122	Pois Japonais............ 175
Manioc................. 351	Pois Ramé.............. 407
Marjolaine.............. 194	Poivre................. 253
Marrube................ 173	Pomme de terre.......... 262
Mauve................. 193	Potiron................ 75
Mélilot................. 196	Potiron gourge........... 281
Mélisse................. 27	Pouliot................ 253
Melon d'eau............. 401	Pourpier............... 283
Melon Muscat............ 211	Primevére.............. 289
Menthe................. 196	Quatre Épice............ 5

	PAGE		PAGE
Radis	283	Sclarée	112
Radis Madras	192	Scorpiure	89
Raifort	173	Scorsonóre	321
Raiponce	288	Seigle	311
Réglisse	189	Sel	319
Rhubarbe	290	Semoule	324
Rhubarbe des Moines	240	Sieve (Petite Fóve)	328
Riz	293	Tanaisie	350
Rocambole	308	Tanaisie Barbotine	134
Romaine	133	Tapioca	351
Romaine Blanche	407	Thé	352
Romarin	309	Thym	355
Roquette	308	Tilleul	191
Rose Trémiere	171	Tisane	147
Rue	310	Tomate	355
Sachet	260	Tomate (fraize)	345
Saffran	312	Tonka (Féve de)	368
Sagou	314	Topinambour	17
Salep ou Saloop	318	Truffe	368
Salpêtre	319	Turmeric	373
Salsifis	316	Tussilage	119
Salsifis	333	Unicorn	382
Sarrasin	57	Valeriane	383
Sarriette	320	Vanille	383
Sauge	313	Vesce	401
Scarole	157		

GERMAN.

	PAGE		PAGE
Adsung	171	Baldrian	383
Alant	157	Bärenzuker	189
Alantwurzel	157	Basilikum	29
Amaranth	109	Bataten	346
Ambrosia	1	Baumgamander	220
Andorn	173	Bene	51
Angelika	2	Bind Salat	133
Anis	3	Blätter Kohl	176
Aromatishe und Medizinishe, Gräuter	4	Blaukraut	290
		Blumen Kohl	90
Arrowmehl	193	Bohne	30
Artishoke	6	Bohne (Lima)	189

	PAGE		PAGE
Bohne (Sieva)	328	Gemüse	384
Boretsch	53	Gerste	27
Brier blätter	53	Gesse	109
Brocoli	53	Gurke	137
Brunnen Kresse	136	Hafermehl	221
Buchweitzen	57	Haferwurz	333
Camomile	105	Haferwurz	316
Catchup	89	Haferwurzel	321
Cepes	52	Hohllauch	110
Cepes	208	Holunderbeere	156
Champignon	199	Hopfen	171
Champignon (Clavaria)	113	Huflattish	119
Chich	108	Indishe Kresse	217
Chineschen Kohl	259	Ingwer	167
Cichorie	157	Iris	239
Cigorien	109	Isop	175
Cocoa	113	Japan Erbse	175
Curcumei	373	Kaffee	116
Diätetishe Getränke	147	Kalaminth	75
Dill	147	Kapor	78
Dragun	352	Kardon	79
Egyptishe Gurke	156	Kari	145
Eierpflanze	151	Kartoffeln	262
Einhornwurzel	382	Kastanie	106
Endive	157	Katzenkraut	89
Erbsen	246	Kleberkraut	168
Erdartishoke	17	Knoblauch	166
Erdnus	111	Knol Selleri	94
Erdnus	245	Knotig Gartenkerbel	382
Ertshwamm	199	Knotig Gesse	372
Essiggurke	167	Kohlrübe	380
Essiggurken	259	Kopfkohl	60
Extrakt	165	Koriander	120
Farina	160	Korn	122
Fecula	163	Korn	311
Fenchel	164	Korn	404
Forellen Salat	133	Kornrose	120
Frauenhaar Syrup	78	Kräuter	169
Frauenmünze	134	Kresse	136
Frauenmünze	333	Kuckuk's Blume	145
Garbür	166	Kugulgurke	168
Gartenampfer	244	Kümmel	79
Gartenkerbel	106	Kümmel	145
Gartenmünze	196	Kürbis	75

	PAGE		PAGE
Kürbis	281	Palm Kohl	240
Kürbis	339	Paradiesfeige	57
Lämmersalat	121	Pastinake	242
Lattichsalat	182	Petersilie	241
Lauch	178	Pfeffer	253
Lavendel	178	Pfeffergurke	167
Liebesapfel	355	Pfeffermünze	258
Liebesapfel (erdbeere)	345	Picridium	260
Liebstöckel	191	Pillenfarn	135
Linde	191	Piment	5
Linse	180	Pimpinelle	59
Löffelkraut	322	Poke	260
Lorbeerblatt (common)	30	Polei	253
Lorbeerblatt (Larustino)	30	Portulak	283
Löwenzahn	146	Portugal Kohl	261
Mailander Kohl	321	Queckengrass	133
Mïas	122	Rapunzel	288
Malve	193	Raupenpflanzen	89
Mangold	322	Raute	310
Marjoram	194	Reis	293
Meerettig	173	Rettig	283
Meerfenchel	319	Rettig (Madras)	192
Meer Kohl	323	Rhabarber	240
Mehl	165	Rhabarber	290
Mehl Graham	169	Rocambole	308
Melisse	26	Roggen	311
Melisse	27	Rosenpappel	171
Mellilot	196	Rosmarin	309
Melone	75	Roth Kohl	290
Melone (Muskat)	211	Rübe	373
Möehre	83	Rübesamen	289
Mohnsamen	261	Runkel Rube	47
Moosbeere	134	Saffran	312
Morchel	197	Sago	314
Morcheln (Cepes)	52	Salbei	313
Muskatenblüthe	192	Salat Kräuter	316
Muskatennus	219	Salep	318
Nelken	113	Saltpeter	319
Nessel	218	Salz	319
Ochsenzunge	59	Sammetpappel	195
Ocher	223	Saturei	320
Orrach	237	Sauerampfer	329
Oxalis	239	Savoyer Kohl	321
Pak-choi	240	Seekohl	323

INDEX TO ARTICLES.

	PAGE		PAGE
Selleri	97	Tausendgüldenkraut	105
Semoule	324	Thee	352
Senf	215	Thymian	355
Scharlei	112	Tonkabohne	368
Schlangengurke	329	Trüffel	368
Schlüsselblume	289	Vanille	383
Schnittlauch	111	Vermouth	408
Shallotte	326	Wachholderbeere	176
Smyrnenkraut	1	Wassermelone	401
Sourklee	407	Weiserendivien	407
Spanish Kerbel	112	Weitzen	404
Spargel	18	Wicke	401
Spargel Bohne	26	Wilde Krausemünze	55
Spargel Erbse	407	Winterkresse	308
Spargel Kohl	53	Wolfsbohne	191
Spinat	336	Wollkraut	199
Spinat (Belle dame)	219	Wurmkraut	350
Sprossen Kohl	55	Würze	334
Stabwurz	332	Yamwurzel	110
Steckrübe	310	Yasmin	176
Sternanis	175	Younge mangoldpflanze	350
Süshols	189	Zimmet	112
Tapioca	351	Zuckerwurzel	328
Täschelkraut	327	Zwiebeln	225

GLOSSARY

—OF—

WORDS AND TERMS USED IN THIS BOOK.

Allemande.—Allemande sauce is not of German origin, as the name would imply, but is the mother and stock of the white French sauces. It is made with veal and chicken broth, and is then called Veloutée. After this the yolks of eggs, lemon juice, and essence of mushrooms are added. It is fully described in the "Book on Sauces." When this sauce can not be made conveniently a substitute can be made by thickening a veal or chicken broth, the same as for butter sauce, letting it boil for fifteen minutes. Put the yolks of four raw eggs in a saucepan with four spoonfuls of cream, and mix in slowly one quart of the thickened veal or chicken sauce. Add the juice of one lemon, season with salt, pepper, and nutmeg, and set it on the fire. Stir it continually until it boils, then strain it through a sauce towel. Put it in a saucepan and place small pieces of butter on top to prevent a crust from forming.

Annual.—Annual plants are those that must be sown every year.

Aroma.—The quality or principle of plants or seeds that constitutes their fragrance. An agreeable odor.

Aromatic.—A plant characterized by a pleasant smell, and usually by a warm, pungent taste.

Bain-marie.—Literally a hot water bath. A Bain-marie is a square pan in which hot water is kept, and is used to keep saucepans in that contain sauces or stews, that are to be kept warm before serving. The water must be kept almost at the boiling heat, but never allowed to boil. The name Bain-marie is also applied to the high saucepans that are made expressly to sit in the above mentioned Bain-marie pans.

Biennial.—Biennial plants are those that last for two years and then perish.

Blanch.—To whiten the stalks or leaves of a plant by earthing them up or tying them together to exclude the light.

Braise.—To cook or stew in a close-covered saucepan or other vessel on a slow fire. Formerly hot coals were put on the cover to keep the heat even, but an oven is much better and warms the vessel thoroughly.

Brisk Fire.—One burning with a quick, free action.

Butter.—When the expression "add a piece of butter" is used, it depends on the quantity of vegetables cooked. For four persons, add a piece as large as a walnut. For soups, add from four to six ounces. When it is added, toss the vegetables well over until the butter is melted. In soups, keep stirring until the butter is melted. In this way it thoroughly permeates the article being cooked, and gives it a glossy, velvety appearance. If it is not stirred, it will remain on the top and impart a greasy appearance to the food.

Calyx.—The outer covering of a flower.

Capsule.—The seed vessel of a plant.

Catechu.—A dry, brown, astringent extract, obtained by decoction and evaporation from the *Acacia Catechu*, in India. It contains a portion of tannin or tannic acid.

Cellulose.—The substance left after the action of solvents on vegetable tissues. It is convertible into starch and sugar.

Chopped.—The term "chopped" parsley or onions is used often. Before being chopped, parsley must be washed, then dried in a towel; the large stems must be removed, and then the leaves are chopped. Then put it in a towel and wring out the moisture; after this dip it in boiling water for a minute, then immerse it in cold water and squeeze it dry. By doing this it will retain its green color in cooking. Onions should not be chopped or they will turn black; they should be cut finely. Parboiled vegetables, such as spinach or cabbage, should be drained first and then dried before being chopped on a board. Garlic has a stronger flavor when mashed than when chopped.

Clarify.—To make clear. Applied principally to butter, which should be melted over a slow fire and then strained through a napkin.

Coagulate.—To curdle or thicken; to change from a liquid to a solid mass.

Colander.—A vessel with the bottom perforated with little holes for straining.

Comfrey.—A genus of plants that abound in mucilage. An emollient drink is made from the roots.

Conical.—Fruit, roots or nuts that have the form of a cone; round and decreasing to a point.

Corsican Sea Moss.—A marine plant which, when boiled in water, is used in diet drinks and apozems.

Cutters.—There are several kinds of cutters for cutting vegetables for garnitures. They are made of tin in various shapes—round, oval, square, etc. A vegetable spoon-cutter is a sort of a knife shaped like a spoon, and of numerous different sizes.

Crow-foot.—A pasture-plant that resembles the common buttercup in its flowers, and has acrid properties. If swallowed in its fresh state it produces heat and pain in the stomach. It is used in diet drinks and apozems.

Decoction.—The strength of leaves, seeds or other matter, extracted by boiling.

Dilute.—To dissolve, such as the yolks of eggs diluted in milk. When they are mixed they should always be strained. Eggs and milk are put in purees for the purpose of thickening them.

Drills.—A light furrow or channel made in the ground to put seed into in sowing.

Esculent.—Any plant that is fit for food, though sometimes used as a general name for edible roots.

Espagnole Sauce.—This is the stock sauce of almost all of the brown sauces. It is made of good stock broth, thickened with cooked flour, and then flavored. It is fully described in the "Book on Sauces." When this sauce cannot be made conveniently, an ordinary brown sauce can be substituted, which is made as follows: Make an ordinary stock broth; then thicken, and flavor it lightly with ham, vegetables and Madeira wine. When done it must be free from grease.

Expression.—The act of pressing or squeezing out.

Faggot.—A term applied to a bunch of vegetables and herbs that are tied together with a string, so it can be removed conveniently when the article is cooked. It is used in soups, sauces, and stews. See No. 1039.

Farina.—Fine dust or powder contained in the anthers of plants.

Farinaceous.—Consisting or made of meal or flour.

Fecula.—The nutritious part of wheat, starch or farina.

Fermentation.—That change of organic substances by which their starch or sugar, under the influence of water, air and warmth are decomposed and their elements are re-combined in new compounds.

Flat Saucepan.—A flat saucepan has a two-inch border, but they come in various sizes. They are used to reduce sauces. Small ones that have the bottom slightly curved are used for tossing.

Fungi.—A natural order of plants, such as mushrooms. Also applied to excrescences on plants.

Fusiform.—Shaped like a spindle.

Garniture.—A decoration placed around or on joints, entreés, etc. They are used hot or cold. Vegetables are sometimes compounded in purees, which are also used as a garniture.

Gentian Root.—The root of the Gentian plant having a yellowish-brown color, and a very bitter taste. It is used in diet drinks and apozems.

Germ.—The ovary or seed-bud of a plant.

Glaze.—To glaze is to baste with a gravy while cooking; to nourish the article being cooked. It also gives it a nice color. The term glaze is also applied to a broth that is reduced as low as possible without being scorched. Cakes are glazed with fine sugar, diluted with wines. Some baked vegetables are glazed with the yolks of eggs, diluted in milk or water.

Glume.—The outer covering of corn, husks, or chaff.

Gluten.—A tough, elastic, gray substance, found in the flour of grain.

Hot Water Bath.—See Bain-marie in Index.

Hybrid.—A plant produced from the mixture of two species.

Iceland Moss.—A kind of lichen found in Europe, having a slightly bitter taste, and being tonic and nutritive in its properties. It is used in diet drinks and apozems.

Immerse.—The expression " immerse in cold water " is applied to vegetables that have been parboiled. The green vegetables are immersed so they will retain their green color, while others are immersed to remove their acidity and crude taste.

Jardiniere.—A well known term for a mixture of vegetables used as a garniture.

Lichen.—One of the order of cellular, flowerless plants that derive their nourishment from the air. They are usually of a greenish or yellowish color, and are used in diet drinks and apozems.

Lupulin.—The fine yellow powder of hops.

Macedoine.—A mixture of vegetables, and is also applied to fruits and jellies.

Macerate.—To steep.

Marsh-Trefoil.—A plant growing in marshy places, having bitter leaves, which are used in diet drinks and apozems.

Menyanthes.—Same as Marsh-Trefoil.

Moisten.—To add a little liquid to prevent scorching or burning.

Mulligatawny.—A combination of East India spices that comes in the form of paste, and is used in soups and preparations of rice.

Orange Blossoms or Leaves.—The petals of the leaves are separated and dried. The leaves are dried in the shade, and kept in boxes in a dry place. They are both used in diet drinks or apozems.

Ovate.—Oval or egg-shaped.

Palmate.—Referring to leaves, and meaning those that spread from the apex of a petiole, so as to represent the hand with outstretched fingers.

Panicle.—A form of inflorescence, in which the cluster is much and irregularly branched.

Parboil.—To cook anything partially by boiling. To boil moderately. It is done to remove the acidity or tartness from vegetables or meats.

Pedicle.—The stem that supports one flower only.

Peduncle.—The stalk that supports the flower or fruit of a plant.

Perennial.—A plant which lives more than two years, whether it retains its leaves or not.

Petal.—The leaf of a flower.

Petiole.—The foot-stalk of a leaf that connects the blade with the stem.

Pinch.—A pinch of sugar or salt is the amount you can hold between three fingers. A small pinch is what the end of the blade of a knife will hold. A pinch of spice is the amount you can hold between the thumb and first finger; but care must always be taken with spice.

Pistil.—An organ of female flowers which adheres to the fruit and encloses the seed.

Pomegranate.—A tropical tree, the roots of which are prepared and used in diet drinks and apozems.

Puree.—A pure liquid soup containing no solid parts. A puree of vegetables is made as follows: Cook the vegetables desired; then drain off all of the moisture and rub the pulp through a fine sieve. Finish as directed in recipes. When used as a garniture they are kept firmer than when used for a sauce. Soup-purees are thickened soups diluted with broth to their proper consistency.

Purge.—To put vegetables in cold water for a certain time to extract their tartness or acidity.

Reduce.—To diminish the amount of water, broth, or moisture of any kind, in a saucepan or other vessel, over a fire. The moisture is reduced by evaporation. When reducing a sauce or puree, stir it continually until it is reduced, or it will lose its glossy appearance and flavor.

Refresh.—Vegetables are said to be refreshed when they are immersed in cold water after being parboiled. This is done to green vegetables to make them retain their color.

Reniform.—Having the shape of a section of a kidney; being broader than long, and more or less rounded.

Rugose.—Pertaining to leaves that have the veins more contracted than the disk, so that the surface rises into little inequalities.

Saline.—Consisting or partaking of the qualities of salt.

Scape.—The flowering stem of a plant.

Scion.—A young shoot, twig, or the sprout of a tree.

Seedling.—A young plant or root just sprung from the seed.

Sessile.—Applied to a leaf growing on a stem without having any foot-stalk.

Setiform.—Having the shape of a bristle.

Sheath.—A rudimentary leaf of a plant which wraps itself around the stem.

Sieve.—A utensil for separating the fine part of any pulverized or fine substance from the coarse, consisting of a vessel, usually shallow, with the bottom perforated, or made of hair or wire woven in meshes. Brass sieves should never be used for culinary purposes. Hair sieves, or those made of copper, tinned inside and outside, are best. Use wooden spoons, or sieve brushes when rubbing anything through a sieve. Purees of vegetables should be rubbed through quickly.

Simmer.—To boil gently, or until the liquid commences to boil, and the scum gathers on top,

Spermatic.—Consisting of seed, or pertaining to the elements of production.

Spike.—A species of inflorescence in which sessile flowers alternate on a common stalk.

Spiracle.—A small aperture in vegetable bodies through which air passes.

Spoonful.—When the term "spoonful" is used, it means the contents of a kitchen spoon, which holds about double the quantity of a tablespoon.

Spore.—The part of flowerless plants which performs the functions of seeds.

Standard.—A shrub or plant which stands singly, without any support.

Stellate.—Arranged in the form of a star around a common centre.

Stirring.—When any preparation containing solid matter is put in a saucepan, it should be stirred until it boils, or it will burn. All farinaceous preparations should be stirred well while cooking until they cook. When butter and flour is put in a saucepan to get browned, stir it constantly until done.

Stool.—The root or stem of a tree or plant cut off near the ground, from which the shoots spring up.

Straining—Is to pass anything through a sieve, colander strainer, or towel, in order to have it clear of impurities.

Sub-sessile.—Having very short foot-stalks.

Sub-soil.—The bed or layer of earth which lies beneath the surface soil.

Succulent.—Juicy, or full of juice.

Sucker.—The shoot of a plant from the roots or lower part of the stem.

Sward.—The grassy surface of land; turf.

Tassels.—The flower ribbons or heads of plants such as corn.

Tepid.— Moderately warm.

Toss.—(Sauté)—Means to cook on a brisk fire, without any moisture other than butter, oil, or lard.

Trench.—A plowed furrow, ditch, or channel.

Triennial.—Plants that last for three years.

Trifoliate.—Having three leaves or leaflets.

Tuberous.—Consisting of or containing a fleshy, roundish stem or root (called a tuber).

Tunicated.—Covered with a tunic or layers.

Valve.—A division of the fruit of a plant.

Vexillum.—The upper single petal of a flower, like that of a pea.

Violet.—The flowers of this well-known plant have an agreeable flavor, and are used in diet drinks and apozems.

White Archangel Nettle.—The flowers of this plant are dried in the sun after being picked on a dry day, and are used in diet drinks and apozems.

Wooden Spoon.—Wooden spoons should always be used in preparing dishes, or in cooking purees of vegetables or cranberries, or when rubbing forced meats through a sieve. In reducing sauces a special kind of wooden spoon is used, which has a long handle, terminating like a paddle, with a flat surface. An iron spoon will scratch the tin in a saucepan, and generally imparts an unpleasant taste to the food.

PRACTICAL AMERICAN COOKERY.

ARTICLE I.

French   **ALEXANDER.**   **German**
Alisandre.   *Smyrnenkraut.*

No. 1.—Is a hardy biennial plant, cultivated for its leaf stalks, which, after being blanched are used as a salad. In habit and foliage it resembles the Celery somewhat. It has a pleasant aromatic taste and odor.

CULTURE.

No. 2.—It is raised from seed annually, in light, deep loam, in drills four feet apart, covering its seeds an inch deep. When three inches high thin to ten inches apart; when well advanced earth up about the stems gradually, same as for Celery, like which they are also gathered for use and preserved during winter.

PERFOLIATE ALEXANDERS.

No. 3.—A variety, originally from Italy, of superior quality It blanches better and is more crisp and tender, and not so harshly flavored. The stems are about three feet high.

ARTICLE II.

AMBROSIA.

Ambrosie.   *Ambrosia.*

No. 4.—Is an herb similar to Basil, and is used with Basil and Balm for the preparation of aromatic vinegar, and also used in faggots of Parsley when used for stewed game and small birds. Cultivation same as Balm, Article XI.

ARTICLE III.

French ANGELICA. **German**
Angelique. *Angelika*

No. 5.—Is is a hardy biennial aromatic plant, and is said to have originated in Syria, where it grows along the banks of rivers near high mountains. It is cultivated in the United States but is of inferior quality. The plant is highly esteemed in its preserved state, and much used by pastry cooks and confectioners. The best Angelica now preserved comes from Niort, where the old formula is adhered to, as when made by the Nuns of the "Visitation of St. Mary," which gave it a world-wide reputation. The tender leaf-stalks and flavoring shoots of the native grown Angelica are used as a basis for sweet-meats, and the seeds for flavoring liquors.

CULTURE.

No. 6.—The plants thrive best in damp localities, but may be grown in well enriched soil. Sow in drills, ten inches apart. Allow the young plants to remain until the following spring, then set them out two feet asunder, in each direction. The stalk, which is a cylindrical, hollow, herbaceous stem, will be fit for use by June of the following year. If the flower stem is removed, as it makes its appearance, the plants will put forth fresh sprouts from the sides of the root, and survive three years, but when allowed to blossom and perfect their seeds the plants soon perish.

ANGELICA SYRUP.

No. 7.—Trim one pound Angelica stems, parboil them for ten minutes, then immerse them in cold water. Peel and dry them on a napkin, cut in small pieces, put in a glass jar with two quarts of Spirits of Wine, at fifty degrees; cover, and let stand for ten days. Then add a half pint of syrup, at thirty degrees. Filter the next day, put it in a bottle and cork well.

PRESERVED OR CANDIED ANGELICA.

No. 8.—Cut the Angelica in stems twelve inches long, then throw them into boiling water, letting them boil twenty minutes, then immerse them into cold water. Peel and dry them on a napkin, and when all are prepared put them into an earthen bowl. Make a syrup with five pounds of sugar to five pounds of water. Pour it over the

Angelica boiling hot, and cover. Next day draw off the syrup, make it boil again, skimming it well, and pour over the Angelica again. Repeat this four times in all, and the fifth time let the syrup cook to a boil, then add the Angelica, letting it cook until it gets firm. Then take out one piece at a time and put them in a warm place to dry.

Article IV.

French ANISE. **German**
Anis. *Anis.*

No. 9.—Is an annual aromatic plant, and is cultivated for its seeds and leaves, which are used for seasoning and flavoring. The seeds have a fragrant odor, a pleasant warm taste, and are used by confectioners and bakers, and also for medicinal purposes—in cases of dyspepsia and colic, and to correct griping when taking unpleasant medicine. The green leaves are used like fennel for seasoning and garnishing salads.

ANISETTE CORDIAL.

No. 10.—A liquor distilled from anise seeds. The most renowned comes from Amsterdam, and is partaken after dinner with black coffee, and is also used for creams, jellies and punches.

PUMPERNICKEL.

No. 11.—A kind of bread made in Germany called pumpernickel, in which anise seeds are mixed, and much relished when eaten with stewed prunes, figs or pears.

CULTURE.

No. 12.—Sow in warm mellow or garden soil early in spring in drills ten inches apart and one inch deep. When the plants are about an inch high, thin to four inches apart and keep the ground between the rows loose and free from weeds. When the seeds are ripened the plants should be pulled up and spread in a sunny place to dry. Then thresh the seeds from the heads, riddle and winnow them and again expose to the sun to evaporate any remaining moisture.

ARTICLE V.

AROMATIC, MEDICINAL AND POT HERBS.

French *Plante Médicinal, Aromatique et herbe.* **German** *Medizinishe Aromatishe, Kräuter.*

No. 13.—Care should be taken to harvest them properly. This should be done on a dry day just before they come into full bloom. Then dry them and pack closely entirely excluded from the air. They are used for culinary and medicinal purposes. For further information see each under its classification.

CULTURE.

No. 14.—Most of the varieties thrive best in rich sandy soil, which should be carefully prepared and well cultivated, as the young plants are for the most part delicate, and are easily choked out by weeds. Sow as early as the ground can be made ready, in drills sixteen inches apart, or they may be planted as a second crop, the seeds sown in beds in April and the plants set out in June.

No. 15.—The following constitutes some of the various varieties of aromatic, medicinal and pot herbs:

Ambrosia,	Coltsfoot (common),
Angelica,	Coriander,
Anise,	Couch grass or Wheat grass,
Balm,	Costmary or Alecost,
Balm Mint,	Cuckooflower Cress,
Basil Sweet,	Cumin,
Ben,	Dill,
Borage,	Elecampane,
Bugloss,	Fennel Sweet,
Burnet,	Fennel Flower (field),
Carraway,	Garlic,
Catnip,	Hop,
Chamomile,	Horehound,
Chervil,	Hyssop,
Chives or Welch Onion,	Lavender,
Chives,	Licorice,
Cicely Sweet,	Lupine,
Clary,	Mandrake or May Apple,

Marjoram Sweet,
Melilot,
Mint,
Palmate Leaved Rhubarb,
Parsley,
Penny Royal,
Peppermint,
Picridium (garden),
Poppy or maw,
Purslain,
Rosemary or Rosemarine,
Rue,
Saffron,
Sage,
Samphire,
Samphire (sea),
Savory,
Scallion,
Southerwood,
Spearmint,
Tansy,
Tarragon,
Thyme,
Wormwood.

Article VI.

ALLSPICE OR AROMATIC NIGELLE.

French
Piment ou Quartre Épices.

German
Piment.

No. 16. Is a hardy annual plant from the East Indies. It is cultivated for its seeds, which are produced in a roundish capsule and are somewhat triangular, wrinkled, of a yellowish color, and have a pungent, aromatic taste. There are species cultivated, the seeds of which are black. The seeds have a warm, aromatic taste, and are used in the kitchen under the name of allspice or the four spices.

CULTURE.

No. 17.—Sow in April, in light, warm soil, in drills fourteen inches apart and half an inch deep. When the plants are two inches high thin them to six inches apart in the rows, keeping the soil loose and watering occasionally, if the weather is dry. When the seed ripens cut off the plants at the roots, and spread them in an airy situation to dry. When dried thresh out, after which spread out the seeds again for a short time to evaporate any remaining moisture, when they will be ready for use.

ARTICLE VII.

French
Artichaut.

ARTICHOKE.

German
Artishoke.

No. 18.—Artichokes were first discovered in Italy, but are now planted in all large gardens in the United States, and are used as a vegetable, and prepared for the table in various ways. There are five kinds of Artichokes, viz: The Violet, the White, the Green, the Red, and the Sweet. They are called the Globe Artichokes, which differ from the Jerusalem Artichoke. The Sweet Artichoke is preferable to all others for its delicious flavor. It grows very small, and its plants are very productive for two years. It is rare yet in this country. The Green, which is the variety in general use, is large and juicy. The Red, which is more delicate than the Green, is picked when young, and is mostly used for eating in the raw state, or in salad. The Violet grows as large as the Green, but is not as profitable in culture. The White is very productive, but very troublesome to raise, and owing to this is very rare in the market.

Artichokes when eaten raw take long to digest, but when cooked are very agreeable. They are cooked in various ways as a vegetable for the table, and are used for garnitures and soups.

CULTURE.

No. 19.—Sow in April in rich soil, and transplant the following spring to permanent beds, in rows or drills, three feet apart and two feet between the plants. The first season will only give a partial crop, but as it is a perennial, after being once planted the beds will remain in bearing for years. They should be protected in winter by a covering of leaves or coarse manure.

GREEN LARGE GLOBE.

No. 20.—Is the best for general culture and use. The edible portion is the undeveloped flower heads, which should be used before they begin to open, and the stalk should then be cut to the ground, for if the flowers expand they weaken the plant. In the large Globe the buds are large—nearly round; scales deep green, shading to purple, very thick and fleshy, the bottom of which is the edible part.

HOW TO PREPARE ARTICHOKES FOR COOKING.

No. 21.—Do not use Artichokes when they have developed. If once open they are not good for cooking. Cut off the stem, trim off the hard leaves around the bottom, and cut off the upper quarter of the Artichoke leaves. Then scoop out the fibrous part in the middle and put them in a pan of cold water acidulated. When thus prepared put them in boiling water, add a little salt and lemon juice, and cook until tender. When done drain them on a napkin.

ARTICHOKES WITH HOLLANDAISE SAUCE.

No. 22.—Prepare one dozen Artichokes as in No. 21. Then put them in boiling water with a little salt and the juice of two lemons, cover the saucepan and let them boil for twenty-five minutes on a brisk fire. When ready to serve drain them on a napkin, upside down, so as to absorb all the moisture from them, then dish them up on a napkin, and serve the Hollandaise Sauce separately.

ARTICHOKES WITH BUTTER SAUCE.

No. 23.—Prepare the Artichokes same as for Hollandaise, and serve the butter sauce separately in a sauce bowl.

ARTICHOKES WITH MAYONNAISE OR VINAIGRETTE.

No. 24.—Prepare same as for Hollandaise, serve Mayonnaise or Vinaigrette sauce separately.

ARTICHOKES, WITH OIL OR POIVRADE SAUCE.
FOR RELISH OR SIDE DISH.

No. 25.—The small tender ones are served raw, after being cleaned of the fibrous parts and dished up on a napkin. The large ones are cut into quarters, trimmed of the hard leaves. Removing all the fibrous parts, keep them in cold water, in which add a little vinegar. Serve them in a relish dish, adding the juice of lemons which will keep the artichokes from turning black. Serve the sauce separately in a sauce bowl.

ARTICHOKES, WITH OIL AND VINEGAR SAUCE.

No. 26.—Take the yolks of two hard boiled eggs, mash them into a fine paste, put them into a bowl with two fine chopped shallots, add in slowly, while stirring with a wooden spoon, three spoonfuls of vinegar. Season with salt and pepper, then add two spoonfuls of sweet oil, mixing it well together and serve with artichokes, raw or plain boiled.

ARTICHOKES—BARIGOULE.

No. 27.—Trim one dozen middle sized artichokes, cut the top leaves off in the middle, trim the bottom round and with a teaspoon scoop out all the fibrous part. Put them in cold water with a little vinegar, and when all cleaned parboil them for a few minutes, then immerse them in cold water. Drain them on a napkin to absorb all the moisture from them. Chop eight shallots very fine and put them in a saucepan with two ounces of scraped fresh fat pork. Fry lightly, then add a quarter of a pound of fine chopped mushrooms, one handful of fresh bread crumbs and a little chopped parsley; season well. Fill the centre of the artichokes with this preparation, cover each with a thin slice of fat pork, place them in a deep flat saucepan lined with a layer of thin sliced fat pork. Moisten with a clear madeira wine sauce (or mirpoix), put on the lid and simmer gently in the oven for three quarters of an hour. When done and ready to serve remove the fat pork, strain the gravy, take off the grease and then add the gravy to a brown Italian sauce and reduce it to its consistency. Put a teaspoonful of sauce in each artichoke and serve the rest separately in a sauce bowl.

ARTICHOKE BARIGOULE—ANOTHER WAY.

No. 28.—Prepare the artichokes same as in No. 27. Chop eight shallots very fine and put them in a saucepan with a piece of butter. Fry them lightly, then add a little garlic, a quarter of a pound of fine chopped mushrooms, one handfull fresh bread crumbs and a little chopped parsley. Season with salt and pepper, and a pinch of nutmeg. Mix all well together, then fill the centre of the artichokes with this preparation. Sprinkle fresh bread crumbs over each of them, arrange them in a deep buttered flat saucepan, put a piece of butter on each artichoke and bake in the oven until nicely browned. Serve with a white Italian sauce reduced with a glass of white wine.

ARTICHOKES, ITALIAN STYLE.

No. 29.—Prepare the artichokes as in No. 31. Then put them in a flat saucepan. Season with salt and pepper and a pinch of sugar. Moisten with a glass of white wine and some white broth.

Then let them cook on a brisk fire, and when done the broth must be reduced to a half glaze. Then add four spoonfuls of white Italian sauce, and serve.

FRIED ARTICHOKES, ITALIAN STYLE.

No. 30.—Prepare the Artichokes as in No. 31. When dried, put them in an earthen bowl and season with salt and pepper, the juice of two lemons and a small wine glassfull of olive oil. Let them macerate for half an hour, then drain them on a strainer, flour them, dip each piece in beaten eggs and fry in clarified butter. Dish them on a napkin, and garnish with fried parsley. Serve with Brown Italian sauce.

ARTICHOKES, LYONNAISE.

No. 31.—Cut one dozen Artichokes in four parts, trim off the hard leaves, cut the others close around the bottom, take off the fibrous part, and put them in cold water with a little vinegar, so as to retain their color. When all prepared, parboil for five minutes, then immerse them in cold water and drain them dry on a napkin. Then put the Artichokes in a flat saucepan, well buttered, season with salt and pepper and a pinch of sugar, put on a brisk fire, turning them over occasionally, and moisten with a half bottle of white wine and the same quantity of good white broth. Cover the saucepan. When cooked, the broth must be three-quarters reduced. Dish the Artichokes on a dish, with their bottoms upwards, strain the gravy, take off the grease, add four spoonsful of Allemande sauce, reduced to its consistency, a piece of butter, a little glaze and the juice of half a lemon, and pour the sauce over the Artichokes.

STUFFED ARTICHOKES, BORDELAISE.

No. 32.—Prepare one dozen Artichokes as in No. 27. Chop one large white onion fine, put in saucepan and fry it lightly in sweet oil. Then add the bottoms of five cooked Artichokes cut in small square pieces, the same quantity of cooked ham, and a quarter of a pound of mushrooms. When the moisture is reduced, drain off the sweet oil and add one handful of fresh bread crumbs, a little chopped parsley, and season with salt and pepper. Mix all well together, adding three spoonfuls of reduced Madeira wine sauce. Fill the centre of the Artichokes with this preparation, and cover each with a fine slice of fat pork. Line a deep, flat saucepan with thin slices of fat pork, two sliced onions, one carrot, and a faggot of parsley garnished. Put the Artichokes in, moisten with a glass of white wine and good stock broth, make it boil, put on the lid and set it in the oven. When cooked take them out, place them on a dish, strain the gravy, take off the grease, reduce it to a half glaze, add the juice of one lemon, a little fine chopped parsley and a piece of butter. Put a teaspoonful of the sauce over each Artichoke, and serve the rest in a sauce bowl, separately.

STUFFED ARTICHOKES, AMERICAN STYLE.

No. 33.—Prepare one dozen Artichokes as in No. 27. Chop one large onion in fine pieces, and put them in a saucepan with a piece of butter. Fry them lightly, then add a quarter of a pound of fine chopped braized veal, same quantity of cooked Artichoke bottoms cut in small square pieces, a handfull of fresh bread crumbs, a little fine chopped parsley and chives. Season with salt and pepper and two spoonfuls of reduced Allemande sauce. Mix all well together and stuff the Artichokes with this preparation. Sprinkle fresh bread crumbs over them. Arrange them on a buttered pan, place a small piece of butter on each, and bake in a hot oven. Serve with, or separately, a reduced Madeira wine sauce, in which add some fine herbs.

ARTICHOKES, TOSSED (SAUTÉ) IN BUTTER.

No. 34.—Cut one dozen Artichokes in quarters, trim off the hard leaves, take off all the fibrous parts, leaving three leaves on each piece, nicely trimmed. Arrange them in a deep flat saucepan, with six ounces of butter, cover the saucepan and let them simmer for twenty-five minutes. When tender dish them up in the form of a circle, then add one large spoonful of fresh bread crumbs to the butter. Fry it lightly, season with salt and pepper, the juice of one lemon, and a little fine chopped parsley. Pour the sauce in the middle and serve hot.

HOW TO PREPARE ARTICHOKE BOTTOMS.

No. 35.—Use medium or large sized Artichokes. They are used for garnitures of meats and soups, and as a vegetable are preferable to the others—as all is edible. In the others the leaves have to be picked, and are very annoying to persons not accustomed to eating Artichokes. Take one dozen even sized Artichokes, cut off the stem and three-quarters of the top, scoop out the fibrous part with a small sharp knife, round the Artichoke even to the fleshy part, and put them in a pan with cold water acidulated. Put in a saucepan a quarter pound of butter, add two spoonfuls of flour, and mix it well. Then add two quarts of boiling water, stirring it well until it boils, not allowing it to get lumpy. Add the juice of four lemons, a little salt, then the Artichokes, and let them cook slowly until tender. When cooked and not ready for use, put them in an earthen bowl with the liquid, and cover with a paper cover. When ready for use take them out one by one and dip them in lukewarm water and prepare them as needed.

STUFFED ARTICHOKE BOTTOMS.

CLARA LOUISE KELLOGG STYLE.

No. 36.—Prepare the Artichoke bottoms as in No. 35. Cut one large white onion in small square pieces, put them in lukewarm water for two minutes, then immerse them in cold water, after which put them in a napkin and dry them well. Then put them in a saucepan with a piece of butter and fry. When nicely browned, season with salt and pepper and a little chopped parsley or chives. Put this preparation on a plate to get cold, then fill the bottom of the Artichokes, sprinkle some fresh bread crumbs and grated Parmesan cheese over them; arrange them on a buttered pan with a few drops of olive oil over each, and put in the oven until lightly browned. Serve with a Soubise sauce.

STUFFED ARTICHOKE BOTTOMS, PIONEER STYLE.

No. 37.—Prepare one dozen Artichokes as in No. 35. Chop one large onion fine and put it in a saucepan. Fry it nice and brown, and season with salt and pepper. Add a quarter of a pound of fine chopped roast veal, two spoonfuls of reduced Allemande sauce, and two spoonfuls of fresh bread crumbs, mix all well together. Take it off the fire, add the yolk of two raw eggs, stuff the Artichoke bottoms, then shake some light colored raspings of bread over them. Arrange on a buttered pan with a piece of butter on each bottom, and bake in oven. Serve with a thickened veal gravy.

STUFFED ARTICHOKE BOTTOMS, ITALIAN STYLE.

No. 38.—Prepare one dozen large Artichokes as in No. 35. Fill them with stuffing of forced meat of chicken or veal, in which add some cooked fine herbs. Sprinkle fresh bread crumbs over each, and a few drops of sweet oil. Arrange them in a pan, on which put some light Espagnole sauce (or gravy), bake them slowly to a nice brown color, and dish them up, adding to the sauce a piece of butter, the juice of one lemon and a little chopped parsley, Put a teaspoonful over each Artichoke bottom, and serve the rest separately.

ARTICHOKE BOTTOMS, FRICASSEE.

No. 39.—Prepare the Artichokes as in No. 35. Then cut them in quarters and put them in a saucepan with a piece of butter. Toss them in the pan over the fire, then add some Allemande sauce, the juice of one lemon, and a little finely chopped parsley.

FRIED ARTICHOKE BOTTOMS, VILLEROI STYLE.

No. 40.—Prepare one dozen Artichokes as in No. 35. When well dried dip them in some cool Villeroi sauce, then place them on a plate and put them in a cool place, so the sauce may get cold and adhere to the bottom. Then roll them lightly in fresh bread crumbs, dip in beaten eggs and bread them again, being careful in the handling of them. Fry in clarified butter or lard to a nice brown color, and dish up in a napkin with fried parsley to garnish.

ARTICHOKE BOTTOMS, SPANISH STYLE.

No. 41.—Prepare one dozen Artichokes as in No. 35. When all are trimmed put them in a deep flat saucepan, lined with thin slices of fat pork. Moisten by covering with veal broth and a wineglassful of white wine and the juice of one lemon. Season with salt and pepper, cover the saucepan and let them cook slowly. When tender take out the Artichoke bottoms, dish them on a plate, strain the gravy, reduce it on a brisk fire, adding two spoonfuls of Espagnole sauce and one of Tomato sauce. When reduced to the proper consistency take it off the fire, add a few drops of lemon juice, a piece of butter, and a little fine chopped parsley, then pour the sauce over the Artichoke bottoms.

ARTICHOKE BOTTOMS, MACEDOINE.

No. 42.—Prepare one dozen Artichokes as in No. 35. Put them in a flat saucepan with a piece of butter, warm them thoroughly, and season with salt and pepper and a pinch of sugar. Prepare separately a small cut Macedoine garniture, with vegetables. Cook and glaze each kind of vegetable separately, then mix them all together, adding two spoonfuls of Allemande sauce. Fill each bottom with the garniture, with a few drops of half glaze over each.

ARTICHOKE BOTTOMS, PROVENÇALE.

No. 43.—Prepare one dozen Artichokes as in No. 35. Parboil them for ten minutes, then immerse them in cold water and dry them on a napkin. Arrange them in a flat saucepan with three spoonfuls of Olive oil, half a dozen cloves of garlic (whole). Season with pepper and salt, and let them simmer until tender, then serve them plain with two lemons cut in halves.

ARTICHOKE BOTTOMS, WITH FINE HERBS.

No. 44.—Prepare one dozen Artichokes as in No. 35. Stuff them with cooked fine herbs, to which add some fresh bread crumbs and chopped fresh mushrooms. Arrange them in a deep flat saucepan, with a small piece of butter in each. Moisten them with a light thickened brown gravy, put in an oven and bake slowly. Baste frequently with the gravy, and when nicely browned dish them up with the gravy.

ARTICHOKE BOTTOMS, STEWED FOR GARNITURE.

No. 45.—Prepare one dozen Artichokes as in No. 35. Cut them in quarters and put in a saucepan with a little reduced Allemande sauce. Season with salt, pepper, a little nutmeg, and a pinch of sugar. Then toss them in the pan gently over the fire, and serve as required.

NOTE.—Very little sauce should be used with vegetable garnitures. All stuffed Artichoke bottoms can be used for garnitures.

ARTICHOKE BOTTOMS, FOR LARGE COLD GARNITURE.

No. 46.—Have some large white Artichoke bottoms cooked as in No. 35. Dry them on a napkin and glaze them with a coating of Aspic jelly. Keep them in a cool place until needed. Fill each with a garniture of small cut vegetables (alternating each vegetable in color), seasoned and glazed with Aspic jelly. Dish them up in a pyramid with finely chopped Aspic jelly around the dish.

ARTICHOKE PUREE, FOR GARNITURE.

No. 47.—Prepare two dozen Artichokes as in No. 35. When cooked drain them and put in a saucepan with a piece of butter. Toss them in the pan over the fire lightly, then add one pint of Cream sauce, or Allemande sauce. Season with salt, pepper, nutmeg, and a pinch of sugar. Rub them through a fine sieve, then put the puree in a flat saucepan, with one wineglassful of double cream, and reduce the puree to its proper consistency. Put it in a Bain-marie saucepan, with a little butter on top to save it from getting a crust. Keep warm in a hot water bath until ready for use, and when ready to serve add a piece of butter, and stir well until the butter is melted.

ARTICHOKE CROQUETTES.

No. 48.—When the Artichoke bottoms are cooked, as in No. 35, drain them dry and cut two dozen in small square pieces. Put in a flat saucepan a piece of butter with four finely chopped shallots. Fry them lightly, then add one pint of cream, or Allemande sauce. Reduce it and add the yolks of six raw eggs. Season with salt and pepper, nutmeg and a little fine chopped parsley. Add the Artichokes and let boil up once or twice. Then mix them gently and put in a place to cool. Then form in any croquette shape desired. Bread in fresh bread crumbs, and dip in beaten eggs and bread again. Fry in hot lard and dish up on a napkin, with fried parsley to garnish.

ARTICHOKE PUREE SOUP.

No. 49.—Peel three dozen large Artichokes as in No. 35. Then cut them in quarters and put in a saucepan with four ounces of butter. Season with salt and pepper and a pinch of sugar. Set them on a slow fire so that they attain a light color, then add some white stock broth to cover them, and a faggot of parsley, garnished with celery, and two onions. Cover the saucepan and cook them until tender. Then add one gallon of thickened chicken or veal broth, and let boil slowly for a half hour. Take out the faggot of parsley and the two onions, skim it and rub it through a fine sieve. Then put back in saucepan to keep warm. Before serving add a piece of butter, stirring it well until melted and serve with it, separately, small fried bread crumbs.

ARTICHOKE CREAM SOUP.

No. 50.—Peel three dozen large Artichokes as in No. 35. Then cut them in quarters and put them in a saucepan, with a quarter of a pound of butter. Toss them in the pan over the fire lightly (not allowing them to get brown). Then cover them with white chicken or veal broth. Add a faggot of parsley well garnished and season with salt, pepper and a little sugar, and let them cook slowly until tender. Take out the faggot of parsley. Add two quarts of cream sauce and pound them through a fine colander and add enough broth so as not to have it too thick, and then strain the whole through a fine sieve. Put back in the saucepan and season to taste, keeping it warm without allowing it to boil. Before serving add four ounces of butter, stirring it well until the butter is melted.

Pour in the soup-tureen the following preparation: The yolks of four raw eggs with a half pint of cream well mixed, and strain through a fine strainer. Then add this in the soup slowly, stirring it well. It is then ready to serve.

PICKLED ARTICHOKES.

No. 51.—Take some fresh picked Artichokes, cut off the stems, trim off the hard leaves, cut off the upper part in the middle, and trim the other leaves close to the bottom. Scoop out all the fibrous part carefully and put the Artichokes in a pan with cold water, in which add a little vinegar. When they are all cleaned parboil for five minutes and then immerse them in cold water. Trim all alike, and rub them with a lemon and arrange in an earthen jar or barrel, the size intended to be filled. When filled, pour over so as to cover them, a brine of water and salt, from sixteen to eighteen degrees (sugar weight.) Twenty-four hours afterwards drain off the water; boil it again, skim and add salt again to bring the brine to its former strength. Then cover the barrel or jar hermetically. When ready to use for cooking, let them soak in luke-warm water from ten to fifteen hours.

HOW TO COOK PICKLED ARTICHOKES.

No. 52.—Put in a saucepan four ounces of butter, and two spoonsful of flour. Mix well together, adding while stirring, one quart of boiling water, letting it boil slowly. Then add the juice of two lemons and the Artichokes (having been prepared as above). Cover the saucepan and let boil slowly and prepare them as needed.

ARTICHOKES PRESERVED WHOLE.

No. 53.—Take freshly picked Artichokes, and see that they are fleshy and sound. Cut off the stem and trim off the hard leaves around the bottom. Cut off the top part in the middle and scoop out the fibrous part carefully. Parboil them for five minutes in water acidulated with a little vinegar, then immerse them in cold water, after which rub the bottom of each with a lemon. Then place them in tin boxes, about five in a box. Cover them with cold boiled water lightly salted. Add the juice of two lemons in each box. Then solder on the cover and boil the boxes in a hot water bath for two hours.

ARTICHOKES PRESERVED IN QUARTERS.

No. 54.—Use middle sized Artichokes. Cut off the stem and trim off all the hard leaves. Cut them in quarters, remove all the fibrous part, round off the bottoms, trim off the edges of the remaining leaves, and parboil them for five minutes. Then immerse in cold water. Rub each piece with a lemon, and cook them in a preparation, same as Artichoke Bottoms, No. 55, and proceed in the same way. Add the juice of two lemons in each quart can, and solder on the cover. Then boil the cans in a hot water bath for one hour.

ARTICHOKE BOTTOMS, PRESERVED IN CANS.

No. 55.—Prepare and clean the Artichokes as in No. 35. When all are cut and free from all fibrous parts, rub them well with a lemon. Parboil them for five minutes, then immerse in cold water. Have ready on the fire a saucepan, in which put a quarter of a pound of melted butter, and the same quantity of flour. Mix them well together, adding two quarts of boiling water, stirring all well until it boils. Then add the juice of three lemons and let boil slowly for twenty minutes, adding the Artichokes. Then cover the saucepan and cook slowly for fifteen minutes. Then take it off of the fire and let it get cold. Take out one Artichoke after another, and dip in lukewarm water. Dry them on a napkin and place in quart tin cans, each to be done the same way, and then covered with cold boiled water slightly salted. Add the juice of two lemons to each can. Solder the cover, and boil in hot water bath for one hour and a half.

ARTICHOKE PUREE, PRESERVED.

No. 56.—Prepare the Artichoke bottoms as in No. 35. Use lemon juice in place of vinegar to keep them white. When they are cooked drain them on a napkin, rub them through a fine sieve, put the puree in pint tin boxes, solder on the cover, and boil in hot water bath for one and one-half hours. When ready to use the preserved puree open the can, and put the puree in a saucepan with half its quantity of Cream, or Allemande sauce. When thoroughly warmed, season with salt, pepper, nutmeg, and a pinch of sugar. Before serving add a piece of butter, mixing it well until the butter is melted.

Article VIII.

French **JERUSALEM ARTICHOKE.** **German**
Topinambour. *Erdartishoke.*

No. 57.—It is entirely different from the Globe Artichoke; its roots are all tubers, which are served as a vegetable; they resemble potatoes but have an Artichoke flavor.

CULTURE.

No. 58.—They are grown exclusively for their tubers, and are cultivated similar to potatoes, only that the rows in which they are planted should be at least four feet apart when they are grown in rich soil.

JERUSALEM ARTICHOKES, WITH BUTTER SAUCE.

No. 59.—Wash them thoroughly in cold water, trim them in the shape of a large olive, boil them in water, lightly salted, adding a piece of butter; when cooked drain them, dish up and pour butter sauce over them.

JERUSALEM ARTICHOKES, ITALIAN STYLE.

No. 60.—Wash and peel the Artichokes, then slice them and put in a flat saucepan with some clarified butter. Fry them lightly, then moisten with white broth, season with salt, pepper, and nutmeg. Then let them simmer slowly until cooked, when the broth must be reduced to a glaze. Add the juice of lemon and serve with Italian sauce over them.

JERUSALEM ARTICHOKES, CRACOVIENNE.

No. 61.—Peel and boil some large sized Artichokes. When cooked slice them, not too thin. Put them in a flat saucepan with clarified butter and fry lightly. Dish them up with fresh bread crumbs and fine chopped onions, fried in clarified butter and poured over them.

JERUSALEM ARTICHOKES, PUREE FOR GARNITURE.

No. 62.—Peel and wash two dozen Artichokes, slice and put them in a saucepan with a piece of butter. Toss them over the fire a few minutes, then moisten them with just enough broth to cover them. Season with salt, pepper and a pinch of sugar. Cook them until the broth is reduced. Then add a half pint of cream sauce and rub through a fine sieve. Put them back in a flat saucepan, and reduce with a little cream to its consistency. Before serving add a small piece of butter and a few drops of meat glaze.

JERUSALEM ARTICHOKES, FOR GARNITURE.

No. 63.—Peel the Artichokes, cut them in any kind of shape you wish, but have them all alike. Put them in a saucepan, with white broth and a piece of butter. Cook them so as to reduce the broth to glaze the Artichokes. Serve them with a half glaze, cream, or Allemande sauce, as may be required.

SOUP PUREE, JERUSALEM ARTICHOKE, PALESTINE.

No. 64.—Put in a saucepan, two fine chopped onions with four ounces of butter. Fry them lightly, then add ten pounds of Artichokes cut in slices. Put on the cover and let them simmer slowly for twenty minutes, then add one gallon of thickened chicken or veal broth, and a faggot of parsley garnished. Season with salt, pepper, nutmeg and pinch of sugar. Let them cook slowly until they are tender. Take out the faggot and rub them through a fine sieve, then put back in saucepan to keep warm. When ready to serve add a pint of cream, in which dilute the yolks of five raw eggs, and a piece of butter, stirring it well until the butter is melted.

Article IX.

French
Asperge.

ASPARAGUS.

German
Spargel.

No. 65.—The Asparagus is one of the best table vegetables, having a delicious flavor, and being easily prepared. It can be had nearly all the year round, but is best when in season. To have them at perfection they need great care in their cultivation. The best flavored and most tender are those raised under cover and kept from the rays of the sun. There are four varieties: the green, violet, white and wild Asparagus. The white is savory and agreeable for eating whole, but contains little substance. The violet grows large and is very substantial and preferred by all gourmets. The green is smaller and more common and is generally used for soups and purees. The wild is used for medical purposes. The water in which Asparagus has been boiled, when cold, is a refreshing drink, and can be used to advantage by persons troubled with kidney complaint.

CULTURE

No. 66.—Sow early in spring, as soon as the ground will admit of working, in rows a foot apart. Keep carefully hoed and clear from weeds, and the plant will be in condition to set out in the succeeding spring. The soil for the permanent beds should be thoroughly manured and trenched or plowed to a depth of at least one foot. Plant in rows, spread the roots well out and let the crown of the plant be set deep enough so that it will be covered from five to eight inches. In heavy soil the covering must be less than in light soil. After sowing the seeds, tread them firmly in with the feet.

COLOSSAL.

No. 67.—The best variety, unrivaled in size, deep green in color, tender and good in quality.

GIANT.

No. 68.—A popular variety, producing green and purple shoots, according to the soil. It grows very hardy but not as large as the Colossal.

CROSSBRED.

No. 69.—It retains the head closed until the stalks are quite long and is of a uniform color, while for tenderness and quality it is unsurpassed. The size is medium large, and uniform.

SMALL DEFIANCE.

No. 70.—Is of a rich green color, very early, good sized, tender, and good quality.

HOW TO PREPARE ASPARAGUS FOR COOKING.

No. 71.—Wash the Asparagus in plenty of cold water, then take a knife and scrape the bottom parts of the stems. Put them in bundles of about ten to fifteen Asparagus in each and see that the heads are even. Tie them with a string and cut them at the bottom so as to have them all the same length. Boil them in boiling water with a little salt. Asparagus to be good should not be overdone, and in serving them when boiled, dish up on a napkin so that it will absorb all the moisture, with sauce separately.

ASPARAGUS, WITH BUTTER SAUCE.

No. 72.—Prepare the Asparagus as in No. 71. Tie them in small bunches. When boiled and tender, drain them on a napkin. Dish them on a hot plate, in a folded napkin, with butter sauce separately in a bowl.

ASPARAGUS, HOLLANDAISE SAUCE.

No. 73.—Prepare Asparagus as in No. 71. Tie them in small bunches. When boiled drain them on a napkin, dish them on a dish with Hollandaise sauce served over the tops of the Asparagus, or serve the sauce separately if in large quantities.

ASPARAGUS PIEMONTAISE.

No. 74.—Prepare Asparagus same as for Hollandaise. Use green Asparagus. When cooked and drained, serve them on a dish with a nut-brown butter sauce.

ASPARAGUS, POMPADOUR.

No. 75.—Prepare three pounds of Asparagus as in No. 71. Tie them in bundles; cut off all the hard part so as to have only the tender part left. Cook them in boiling water seasoned with salt. When cooked, drain them on a napkin and keep warm. While the Asparagus is cooking, make the following sauce: Put in a saucepan one-half pound of best fresh butter, add a little salt, pinch of mace and red pepper, the yolks of four raw eggs, the juice of two lemons and two soup spoons full of cold water. Put the saucepan in boiling water, stirring it with a whisk continually. As soon as it commences to thicken take it off the fire, place a layer of Asparagus on a dish, then a layer of the sauce twice over. This must be served hot; delay will spoil it. The Asparagus must be served with a spoon, and is eaten with the fork.

ASPARAGUS, SPANISH STYLE.

No. 76.—Prepare two dozen bunches of Asparagus as in No. 71. When cooked, drain them on a napkin. When dry, place them on a dish and serve separate, one soft-poached egg for each person, which you poach in the Asparagus water, and a sauce bowl of Vinaigrette sauce.

ASPARAGUS, WITH OIL AND VINEGAR.

No. 77.—When Asparagus is prepared as in No. 71, and cooked, immerse them in cold water until cold, to retain their green color. Then drain them on a napkin and serve as needed with a sauce as indicated in Artichokes No. 26.

ASPARAGUS TOPS—HOW TO PREPARE.

No. 78.—Asparagus Tops are the tender part of the Asparagus. For small garniture, first cut off the heads and then cut the other part of the stem the size of a large pea. Cook each separately in boiling water seasoned with salt, on a brisk fire. When cooked, immerse in cold water, to keep them green; then drain them on a sieve, put them on a plate, cover them with a dampened napkin and keep in a cool place until needed. For large garniture cut all the pieces one inch long. To be served in faggots, leave them from two to four inches long, as may be required.

ASPARAGUS TOPS, WITH SAUCE.

No. 79.—Prepare two pounds of Asparagus tops as in No. 78. Cut one and a half inches long, and when ready for use put them in a flat saucepan with a piece of butter. Toss them gently in the pan over the fire, and when warmed season with pepper, pinch of nutmeg, and sugar. Let boil up once or twice, then add a mixture of the yolks of two raw eggs, diluted with a little cream and a small piece of butter; mix it well together, not letting it boil, and then serve.

ASPARAGUS TOPS, COLBERT.

No. 80.—Prepare one pound of Asparagus as in No. 78. Cut them one inch long; keep the heads separate, and put each part in a saucepan with a small piece of butter. Toss them gently in the saucepan over a brisk fire, then add two spoonfuls of Allemande sauce. Season with salt and pepper. Dish up the stalk part first, with the heads over them, and with a garniture of poached eggs around the dish, with a few drops of glaze on each egg.

ASPARAGUS TOPS, WITH TRUFFLES, IMPERIAL.

No. 81.—Prepare two pounds of Asparagus tops as in No. 78. Cut them one inch long, and when cooked put them together in a flat saucepan with a small piece of butter. Season with salt and pepper, and warm thoroughly, then serve them on a dish, leaving some space in the centre. Fill the centre with a garniture of truffles cut in a Julienne, and finished with a reduced Madeira wine sauce. When dressed sprinkle a pinch of chopped parsley over them.

ASPARAGUS TOPS, WITH MUTTON GRAVY.

No. 82.—Prepare two pounds of Asparagus tops. Cut them one inch long, parboil five minutes, drain and put them in a saucepan with a small piece of butter. Season with salt, pepper, pinch of nutmeg, and add two cupfulls of mutton gravy. Finish cooking them on a brisk fire, and before serving add some finely chopped parsley and chives.

ASPARAGUS TOPS, FOR GARNITURE.

No. 83.—Prepare the Asparagus as in No. 78. For small garniture they may be served in sauce, or tossed in butter in the pan over the fire, and seasoned with salt and pepper and a pinch of sugar. For large garnitures tie them in faggots and dress them in bunches, alternating with other vegetables, as may be required.

ASPARAGUS PUREE, FOR GARNITURE.

No. 84.—Use green Asparagus; break off the tender parts, wash them in cold water, drain and put them in a saucepan of boiling water, adding salt, faggot of parsley garnished, and two whole onions When cooked drain them and take the faggot and onions, put the Asparagus in a flat saucepan with a piece of butter, and season with salt, pepper, nutmeg, and pinch of sugar; add two spoonfulls of cream sauce, and one handful of bread crumbs, previously soaked in milk and pressed dry in a napkin; Let cook for ten minutes, then rub through a fine sieve; put the puree in a flat saucepan, reduce it with a little cream to its proper consistency, if necessary, add some color of spinach to give it a bright green color. Before serving add a piece of butter, stirring it well until melted.

ASPARAGUS TOPS, FOR LARGE COLD GARNITURE.

No. 85.—Slice some Turnips three-eighths of an inch thick, then cut them with a round cutter two and a half inches in diameter, Cut out the centre one and a quarter inches in diameter, parboil them two minutes, and then immerse in cold water. Dry them on a napkin, fill each ring with Asparagus tops, cooked, but not too much so. Cut two inches, or two and a half inches long; arrange in a tin pan so that they will stand up straight; set on ice to get cold, then mask with Aspic jelly. Carrot rings may be used, alternating with the Turnips.

ASPARAGUS SALAD, PLAIN.

No. 86.—Prepare one pound of Asparagus tops as in No. 78. Cut them one inch in length. When cooked and drained put them into a salad bowl, and season with salt and pepper. Add some chopped parsley or chives, vinegar, and olive oil. Mix it carefully, not breaking the tops.

ASPARAGUS SALAD, WITH SHRIMPS.

No. 87.—Prepare the Asparagus as in No. 78. Add one-half their quantity of picked shrimps, season with salt and pepper. Make separately, in a bowl, a sauce with the yolks of three hard boiled eggs. Rub them through a sieve, then put them in the bowl and add in slowly, while stirring with a wooden spoon, one glass of olive oil and a few drops of vinegar. Pour this over the salad, arrange it properly and trim with hard boiled eggs cut into quarters.

ASPARAGUS SALAD, WITH TRUFFLES, ROYAL.

No. 88.—Prepare the Asparagus as in No. 78. Add one-half their quantity of truffles, cut into a short Julienne. Season with salt, pepper, and add the juice of one lemon. Mix all gently together, cover them and set in a cool place for one hour. When ready to serve garnish the salad with fine chopped eggs—the yolks and the white alternating—around the border, and slices of truffles which have been dipped in a reduced cold Madeira wine sauce. Make a crown in the centre and fill with Tartare sauce.

SOUPS.

PUREE ASPARAGUS, CONDE.

No. 89.—Take the tender part of ten pounds of Asparagus, wash them well and parboil for five minutes, then immerse them in cold water and drain them on a sieve. Then put them in a saucepan with one gallon of boiling chicken or veal broth, and add a faggot of parsley garnished with celery. Put this on a brisk fire, and when cooked drain them on a collander; take out the faggot, thicken the broth, and let boil slowly. Then add the Asparagus which you pounded through the colander. Season with salt, pepper, nutmeg, and a pinch of sugar. Let cook for twenty-five minutes, then rub it through a fine sieve, putting it back in saucepan to keep warm. Before serving add half a pound of butter, stirring it until the butter is melted. Serve with a plate full of small fried bread crumbs;

PUREE ASPARAGUS, ROYAL.

No. 90.—Take ten pounds of the tender green part of the Asparagus, and when washed parboil them for four minutes, then immerse in cold water (to retain their green color). Drain them, and put them in a saucepan with a quarter of a pound of butter, then toss them in the pan gently over the fire, and season with salt, pepper, nutmeg, and a little sugar. Add just enough white chicken or veal broth to cook them thoroughly, and a faggot of parsley. Let them boil until tender, and then pound the Asparagus through a colander, and then put into a saucepan with one gallon of thickened chicken or cream, in veal broth. Put it on the fire, stirring it until it boils, then set on side of fire to boil slowly for twenty-five minutes. Skim, and strain through a fine sieve, and then put back into the saucepan to keep warm. Before serving add four ounces of butter and a pint of which dilute the yolks of four raw eggs, while stirring the soup well. Serve with a garniture royal, cut into rings or in small dice shape.

PUREE ASPARAGUS, ST. GEORGE.

No. 91.—Prepare the puree the same as No. 90. In place of a garniture royal add a garniture of Asparagus tops, with small balls of forced meat of chicken, the size of a large pea.

CREAM ASPARAGUS, COUNTESS.

No. 92.—Cut the tender parts of ten pounds of Asparagus, and parboil them. Immerse them in cold water, drain them, and put them into a saucepan with boiling white broth, just enough to cook them. Season with salt and pepper, and add a faggot of parsley garnished with celery. When they are thoroughly cooked add two quarts cream sauce, a little nutmeg, and a pinch of sugar. Pound them through a colander, then rub through a fine sieve; put back in saucepan to keep warm (not letting it boil). Before serving add four ounces butter, a pint of cream, in which dilute the yolks of six raw eggs, stirring it well until the butter is melted. Serve with a garniture of Asparagus tops, and add some green color of spinach to this soup, as it must be of a bright green color.

ASPARAGUS, PRESERVED IN SALT.

No. 93.—Pick out middle sized, sound and fresh cut Asparagus, Put into the bottom of a square water-tight wooden box, which you intend filling, a layer of salt, then a layer of Asparagus, then a layer of salt, a layer of Asparagus, continuing until filled. On the top layer have the salt one-half an inch thick, and have a wooden cover to fit closely on the box, with a weight on top to keep it pressed down, and keep them in a cool dry place. When ready to use them soak them for three hours in cold water, then scrape them the ordinary way, and put them to soak in lukewarm water for five hours, changing the water occasionally, then cook them as required.

ASPARAGUS, PRESERVED IN CANS.

No. 94.—Square boxes, the size of the Asparagus, are much better than the round high boxes generally used by factories. When the boxes are properly made they can be used several times for the same purpose. Each box should contain from twenty-five to thirty Asparagus. After the Asparagus stems are scraped, wash them in cold water, tie them in bundles, and cut them all the same size. Parboil them for five minutes in water lightly salted, then immerse them in cold water, drain them and put on a linen towel to dry. Then arrange them in boxes so that the bottom half will have their heads towards the right, and the top half will have their heads towards the left. Cover them with cold boiled water, lightly salted; solder on the cover and boil the cans in a hot bath for one and one-half hours.

ASPARAGUS TOPS, PRESERVED.

No. 95.—Use fresh green Asparagus, and all the same size. Cut off the heads and keep them separate. Then cut the remaining tender part the size of a large pea. Parboil the heads one minute and the others five minutes. Immerse them in cold water, then drain them and dry on a napkin. Mix them together and put them into round quart tin cans. Cover them with cold boiled water, lightly salted; solder on the cover and boil them in a hot water bath for one hour.

ASPARAGUS SYRUP.

No. 96.—Cut off the tender part of four bunches of Asparagus, and wash them well in cold water. Put them in a saucepan with one gallon of water, letting them cook until it is reduced to five pints of water. Drain them and then strain the liquid through a flannel filter, adding four pounds of cube sugar. Cook to a syrup of 32 degrees, and when cold put in bottles, corked tight.

ARTICLE X.

French
Haricot Asperge.

ASPARAGUS BEAN.

German
Spargel Bohne.

No. 97.—The Asparagus Bean is a distinct variety from the garden bean, being a native of the southern part of South America and China. The pods measure over one foot in length, and the beans are cultivated on account of their long pods, which are crisp and tender, having a rich flavor, and being much esteemed for pickling. The seeds are quite small, and are seldom eaten in their green or ripe state.

ARTICLE XI.

BALM.

Baume. *Melisse.*

No. 98.—Balm is a hardy perennial aromatic plant. Originally from the southern part of Europe. The leaves have a fragrant odor, similar to lemons, and are used for making Balm Tea, for use in fever, and makes a pleasant beverage of Balm wine for diseases of the lungs, being also used in seasoning meats and for flavoring vinegar. A mixture of Balm and honey is sometimes applied to the interior of bee hives just previous to receiving the swarm for the purpose of their settlement, to attract them.

CULTURE.

No. 99.—Prepare a rich sandy soil and keep it clear of weeds. Plant early and thin to ten inches apart. The plants will soon completely cover the ground, and the bed with good management will last several years. When drying, the plants should be cut as they come into bloom, separating the stems at the surface of the ground. Spread them in an airy shady place and allow them to dry gradually. The leaves may be used in their green state directly from the plants, as they are required.

ARTICLE XII.

French
Mélisse.

BALM MINT.

German
Melisse.

No. 100.—The Balm Mint is a hardy perennial aromatic plant, similar to the Balm, but different in flavor, being often taken for Mint, on account of its flavor. It is used for seasoning game and flavoring vinegar and spirituous waters. Culture same as Balm.

ARTICLE XIII.

BARLEY.

Orge. *Gerste.*

No. 101.—The common Barley is a cereal, the flour obtained from its grains containing very little gluten, but an abundance of fecula, also containing a mucilaginous substance. For this reason it produces a bread less savory and less digestible than other flours. The Pearl Barley, when entirely removed of its pellicle, is reduced to a small pearl. It is much used for culinary purposes in replacing rice, and also in making soups for invalids.

COMMON BARLEY.

No. 102.—Barley succeeds best in lands more sandy and lighter than those adapted to wheat. It is sown in the spring and can be grown further north than any other grain. Unless intended for seed, it should be cut before being fully ripe, as it is then heavier, of better quality, and less liable to shell. The land should always be rolled immediately after sowing.

BARLEY MANSURY.

No. 103.—This is a six-rowed Barley with long, heavy well filled heads, containing large plump grains. The straw is bright, very strong, and is not apt to lodge even in the richest lands. Ripens a week later than the common six-rowed Barley, or about the same time as two-rowed Barley.

BARLEY NAKED, OR HULLNESS.

No. 104.—This is a peculiar grain, and not generally known. The corolla is not attached to the grain, and in this it resembles wheat. It is a splendid grain for all the purposes for which Barley is used, and will make an excellent bread when bolted and ground like wheat.

SOUPS.

CREAM BARLEY, NEILSON STYLE.

No. 105.—Put in a saucepan half a pound of butter, and when melted add a handful of flour and four handfuls of Pearl Barley, stirring it with a wooden spoon for fifteen minutes. Then add in slowly one gallon of veal or chicken broth; make it boil, and then set on the side of the fire to boil slowly, adding a faggot of parsley garnished, with two leeks and two green onions. Season with salt and pepper, and let it boil slowly for an hour and a half. Then skim off the grease and take out the faggot. Strain it through a fine sieve and put back in saucepan to keep warm. When ready to serve add the following preparation: Take a pint of cream and the yolks of six raw eggs, mix them well, and strain through a strainer. Add six ounces of butter, stirring it well until the butter is melted. Serve with a garniture royal.

CREAM BARLEY, MARIE LOUISE STYLE.

No. 106.—Prepare the soup same as No. 105. When moistened with the broth and it boils add two raw chickens, letting them boil slowly until they are cooked. Then take out the chickens and the faggot, skim off the grease and strain through a fine sieve. Season with salt and pepper and set on the fire to keep warm. Take the breasts of the chickens and pound them into a fine paste with six ounces of butter. Then rub it through a fine sieve and put it in a saucepan, adding a pint of cream, the yolks of six eggs and a pinch of sugar. Then add the hot soup slowly while stirring briskly with a whisk. Serve with a garniture of green peas.

CREAM OF BARLEY, FARRAGUT STYLE.

No. 107.—Prepare the soup in a similar way to No. 105. When strained set it on the fire to keep warm, and when ready to serve add six ounces of crawfish butter, diluted in their broth, the yolks of six raw eggs and a glass of cream, stirring well until the butter is melted. Serve with a garniture of fried peas.

BARLEY BROTH FOR INVALIDS.

No. 108.—Wash two handfuls of Pearl Barley in cold water. Put in a saucepan on the fire with three quarts of plain chicken broth, and let it boil slowly for two hours. Press the liquid through a fine sieve and season lightly. When common Barley is used for these recipes put on the fire with cold water, and as soon as it boils strain off and proceed as with Pearl Barley.

BARLEY WATER FOR INVALIDS.

No. 109.—Prepare same as No. 108. Use water instead of broth. When cooked press the liquid through a fine sieve. Serve plain or sweeten with sugar.

BARLEY CREAM FOR INVALIDS.

No. 110.—Prepare the Barley as in No. 108. Use milk in place of broth. When well cooked press the liquid through a fine sieve and sweeten with a syrup of marsh mallow or venus hair.

BARLEY WATER FOR GARGLING.

No. 111.—When Barley water is made for gargling with briar leaves and honey, use the plain common Barley without changing the fresh water as with No. 108. When the Barley water is made pour it boiling over the briar leaves, then add a soup spoonful of honey and one of wine vinegar.

ARTICLE XIV.

French
Basilic.
BASIL SWEET.
German
Basilikum.

No. 112.—There are four kinds of Basil. The large sweet Basil is the one principally used for culinary purposes. It is a hardy annual plant, and must be cut before it gets in full bloom. The seeds and stems are dried and used for flavoring soups and sauces, etc. It is also used when young and tender to mix with cooked vegetable salads, such as potatoes, beets, peas, beans, etc.

CULTURE.

No. 113.—All the varieties are annual and grow from seed. Sow as early as the ground will permit, in sandy soil carefully prepared. For winter use the stalks are cut while in flower, then dried, powdered and preserved as other pot herbs.

ARTICLE XV.

BAY LEAVES, OR LAUREL LEAVES (Common).

French — *Laurier Franc ou dappolon.*
German — *Lorbeerblatt.*

No. 114.—These leaves are much used for culinary purposes, being indispensable for stews, etc.. For these purposes they should be used in their dry state, as they then lose their bitter taste. In their green state they are used for pickling, and in imparting an aromatic taste to meats.

ARTICLE XVI.

BAY OR LAUREL LEAVES (Larustine).

Laurier Amande.   *Lorbeerblatt.*

No. 115.—These are not used much for culinary purposes, but in dairies they are frequently used to aromatize the milk. They should be used with precaution. Although they give an agreeable taste to the milk they are dangerous to use, being slightly poisonous.

ARTICLE XVII.

BEANS.

Haricot.   *Bohne.*

No. 116.—This is a vegetable of which there are many varieties. They are prepared for the table in several different ways. Some varieties, when young and tender, are eaten whole, and are known as String Beans. Later on they get hulled, when the seeds are ripe, and are called the Shell Bean (French, *Flageolet*). Next they are dried and then prepared in various ways. The White Marrow Fat, the Golden Wax, and the Dwarf Soisson are among the best varieties. To have Beans well cooked pure water must be used, some varieties having hard shells, which will not boil tender. This can be remedied by adding some carbonate of soda while they are being boiled. For early cultivation the American Garden Bush Bean is the earliest and hardiest. The Garden Bush or Pole Running Beans are tender annual plants, originally from the East Indies. The dwarf varieties require no poles or sticks for their support.

CULTURE OF THE DWARF OR BUSH BEAN.

No. 117.—A succession of sowing can be made according to the latitude. Plant in drills about two inches deep, and from eighteen inches to two feet apart, according to the richness of the soil.

EARLY FEEGEE.

No. 118.—The earliest variety and very prolific.

EARLY RED VALENTINE.

No. 119.—Tender and succulent, and of excellent flavor. They continue longer in their green state than most varieties.

WHITE VALENTINE.

No. 120.—Similar in growth to the red valentine. It is a very prolific bearer, and the fact of the bean being white gives it additional value, as it enables it to be used as a shell bean.

GALLEGA, OR LARGE REFUGEE.

No. 121.—A standard sort for market or private use. Is very prolific; pods and beans are large.

EARLY MOHAWK.

No. 122.—An excellent early variety, very productive, and of good quality.

BLACK WAX, OR BUTTER.

No. 123.—The pods when ripe are of a waxy yellow transparent color, very tender, excellent, and delicious.

WHITE WAX.

No. 124.—A variety similar to the black wax, except in color.

IVORY POT WAX.

No. 125.—The pods are long, and almost of a transparent waxy white color, and are entirely stringless. In tenderness it excels almost all the other kinds. The beans when ripe are of medium size, white, and oval. It is an excellent Shell Bean for winter use.

CANADIAN WONDER.

No. 126.—Produce very large pods with great abundance; very fleshy, and exceedingly tender when cooked.

GOLDEN REFUGEE.

No. 127.—Pods perfectly round, and of a very light color. It is particularly well suited for pickling.

CRYSTAL WHITE WAX.

No. 128.—Produces pods of fair size of exceedingly rich and tender flavor. In color waxy white, and almost as transparent as glass. It is a stringless variety, very productive, and the pods though quick to develop are slow to harden.

GOLDEN WAX.

No. 129.—Is an entirely different variety, the pods are large, long, and brittle, and entirely stringless. As a snap bean it excels all others in richness and tenderness of flavor, and has the further merit of being one of the best shell beans grown for winter use.

REFUGEE OR A THOUSAND TO ONE.

No. 130.—Very productive, though not early. The young pods are extremely tender and of fine flavor.

LARGE WHITE KIDNEY.

No. 131.—An excellent shell bean, green or ripe.

WHITE MARROWFAT.

No. 132.—Extensively grown for dry state. Of average quality as a string bean, but excellent when shelled either green or dry.

DWARF SOISSON.

No. 133.—Is an early variety. They blossom six weeks after planting. Can be used with pods after seven weeks, and ripen in ninety days. The seeds are white kidney shaped, often flattened, bent, or distorted. They are productive, and the young pods are of fair quality. The seeds are excellent, whether used green or ripe. The skin is thin. They are much esteemed for their whiteness and delicate flavor.

BEANS, POLE RUNNING.

No. 134.—They are more tender and require rather more care in culture than the Bush Beans. They succeed best in sandy loam, which should be liberally enriched with short manure in the hills, which are formed according to the variety, from three to four feet apart.

LARGE WHITE LIMA.

No. 135.—They are considered the best of all the Pole Beans, and are almost universally grown.

SMALL LIMA, OR SIEVA.

No. 136.—It is earlier and more hardy than the large White Lima.

DREER'S IMPROVED LIMA.

No. 137.—This is an extra quality of bean which matures early, and yields largely. It produces more shelled beans to the pole than the large Lima.

DUTCH CASE KNIFE.

No. 138.—A very productive variety, and one of the earliest. Sometimes used as a snap bean, but generally shelled.

SPECKLED CRANBERRY.

No. 139.—A popular variety, serviceable in its green state or when shelled.

SCARLET RUNNER.

No. 140.—A great favorite in gardens, both as an ornamental plant and useful vegetable.

GIANT WAX.

No. 141.—Pods long and clear, with a waxy color, thick and fleshy, and very productive When cooked they are tender and delicious.

GERMAN WAX POLE.

No. 142.—One of the best varieties, either for snap or shelled in the green state.

French **BEANS, ENGLISH OR BROAD.** **German**
Fève. *Gartenbohne.*

No. 143.—This class is very hardy, and is said to be the most ancient of all esculents. It originated in Egypt. Should be planted as soon as the soil is in good condition, in Spring. Plant four inches apart and two inches deep, in drills four feet apart. To insure well filled pods, pinch off the tops as soon as the lower pods begin to set. In their young state they are best for the table, being then digestible. When old the skin must be removed, else they are hard to digest.

EARLY MAZAGAN.

No. 144.—A very early and healthy variety.

BROAD WINDSOR.

No. 145.—Best for general use. Suitable for field and garden culture.

SWORD LONG POD.

No. 146.—An excellent variety, similar to the Broad Windsor.

HOW TO PREPARE STRING BEANS FOR COOKING.

No. 147.—To have good beans they must be perfectly fresh. Break off the ends and string them carefully, or pare both edges, to be certain that none of the tough fibre remains (this should be done carefully and at all times). Wash them in cold water. When young and small leave them whole. When large split the beans lengthwise, or cut them in pieces an inch long.

STRING BEANS, ENGLISH STYLE.

No. 148.—Prepare the Beans as in No. 147, and when ready for cooking throw them in boiling water, lightly salted. Boil them on a brisk fire until tender (never cover the pot while cooking beans, as that has a tendency to tinge them yellow). Drain them on a colander and serve them with a piece of butter in the centre and a piece on top.

STRING BEANS, MAITRE D'HOTEL.

No. 149.—Cook them as in No. 148. When done immerse them in cold water. Drain them on a colander and place them on a napkin to absorb all the moisture. Put them in a flat saucepan with a piece of butter, and season with salt and pepper. Toss them over the fire until thoroughly warm, and then add a little fine chopped parsley and a few drops of lemon juice.

STRING BEANS, WITH FINE HERBS.

No. 150.—Prepare the Beans as in No. 148. Put in a flat saucepan a piece of butter, two fine chopped shallots, and fry them lightly. Add the String Beans, and season with salt, pepper, and a little nutmeg. Toss them over the fire until thoroughly warmed, then take them off of the fire and add a piece of butter, some fine chopped parsley, and a few drops of lemon juice—tossing them over until the butter is melted.

STRING BEANS, LYONNAISE.

No. 151.—When the Beans are prepared as in No. 148, put in a flat saucepan a piece of butter, one onion cut in half and sliced fine. Fry lightly and then add the Beans. Season with salt and pepper, and add two spoonfuls of Espagnole sauce. Toss them over the fire, and when serving add a little fine chopped parsley.

STRING BEANS, POULETTE.

No. 152.—When the Beans are prepared as in No. 148, put them in a saucepan with a piece of butter. Season with salt, pepper, and nutmeg. When thoroughly warmed add two spoonfuls of Allemande sauce. Toss them well together, and when ready to serve add a few drops of lemon juice and some fine chopped parsley.

STRING BEANS, BRETONNE.

No. 153.—Prepare the Beans as in No. 148. Cut two onions in half, trim off the ends, and slice them fine. Then put them in a saucepan with a piece of butter, and fry them to a light brown. Then add four spoonfuls of vinegar, and cook until it is two-thirds reduced. Then add four spoonfuls of Espagnole sauce, the Beans, and season with salt and pepper, and cover the saucepan, letting them simmer slowly for twenty minutes.

STRING BEANS, GERMAN STYLE.

No. 154.—Put in a saucepan a piece of butter, and add one fine sliced onion. Fry lightly. Add young Beans, and season with salt, pepper, and a pinch of sugar, and add a faggot of parsley garnished, and two spoonfuls of white broth. Cover the saucepan, and let them simmer for fifteen minutes. Then sprinkle a little flour over them, tossing them over well and cooking for fifteen minutes longer.

STRING BEANS, WITH CREAM.

No. 155.—Prepare the Beans as in No. 148. Put them in a flat saucepan with some fine scraped fresh fat pork. Season with salt and pepper and add a faggot of parsley. Let them simmer slowly for half an hour, and when ready to serve add a glass of cream, into which dilute the yolks of two raw eggs and a piece of butter. Toss them well together. Take out the faggot and then serve.

STRING BEANS, COUNTRY STYLE.

No. 156.—Prepare the Beans as in No. 148, then put them in a saucepan with a piece of butter. Add some fine chopped parsley and chives. Sprinkle them with flour. Toss them over and add some broth. Let them simmer for half an hour, and when the moisture is nearly reduced, add a glass of milk, into which dilute the yolks of two raw eggs. Mix all well together and serve with pieces of sliced fat pork cooked separately.

STRING BEANS, PRESERVED IN SALT.

No. 157.—Use small fresh plucked Beans. Cut off the ends and string them. Parboil them for two minutes in plenty of water.

Immerse them in cold water and drain them on a sieve, then dry them on a towel. Put in a keg or barrel a layer of salt, then one of Beans, alternating until the keg or barrel is full. Put on the cover to press them. Fill up next day with Beans, as they will have settled. If they show too much water, drain half off and add more salt. Cover with a cloth and put the top on tight. Keep in a cool place.

STRING BEANS, PRESERVED IN BRINE.

No. 158.—Prepare the Beans as in No. 157. Put them in layers in a glass jar and then cover them with strong cooked brine. Twenty-four hours after drain off the brine, boil it, add more salt, and when cold pour it over the Beans. Three days after this boil the brine again, adding salt, and when cold pour it over the Beans again, cover them tight and keep in a cool place.

STRING BEANS, PRESERVED IN CANS.

No. 159.—Prepare the Beans as in No. 157, and when dried arrange them in layers in tin cans holding one pound of Beans. Boil some water, lightly salted, and when cold cover the Beans, solder on the cover, and boil in a hot water bath for an hour and a quarter.

HOW TO PREPARE SALTED STRING BEANS FOR COOKING.

No. 160.—Soak them in cold water for four hours, changing the water once or twice. Then put them with fresh water on the fire to warm slowly. When the water intends to boil, drain it off and put on fresh cold water and let them boil. Cook until tender and prepare as needed.

STRING BEAN SALAD.

No. 161.—Cook some small String Beans as in No. 148. When cold put them in a salad bowl with some fine sliced cooked onions. Season with salt, pepper, vinegar and oil, and add some fine chopped parsley. Mix all together without breaking the Beans, and garnish with beets cut in rounds.

STRING BEAN SALAD, GERMAN STYLE.

No. 162.—Prepare same as in No. 161. Garnish with fillet of anchovies around the border, and cover the centre with a Remoulade sauce.

STRING BEANS FOR GARNITURE.

No. 163.—String Beans, when used for large garniture, are cooked as in No. 148, immersed in cold water, then thoroughly warmed and seasoned. Dress them in bunches, alternating with other vegetables.

For small garniture, cut them diamond shape an inch long, and boil them the usual way. Then put them in a sauce-pan with a piece of butter. Season and toss them over the fire for a few minutes. Dress plain or with sauce as may be desired. Care should be taken in cooking to keep them green. In order to do this, instructions as given in No. 148 must be taken.

WAX BEANS, MAITRE D'HOTEL.

No. 164.—When the Beans are shelled wash them in cold water; then put them in boiling water on a brisk fire. Have the water lightly salted, and add a small piece of butter. When cooked drain them, and put them into a saucepan with a few spoonfuls of Allemande sauce. Season, and toss them until well mixed before serving, and add a little fine chopped parsley and a piece of butter. Serve hot.

WHITE OR KIDNEY BEANS, WITH PUREE OF ONIONS, SOUBISE.

No. 165.—Cook the Beans as in No. 164, and when cooked put them into a saucepan with a piece of butter. Season with salt and pepper, and add a few spoonfuls of puree of onions, white or brown. Let them simmer for fifteen minutes, and in serving garnish with scallops of Artichokes around the dish.

WHITE BEANS, COUNTRY STYLE.

No. 166.—After the Beans are shelled and washed, put them into a saucepan to boil, and add a piece of butter and a little salt. When done drain them and then put in a saucepan a piece of butter. Add the Beans, season with salt and pepper, and add a little fine chopped parsley and chives. Toss them well together, and if they should get too thick add a little broth.

GREEN FLAGEOLET BEANS, MAITRE D'HOTEL.

No. 167.—Prepare the same as White Beans in No. 164, and after they are boiled immerse them in cold water. Drain them and keep in a cool place for use when needed.

GREEN FLAGEOLET BEANS, GERMAN STALE.

No. 168.—When the Beans are boiled drain them. Then put them into a flat saucepan with a piece of butter and season with salt and pepper. Toss them over the fire, adding two spoonfuls of Allemande sauce, and in seasoning sprinkle a little fine chopped parsley over them.

GREEN FLAGEOLET BEANS, WITH STRING BEANS.

No. 169.—When the Flageolet Beans are boiled, drain them. Then have the same quantity of string beans, cut diamond shape (the same size as the Flageolet Beans), boiled and drained. Put both of them into a flat saucepan with a piece of butter, and season with salt and pepper. Toss them over the fire until thoroughly warmed; after which add two spoonfuls of cream sauce and some fine chopped parsley.

PUREE OF NEW BEANS FOR GARNITURE.

No. 170.—Shell as many Beans as needed. Boil them as soon as they are shelled, in water lightly salted, with a faggot of parsley garnished with green onions. When the Beans are cooked, drain them on a colander. Take out the faggot and put the Beans into a saucepan with a few spoonfuls of cream or Allemande sauce. Season with salt, pepper and nutmeg, and when well mixed rub them through a fine sieve. Then put the puree in a flat saucepan to reduce it. If needed, add a pinch of sugar and a piece of butter before serving.

PUREE OF GREEN FLAGEOLET BEANS FOR GARNITURE.

No. 171.—Prepare and cook as in No. 170. Rub them through a fine sieve, and reduce in a flat saucepan to its proper consistency. Add a little glaze and butter before serving.

FLAGEOLET BEANS PRESERVED IN CANS.

No. 172.—The green shelled Flageolet Beans are the best. Pluck them while young and tender. Wash them and then parboil them in water, lightly salted, until three-quarters cooked. Drain them in a colander and spread them on a towel, and when cold place them in cans holding a pint. Boil some water, lightly salted, and when cold cover the Beans with it. Add to each can a pinch of carbonate of soda. Solder on the cover and then boil in a hot water bath for one hour.

DRY WHITE BEANS, MAITRE D'HOTEL.

No. 173.—All dry beans must be carefully picked and then washed in cold water. Soak the quantity needed in cold water over night, then drain them the next day and put them in a saucepan, having them well covered with water. When they boil add a piece of bacon or salt pork (previously parboiled for a few minutes). Cover the saucepan and let the Beans cook continuously and slowly until tender. Then take out the pork or bacon and drain half of the liquid from the Beans. Season with pepper and salt, and, if needed, add a piece of butter with fine chopped parsley. Toss them well over until the butter is melted.

DRY WHITE BEANS, GERMAN STYLE.

No. 174.—Cook them the same as in No. 173, and when done drain off the broth. Add Allemande or butter sauce and mix well. When serving add fine chopped parsley, and slice the bacon or pork to garnish the dish.

DRY WHITE BEANS, WITH CREAM SAUCE.

No. 175.—Cook the Beans as in No. 173. When cooked drain them and put them in a saucepan with Cream sauce. Season well and let them simmer for ten minutes.

DRY WHITE BEANS, BRETONNE.

No. 176.—Cook the Beans as in No. 173, and when cooked drain them in a colander. Put in a saucepan two onions, cut in half and sliced fine. Fry them in butter to a light brown color, and add a wine-glassful of vinegar; and when reduced one-third add a few spoonfuls of Espagnole sauce and the Beans. Season with salt and pepper. Cover the saucepan and let it simmer for half an hour.

DRY WHITE BEANS, ROBERT.

No. 177.—Cook the Beans as in No. 173, and when cooked drain them in a colander. Put into a saucepan a piece of butter and two fine chopped onions. Fry them lightly and drain off the butter. Add three teaspoonfuls of mustard flour, diluted with four large spoonfuls of Espagnole sauce. Then add one quart of the Beans and season with salt, pepper, and nutmeg. Cover the saucepan and let it simmer for twenty minutes. Before serving add a piece of butter and toss the Beans well over until it is melted.

DRY WHITE BEANS, WITH BACON.

No. 178.—Pick and wash two quarts of white Beans, and soak them as usual. Then put them in a saucepan with one pound of bacon cut in square pieces. Have the whole well covered with water. Season with salt and pepper, then cover the saucepan, and let them boil slowly. This is a simple but very nourishing dish.

DRY WHITE BEANS, WITH MARROW.

No. 179.—When the Beans are cooked, as in No. 173, drain them in a colander. Put into a flat saucepan some marrow cut in small pieces. Fry it lightly, and then add the Beans. Season well, adding some fine chopped chives, tossing the whole well together, and serve immediately.

HOW TO BAKE BEANS IN POTS.

No. 180,—Pick two quarts of Beans. Wash them in cold water and let them soak in fresh water over night. Then drain them and put them in a saucepan with fresh water. Add two pounds of salt pork (previously washed). Let them boil for half an hour and drain them in a colander. Put the Beans in a pan and season with salt and pepper, to taste. Add four spoonfuls of molasses, mixing it well with the Beans. Then put the Beans in earthen pots with a piece of the pork in the centre of each pot of Beans. Moisten with enough boiling water to cover them, and place them in an oven to bake slowly over night.

DRY WHITE BEAN SALAD.

No. 181.—When the Beans are cooked as in No. 173, drain them, and when cold put one quart of Beans in a salad bowl, with two fine chopped onions, which you will have parboiled for two minutes and immersed in cold water, and then pressed dry in a napkin. Season with salt, pepper, vinegar and a little oil, adding some chopped parsley or chives. Mix the whole well together, and garnish with beets and eggs.

DRY WHITE BEANS FOR GARNITURE.

No. 182.—When the Beans are cooked as in No. 173, drain them and put them in a saucepan with a piece of butter. Season with salt and pepper. Toss them over the fire and add some fine chopped parsley, or with butter, Cream, Allemande or Espagnole sauce if desired.

PUREE OF DRY WHITE BEANS—WHITE.

No. 183.—Cook the Beans the same as in No. 173, and drain them in a colander. Put in a saucepan one white onion chopped fine, and fry it lightly. Add one quart of the Beans with four spoonfuls of Allemande or Cream sauce. Season with salt and pepper, and rub the puree through a fine sieve. Then put it back into a saucepan to keep warm, and before serving, put in a piece of butter, at the same time stirring the puree well up.

PUREE OF DRY WHITE BEANS—BROWN.

No. 184.—Prepare the same way as in No. 183—but in place of Allemande or Cream sauce, use Espagnole sauce, with an essence of ham or game.

PUREE OF DRY WHITE BEANS, WITH CELERY.

No. 185.—Prepare the puree the same as in No. 173, and when rubbed through a sieve put it into a flat saucepan and reduce it to its consistency with one glass of cream. Prepare separately a small cut Julienne of celery, cooked and glazed, and when done add it to the puree.

RED BEANS, BOURGUIGNONNE.

No. 186.—After the Beans are washed and cleaned put them into a saucepan with two onions, two carrots, a faggot of parsley well garnished, and a piece of lean bacon. Moisten to cover with cold water. Make it boil, then skim and let it cook slowly. When the Beans are three-quarters cooked take out the onions, carrots and faggot, and drain off half the moisture. Add the same quantity of claret wine. Cover the saucepan and let them simmer slowly until cooked. Before serving add a piece of butter, tossing them well over, and serve with the bacon sliced.

RED BEANS, CARDINAL—FOR FAST DAYS.

No. 187.—Prepare the Beans the same as in No. 173, leaving out the bacon, and when the Beans are done dish them up with turnovers of fish as a garniture.

RED BEANS, DONOHOE STYLE—FOR FAST DAYS.

No. 188.—Cook the Beans the same as in No. 173, leaving out the bacon; and when the Beans are cooked dish them with a garniture of fried oysters, shad roes, or milts of carp.

BLACK BEANS, WITH BUTTER.

No. 189.—Wash and clean the Beans well. Cook them the same as in No. 173, and when done put them in a saucepan with a piece of butter, tossing them well over the fire, seasoning them with salt and pepper.

BROAD BEANS.

No. 190.—Are best when young and prepared the same as the other Beans. After they are boiled drain them and put them in a saucepan with a piece of butter. Season with salt, pepper, nutmeg and a pinch of sugar. Toss them over the fire and serve.

BROAD BEANS, WITH CREAM POULETTE.

No. 191.—When shelled, wash them. Boil them as usual, then immerse them in cold water and drain them in a colander. Put into a saucepan four ounces of butter and the same quantity of flour. Stir with a wooden spoon and allow it to cook for ten minutes. Dilute the butter and flour with one quart of white broth and add the Beans. Season with salt and pepper, and add a faggot of parsley garnished with a sprig of summer savory. Let the whole simmer slowly for twenty minutes. Before serving add a glassful of cream, letting it boil up once, and serve with some fine chopped parsley thrown over the Beans.

LIMA BEANS.

No. 192.—When shelled should be allowed to lay in cold water a short time before cooking. Boil them on a brisk fire in plenty of water, lightly salted, until tender. Then drain them and return them to the saucepan. Add a piece of butter, salt and pepper, tossing the whole well together and serve.

LIMA BEANS, WITH BUTTER SAUCE.

No. 193.—When cooked and drained as in No. 192, add a few spoonfuls of Butter sauce. Season with salt, pepper, the juice of one lemon and add a little fine chopped parsley. Toss them well over the fire and serve.

LIMA BEANS, FRENCH STYLE.

No. 194.—Cook the Beans the same as in No. 192, and before serving add a glass of cream, into which dilute the yolks of three raw eggs and a piece of butter. Toss the whole well together over the fire and serve with fine chopped parsley over them.

LIMA BEANS, MACEDOINE.

No. 195.—Put into a saucepan a piece of butter, two fine chopped shallots and a handful of sliced fresh mushrooms. Cover the saucepan and cook them lightly. Then add two soup spoonfuls of flour and dilute the whole with a pint of white broth, stirring it so as to have no lumps. Add a faggot of parsley, garnished with summer savory. Put with this two quarts of the Beans (previously boiled as in No. 192) and put on the lid and let them simmer slowly for twenty minutes. Take out the faggot and add a quarter of its quantity of boiled artichoke bottoms cut into pieces the size of the Beans. Season with salt and pepper. Allow them to simmer for ten minutes longer and before serving add a little fine chopped parsley or chives.

SOUPS.

PUREE OF GREEN FLAGEOLET BEANS, SAINT GERMAIN.

No. 196.—Take one quart of Green Flageolet Beans and put them in a saucepan with two quarts of boiling water lightly salted. Add a piece of butter and a faggot of parsley garnished with leeks. Cook them on a brisk fire, and when tender drain them. Then return the Beans to the saucepan and add two quarts of thickened chicken or veal broth. Season with salt, pepper and a pinch of sugar. Let them cook slowly for twenty minutes. Then skim it well, take out the faggot and rub the soup through a fine sieve. Put it back in a saucepan to keep warm, and before serving add a piece of butter, stirring it well until melted. Serve with boiled rice separately.

PUREE OF GREEN FLAGEOLET BEANS, SOUBISE.

No. 197.—Cook the Beans as in No. 196, and when cooked, drain and return them to the saucepan, adding one quart of cream and one pint of Soubise sauce diluted to its proper consistency with chicken broth. Season with salt, pepper and a pinch of sugar. Rub it through a fine sieve and return it to the saucepan to keep warm (not letting it boil). Before serving, add a piece of butter and some fine cut chives. Serve separately with small fried bread crumbs.

PUREE OF FRESH WHITE BEANS, NEWTON STYLE.

No. 198.—Prepare the puree the same as in No. 196, and before serving add a pint of cream, into which dilute the yolks of four raw eggs, and a piece of butter, stirring the puree well. Add some fine cut chives or parsley. Serve with a garniture of forced meat of chicken, rolled into balls of the size of a pea, poached separately in broth.

PUREE OF FRESH BLACK BEANS, FAUBONNE.

No. 199.—Prepare the puree the same as in No. 196. Add a thickened beef broth, and when ready to serve add a garniture of small vegetables, cut with a spoon cutter, cooked and glazed.

CREAM OF GREEN FLAGEOLET BEANS, LELAND STYLE.

No. 200.—Put one quart of Beans in a saucepan with two quarts of boiling water. Add a faggot of parsley, garnished with celery and leeks, one onion, into which stick three cloves, one carrot, and a little salt. Cook on a brisk fire until done, and then take out the carrot, onion, and faggot, and add two quarts of Cream sauce, rubbing the whole through a fine sieve. Put it back into a saucepan to keep warm. Season to taste, and before serving add a pint of cream, into which dilute the yolks of five raw eggs and a piece of butter, while stirring the soup well. Add to this soup some green of spinach, so as to give it a bright green color. Serve separately with some fried peas, as explained in the garniture for soups.

PUREE OF DRY WHITE BEANS, PIONEER STYLE.

No. 201—Take one quart of dry white Beans. Wash and pick them well, allowing them to soak overnight in cold water. Drain them, and put them into a saucepan with three quarts of fresh water, two quarts of broth, and one pound of salt pork (that has been previously washed and parboiled for five minutes), a piece of raw ham bone, two onions and two carrots. Cover the saucepan and cook slowly until well cooked. Then take out the pork, ham bone and carrots, and pound the soup through a fine colander. Put it back into the saucepan and season with salt and pepper, adding a piece of butter.

Cut the pork into small square pieces and fry it, and when serving add it to the soup with small fried bread crumbs.

PUREE OF DRY WHITE BEANS, ST. GEORGE.

No. 202.—Prepare it the same as in No. 201, leaving out the ham bone, and when cooked rub it through a fine sieve. Put it back into the saucepan to keep warm. When ready to serve add a pint of cream, a piece of butter, some fine cut chives and fine chopped chervil. Serve separately with some fried bread crumbs.

PUREE OF DRY RED BEANS, CONDE.

No. 203.—Take one quart of Beans. Pick and wash them well and then soak them for three hours in two quarts of fresh water. Drain them and put them into a saucepan with two quarts of water, and one of broth, and put them on the fire to boil. Add a faggot of parsley, garnished with leeks and celery, two carrots, two onions, into which stick four cloves, a piece of raw ham bone, and a little salt. Cover the saucepan and cook them slowly until thoroughly well done. Then take out the ham bone, the faggot, the onions, and the carrots, and pound the soup through a colander. Add two quarts of game broth and rub the whole through a fine sieve. Put it back into the saucepan and set it on the fire, stirring it well until it boils, then set it on the side of the fire and continue boiling slowly for half an hour. Skim it, and when ready to serve add a piece of butter. Serve with boiled rice or fried bread crumbs.

PUREE OF BEANS, FOR FAST DAYS.

No. 204.—All of the purees of beans described in this book, may be prepared without using meats or broth, if desired. In this case use water, carrots, onions, leeks and celery, and a faggot of parsley, well garnished with herbs. When the beans are three-quarters cooked add to them the crumbs of a loaf of bread. When thoroughly cooked remove the faggot and carrots, leaving the leek, celery, and onions, if desired. Then rub the soup through a fine sieve and season it properly.

NOTES ON BEANS.

No. 205.—When beans are boiled with salt pork they should not be seasoned too much, as the pork itself contains considerable salt.

The pork should be washed in cold water and care taken not to use any that is rancid.

When bacon is used, trim it and then parboil it for five minutes. Then immerse it in cold water to remove the smoky taste.

Dry Beans should first be carefully picked, as there are always small stones and pieces of earth mixed with them. Wash them well in cold water, and allow them to soak in fresh water over night.

When dry Beans are soaked in lukewarm water, and the water is several times renewed, they will cook much quicker than when soaked in cold water.

Article XVIII.

French
Betterave.

BEETS.

German
Runkel Rube.

No. 206.—The Beet is a hardy biennial root plant of a blood-red color. It contains a large substance of sugar and is much used as a vegetable, for salads, and as a relish. It is refreshing and nutritious when properly prepared. There are five varieties of Beets. The Swiss chard, or sea-kale Beet, is a distinct vegetable and much superior to the common Beet for greens. If sown at the same time as the common varieties, it will be fit to use before them. Later on the plants form broad, flat, beautiful white and wax-like stems to the leaves, which are very delicious when cooked. The young leaves of the common varieties are cooked with sorrel, or cooked and prepared the same as spinach. Still another variety is called the mangel, which is seldom used for the table.

CULTURE.

No. 207.—The soil which is suitable for the culture of the Beet is that which is rather light than otherwise, provided always that it is thoroughly enriched by manure. Sow them in drills one foot apart and two inches deep. When the plants have attained three or four leaves then thin them out so they may stand five or six inches apart. Keep them free from weeds by hand weeding or hoeing. In October the roots may be taken up and stored in the cellar or in pits outside, like potatoes, care being taken that they are not bruised or injured in the process.

EGYPTIAN BEET TURNIP.

No. 208.—The earliest Beet and one of the leading market sorts, having a deep crimson color.

BASTIAN'S BLOOD TURNIP.

No. 209.—An early variety of a blood red color, when properly cooked.

DEWING'S BLOOD BEET.

No. 210.—The roots are of a deep blood red color. It is of fine form and flavor, very early and an excellent variety.

EARLY FLAT BASSANO.

No. 211.—Chiefly valuable for its earliness.

LONG SMOOTH BLOOD RED.

No. 212.—An excellent late variety.

EARLY YELLOW BEET.

213.—Similar to the blood red, but different in color. The flesh is yellow, tender and sweet.

PINE APPLE BEET.

No. 214.—A highly esteemed English variety of rich deep crimson color.

BRAZILIAN VARIEGATED.

No. 215.—Beautiful for garnishing and flower garden decoration. The stems and veins are richly colored with crimson, yellow and white.

SWISS CHARD, OR SEA KALE BEET.

No. 216.—This variety is cultivated solely for its leaves. The midrib is stewed and served the same as asparagus, and the other parts of the leaves are used like spinach. If it is cut often, new and more tender leaves will be produced.

HOW TO PREPARE BEETS FOR COOKING.

No. 217,—Beets when young are prepared as a vegetable for the table. They must be boiled whole, without having anything cut from them except the tops. These must always be cut an inch from the root and care taken not to injure the root, for if it is in any way injured the beet will lose its flavor and color. When boiled let them get cold, then peel or rub off the skin and prepare as needed.

BOILED BEETS STEWED.

No. 218.—Boil the Beets, and when done skin and slice them. If large, cut them in two and put them in a saucepan. Season with salt and pepper and add a piece of butter, tossing them over the fire. Serve hot, or boil a glass of vinegar with a piece of butter, seasoned with salt and pepper, and pour it over the Beets.

STEWED BEETS, HANOVERIAN STYLE.

No. 219.—Boil one dozen ordinary sized Beets and when done skin and slice them. Put into a saucepan one fine chopped white onion with a piece of butter. Fry it lightly and then add a wine-glassful of vinegar. When it boils add the sliced beets and four ounces of butter. Season with salt and pepper. Toss them over occasionally until thoroughly warmed, and before serving add some fine chopped parsley.

STEWED BEETS, WITH CREAM SAUCE.

No. 220.—Make a Cream sauce seasoned with salt, pepper, nutmeg and coriander. Add the sliced Beets, and, when thoroughly warmed, serve them.

STEWED BEETS, WITH BUTTER SAUCE.

No. 221.—Prepare the Beets as first described in No. 218. Add a few spoonfuls of Butter sauce, tossing them well over, and before serving add some fine chopped parsley.

STEWED BEETS, ST. IGNATIUS.

No. 222.—Chop a white onion fine and put it into a saucepan with four ounces of butter. Fry it lightly and then add two soup spoonfuls of flour. Cook to a light brown, while stirring it with a wooden spoon. Dilute this with a small wine-glassful of vinegar and some white broth to make a light sauce. Add three dozen young boiled Beets, cut into quarters, allowing them to simmer for fifteen minutes.

ROAST BEETS.

No. 223.—Use medium sized Beets. Rub them with a towel well impregnated with brandy, lay them on a wire crate and place it into a roasting pan. This mode will permit them to cook more evenly, as it takes about six hours to have them properly done. The crust of the Beet will then be carbonized. In cooking Beets in this manner all the sugary substance of the Beet concentrates in the center. It makes a most delicious dish, but is seldom prepared in this way in consequence of the time used in cooking.

BEETS FOR GARNITURE.

No. 224.—When the Beets are boiled, rub off the skin and trim them. Place them whole in earthen jars, covering them with vinegar, and when garnishing salads with them they are cut into various fancy shapes.

BEET FRITTERS, CHARTREUSE.

No. 225.—When the Beets are boiled, peel them and then slice them, but not too thin. Spread them on the table and cover half the sliced Beets with a thin slice of onion. Then season them with salt and a little nutmeg and sprinkle over them a little fine chopped parsley or chives. Then cover each of these with the other slices of Beets, pressing each of them well together. Dip them into frying batter and fry in hot lard. Drain them on a napkin and dish them up and garnish with fried parsley.

NOTE.—Burnet or chives finely chopped may be used with the parsley in seasoning them.

BEET SUGAR.

No. 226.—Beets are largely cultivated for the manufacture of sugar, which was first made about 1812, by a French chemist, during the blockade and siege of the First Empire. Beet sugar is cheaper than that made from the cane, but is not so profitable in its use.

BEET JUICE FOR SOUPS.

No. 227.—Beet juice is made for certain kinds of Polish soups, as is explained in the book on soups. Peel and cut in quarters enough of the finest kind of red beets to fill a small barrel. After putting them in the barrel pour in a sufficient quantity of cold water to cover them. Then put a linen cloth over the top and the cover over that. Place the barrel where the temperature is mild, to allow the liquid to ferment. In eight or ten days drain off the liquid and use it as directed. If bread crumbs or barley is used it will bring on fermentation much quicker.

BEET SALAD WITH VEGETABLES.

No. 228.—Beets mixed with corn salad, lamb lettuce or celery make a fine salad.

Young Beets sliced, with an equal proportion of artichoke bottoms, potatoes, white beans and glazed onions, and seasoned with salt, pepper, vinegar and olive oil, and nicely arranged in a salad bowl garnished with water cress, makes a fine breakfast salad.

PICKLED BEETS.

No. 229.—When the Beets are boiled, slice them and lay them in jars, alternating each layer with sliced onions, a little horse-radish, and a few cloves. When the jar is full, cover them with vinegar. These pickled Beets are for immediate use.

PICKLED BEETS FOR RELISHES, GERMAN STYLE.

No. 230.—When the Beets are boiled, peel them and cut them into slices one-eighth of an inch thick. Lay the slices in layers in an earthen jar, alternating each layer with some fine sliced onions, a few grains of pepper and coriander (or cumin if desired). When the jar is full, pour over the Beets some cold boiled vinegar, into which you add (while boiling it) four ounces of sugar to each quart of vinegar. Cover them tight and keep in a cool place.

NOTE.—If prepared with cumin, leave out the onions.

BEETS FOR RELISHES, AMERICAN STYLE.

No. 231.—Slice fine four cold boiled Beets, and season them with salt and pepper. Dish them in relish dishes and set in a cool place. Mash the yolks of two hard-boiled eggs fine, and dilute them with two soup-spoonfuls of oil and vinegar. When ready to serve, pour the sauce over the Beets, and garnish with fine chopped hard-boiled eggs.

ARTICLE XIX.

French   **BENE.**   German
Ben.   *Bene.*

No. 232.—Bene is said to have been introduced from Africa. It is a hardy annual plant, much used in the Southern States. The seeds are used for food (being first parched), stewed with meats, and are also used for puddings—the same as rice. An oil is extracted from the seed, which does not easily become rancid, and is used for softening and whitening the skin. The leaves, if immersed in a tumbler of water, will convert it into a mucilaginous drink, very beneficial in cases of cholera-infantum and diarrhœa.

CULTURE.

No. 233.—Sow in spring, as soon as the weather is settled, in rich, sandy soil, carefully prepared, and allow the plants to stand two feet apart, keeping the ground loose and free from weeds. The plant will yield a greater amount of herbage if the top is broken or cut off when three-quarters grown.

BI-FORMED LEAVED.

No. 234.—The plant is large. The lower leaves are two-parted, while those of the upper part of the stalk are oval and entire.

OVAL LEAVED.

No. 235.—The stem is about two feet high, with a few short branches. The leaves are oblong, and entire on the borders.

TRI-FIDE LEAVED.

No. 236.—This is taller and more vigorous than the preceding kinds. The leaves are tri-fide, or three-parted.

ARTICLE XX.

French — Cêpes.   **BOLETUS (Esculent).**   German — Morcheln.

No. 237.—This is a variety of the Mushroom family, comprising only two species that are eatable.

The Boletus *etulis* is very palatable, resembling the common mushroom in taste.

The Boletus *scaber* is of good quality, when young and fresh, but is of little value when dried, as it loses much of its odor and becomes insipid and unfit for use. For preparation, see Mushrooms.

Article XXI.

French   **BORAGE.**   **German**
Bourrache.   *Boretsch.*

No. 238.—Borage is a hardy annual plant, being used as a pot herb and for bee pasturage. The leaves, immersed in water, give an agreeable taste and flavor. It is used sometimes for medicinal purposes. The leaves when young are often used for salads. The flowers are dried in the shade and used for tisanes. The flower is star shaped, colored blue, white or red, and is occasionally used by female cooks to garnish dishes.

CULTURE.

No. 239.—Sow in April in rich sandy soil, carefully prepared, in drills ten inches apart and half an inch deep. The stalk and foliage contains a large proportion of nitre, and when dry they burn like match paper.

Article XXII.

BRIAR LEAVES.

Feuille de R nce.   *Brier blätter.*

No. 240.—Briar Leaves are used in diet drinks (tisanes) for colds and sore throats. The leaves are dried, placed in boxes, and kept in a dry place until used.

Article XXIII.

BROCOLI.

Choux Broccoli.   *Brocoli or Spargel Kohl.*

No. 241.—Brocoli resembles cauliflower, but is more hardy. In parts of this country, where the winter is not severe, it is to be had from November to March. It is one of the best vegetables, has a fine flavor and is easily digested. There are two kinds, the white and the purple. The Brocoli is not as compact as the cauliflower, its branches being longer and separate. It is prepared in all the styles that cauliflower is prepared in.

CULTURE.

No. 242.—In the Northern States sow them in May and transplant in June. In the Southern States sow them in July and transplant in August, as they dislike summer heat more than cold weather. They succeed best in a moist and rather cool atmosphere. Sow in deep rich soil, with an abundance of moisture, which in dry seasons must be applied artificially.

WHITE CAPE.

No. 243.—The heads are of medium size; close, compact, and of a creamy white color. One of the most certain to head.

PURPLE CAPE.

No. 244.— One of the hardiest and most popular varieties, most certain to form a good head, and is the earliest of the purple varieties.

BROCOLI, ITALIAN STYLE.

No. 245.—Cut the flower buds of the Brocoli in small bunches, boil them in water, lightly salted, and when tender drain them. Put them into a saucepan with a piece of butter, and season with salt and pepper, tossing them over a brisk fire. Before serving them pour over them some Anchovy butter sauce, in which add the juice of a lemon and some finely chopped parsley.

BROCOLI WITH HOLLANDAISE SAUCE.

No. 246.—Trim and boil them the same as in No. 245. When boiled drain them on a napkin, and then pour a Hollandaise sauce over them. Serve hot.

BROCOLI FOR GARNITURE.

No. 247.—Cut the flower buds in small pieces and boil them as in No. 245. Drain them and serve them in bunches around the intended dish, with some reduced Cream or Allemande sauce over them.

BROCOLI CREAM SOUP.

No. 248.—Prepare them the same as the soup of cream of cauliflower. See article on Cauliflower.

ARTICLE XXIV.

BROOKLINE OR SPEEDWELL.

French — *Cressnoée Veronique.*
German — *Wilde Kruosemünze.*

No. 249.—Brookline is a hardy perennial plant, and grows naturally in ditches and streams of water. The stem is thick, smooth and succulent. It sends out roots at the joints, by which the plant spreads. The whole plant is used as a salad, in the same manner, and for the same purpose as water cress. It is excellent as an anti-scorbutic.

ARTICLE XXV.

BRUSSELS SPROUTS.

Choux de Bruxelles. *Sprossen Kohl.*

No. 250.—Brussels Sprouts are small cabbage sprouts the size of a nut. They get green in the latter part of the fall, and are one of the best of winter vegetables, gradually becoming more and more appreciated in the United States. The plant grows from two to three feet in height, and produces from the axils of the leaves, an abundance of sprouts, which have an excellent and mild flavor.

CULTURE.

No. 251.—The culture is the same as for cabbage. If early plants are raised in hot beds they will perfect themselves in September. When the winters are not very severe they may remain in the ground, to be cut as needed.

TALL FRENCH.

No. 252.—A variety producing an abundance of sprouts.

DWARF IMPROVED.

No. 253.—A variety producing compact sprouts of excellent quality.

HOW TO PREPARE BRUSSELS SPROUTS FOR COOKING.

No. 254.—Wash the Sprouts in plenty of cold water, take off the outer leaves, drain them and put them into a saucepan with boiling water lightly salted. Let them cook on a brisk fire until tender, and then immerse them in cold water, and when cold drain them, discarding the fallen leaves from the sprouts. If used as a garniture they should not be boiled as much as when used as a vegetable.

BRUSSELS SPROUTS WITH FINE HERBS.

No. 255.—After the sprouts are boiled as in No. 254, spread them on a pan and pick off the outer leaves. Put the sprouts into a saucepan with a piece of butter and season them with salt and pepper. Warm them thoroughly and when ready to serve add some fine chopped parsley.

BRUSSELS SPROUTS WITH SAUCE.

No. 256.—After the sprouts are prepared as in No. 255, add some Allemande sauce, tossing them well together. Serve with some fine chopped parsley over them.

BRUSSELS SPROUTS, SPANISH STYLE.

No. 257.—When the sprouts are boiled as in No. 254, put them into a flat saucepan with a piece of butter. Season them with salt, pepper and a pinch of sugar. Toss them over the fire until thoroughly warmed, then add some Espagnole sauce. Serve them with a garniture of roast chestnuts and small fried sausages around the dish.

BRUSSELS SPROUTS FOR GARNITURE.

No. 258.—When the sprouts are boiled as in No. 254, put them into a saucepan with a piece of butter. Season them with salt and pepper and toss them over the fire until thoroughly warmed. Dress them in bunches around the dish.

BRUSSELS SPROUTS FOR GARNITURE, WITH BROILED MEATS.

No. 259.—Prepare them the same as in No. 254, adding some butter or Allemande sauce, the juice of a lemon and some fine chopped parsley. Serve in the center of the dish.

PUREE OF BRUSSELS SPROUTS FOR GARNITURE.

No. 260.—When the sprouts are boiled, drain them. Then put them into a saucepan with a piece of butter. Season them with salt, pepper and a little nutmeg. Toss them over the fire, adding some Cream sauce. Should the sprouts not be of a bright green color add some green of spinach. Rub the whole through a fine sieve. Return them to the saucepan and add a piece of butter and a few drops of meat glaze.

ARTICLE XXVI.

BUCK'S-HORN, OR COCK'S-HEAD PLANTAIN.

French
Plantain ou Corn de Serf.

German
Paradiesfeige.

No. 261.—This is a hardy annual. The root leaves are put forth horizontally, and spread regularly about a common center, somewhat in the form of a rosette. The plant is cultivated for its leaves, which are used as a salad. They should be plucked while young and tender, or when half-grown.

CULTURE.

No. 262.—It succeeds best in soil comparatively light. Sow in April in shallow drills, eight inches apart. When the plants are about an inch high thin them to four inches apart.

ARTICLE XXVII.

BUCKWHEAT.

Sarrasin ou blé noir. *Buchweitzen.*

No. 263.—Buckwheat originated in Asia, but it is now universally grown. It is easily cultivated, and in a favorable climate will produce two crops. Its use is healthful and nourishing, and it is easy of digestion, especially when boiled with milk. When cold, after having been boiled, it is cut in slices and fried. When the

Buckwheat flour is made into batter, it makes a winter breakfast dish well known to and appreciated by all Americans. Buckwheat, when made into bread, is only good while in its fresh state, for as soon as it becomes dry it splits, and on being cut, crumbles into small pieces and becomes hard to digest.

COMMON BUCKWHEAT.

No. 264.—Buckwheat should be sown about the middle of June, and should be threshed as soon as it is dry, on the ground of a barn floor. If allowed to stand in mass it quickly gathers moisture.

SILVER HULLED BUCKWHEAT.

No. 265.—This variety is a great improvement on the ordinary Buckwheat. Sown at the same time as the common Buckwheat, it continues in bloom longer, matures earlier, and yields nearly double under the same conditions. The grain is of a beautiful light gray color, varying slightly in shade, and the corners are much less prominent than in the ordinary variety, while the husk is thinner, thereby saving twenty per cent. in the process of manufacturing into flour.

BUCKWHEAT CAKES WITH YEAST.

No. 266.—Put three pounds of Buckwheat flour into a pan, and make a hole in the center of the flour. Pour into this three pints of water, two ounces of dissolved compressed yeast, and two tablespoonfuls of salt, and mix them slowly to make a light batter without lumps. Gather the sides together, cover the pan with a cloth and set it in a warm place overnight to raise. Next morning mix it up gently before baking.

NOTE.—When a little syrup is added to the batter in the morning, they will bake to a nicer color. A handful or two of corn meal is often added while mixing the Buckwheat flour.

BUCKWHEAT CAKES WITH BAKING POWDER.

No. 267.—Put into a pan three pounds of Buckwheat flour and three soup-spoonfuls of baking powder. Mix them up well, and make a hole in the center of the flour, into which pour three pints of luke-warm water and two tablespoonfuls of salt and mix to a light batter. Ten minutes after mixing, bake it. Should the cakes not be light enough, add a little more baking powder, as the majority of baking powders are very unreliable.

NOTE.—There is to be had a prepared Buckwheat flour, which is much preferable for small families. This flour is easily prepared, it being only necessary to use luke-warm water and salt, but the batter must be used as soon as mixed.

BAKING OF BUCKWHEAT CAKES.

No. 268.—Much depends on the cooking of the cakes to have them done properly. First, the griddle must always be very clean, heated evenly, and should not be allowed to get burning hot. Grease it lightly with leaf lard, and drop enough batter to make ordinary sized cakes. Let them cook on one side before turning them, and serve them hot with sugar or syrup.

ARTICLE XXVIII.

French
Buglose.

BUGLOSS.

German
Ochsenzunge.

No. 269.—Bugloss is a medical and pot herb plant. It is used to make refreshing broths for invalids and in depuratives and apozems. The flower of the Bugloss is used for garnishing salads and cold relishes.

CULTURE.

No. 270.—Same as other pot herbs.

ARTICLE XXIX.

BURNET.

Pimprenelle.   *Pimpinelle.*

No. 271.—Is a hardy perennial plant. The leaves, proceeding directly from the root, are produced on long stems and are composed of from eleven to fifteen smaller leaves, which are of an oval form, regularly toothed, and not uniformly smooth. The leaves have a warm, piquant taste, and are used in salads and occasionally as an ingredient in soups. The roots, after being dried and pulverized, are used in cases of internal hemorrhage. There are three varieties—the hairy leaved, the large seeded, and the smooth leaved Burnet.

CULTURE.

No. 272.—Same as other herbs.

Article XXX.

French
Choux pommé.

CABBAGE.

German
Kopf kohl.

No. 273.—The Cabbage is a biennial plant and is propagated from seed sown annually. Cabbage is a plant extensively used and is prepared in various ways. It is very nutritious and there are many varieties. The white, the green and the red may be had all the year round. The cauliflower, brocoli, Brussels sprouts and kale all belong to the Cabbage family. Cabbage should be well cooked, otherwise it will cause indigestion. In boiling Cabbage, if the water is changed, it will remove that strong odor disliked by many. To preserve Cabbage during winter, pull them on a dry day and turn them over on their heads for a few hours so as to let them drain. Set them in a cool cellar or bury them with their heads down in long trenches in a dry situation. In the Middle States bury the heads and parts of the stamp in the open ground, placing over them a light covering of straw or boards to protect them from severe weather. The Savoy Cabbage is the best of the white sorts. The red Cabbage is formed the same as the other Cabbages, and only differs from them in color, and is preferred by many to the other sorts. It is best in the fall and throughout winter and keeps well, but the outer leaves must be occasionally removed, or else they will decay.

CULTURE.

No. 274.—For the successful culture of Cabbage the very best quality of seed must be used. A heavy moist and fresh loam is most suitable, and should be highly manured, as well as deeply worked. The early sorts should be sown very early in hot beds, hardened off and transplanted eighteen to twenty inches apart, early in the spring. In the South, sow them from the middle of September to the middle of October, and transplant into cold frames, to preserve them through the winter, setting them into open ground as early as possible. The late autumn and winter varieties may be sown from the middle to the last of spring, and transplanted when about six inches high, three feet apart each way. Shade and water the late sowings in dry weather to get them up. It is important that the plants should stand thinly in the seed bed, or they will run up weak and slender, and be liable to make long stumps. In transplanting they must be set in the ground up to the first leaf, no matter how long the stem may be. Cabbages should be hoed every week, and the ground stirred deeper as they advance in growth, throwing up a little earth to the plant each time, until they begin to head, when they should be thoroughly cultivated and left to mature. Loosening the roots will often retard the bursting of full grown heads.

EARLY JERSEY WAKEFIELD.

No. 275.—The heads are very compact, of medium size, conical and early, as well as sure as a heading sort.

EARLY ETAMPES.

No. 276.—This matures nearly or quite as early as the Jersey Wakefield, but is not as pointed. It forms small, compact heads as early as the earliest, and is of excellent quality.

EARLY YORK.

No. 277.—A very valuable early variety, with small, heart-shaped, firm and tender heads, of a very dwarf growth.

EARLY LARGE YORK.

No. 278.—It succeeds the Early York and is equally desirable. It is of larger size, more robust, and bears the head better.

EARLY SUGAR LOAF.

No. 279.—A very compact growing variety. The plants may set as close as sixteen inches apart. It is more affected by the heat than most of the early varieties.

LITTLE DIXIE.

No. 280.—The heads are small, very hard and of very fine flavor. The plant is small but vigorous.

HENDERSON EARLY SUMMER.

No. 281.—This is the earliest large heading Cabbage grown. It is so compact that it may set as close as the smaller sorts. The heads are large, flat or slightly conical. They keep longer without bursting than most of the other sorts.

EARLY FLAT DUTCH.

No. 282.—The favorite second early sort. The heads are large and solid, broad and roundish, very tender, fine grained and of the best flavor, and are also well adapted for second crop for fall or winter use.

EARLY DWARF, FLAT DUTCH.

No. 283.—An excellent second early variety, which does particularly well in the Southern States. The heads are of medium size, solid and flat. It grows slow on the stump and is of good flavor.

EARLY WINNINGSTADT.

No. 284.—This is one of the best for general use, being a very sure header, and will grow a hard head under circumstances where most kinds would fail. The heads are regular, conical shaped and very hard. It keeps well both in summer and winter.

EARLY BLEICHFIELD GIANT.

No. 285.—This is a new German variety of Cabbage that has been highly recommended wherever tried, and is worthy of extensive cultivation. It is short stemmed, and is a reliable and very solid header of the highest quality.

FILDER KRAUT.

No. 286.—This is similar to the Winningstadt, but larger and more pointed. It is highly esteemed for making kraut, and is good either for the first or second crop.

DRUMHEAD SHORT STEM.

No. 287.—This is an excellent second early sort and is particularly recommended for the South, as it withstands the heat well. It is a sure header. The heads are low on the stump, being compact and solid.

EARLY LARGE SCHWEINFURT.

No. 288.—It forms a very large showy head of excellent quality, but does not stand the heat well. When grown in perfection it is one of the handsomest of the second early sorts.

IMPERIAL FRENCH OX HEART.

No. 289.—This grows low on the stump. The heads are very close and firm and of a yellowish green color.

RED DUTCH, FOR PICKLING.

No. 290.—This is excellent for pickling or eating raw. It forms very hard oblong heads, round at the top and of a dark or purple color.

FINE BLOOD RED.

No. 291.—A Cabbage of a remarkably deep blood red color and a great favorite.

MARBLEHEAD.

No. 292.—It is characterized by its sweetness and delicacy of flavor and by its reliability in forming a large head. It is very hardy and will endure the cold of an extreme northern climate.

LATE FLAT DUTCH.

No. 293.—This is a low growing variety, with large heads of a bluish green color; round, solid, broad and flat on the top. It is often tinted with red and brown. An excellent fall and winter variety and a good keeper.

LARGE DRUMHEAD.

No. 294.—The drumhead Cabbage is a large fall or winter variety, with a broad, flat, round head and short stump. It is tender and of good flavor and is an excellent keeper.

MARBLEHEAD MAMMOTH DRUMHEAD.

No. 295.—The largest Cabbage known, weighing, under good cultivation, from thirty to fifty pounds each.

GREEN GLAZED.

No. 296.—A standard late variety in the South, not being affected by the heat. The heads are large but rather loose and open. It is very desirable on account of its immunity from the attacks of insects.

EARLY DWARF ULM SAVOY.

No. 297.—This is one of the earliest and sweetest of the Savoy Cabbages, with small, round and solid heads. The leaves are small, thick, fleshy and of a fine deep green color, and of most excellent quality.

GREEN GLOBE SAVOY.

No. 298.—This does not make a firm head, but the whole of it, being very tender and of pleasant flavor, is used for cooking. The leaves are wrinkled and dark green. It is very hardy, being improved by frost.

AMERICAN SAVOY.

No. 299.—This closely approaches the cauliflower in its delicacy and delicious flavor, and is the best of all the Savoys. It has a short stump and grows to a large size, being compact and solid, and is a sure header.

DRUMHEAD SAVOY.

No. 300.—This grows to a large size, with heads that are nearly round, but a little flattened on top. Color, dark green.

BOILED CABBAGE.

No. 301.—Wash and clean two heads of Cabbage. Then cut them in quarters, cutting out the stalks, and put them in a saucepan with boiling water on a brisk fire, to which add a piece of bacon or salt pork (the bacon or pork having been parboiled for five minutes). When the Cabbage is well cooked drain it on a colander and put the Cabbage into a saucepan, season it with salt and pepper. Serve with the bacon or pork nicely trimmed.

NOTE.—If the Cabbage is used as a plain vegetable, add a piece of butter. Pig's jowl or corned beef may be cooked with the Cabbage in the same way.

CABBAGE WITH POTATOES, FLAMANDE.

No. 302.—When the Cabbage is cooked, as in No. 301, drain it on a colander, chop it fine, and put it into a saucepan with one quarter of its quantity of mashed potatoes. Mix the whole well together and season it with salt and pepper. Add a few spoonfuls of thickened veal gravy and let it simmer for half an hour.

BRAIZED CABBAGE, FRENCH STYLE.

No. 303.—Trim and wash two heads of Cabbage, cut them into quarters and parboil them for fifteen minutes. Then immerse them in cold water, drain them on a napkin, and cut out the stalks. After this season them with salt and pepper, and then roll each quarter together, covering each one with a thin slice of fat pork, which must be tied on with a string. Line the bottom of a deep, flat saucepan, with thin slices of fat pork. Slice one carrot and one onion fine, and place them on the pork, adding a few grains of pepper and cloves, a bay leaf, and a faggot of parsley garnished with a sprig of thyme. Place the Cabbage on top of this, and then moisten it all with sufficient broth to cover it. Put the cover on the pan and place it on the fire to boil. When it boils, set it on the side of the fire to simmer slowly. When it is all thoroughly cooked, take the Cabbage out, remove the string and pork, and put the Cabbage in another flat saucepan to keep warm. Then strain the gravy to take off the grease, and add three spoonfuls of Allemande sauce to reduce it to its consistency. When it is ready to serve, dish up the Cabbage and pour the sauce over it.

CABBAGE, GERMAN STYLE.

No. 304.—Trim and wash two heads of Cabbage. Cut out the stalks and cut the leaves in shreds. Put into a saucepan two finely chopped onions and four ounces of butter or lard. Fry them lightly, not letting them get brown. Then add the Cabbage and season it with salt and pepper. Put on the lid and cook slowly for twenty minutes, stirring the Cabbage occasionally, and then add a wine-glassful of vinegar. When the moisture is reduced, add a few spoonfuls of topping from the stock-pot to nourish the Cabbage. Let it cook until thoroughly done.

CABBAGE WITH BACON, FAMILY STYLE.

No. 305.—Trim and wash two heads of Cabbage, quarter them and remove the thickest part of the stalk. Put the Cabbage in a saucepan with a piece of parboiled bacon or salt pork, and half a dozen sausages. Add to this two carrots, three onions (each garnished with four cloves), and a faggot composed of parsley, celery, a sprig of thyme, and one bay leaf. Cover it all with boiling water and season with salt. Place the saucepan on the fire to boil, then cover it and let it boil slowly until the Cabbage is thoroughly cooked. Then remove the faggot and the onions. When it is ready to serve, put the Cabbage on a dish, with the bacon on top, garnish it with the sausages and carrots cut in thin slices, and pour a little of the gravy over it.

STUFFED CABBAGE.

No. 306.—Trim off the first outer leaves of two middle-sized solid heads of Cabbage. Then parboil the Cabbages for twenty minutes, after which immerse them in cold water and drain them on a napkin. Then cut out the stalk and turn the leaves carefully out from the center. Have a stuffing prepared, composed of two pounds of sausage meat seasoned with salt, pepper and spices, with which add some cooked fine herbs, the yolks of four hard-boiled eggs chopped fine, and two dozen roasted chestnuts. Put this stuffing into the center of the Cabbages and replace the leaves so as to form the shape of the Cabbage. Cover the opening with a thin slice of fat pork and tie up the Cabbages with a string so that they may retain their shape. Have a saucepan large enough to hold the Cabbage, and line it with thin slices of pork. Put the Cabbages into the saucepan, leaving the opening on top. Garnish them with one sliced carrot, two whole onions (into which stick half a dozen cloves), a faggot of parsley, with a sprig of thyme and one bay leaf. Season with salt and pepper. Cover them with broth and set the pan on the fire to boil. Then put on the lid and let it cook slowly until the Cabbages are thoroughly done. After which take out the Cabbages carefully, remove the string and dish up the Cabbages. Strain the gravy into another saucepan, take off the grease, reduce and thicken it lightly, and when ready to serve pour the gravy over the Cabbage.

STUFFED CABBAGE, HUNTERS' STYLE.

No. 307.—Prepare two heads of Cabbage the same as in No. 306, and fill the center with small sausages prepared in chipolata style, roast chestnuts and some boned reed birds. Arrange the leaves of the Cabbage and finish them as in No. 306. Put them into a saucepan, lined with thin slices of fat pork, and garnish them with two carrots, two onions, a faggot of parsley, and some trimmings of ham and veal. Season with salt and pepper, and moisten with broth to cover. Put on the lid and let them cook slowly until the Cabbages are well cooked and glazed. Then take out the Cabbages, remove the strings and dish them up. Strain the gravy into another saucepan, remove the grease, and add four spoonfuls of Espagnole sauce, reducing this to its consistency. Cook some marrow, separately, cut it into slices, and add it to the sauce which is served with the Cabbage.

CABBAGE, BISMARCK STYLE.

No. 308.—Trim and wash two heads of Cabbage, quarter them and cut off the thickest part of the stalk, parboil them for ten minutes, and immerse them in cold water. Press each quarter in your hand so as to squeeze out the water, then tie each one with a string, so that they may keep their shape. Put them into a saucepan and season with salt and pepper. Add a piece of butter, two dozen small onions, and a faggot of parsley, garnished with bay leaves, thyme, and a few grains of pepper. Moisten them with broth to cover, letting them cook slowly. When the Cabbages are nearly cooked, add one dozen small sausages, and when thoroughly cooked, take out the Cabbages and dish them up on pieces of toast, with the onions and sausages around the Cabbages. Strain the gravy into another saucepan, remove the grease, then reduce and thicken the gravy lightly and pour it over the Cabbages.

CABBAGE WITH CREAM.

No. 309.—Trim and wash two heads of Cabbage, quarter them and remove the stalks. Cook them in water lightly salted, and when cooked drain them and place them upon a chopping-board and chop them finely. Put into a saucepan a piece of butter, and when it is melted add the Cabbage. Season it with salt, pepper and nutmeg. Fry lightly for ten minutes, not letting the Cabbage get scorched. Then add one pint of cream, reducing it on a brisk fire. Before serving add a piece of butter.

STEWED CABBAGE, SPANISH STYLE.

No. 310.—Trim and wash two heads of Cabbage, quarter them, remove the stalks and cut the leaves into fine shreds. Parboil them for five minutes and immerse them in cold water, then drain and press them dry. Put into a saucepan a piece of butter, and when melted add the Cabbages. Cover the saucepan and let them simmer, to reduce the moisture. Prepare separately, and put into a saucepan one sliced carrot, one sliced onion and a faggot of parsley, garnished with a sprig of thyme, one bay leaf, three cloves, and two cloves of garlic. Fry them lightly in some clarified butter, to which add one quart of broth and a wine-glassful of Madeira wine. Let this cook until it is reduced three-quarters. Strain the gravy and remove the grease, adding the gravy to the Cabbage, after the moisture of the latter has been reduced. Let it simmer until the Cabbage is tender and nicely glazed. Before serving drain off the butter, dish up the Cabbage, and garnish it with glazed chestnuts and fried sausages. Serve separately, a reduced Espagnole sauce.

CABBAGE WITH QUAILS OR PARTRIDGES.

No. 311.—Trim and wash four heads of Cabbage, quarter them and cut out the stalks. Parboil the Cabbages in water, lightly salted, until they are three-quarters cooked and then drain them on a colander, pressing out the water. After this spread them on a table and cut them coarsely, seasoning with salt, pepper and nutmeg.

Dress four partridges, or one dozen quails, as you would for roasting. Parboil them for two minutes, then drain and wash them in cold water.

Now line a saucepan with thin slices of fat pork. Put a layer of Cabbage in the bottom and around the sides of the saucepan. Then arrange on this six quails, four young carrots and two whole onions, into which stick six cloves. Cover this with a layer of Cabbage. Then lay on this the other quails, one-half a pound of parboiled bacon and half a dozen small smoked sausages. Cover this with the rest of the Cabbage. Put on this a thin layer of sliced pork and moisten with drippings of the stock broth. Then put on a buttered paper cover, and on this the lid of the saucepan. Set it on the fire, and, as soon as it boils, set it on the side and let it cook slowly for one and a half hours, after which take off the buttered paper and pork. Then remove the Cabbage and put it in a colander to drain, keeping the quails, sausages, bacon and carrots separate. Dish up the Cabbage with the quails, placing the latter so that only their breasts are exposed. Cut the bacon and carrots in slices and split the sausages in half and garnish the Cabbage and quails with them.

HOT SLAW.

No. 312.—Trim and wash two heads of Cabbage. Cut them in quarters and cut out the stalks, then cut the leaves into fine shreds. Season with salt and pepper. Put into a saucepan half a pound of fat pork cut into small pieces, and fry it until nicely browned. Add to this a wine-glassful of vinegar and the Cabbage, and cover the saucepan immediately. Let it simmer slowly for twenty-five minutes. Serve as a vegetable or a garniture for roast pork.

COLD SLAW.

No. 313.—Cut the leaves of a head of Cabbage into fine shreds, and season with salt, pepper, oil and vinegar.

NOTE.—Cold Slaw is generally served with oysters. A very nice way is to mix red and white cabbage and have a cream dressing for it.

CABBAGE SALAD.

No. 314.—Trim and wash one head of Cabbage. Quarter it and remove the stalks and the hard rib of the leaves. Then cut the leaves into fine shreds and parboil them for five minutes. Then immerse them in cold water and dry them on a napkin. Put them in a salad bowl, and season with salt, pepper, oil and vinegar, mixing the whole well together.

Red Cabbage may be prepared in the same way, or it may be mixed with white, using half of each kind, and dressed with a mustard dressing. Garnish with pickled beets and hard-boiled eggs.

CABBAGE SALAD, BOSTON STYLE.

No. 315.—Cut the Cabbage leaves into fine shreds. Put them in a bowl and season with salt and pepper. Put into a saucepan a wine-glassful of vinegar and a piece of butter, and set it on the fire to boil. Then pour the hot vinegar over the Cabbage and cover the bowl. When cold, add a cupful of cream and mix the whole well together. Arrange it in the salad bowl and garnish with eggs.

CABBAGE SALAD WITH CREAM, AMERICAN STYLE.

No. 316.—Cut the hearts of two heads of Cabbage into fine shreds. Put into a saucepan a glass of white wine vinegar, and when it boils, add one ounce of butter, and salt and pepper enough to season the Cabbage, a teaspoonful of powdered sugar, and then the Cabbage. Let it get thoroughly warm, then put it into an earthen bowl. Dilute the yolks of four raw eggs in a little cold milk, strain it through a sieve, and add it to a pint of boiling milk while stirring it. As soon as it thickens, take it off of the fire, pour it over the Cabbage, and mix it well. Cover the bowl, and when cold put it into a salad bowl. Dress it in its proper shape, and garnish with beets and hard-boiled eggs cut in quarters.

RED CABBAGE SALAD.

No. 317.—Cut the leaves of a small head of red Cabbage into fine shreds. Wash them in cold water, drain them on a napkin, and put them into a salad bowl with six hard-boiled eggs chopped up finely. Make a dressing of salt, pepper, oil, vinegar, mustard, and a pinch of sugar. Pour it over the Cabbage and mix the whole well together. Arrange it properly, and garnish it with hard-boiled eggs, cut in quarters. If oil is not desired, add clarified butter.

RED CABBAGE, GERMAN STYLE.

No. 318.—Trim and wash two heads of Cabbage, cut out the stalks, and cut the leaves into fine shreds. Put into a saucepan four ounces of butter, with two finely-chopped onions. Fry them lightly and add the Cabbage. Season with salt and pepper, cover the saucepan, and let it cook slowly until the moisture is reduced Then add a wine-glassful of vinegar and half a bottle of red wine. Let it cook until the moisture is nearly reduced, when the Cabbage should be well cooked.

RED CABBAGE, HOLLANDAISE STYLE.

No. 319.—Trim and wash two heads of red Cabbage, cut them into quarters, remove the stalks and cut the leaves into fine shreds. Parboil them for five minutes and then drain them. Put into a saucepan a piece of butter with two finely-chopped onions. Fry them lightly, and add the Cabbage, with half a dozen peeled, sliced apples. Season with salt, pepper, a little fine sugar, and a faggot of parsley well garnished. Let them simmer slowly for one hour, then add a large glassful of Burgundy wine, and let them cook half an hour longer. When ready to serve, take out the faggot, add a piece of butter, and toss well together.

RED CABBAGE, VALENCIENNE STYLE.

No. 320.—Cut into small pieces two pounds of salt pork or bacon, and fry them lightly. To this add two heads of red Cabbage, cut into fine shreds. Season with salt, pepper and nutmeg, and moisten with half a pint of broth and half a glassful of Kirschwasser. Then lay half a dozen sliced and peeled apples on top of the Cabbage. Cover the saucepan and let them cook slowly for one and a half hours, without stirring them, but care must be taken not to let the Cabbage adhere to the bottom. When ready to serve, toss it all well together and garnish with small, fried sausages.

CABBAGE FOR GARNITURE.

No. 321.—The Cabbage as prepared in Nos. 302, 303, 304, 309, and 318, can be used for garniture, as may be required. They are generally served with sucking pigs, roast pork, boar, geese, etc.

CABBAGE SOUP.

No. 322.—Trim the outer leaves of two heads of young Cabbage, cut the heads into quarters, remove the stalks, and wash the heads in cold water. Parboil them for fifteen minutes with one pound of bacon or salt pork. Immerse them in cold water, drain them in a colander, and then press the Cabbages dry. Put into a saucepan two pounds of beef from the breast bone or the rump, and arrange the cabbages around it. Add a faggot of parsley, garnished with a head of celery, two leeks and one bay leaf, two onions, into which stick six cloves, two carrots, and the bacon or pork. Add to this one gallon of cold water, then set it on the fire to boil. Skim it and season lightly with salt, letting it boil slowly for three hours. Then take out the Cabbages and cut them in small pieces. Place them in a soup tureen with pieces of toasted French bread, cut to the size of half a dollar. Strain the broth, season to taste, and pour it into the tureen. Serve hot.

CABBAGE SERVED WITH BROTH, GARBURE.

No. 323.—Trim and wash two young heads of Cabbage, cut them in half and remove the stalks. Parboil them in water, lightly salted, until three-quarters cooked. Then drain them, separate the leaves, and place a layer of them in a silver or earthen baking dish. Put on this a layer of thin slices of Gruyere or Swiss cheese, and over the cheese put thin slices of bread, alternating this way until the dish is full, seasoning each layer with salt, pepper, and a little nutmeg. Moisten it to cover with good beef broth, and set it in an oven to gratinate for an hour. Serve with a soup tureen of good beef broth.

PICKLED CABBAGE.

No. 324.—Trim the outer leaves of two heads of Cabbage, cut them into quarters and remove the stalks. Cut the tender leaves into fine shreds and put them into an earthen bowl, with half a pound of fine salt to two pounds of Cabbage, and mix well. After three days drain off the liquid, and put the Cabbage into glass jars, filling them three-quarters full. Add a few grains of pepper and two bay leaves to each jar holding two quarts. Pour into each jar enough of the best wine vinegar to cover the Cabbage well. Close the jars tight and keep them in a cool place. After using, be sure to tightly cover each jar.

PICKLED RED CABBAGE, ENGLISH STYLE.

No. 325 —Prepare the red Cabbage the same as in No. 324. When putting the Cabbage in the jar, add some small, peeled and parboiled onions, a few cloves, some small green peppers, and a little ginger.

SAUER KRAUT.

No. 326.—Sauer Kraut is a German preparation and is highly esteemed by them, when well prepared. It is made in large quantities in this country, especially in the Northern States. It is seldom made in private families here, as it can be so readily procured of dealers at all times. To make good Sauer Kraut, only the best of cabbage heads should be used. When prepared to keep for a certain length of time, use new barrels, or those which have contained vinegar or white wine. Sauer Kraut is cabbage cut into fine shreds, pickled in salt, and made to ferment in the barrel. To keep it well preserved, it must be kept in a cool and even temperature, and must be kept well pressed under the brine. It is an agreeable vegetable to be eaten with salted meats.

SAUER KRAUT, HOW TO MAKE.

No. 327.—Take a barrel and knock out the head. Then set it in a stationary place half a foot from the ground, in a cool and even temperature. Bore a hole in the barrel, about two inches from the bottom, and put therein a wooden faucet with a strainer inside of the barrel. Now select as many cabbages as are needed to fill the barrel, using only the best, solid white sorts procurable. Trim off the green leaves and cut out the stalks, then cut the cabbage into fine, short shreds, using a slide-board which has three or four knives, which are made for such a purpose. Place the slide-board over a wooden tub to receive the cabbage when it is cut up. Put a layer of salt in the bottom of the barrel, and then a layer of cabbage two inches thick. Add salt again, then cabbage, and thus alternate until the barrel is full. To every thirty pounds of cabbage use one and a half pounds of fine salt.

NOTE.—A few bay leaves, carraway or anise seed, may be added with the layers of cabbage, but should be used only with moderation.

When the barrel is full, cover the top with a layer of cabbage leaves, and spread a linen cloth over this, placing on top of the cloth a wooden cover, made to go inside the barrel, and on this cover place some heavy weight that will press the cover down very tight. Five days after let the brine run off and add the same quantity of fresh brine, changing it once every sixth day until the brine has been changed four times, or until the brine runs clear and without odor. To keep Kraut from moulding, the brine must always cover the cabbage. Two months after the Kraut is first put in the barrel it will be ready for use. Care must be taken to always keep the Kraut covered after any of it has been taken from the barrel for use.

SAUER KRAUT, HOW TO PREPARE FOR COOKING.

No. 328.—Before cooking the Sauer Kraut, soak it in fresh cold water for two hours. If it has a strong odor, change the water. When ready for cooking drain it.

SAUER KRAUT, GERMAN STYLE.

No. 329.—Prepare three pounds of Sauer Kraut as in No. 328. Chop one large onion fine and put it into a saucepan with two spoonfuls of drippings from the stock-pot or roast meats. Fry it to a light brown and then add the Sauer Kraut, three peeled fine-sliced apples, one tumblerful of white wine and a pint of broth. Cover the saucepan and let it simmer slowly on the fire for two hours. Then sprinkle two soup spoonfuls of flour in it, mix it up well, and if necessary add a little more broth and let it simmer for half an hour longer. When ready, serve it in a deep dish and garnish with pig's jowl or fried sausages.

The pig's jowl may be cooked with the cabbage or separately.

SAUER KRAUT, FRENCH STYLE.

No. 330.—Prepare the Sauer Kraut as in No. 329. Add to it some salted or pickled spare-ribs of pork and one smoked sausage. When this is all well cooked, dish up the Sauer Kraut and garnish it with the spare-ribs and the sausages cut in slices. Always prepare more than is required for one meal. What is left can be set aside in a cool place, and when warmed over two or three days after, it will be relished much more than at first.

SAUER KRAUT, BAVARIAN STYLE.

No. 331.—When the Sauer Kraut is prepared for cooking, as in No. 329, add to it two pounds of fresh pork from the loin or leg. When it is well cooked dish it up with the pork. Serve separately a dish of potato balls (Kartoffelshnitzhen), poached in broth, lightly salted. Dish these up with fine chopped onions, fried in clarified butter. Put the latter over the potato balls.

SAUER KRAUT, FLEMISH STYLE.

No. 332.—Prepare the Sauer Kraut as in No. 329. When it is well cooked, drain it in a colander and put the Sauer Kraut into a mould to fit the dish intended to serve it on. Press it into the mould solidly and keep it warm until ready to serve. Then turn it on to the dish, care being taken to keep the Kraut well together. Dish on top of it a salmis of snipes or partridges, with a well-reduced sauce, and garnish the dish with toasted bread, cut into fancy shapes and buttered with lobster butter, into which add a little puree of anchovies.

SAUER KRAUT BAKED, DUFOUR.

No. 333.—Cut in small scallops an equal quantity of cooked smoked beef tongue, calf's head, mushrooms and breast of partridges. Add to this a reduced Madeira wine sauce. Cook the quantity of Sauer Kraut necessary, as in No. 329, and when cooked put it into a colander to drain it of its moisture. Then put a layer of the Kraut into a baking dish, hollow the middle and add the above preparation. Cover this with the rest of the Sauer Kraut, filling the dish up nicely. Sprinkle on top some fresh bread crumbs and some butter, divided into small pieces. Wipe the borders and bake in a slow oven until nicely browned.

SAUER KRAUT BAKED WITH FILLET OF SOLES.

No. 334.—Cook the quantity of Sauer Kraut necessary, as in No. 329. Drain it in a colander and press it dry. Then put it into a saucepan (to a pound of Sauer Kraut add half a pint of reduced cream sauce), with four ounces of lobster butter. Mix this well together off of the fire.

Take out the fillet from six medium-sized soles (or flounders). Remove the skin and season and bread them, frying them in hot lard. Drain them on a napkin and let them get cold.

Place a layer of the Kraut in a baking dish, and on top of this a layer of the fried fillet, cut in scollops. Alternate thus until the dish is full and cover the top with Sauer Kraut. Sprinkle on this some fresh bread crumbs and some lobster butter, divided into small pieces. Wipe the borders, bake in an oven, and serve hot.

SAUER KRAUT WITH PARTRIDGES OR QUAIL.

No. 335.—Cook the Sauer Kraut as in No. 329. When nearly done, drain off the moisture. Have ready two roasted partridges, or six quails, three-quarters cooked. Add them to the Sauer Kraut and cover the saucepan tight. Let them simmer slowly until the birds are tender. When ready to serve, dish up the Sauer Kraut, with the birds nicely arranged on top.

Article XXXI.

CALABASH, OR COMMON GOURDS.

French   German
Citrouille ou Potiron.   *Kürbis.*

No. 336.—The Calabash is of the same family as the squash and pumpkin. The fruit, when young, is hairy on the outside, and quite soft and tender. The surface, however, becomes hard, smooth and glossy when the fruit is ripe. The fruit is only fit for use when young, and it is then pickled in vinegar, the same as cucumbers. The flesh, when fully ripe, is worthless, but the shells, which are hard, light, compact and very strong, are used in the manufacture of baskets and for many ornamental purposes. There are four varieties: the Bottle Gourd, the Hercules Club, the Powder Horn, and the Siphon Gourd. They are cultivated in the same manner as squash or pumpkins.

Article XXXII.

CALAMINT.

Calament ou Calamus.   *Kalaminth.*

No. 337.—Calamint is an aromatic root, of the Orris variety, having a delicate, violet odor, and is used as a substitute to impart a violet flavor.

To make the flavor, by infusion, cut the roots in small pieces, put them in a bottle, pour alcohol over them, and then cork the bottle tight. Pastry cooks use the roots for flavoring when they are dried and pulverized.

Article XXXIII.

CANTALOUPE OR PERSIAN MELONS.

Cantal up.   *Melone.*

No. 338.—Cantaloupes differ remarkably from the common varieties usually cultivated. They are destitute of the thick, hard rind which characterizes the common melons and which renders so large a portion of the melon useless. The skin of the Persian Melon is thin and delicate, the flesh being extremely tender, rich and sweet, flowing copiously with a cool juice that renders them still more grateful. They are not an early melon, and for their perfection require a long and warm season.

GERMEK.

No. 339.—This is a handsome, large-sized fruit, with a deep green skin, closely netted. The flesh is from one to two inches deep, and is of a clear green color, firm, juicy, and highly flavored. It is an excellent variety and an abundant bearer.

GEREE.

No. 340.—This is a handsome, green fruit, oval-shaped, with a short stalk. The flesh is about two inches thick, of a bright green color, being very sweet and highly flavored. It is a good bearer, requiring a long, warm season.

DAREE.

No. 341.—This resembles the Geree in shape. The flesh is white, thick and crisp, melting when fully ripened. If imperfectly matured, it is generally insipid, but always remains cool and pleasant.

GREEN HOOSAINE.

No. 342.—This is a handsome, egg-shaped fruit. When unripe it is of a deep green color, but in maturity it acquires a fine, even, light green, regularly netted surface. The exposed side becomes rather yellow in color. The flesh has a pale green and white tint, and is tender and delicate and full of highly perfumed, sweet juice. It is a hardy variety, of great excellence, and a good bearer.

GREEN VALENCIA.

No. 343.—A desirable winter variety, of much excellence, a great bearer and very hardy. Though not rich in flavor, it is firm, saccharine and juicy.

ISPAHAN.

No. 344.—This is said to be the most delicate of all Melons. It is egg-shaped, weighing from six to eight pounds. The skin is nearly smooth and of a deep sulphur yellow color. The flesh, which extends nearly half way to the center, is nearly white in color and is crisp, sugary and very rich.

MELON OF KEISING.

No. 345.—This differs from the sweet Ispahan in being a closely netted Melon, egg-shaped, and regularly and handsomely formed, though extremely delicate. The skin is of a pale lemon color, and the flesh nearly white and from one to two and a quarter inches thick. It flows copiously with juice, and is sweet and high flavored. The rind is thin but firm.

MELON OF SEEN.

No. 346.—An oval-shaped Melon, of handsome appearance, with a small mamelon at the apex. The surface has a pale, dusky yellow color, and is regularly and closely netted, except the mamelon. The rind is very thin, and the flesh is from an inch to two inches thick, of a pale green color, sometimes becoming reddish towards the center. It is exceedingly tender, and has sweet and delicately perfumed juice. It bears well, but requires a long season.

HOW TO SERVE CANTALOUPES.

No. 347.—Cantaloupes are served before breakfast, and before dinner as a relish, or after dinner as a dessert. They should always be kept in a cool place an hour before serving. Select a Melon not over ripe, cut it in half and take out the seeds. Then cut it in ordinary sized slices and pass a knife under the flesh, without detaching it altogether from the rind. Serve it on a napkin, with salt and pepper.

MELONS PRESERVED IN CANS.

No. 348.—All of the varieties of Melons can be preserved. The best are preferred, and they must not be too ripe. Cut the Melons in slices and remove the seeds and the softest part of the Melon. Then peel the outside of the rind and cut the hard part of the Melon in scallops, parboil them until tender and drain them. Put them in an earthen jar and cover them with a light syrup for three hours. Then take them out, arrange them in quart cans and cover them with a vanilla flavored syrup of thirty-two degrees. Then solder on the covers and boil them in a hot water bath for half an hour.

PRESERVED MELONS IN SYRUP.

No. 349.—Select Melons that are not too ripe. Cut them in slices, remove the seeds and peel off the rind. Cut the slices in three or four pieces, parboil them until tender, and then immerse them in cold water for two hours. Then take them out, trim the pieces of Melon and put them in an earthen jar. Cover them with a cold syrup at fourteen degrees for two hours and then drain off the syrup. Cook it to sixteen degrees, and when lukewarm turn it over them again. Repeat this four times, twice a day. The fifth time cook the syrup to thirty-two degrees and put in the Melon. Let it boil up once and then let it stand on the side of the fire for one and a half hours. Then take it off, and when cool put them in jars, covered tight, and set them in a cool dry place. If, after a certain time, they should ferment, boil them over again.

Article XXXIV.

French	CAPERS.	German
Câpre.		*Kaper.*

No. 350.—The Caper bush grows in warm climates. The young buds are picked and then pickled for use. They are preferred when small, and of a bright green color. They have a warm, aromatic taste, and are used in sauces, salads, and various other culinary preparations.

CAPERS PICKLED IN VINEGAR.

No. 351.—Pick out small Capers, all of the same size, as they are the best. Those developed are not fit for use. Pick off the stems and put the Capers in jars or bottles, and cover them with cold, boiled vinegar. A sprig of Tarragon in each bottle will afford an excellent flavor. Keep the bottles corked tight, and in three or four weeks the Capers will be ready for use.

CAPER SAUCE.

No 352.—This is simply a butter sauce with Capers added, and is generally served with boiled mutton and fish.

Article XXXV.

CAPILLARY OR VENUSHAIR.

Capillaire. *Frauenhaarsyrup.*

No. 353.—There are three varieties—the white, black, and Canadian—the latter kind being used most. They are diuretic, stomachic, and principally bechic. The Capillary syrup has all the virtue of the plant, and is used by pastry cooks for Bavarian creams, etc. The Capillary syrup and the syrup of marsh mallow have the same properties, and are used for the same purposes.

CAPILLARY SYRUP.

No. 354.—Take seven pounds of sugar and boil it to a light syrup. When it is boiling hot pour it over six ounces of Capillary. Then cover it and let it lay until next day, when you will drain off the syrup, boil it again to thirty-two degrees, and then pour it boiling hot over the Capillary again. When it is cold, strain it and put it in bottles.

NOTE.—When the Capillary is boiled with the syrup, its flavor evaporates somewhat, and leaves a disagreeable taste.

ARTICLE XXXVI.

French — Carvi. **CARAWAY.** German — Kümmel.

No. 355.—Caraway is a biennial plant of the parsley family. The seeds have an aromatic flavor and a warm pungent taste. Caraway is cultivated for its seeds, which are used by bakers, confectioners, and distillers, and also in medicine—as a carminative.

CULTURE.

No. 356.—Sow it in August, and the plant will give a fair crop of seed the next season. Plant it in drills and thin it to six inches apart.

ARTICLE XXXVII.

CARDOON.

Cardon. Kardon.

No. 357.—There are two kinds of Cardoons—the Spanish and the ordinary—of which there are several species—which are cultivated for the stems and midribs. The Spanish variety is preferred, as the stems are thicker than the ordinary, the latter having the flavor of artichokes. It is a vegetable much esteemed in Europe, though seldom used in this country, but it is becoming popular here. The flowers are gathered and dried in the shade, and are used to coagulate milk.

CULTURE.

No. 358.—Cardoon is grown for the midribs of the leaves, which require to be blanched the same as celery. When the plants are to remain, sow them early in spring, in drills three feet apart and an inch and a half deep. Then thin out the young plants to a foot apart in drills.

LARGE SPANISH.

No. 359.—The ribs are longer than in the ordinary Cardoon, and the whole plant is much stronger. It runs up to seed quicker than the other variety.

THE ORDINARY.

No. 360.—This is of a shiny green color, the stems growing about five feet high. Its leaves are large and strong.

ARTICHOKE LEAVED.

No. 361.—This is remarkable for its strong growth and the thickness of its midribs, which are almost solid. It is a tender and fine variety.

LARGE TOURS SOLID.

No. 362.—The midribs are large and solid, yet tender and delicate. Notwithstanding the inconvenience arising on account of its numerous and rigid spines, it is considered one of the best varieties.

CARDOONS WITH MARROW.

No. 363.—Take six white and solid Cardoon stems (the hard and hollow ones are of no use) and cut them four inches in length. As you prepare them put them in a pan of cold water, acidulated. Have a saucepanful of boiling water on the fire, in which you will put the juice of five lemons. Put the pieces of Cardoon in this water and parboil them until you can peel off the outer surface easily. Take them off of the fire to peel and trim them, adding sufficient cold water to allow you to put your hand in the water. Then put the peeled Cardoons in fresh water and drain them on a napkin. Prepare a deep flat saucepan lined with fine slices of fat pork, in which you will put the Cardoons. Season them well with salt, pepper and a pinch of sugar, and moisten with enough broth to cover them. Add the juice of two lemons and cover the Cardoons with thin slices of fat pork. Put on the lid and let them boil, after which let them cook slowly. When done drain them on a napkin. Dish them up and then pour a reduced Espagnole sauce over them, garnish around the dish with small patties or buttered toast filled with scallops of marrow cooked with fine herbs. Then serve.

CARDOONS WITH PARMESAN CHEESE.

No. 364.—Prepare and cook them the same as No. 363, and when done drain them on a napkin and trim them. Arrange a layer of Cardoons in a buttered baking dish, add a little reduced Espagnole sauce and sprinkle it with Parmesan cheese. Make three layers like this and sprinkle the top with Parmesan cheese and fresh bread crumbs mixed together. Wipe off the border, put a little butter on the top, and then bake it in the oven.

CARDOONS, WITH CREAM SAUCE.

No. 365.—Prepare and cook them the same as in No. 363, and when cooked drain them on a napkin. Dish them up and then pour over them a Cream sauce, to which add a spoonful of half glaze.

CARDOONS, WITH ESSENCE OF HAM.

No. 366.—When the Cardoons are parboiled and cleaned, as in No. 363, put them in a flat saucepan with a glass of white wine and some broth to cover them. Season with salt, pepper, and a pinch of sugar, and let them cook until the moisture is reduced, and they are nicely glazed. Then put them in a dish, and pour over them a reduced brown sauce, with essence of ham.

CARDOON FRICASSEE.

No. 367.—Cook the Cardoons as in No. 368, and reduce the moisture without letting them get brown. Take out the faggot and add a few spoonfuls of Allemande sauce and the juice of one lemon. Toss it all well together, and serve with a garniture of buttered toasted bread, cut in fancy shapes.

CARDOONS FOR GARNITURE.

No. 368.—Cut the Cardoons in pieces one and a half inches long. Parboil and clean them as in No. 363, and drain them on a napkin.

Put them in a flat saucepan, with a small piece of butter. Moisten them with white broth, and season with salt, pepper, and a pinch of sugar, and add the juice of a lemon and a faggot of parsley, garnished with a piece of lean ham. Let them cook slowly until tender, and then take out the faggot. The moisture must be well reduced. Take the pan off of the fire, and add a small piece of butter and a little chopped parsley. Toss them well together until the butter is melted, and then serve as required.

PUREE OF CARDOONS.

No. 369.—Prepare and cook them as in No. 368. When well cooked take out the faggot, reduce the broth, and add two spoonfuls of Allemande or Cream sauce. Rub them through a fine sieve, put them back in the saucepan, and before serving add a small piece of butter.

CARDOON SALAD, SPANISH STYLE.

No. 370.—Prepare and cook the Cardoons the same as in No. 363. Then cut them in scollops an inch long and drain them on a napkin. Put them in a salad bowl and season them with salt and pepper. Then chop two cloves of garlic very fine and put them in a frying pan with a little sweet oil. Fry them lightly (not letting them get brown), and add immediately some bell peppers, chopped fine, and some vinegar. Then let them boil up for two minutes and pour the dressing over the Cardoons, mixing them well together, and then serve.

CARDOONS PRESERVED.

No. 371.—Prepare and clean the Cardoons as in No. 363. Cut them all the same size and drain them. Then put one gallon of water in a saucepan, and when it boils, add two spoonfuls of flour, diluted in cold water, a little salt, and the juice of two lemons. Stir it until it boils, so it will not get lumpy. When it boils, add the Cardoons, and cook them until tender. Take the saucepan off of the fire and let the Cardoons get cold. Take each piece out and dip them in lukewarm water, and place them in quart tin cans. Cover them with cold-boiled water, lightly salted. Then solder on the cover, and cook them in a hot bath for two hours.

CARDOONS PUREE, PRESERVED.

No. 372.—Prepare and cook the Cardoons as in No. 363. When they are cooked tender, drain them. Rub them through a fine sieve, and put the puree in pint tin cans. Solder on the covers and boil the cans in a hot water bath for one hour and a half.

Article XXXVIII.

French
Carrote.

CARROT.

German
Möehre.

No. 373.—The Carrot is a biennial root, somewhat hardy, and is one of the most healthful and nutritious of garden roots. It is extensively used as a vegeteble for the table, and for seasoning and garnitures. It contains a certain amount of sugar, which adds to its nutritious quality. There are several different varieties, all of which can be obtained all the year round. The larger varieties are also cultivated as an agricultural root, and are better suited than other kinds of food for dairy cattle, not alone because they are nutritious, but because they impart a good color and flavor to the butter.

CULTURE.

No. 374.—The Carrot succeeds best in light, sandy loam, made rich by manuring the previous year. The roots often grow pronged and ill-shaped, in imperfectly manured ground. It is better to sow as early in spring as the ground can be got ready, but if planting is necessarily delayed until late in the season, the seed must be soaked in tepid water twenty-four hours, then dry it by mixing in sifted ashes, and sow it in fully prepared soil.

EARLY FRENCH FORCING.

No. 375.—This is the earliest variety, is valuable for forcing, and has a small root of fine flavor.

EARLY SCARLET HORN.

No. 376.—An old and favorite variety, much esteemed for summer use.

HALF LONG RED (STUNTED ROOTS).

No. 377.—A variety intermediate in size, with stunted roots. Its period of maturity is between the Early Scarlet Horn and the Long Orange.

HALF LONG SCARLET (POINTED ROOTS).

No. 378.—This is similar to the Half Long Red with stunted roots, except that the roots are pointed.

EARLY HALF LONG SCARLET CARENTON.

No. 379.—An early variety without core, and is excellent for forcing, or is used as an early kind for planting in the open ground.

LONG ORANGE.

No. 380.—It is adapted for garden or farm culture, and has large-sized roots.

DANVERS.

No. 381.—This is a valuable variety having the smallest root of any kind grown, but it will yield the greatest bulk. Its color is a rich shade of orange and it grows very smooth and handsome.

ALTRINGHAM.

No. 382.—An excellent variety, large and finely flavored.

LARGE WHITE BELGIAN.

No. 383.—A very productive variety, but grown almost exclusively for stock.

YELLOW BELGIAN.

No. 384.—When young, the roots are mild, delicate and of good flavor; when full grown, it is only valuable for stock.

HOW TO PREPARE CARROTS FOR COOKING.

No. 385.—Carrots should always be scraped, and should only be prepared when ready for use. When young use them as a vegetable, and prefer those that are stunt rooted. Cook them whole, or cut them in small parts. The large carrots are cut in different shapes, with spoon cutters, for garnitures, but when used as a vegetable, cut them in a short, thick Julienne. When used for Julienne soup, cut them two inches crosswise; then slice them, and cut them lengthwise in small stems. When they get older, use only the red part, which you peel off by cutting it the same thickness. In this way the pieces will stay whole, but in the other way the pieces will break off when cooked.

CARROTS MAITRE D'HOTEL.

No. 386.—Take three dozen young carrots and cut each one in half, then put them in water lightly salted, and when three quarters done, drain them. Put them in a saucepan with a piece of butter and a pint of broth, and season with salt and pepper and a pinch of sugar. Then put them over a brisk fire, and when the moisture is reduced, the carrots must be cooked. Add two spoonfuls of Allemande sauce and a little parsley chopped fine, then toss them well together and serve. When large carrots are used, slice and prepare them as you would young carrots.

CARROTS STEWED, GERMAN STYLE.

No. 387.—Prepare the carrots the same as in No. 386. When the broth is reduced, add a piece of butter, in which you will mix two spoonfuls of flour. Dilute it with some broth, then let it simmer slowly for ten minutes, add some fine chopped parsley, and then serve.

CARROTS, WITH BUTTER SAUCE.

No. 388.—Cut the Carrots in any shape desired, then boil them in water lightly salted, and when tender drain them. Then put them in a saucepan and season with salt, pepper, a little nutmeg and a pinch of sugar, and add a piece of butter. Toss them over the fire a few minutes, then add four spoonfuls of Butter sauce and serve.

CARROTS WITH GREEN PEAS, STRASBOURGEOISE.

No. 389.—Parboil two dozen young Carrots for five minutes, then drain them. After this put them in a saucepan with a piece of butter, then toss them over the fire and season with salt, pepper and a pinch of sugar. Moisten them with white broth, and when they are half cooked add as much green peas as you have Carrots, and a faggot of parsley garnished. Cover the saucepan and cook them on a brisk fire. When tender add two spoonfuls of Cream sauce. Toss them well together over the fire and add a piece of butter before serving.

STEWED CARROTS, INDIAN STYLE.

No. 390.—Cut and trim two dozen young Carrots, all of even size. Put them in water to cover them. Then season with salt, pepper and sugar, and add a piece of butter. Cook them until tender. Then slice an onion and put it in a saucepan with a piece of butter. Fry it lightly, adding a soup-spoonful of flour and a teaspoonful of curry powder. Let it cook for a minute, while stirring it well, and mix with it a glassful of cream and some of the Carrot broth to make a clear sauce. Add the Carrots then, and season with salt and pepper, and let them simmer for fifteen minutes.

CARROTS STEWED FOR GARNITURE.

No. 391.—Cut three dozen Carrots in a short, thick Julienne. Boil them, and when done, drain them. Put in a flat saucepan a piece of butter, and set it on the fire. When the butter commences to get brown, add the Carrots. Toss them well over the fire, add some chopped parsley, season with salt and pepper, a pinch of sugar, and add two spoonfuls of butter sauce.

CARROTS FOR LARGE GARNITURE, FLAMENT.

No. 392.—Take three dozen young Carrots, trim them in nice shape or cut them with large spoon cutters. Parboil them for five minutes and then drain them. Then put them in a saucepan with a piece of butter, a pinch of sugar and a pint of white broth. Cook them until the broth is reduced and the Carrots glazed. Serve them as needed.

CARROTS FOR SMALL GARNITURE, OLIVE-SHAPED.

No. 393.—Cut as many Carrots as are needed, in olive shape, with a spoon cutter. Cook them the same as in No. 392, and when glazed add four spoonfuls of Cream, Allemande or Brown sauce, which-ever may be desired.

CARROT GARNITURE, NIVERNAISE.

No. 394.—Cut the Carrots with a channelled spoon cutter, the size of a small olive. Cook them the same as in No. 392. When well glazed, add a small piece of butter and a little chopped parsley. Toss them well together, and serve with articles needed in Nivernaise style.

CARROT PUREE FOR GARNITURE.

No. 395.—Use young carrots or only the red parts of old ones. When washed and cleaned, parboil them for fifteen minutes, and then drain them in a colander. Put them in a saucepan with a piece of butter, and season with salt, pepper, a pinch of sugar and a little nutmeg. Put on the lid, set them over a slow fire and let them simmer, turning them occasionally, not letting them get brown. Moisten with a little broth, and when cooked and lightly glazed, add a reduced Allemande or cream sauce. Then rub it through a fine sieve, put it back in the saucepan and warm it thoroughly. Before serving, add a piece of butter.

CARROT SOUP PUREE, AURORE.

No. 396.—Take three dozen young Carrots, or the red parts of old ones, and slice them in fine pieces. Put them in a saucepan with a piece of butter, two onions, two pieces of celery, a faggot of parsley garnished with a leek, a little salt and a pinch of sugar. Cover the saucepan and let them simmer until the moisture is reduced, not letting them burn or get browned. Then add one quart of broth, and cook slowly until done. Then add one gallon of thickened veal or chicken broth, and let it all boil slowly for twenty minutes. Then take out the faggot, skim the top, and rub the puree through a fine sieve. Put it back into the saucepan to keep warm, and before serving add a piece of butter, stirring it well until melted. Serve with small fried bread-crumbs, separate.

CARROT SOUP PUREE, STANLEY

No. 397.—Prepare the puree the same as in No. 396. Before serving, add a pint of cream, in which dilute the yolks of six raw eggs and a piece of butter. Then add a garniture of balls of forced meat of chicken, green peas and asparagus tops, cooked separate.

CARROT SOUP PUREE, GERMAN STYLE.

No. 398.—Prepare the Carrots as in No. 396. When the moisture is reduced add two quarts of broth and the crumbs of a loaf of white bread. Let them cook slowly until the Carrots are thoroughly done. Then add two quarts of cream sauce while stirring it with a wooden spoon, and if it is too thick add some broth, to bring it to the proper consistency. After fifteen minutes, rub it all through a fine sieve, put it back on the fire to keep warm, then add a piece of butter and season to taste. Before serving, add some Vermicelli or Noodles cooked in broth.

SOUP PUREE, CRECY.

No. 399.—Cut the red part of two dozen Carrots in small pieces, parboil them for two minutes and drain them in a colander. Put them in a saucepan with a piece of butter and add two white onions sliced and the white part of two leeks. Let them simmer for five minutes until the moisture is reduced, stirring it occasionally. Then add two quarts of white broth, half a pound of rice or the crumbs of one square loaf of bread. Cook them slowly until well cooked, and add three quarts of chicken or veal broth, seasoned with salt, pepper and sugar. Rub the puree through a fine sieve, then put it back in the saucepan, stirring it until it boils. Then let it cook slowly for half an hour, then skim it and add a piece of butter. Serve it with small fried bread crumbs. In this soup boiled rice or any other paste may be used.

CARROT SOUP PUREE, CRECY, FOR FAST DAYS.

No. 400.—Prepare it the same as in No. 399. Use vegetable consomme in place of chicken or veal broth.

CARROTS PICKLED.

No. 401.—Use small young Carrots. Trim them, parboil them two minutes, and then peel them. Put them in a saucepan with boiling water lightly salted. Cook them until nearly done, then drain them and put them in earthen jars with enough cold boiled vinegar to cover them. Let it lay until next day, when you will draw off the vinegar and boil it, adding a little salt. Put the Carrots in a two-quart jar and pour the vinegar, when cold, over them (just enough to cover them). Then add half a dozen cloves and three bay leaves. Cover the jar tight and keep it in a cool place. Use them for garnishing, the same as beets.

CARROTS PRESERVED FOR GARNITURE.

No. 402.—Use young Carrots and cut them in any shape, but nearly all of the same size. Parboil them until half cooked, in water lightly salted. Drain and then dry them on a towel, and when cold put them in quart tin cans. Cover them with boiled water lightly salted. Then solder on the covers and boil in a hot water bath for one hour and a half. If you use whole Carrots, you must boil them for two hours.

PUREE OF CARROTS PRESERVED FOR SOUPS OR GARNITURES.

No. 403.—Use only the red part of four dozen Carrots. Slice them in fine pieces, parboil them five minutes, then drain them. Put them in a saucepan with two quarts of plain veal broth. Let them cook until the Carrots are well cooked, and then rub them through a fine sieve. Then put the puree in quart tin cans, solder on the covers, and boil in a hot water bath for an hour and a half.

ARTICLE XXXIX.

French — CATERPILLAR. — German
Scorpiure. *Raupenpflanzen.*

No. 404.—A hardy annual plant with creeping stems, that are about two feet in length. The seeds are produced in pods. No part of the plant is eatable, but the pods, in their green state, are placed upon dishes of salad, and so closely do they resemble a real caterpillar, that they will oftentimes deceive the uninitiated.

CULTURE.

No. 405.—Sow them in April, fifteen inches apart, in rows that are fifteen inches wide.

ARTICLE XL.

CATNIP.
Nepeta. *Katzenkraut.*

No. 406.—This is a hardy perennial plant, well known as a mild nervine for infants. The plant should be pulled up by the roots when in full flower, and dried in the shade.

CULTURE.

No. 407.—The seeds may be sown in drills, twenty inches apart, either in the fall or in spring.

ARTICLE XLI.

CATSUP.
Catsup. *Catchup.*

No. 408.—Too much care cannot be taken in buying Catsup, as there are many spurious imitations made that are deleterious to health, often producing dyspepsia, etc. It is made of tomatoes, mushrooms, walnuts, etc., as described elsewhere in this book and can be made in any family far superior to that which is purchased in stores, and having the advantage of being pure and healthful.

Article XLII.

French
Choufleur.
CAULIFLOWER
German
Blumen Kohl.

No. 409.—The Cauliflower, like Brocoli, is an annual plant, being delicious in flavor. It requires a cool, moist atmosphere to bring it to perfection, and if this condition occurs when the plant is about to head, fine large heads will result, whereas, if the air is hot and dry, failure will result in spite of the best of seeds and cultivation. Brocoli is a species of Cauliflower, and both are prepared in the same style. See Brocoli, Article XXIII.

CULTURE.

No. 410.—For the spring or summer crop, sow the early varieties, about the last of winter, in hot-beds, and transplant them into the open air as soon as the ground can be worked. For the late autumn crop, sow the late varieties about the middle of spring, and transplant them as you would winter cabbages. In dry weather water them freely, and as they advance in growth hoe deep and draw earth to the stems. After they begin to head they should be watered every other day. In two or three weeks the strongest will begin to form flower heads, which should be cut for use while the curd is close and compact. It is then tender and delicious, but later on the head opens and separates into branches and soon becomes coarse, fibrous, strongly flavored, and unfit for use. The leaves should be gathered and tied loosely over the tops of the heads to facilitate blanching. On the approach of frost, those plants that have not headed may be set out in a cellar and can be aired in mild weather.

EARLY SNOWBALL.

No. 411.—This is the earliest of all Cauliflowers. Its heads measure from 8 to 9 inches in diameter. Every plant forms a fine head. Its dwarf habit and short interleaves allow it to be planted as close as 18 inches apart each way. This variety does equally well for late planting.

EARLY DWARF ERFURT.

No. 412.—An early dwarf variety, having large white compact heads of the finest quality.

EARLY PARIS.

No. 413.—An excellent variety.

NONPAREIL.

No. 414.—A half early variety and one of the best.

EARLY LONDON.

No. 415.—An excellent and very early variety.

LENORMAND SHORT STEMMED.

No. 416.—A large late variety, with well-formed heads of superior quality.

WALCHEREN.

No. 417.—An old and favorite variety.

ALGIERS.

No. 418.—An excellent late variety, in general favor.

WEITH'S AUTUMN GIANT.

No. 419.—A valuable late variety, particularly in the Southern States and California.

HOW TO PREPARE CAULIFLOWER FOR COOKING.

No. 420.—Cut the root close to the stem, then trim off all of the leaves and wash them carefully in cold water, as there are often some insects among the stems and buds.

CAULIFLOWER, WITH BUTTER SAUCE.

No. 421.—Wash and trim them as in No. 420. Put them in a saucepan with enough water to cover them, and add a little salt when they boil. Let them cook slowly, adding a little milk and a piece of butter. When cooked, drain them on a napkin and be careful not to break the flowered buds. Serve on a napkin, with Butter sauce separate.

CAULIFLOWER, HOLLANDAISE.

No. 422.—Prepare the same as in No. 420. When cooked, drain them on a napkin. Put the Cauliflowers on a dish and put Hollandaise sauce over them.

If they are small and detached, put them in a bowl with the heads downward. Press them lightly, moulding them together, as it were, in the bowl, so they will all form together, making one large head. Then put it on a plate with the head up, and pour Hollandaise sauce over it.

CAULIFLOWER BAKED, AU GRATIN.

No. 423.—Cook the Cauliflowers as in No. 421. Drain off all the moisture and season them with salt, pepper and nutmeg. Then put them in a buttered baking dish, evenly formed, and pour over them a reduced cream or Allemande sauce, to which add some grated Parmesan cheese. Sprinkle fresh bread crumbs over them and put a small piece of butter on top. Wipe the borders off clean, and then bake in an oven.

CAULIFLOWER FRIED, VILLEROI.

No. 424.—Cook the Cauliflowers the same as in No. 421. After you drain them, cut off the flowered heads in small bunches and dip them in Villeroi sauce. Set them in a cool place, so the sauce will adhere to the Cauliflower. Then bread them with fresh bread crumbs. After this, dip them in beaten eggs and bread them again. Fry them in hot lard, until nicely browned, and serve them on a napkin, with fried parsley as a garniture.

CAULIFLOWER FRIED IN BATTER.

No. 425.—Cook the Cauliflowers as in No. 421. Then drain them and cut the flowered buds in small bunches. Put them in an earthen bowl, season them with salt and pepper, and add a little vinegar, some finely chopped parsley and chives, and cover them to macerate for two hours. Then place them on a towel to absorb all the moisture, and afterwards dip them in a light batter and fry them in hot lard to a nice brown color.

CAULIFLOWER, ITALIAN STYLE.

No. 426.—Cut off the flowered buds of the Cauliflower in small bunches. Then boil them in water lightly salted, and when tender drain them. Then put them in a flat saucepan with a piece of butter, and toss them over a brisk fire, seasoning them with salt, pepper, and a little nutmeg. When thoroughly warmed, dish them up and pour over them some Anchovie butter sauce, in which add the juice of one lemon and a little parsley chopped fine.

CAULIFLOWER FOR GARNITURE.

No. 427.—Cut off the flowered buds, boil them, and when done drain them. If you wish a small garniture, cut them small. If for a large garniture, leave them in bunches. For a large garniture dress them in bunches around the dish with other vegetables, and mask them lightly with a white sauce.

CAULIFLOWER PUREE, FOR GARNITURE.

No. 428.—Boil two heads of Cauliflower as in No. 421. Drain them and put them in a saucepan with four spoonfuls of Cream or Allemande sauce. Season with salt, pepper and nutmeg. Mix them well together, rub it through a fine sieve and put it in a flat saucepan. Reduce it with a glass of cream to its proper consistency, and before serving add a small piece of butter.

CAULIFLOWER SALAD.

No. 429.—Boil two heads of Cauliflower in water lightly salted. When cold cut off the flowering buds, dividing them in small tufts. Put them in a salad bowl, season with salt and pepper, and pour over them a light Mayonnaise or cream dressing. Mix gently, so as not to break them, and garnish with beets and water cress.

SOUP—CREAM OF CAULIFLOWER.

No. 430.—Cook four heads of Cauliflower as in No. 421. When drained put them in a saucepan with two quarts of Cream sauce. Dilute it to its proper consistency with chicken or veal broth, and season it with salt, pepper and nutmeg. Rub it through a fine sieve, then put it back in the saucepan to keep warm, not letting it boil. Before serving add a piece of butter, stirring it in well until the butter is melted. Then add some chives chopped fine. Cauliflower soup should only be made when you have fresh plucked young Cauliflower.

CAULIFLOWER SOUP PUREE.

No. 431.—Cook four heads of Cauliflower as in No. 421, and when drained put them in a saucepan with one gallon of thickened chicken or veal broth. Season it with salt and pepper, then rub it through a fine sieve and put it in a saucepan to boil for ten minutes. Before serving add one pint of cream diluted with the yolks of six raw eggs and a piece of butter. Add some small square pieces of breast of boiled chicken.

CAULIFLOWER PICKLED.

No. 432.—After you have picked and washed a number of Cauliflowers, cut off about three pounds of the flowered buds and arrange them in small bunches all of the same size. Put them in a pan of cold water. Then put some lightly salted water in a saucepan, and when it boils add the Cauliflowers. Let them boil for six minutes, then drain them and put them in an earthen jar. Then pour hot boiling vinegar over them and keep the cover on the jar until the next day, when you will drain off the vinegar. Then boil the vinegar again, adding a little salt, and pour it hot over the Cauliflower in the jar. When cold cover them tight and set them in a cool place. If glass jars are used pour the vinegar in slowly at first, as the glass is liable to crack.

CAULIFLOWER PRESERVED IN BRINE.

No. 433.—After you have picked and washed the Cauliflowers cut off the flowering buds in large bunches. Parboil them six minutes, then immerse them in cold water and afterwards drain them. Put them in earthen jars with a boiled salt brine of 18 degrees (sugar weight). Two days later drain off the brine and boil it over again, adding salt to bring it to 18 degrees. Pour it over the Cauliflower and cover the jar tight. When ready to use soak them in cold water for five hours, boil in fresh water, and serve as needed.

Article XLIII.

French **CELERIAC, OR TURNIP ROOTED CELERY.** **German**
Celeri Rave. *Knol Selleri.*

No. 434.—This variety has a brownish, irregular root, at the base of the leaves near the surface of the ground. It is much hardier than the common variety of celery. Those required for winter use should be drawn, packed in sand, and stored in the cellar before severe weather sets in. It is used in the same manner as the common celery. Its root, or bulb, is the only part eaten. Its flesh is white and tender, having the flavor of the stalks of common celery, though less mild and delicate. The leaf-stalk is used most for flavoring soups, and the bulbs are stewed or used in salad the same as celery.

CULTURE.

No. 435.—Sow it early in spring, in light, rich soil, and transplant it in May into beds, and water it freely in dry weather. When the plants are almost full grown, it is customary to earth up the bulbs to the height of four or five inches. In about a month they will be sufficiently blanched for use. The roots, which resemble turnips, will be ready in October, and may be preserved in sand during winter. It is a vegetable that is much esteemed for culinary purposes.

LARGE ERFURT.

No. 436.—This is a variety of Celeriac, having turnip-shaped roots, which may be cooked and sliced, and used with vinegar, to make an excellent salad. It is more hardy, and may be used in the same manner as celery.

APPLE-SHAPED.

No. 437.—This is a great improvement over the old variety, having small foliage, and large, round and smooth tubers.

CELERIAC FRIED, VILLEROI.

No. 438.—Pare and then wash six Celeriac roots in cold water and cut them in quarters. Take off the hard part, trim them in scallops, parboil them for 15 minutes, and drain them. Then put them in a flat saucepan lined with slices of fat pork and moisten them with white broth. Season with salt, pepper, nutmeg and a pinch of sugar. Then cover them with thin slices of fat pork, put them on the fire and let them cook slowly. When cooked take out the Celeriac and dry them on a napkin. Then strain the gravy in another saucepan and add four spoonfuls of Allemande sauce. Reduce it on a brisk fire and when cool dip the Celeriac in the sauce. Then arrange them in a pan and set them in a cool place, and when they are cold and the sauce adheres to the Celeriac, bread them in fresh bread crumbs. Then dip them in beaten eggs and bread them again. Fry them in hot lard and serve on a dish having a puree of Celeriac in the center.

CELERIAC PUREE FOR GARNITURE.

No. 439.—Prepare the Celeriac the same as No. 438. When the Celeriac is cooked strain and remove the gravy, then add four spoonfuls of Cream or Allemande sauce. Rub it all through a fine sieve and put it back in the saucepan. Then add a glass of cream to reduce it to its consistency. Before serving add a piece of butter and a few drops of meat glaze.

CELERIAC STEWED, SPANISH STYLE.

No. 440.—Cut the Celeriac roots in scallops and prepare them the same way as Celery No. 463.

CELERIAC STEWED, WITH ALLEMANDE OR CREAM SAUCE.

No. 441.—Cut the Celeriac roots in scallops and prepare them the same way as Celery Nos. 464 and 465.

THE USE OF CELERIAC TOPS.

No. 442.—Celeriac tops are used principally for garnishing faggots and for flavoring soups, etc.

CELERIAC WITH GRAVY (HALF-GLAZE).

Fo. 443.—When the Celeriac roots are peeled, cut them in quarters, then trim them all alike, and cook and serve them the same as Celery, No. 462.

CELERIAC, FOR SOUPS.

No. 444.—Prepare the same as those with common celery. Celeriac should always be added with the common celery in soups or purees, as it gives it a better flavor. The roots are also used for all of the other vegetable soups when celery is used in their combination.

CELERIAC, PRESERVED.

No. 445.—Peel and wash one dozen Celeriac roots and cut them in quarters. Trim them all the same size and parboil them for five minutes. Put two gallons of water in a saucepan, and when it boils put in it three spoonfuls of flour (diluted with a little cold water), the juice of three lemons and a little salt, and then add the Celeriac roots. When three-quarters cooked, take them off of the fire and let them cool. Then take out the Celeriac roots, dip them in lukewarm water, and arrange them in quart tin cans. Cover them with cold-boiled water, lightly salted. Then solder on the covers and boil the cans in a hot water bath for one hour and a half.

CELERIAC PICKLED.

No. 446.—Peel one dozen Celeriac roots, and cut them all of even size, not too thin. Parboil them in water lightly salted, until three quarters cooked. Then drain them and arrange them in an earthen jar. Then boil some wine vinegar and pour it over the Celeriac in the jar, while hot. Add a few grains of pepper and a few fennel leaves. Cover the jar and let it stand until the next day, when you will drain off the vinegar and put the Celeriac in glass jars. Put in a bowl four spoonfuls of English mustard flour. Dilute it with vinegar, add some red pepper, and mix it well together, to have a light gravy. Pour it over the Celeriac roots, then cover the jar and put it away.

CELERIAC PRESERVED IN BRINE.

No. 447.—Peel and wash two dozen Celeriac roots, and cut them in quarters. Parboil them until three-quarters cooked. Then immerse them in cold water, drain them, and dry them on a napkin. Put them in earthen jars and cover them with a strong boiled brine, when cold. Cover them and let them lay for two days, and then drain off the brine. Then boil the brine again, adding salt, to have it at about 16 or 18 degrees (sugar weight). When it is cold pour it over the Celeriac in the jars, put the covers on tight and put the jars in a cool place. When you are ready to use them soak them in fresh water for a few hours, and prepare them as required.

ARTICLE XLIV.

French   CELERY.   **German**
Celeri.   *Selleri.*

No. 448.—Celery is a hardy, umbelliferous biennial plant, and is always propagated from seed. The stems of the leaves are the parts of the plant that are used. These, after being blanched, are exceedingly crisp and tender, having an agreeable and peculiar aromatic flavor. They are prepared in various ways, but are generally served raw, for a relish, with salt or with oil, vinegar and mustard sauce. They are almost indispensable for salads.

CULTURE.

No. 449.—Sow the seed in shallow boxes, or in a finely prepared bed out of doors, in straight rows, so that the small plants may be kept free from weeds. When about two inches high, thin them out and transplant them so they will stand two inches apart. When they are about four inches high cut off the tops, which will cause them to grow stocky. The crop is usually an early one, and if good plants are used, they may be set out as late as the middle of August. The best results, however, are obtained by setting them out in the middle of June or the first of July. When setting them out, prepare broad, shallow trenches, about six inches deep and four feet apart, in which the plants should be set six inches apart. Cut off the outer leaves and press the soil firmly about the roots. In about six weeks the plants should be handled, which is done by having one man gather the leaves together while a second man draws the earth about the plant to one-third of its height, being careful that none of the earth falls between the leaves, as that would cause them to rust or rot. In a few days draw more earth around them, and repeat this process every few days until only the tops of the leaves are visible. In a few days more it will be fit for use. Do not disturb the plants when the ground is wet, as that will injure them.

At the approach of severe, freezing weather, take up the plants and put them in a light cellar or an unused frame, where the temperature can be kept above the freezing point. Set them out compactly, so that all but the tops of the leaves can be covered with sand. They will then gradually blanch, and may be used throughout the winter.

DWARF WHITE.

No. 450.—A favorite market variety of close habit, being solid, crisp and tender.

SANDRINGHAM DWARF WHITE.

No. 451.—An excellent variety, remarkable for its fine flavor and solidity.

GIANT WHITE SOLID.

No. 452.—This is of large size, solid and crisp.

WHITE WALNUT.

No. 453.—A dwarf habit seldom attaining a height of more than twenty inches. It is solid and heavy, having a rich walnut-like flavor. Its graceful and feather-like foliage, when blanched, makes it a most beautiful Celery for the table.

HALF DWARF.

No. 454.—A remarkably fine white variety, intermediate in size between the Dwarf and Large White. When blanched it is of a yellowish white color, making it very ornamental for the table. It is entirely solid, possessing a rich nutty flavor.

GOLDEN DWARF.

No. 455.—This is a distinct variety in size, but grows similar to the Half Dwarf, except that when blanched the heart, which is large, is of a waxy golden yellow color, which renders it most striking. It is entirely solid, has an excellent flavor and keeps well during winter.

LONDON RED.

No. 456.—The red Celery is generally superior to the white, being better flavored and more crisp. It is also hardier and keeps better in winter. The London Red is one of the best varieties, having every requisite good quality.

MAJOR CLARK PINK.

No. 457.—There is a disposition to grow red or pink Celery in preference to the white, which is as it should be, for as regards the flavor the red and pink are far superior to the white. The Major Clark Pink is a variety of medium growth of stiff, close habit, having a large heart, remarkably solid and crisp, and of a fine walnut flavor.

HOOD'S DWARF RED.

No. 458.—An excellent dwarf variety, solid and crisp.

HOW TO PREPARE CELERY FOR GENERAL USE.

No. 459.—Trim off the green stems, then cut off the tops, leaving the yellow center leaves. Make two deep incisions in the bottom of the stalk, so as to be able to wash the Celery well in cold water.

CELERY PLAIN, FOR RELISHES.

No. 460.—Trim the Celery, using only the tender hearts. Then put them in a basin, on ice, until ready for use, and then serve them in Celery glasses. Serve with a sauce made of Anchovie paste, diluted with warmed sweet oil, without letting it boil, or plain Anchovie butter. It can also be served after dinner, plain, with the cheese.

DRESSED CELERY.

No. 461.—Trim and wash the Celery in cold water, letting it lay on ice until ready for use. Then dry it on a napkin and cut it in thin sliced sticks, an inch and a half long. Season it with salt, pepper, and a few spoonfuls of cream of mustard dressing.

CELERY WITH GRAVY (HALF-GLAZE).

No. 462.—Clean and wash the celery and cut it in bunches, five or six inches in length from the root. Tie them together, single or double. Then parboil them for three minutes, immerse them in cold water and dry them on a napkin. Put some thin slices of fat pork in a saucepan and arrange the celery on it. Then season with salt, pepper, nutmeg and a pinch of sugar. Moisten it with veal gravy or a light Espagnole sauce, and cover with thin slices of fat pork. Put the saucepan on the fire, let it boil, and then cook slowly until tender and nicely glazed. Then put the Celery in a dish, strain the gravy through a fine sieve, and skim off the grease. Then pour the gravy over the Celery and serve.

CELERY STEWED, SPANISH STYLE.

No. 463.—Clean and wash the Celery and cut the white part in pieces of even size two inches long. Parboil them for three minutes, then immerse them in cold water and dry them on a napkin. Put the Celery in a flat saucepan, with a piece of butter, and season with salt, pepper, nutmeg, and a pinch of sugar. Cover the saucepan and let the Celery simmer until the moisture is reduced. Then cover it with white broth. Let it reduce on a brisk fire to a glaze, when the Celery must be cooked. Then add three spoonfuls of Tomato sauce and one of Espagnole sauce, and let it cook slowly for ten minutes. Add a small piece of butter, some parsley chopped fine, and toss it all well over a fire. Then serve with small toast of marrow around the dish as a garniture.

CELERY STEWED WITH ALLEMANDE SAUCE.

No. 464.—Prepare the Celery the same as in No. 463, and when it is cooked to a glaze add four spoonfuls of Allemande sauce. When it is ready to serve add a small piece of butter, some finely chopped parsley and the juice of one lemon. Toss it well over the fire and serve with small pieces of toast as a garniture.

CELERY STEWED WITH CREAM SAUCE.

No. 465.—Prepare the Celery the same as in No. 464, and add Cream sauce in place of Allemande sauce. Instead of lemon juice add a few drops of meat glaze, and then serve.

CELERY SAUCE.

No. 466.—Cut the tender part of two heads of Celery in pieces one inch long, or smaller if desired. Put them in a saucepan with enough water to cover them and season with salt. Let them boil until tender and then drain off half of the water. Add a pint of boiling milk and when it all boils add four ounces of butter in which you will mix two spoonfuls of flour, stirring it gently until melted. Season with salt, pepper and nutmeg, letting it boil 10 or 15 minutes.

CELERY FRIED, VILLEROI.

No. 467.—When the Celery is trimmed and washed, cut the tender stems in pieces four inches long. Parboil them for five minutes, then immerse them in cold water and drain them on a napkin. Put them in a saucepan with some broth to cover them, and season with salt, pepper and a little sugar. Let them cook slowly until tender, then take them out and drain off the moisture on a napkin. Then dip them in a cool Villeroi sauce, and place them on a pan in a cool place. When the sauce is firm trim them, roll them in fresh bread crumbs, then dip them in beaten eggs and bread them again. Fry them in hot lard and serve them on a napkin, with fried parsley to garnish.

CELERY WITH PARMESAN CHEESE.

No. 468.—Prepare the Celery the same as in No. 464. Add to the Allemande sauce some fine grated Parmesan cheese. Put the Celery in a buttered baking dish or in shells. Sprinkle the top with bread crumbs and grated cheese, and add a small piece of butter on top. Wipe off the borders clean and put it in an oven to bake.

CELERY FOR GARNITURE.

No. 469.—Prepare the same as in Nos. 462, 463, 464, and 465, with but very little sauce. The Celery in No. 462 is used for large garnitures. As a garniture for salad borders use it as follows: Trim all of the green leaves from the bottom of a head of celery, and cut it in pieces two inches long. Then slice it thin and cut the broad stems an inch deep, without detaching them. Then lay them in cold water for an hour, and they will be nicely frizzled. That is, the little shreds will be curled. When using Celery for the center of a salad, take the heart of the Celery and slice it thin a few inches from the top, and lay the pieces in cold water for an hour, when it will be nicely frizzled. This makes an attractive garniture over the salad.

CELERY PUREE, FOR GARNITURE.

No. 470.—Clean and trim six heads of Celery, cut the white parts in small pieces and parboil them for ten minutes. Then immerse them in cold water, drain them dry, and put the Celery in a saucepan with a piece of butter, and season it with salt, pepper, nutmeg, and a pinch of sugar. Add some white broth to cover it, then cover the saucepan and put it on a brisk fire to cook. When the moisture is reduced, and the Celery well cooked, add one pint of Allemande or Cream sauce. Rub it all through a fine sieve, then put it back in the saucepan and add a cup of cream to reduce it to its proper consistency, stirring it well with a wooden spoon. Add a small piece of butter before serving.

CELERY, WITH WHITE OR BROWN SAUCE.

No. 471.—When the Celery is cleaned, cut the tender parts in pieces half an inch long. Parboil them for five minutes, then immerse them in cold water and drain them in a colander. Then put the Celery in a saucepan with a piece of butter, and season it with salt, pepper, nutmeg, and a pinch of sugar. Then cover the saucepan and let the Celery simmer for ten minutes, not letting it get brown. Then moisten it with white broth, letting it reduce so as to glaze the Celery lightly. Then add Espagnole, Allemande or Cream sauce, as may be desired.

CELERY SALAD.

No. 472.—When the Celery is trimmed and washed, cut it in short, thick Juliennes. Season it with salt, pepper, vinegar and oil, and add some chives, chopped fine. Mix it all well together, and when ready for use dress it in a salad bowl and garnish with sliced tomatoes or beets, cut in fancy shapes.

NOTE.—When Celery is used in chicken or lobster salad, cut it in fine slices. It will preserve salad better than lettuce, when the salad is kept a length of time before using.

CELERY BROTH.

No. 473.—Clean and wash four heads of Celery, then cut them in pieces three inches long. Put them in a saucepan with one gallon of water. Let it boil slowly until the broth is reduced to one quart, and then strain it through a napkin. Drink it warm or cold. This is a very good beverage for nervousness.

CELERY SOUP PUREE, SPANISH STYLE.

No. 474.—Clean and wash six heads of Celery and trim off all of the green parts. Cut the tender parts in small pieces, one inch long, mixed with two celery roots sliced fine. Parboil them for five minutes, then immerse them in cold water and drain and dry them. Then put the Celery in a saucepan, with a piece of butter, and season with salt, pepper, nutmeg, and a pinch of sugar. Cover the saucepan and let it simmer until the moisture is reduced. Then add two quarts of white broth and a faggot of parsley, garnished with leeks and green onions. Let it boil until the Celery is well cooked, and then add one gallon of thickened veal or chicken broth. Let it all boil slowly for twenty minutes, then take out the faggot and strain the soup through a fine sieve. Then put it back in the saucepan to keep warm. When ready to serve, add a pint of cream, diluted with the yolks of six raw eggs, four ounces of butter, and some parsley chopped fine. Mix this all well together off from the fire until the butter is melted. Add some small fried bread crumbs before serving.

CELERY CREAM SOUP.

No. 475.—Prepare the celery the same as in No. 474, and when it is thoroughly cooked in the broth add three quarts of Cream sauce. Rub it through a fine sieve and put it back in the saucepan to keep it warm. Before serving it, add half a pound of butter in small pieces, stirring it all well until the butter is thoroughly merged in the soup. Also add some chervil chopped fine. The soup must not be too thick. Farina or vermicelli, cooked in white broth, may be added.

CELERY PUREE, PRESERVED.

No. 476.—Clean and trim six heads of Celery, using only the white, tender part, and four Celery roots. Slice them all in small pieces and put them in a saucepan. Cover them with boiling water and add a piece of butter and a little salt. Cover the saucepan and let them cook until tender. Then rub the puree through a fine sieve and put it in pint tin cans. Solder on the covers and boil the cans in a hot water bath for one hour and a half. When it is to be used, finish it with Allemande or Cream sauce.

PRESERVED CELERY.

No. 477.—Prepare one dozen heads of Celery, cut them in pieces six inches long, and parboil them for five minutes. Immerse them in cold water, and then drain and dry them. Put them in a saucepan with one gallon of water. When it boils, add to it three spoonfuls of flour, diluted in cold water, and also add the juice of three lemons and a little salt. When it is half cooked take it off of the fire and let it get cold. Then take out the Celery, one piece at a time, and dip them in lukewarm water to clean them. Then arrange them in tin cans (same as asparagus), and pour over them some cold-boiled water, lightly salted. Add the juice of one lemon in each can. Solder on the cover, boil the cans in a hot water bath for two hours.

CELERY PRESERVED IN BRINE.

No. 478.—Prepare the Celery and then cut each head in pieces six inches long. Parboil them until they are three-quarters cooked, then immerse them in cold water, then drain and dry them on a napkin. Put them in an earthen jar and cover them with a brine at 18 or 20 degrees (sugar weight), when cold. Cover the jar, and in two days remove the brine and put on the fire to boil. Add more salt, to bring it to the same degree as before. When it is cold, pour it over the Celery to cover it well. Put the cover on the jar tight and set it in a cool place. When ready for use soak the Celery in fresh water for several hours, and prepare it as required.

CELERY VINEGAR.

No. 479.—Cut four heads of Celery in small pieces. Put them in an earthen jar with four ounces of Celery seed, one ounce of pulverized white sugar, and half an ounce of salt. Pour two quarts of boiled vinegar, when hot, over this. Cover the jar, and in two weeks strain it through a filter. Then put it in bottles and cork well.

CELERY FLAVOR.

No. 480.—Put two ounces of Celery seed in a quart bottle and fill it with brandy. Cork it tight and let it lay for two weeks, when it will be ready for use.

ARTICLE XLV.

CENTAURY.

French: *Centaurée.*
German: *Tausendgüldenkraut.*

No. 481.—This is a small annual herbaceous plant, which grows wild. It is about a foot high, having a branching stem which divides above into pairs, and bears oval, smooth pointed leaves, direct from the stem. The flowers are rose colored. The herb has no odor, but has a strong bitter taste, and its tonic properties are similar to those of gentian. It is used in cases of dyspepsia and fever. The roots make a valuable yellow dye. The flowers are gathered in bunches, hung in a dark, airy, warm room, and when thoroughly dried are kept in boxes, in a dry place. They are used in diet drinks (tisanes), see Article LXXXII.

ARTICLE XLVI.

CHAMOMILE.

Camomille.   *Camomile.*

No. 482.—The single and double flowering Chamomile are propagated by slips, with a few of the small roots attached, both kinds being claimed as hardy perennials. In the Northern States the plants are frequently destroyed by severe frost. The single Chamomile, though considered more efficacious for medicinal purposes, is not cultivated as much as the double flowering variety. They may be grown from leaves or slips. The leaves, when cut fine and burned, emit a peculiar, pungent odor. The flowers, which are the parts generally used, are in high repute, both in the popular and scientific materia medica, and give out their properties by infusion in either water or alcohol. The flowers are also used in the manufacture of bitter beer, and along with wormwood are used to a certain extent as a substitute for hops. It is considered a safe bitter and tonic, though strong infusions, when taken warm, act sometimes as an emetic.

CULTURE.

No. 483.—Chamomile flourishes best in light poor soil, and is generally propagated by dividing the roots and setting them in rows that are a foot apart with the plants ten inches from each other. They grow fast and soon entirely cover the ground.

ARTICLE XLVII.

French
Cerfeuil.

CHERVIL.

German
Gartenkerbel.

No. 484.—Chervil is an aromatic plant that is used for aromatizing certain dishes, but should be used with moderation in soups and salads.

CULTURE.

No. 485.—Sow it thinly in May in drills half an inch deep and one foot apart.

TUBEROUS ROOTED.

No. 486.—Sow this variety in April and treat it the same as carrots.

ARTICLE XLVIII.

CHESTNUT.

Chataigne.   *Kastanie.*

No. 487.—The Chestnut is the fruit of the chestnut tree. It contains a large proportion of sugary matter, and is eaten either green or roasted. It is used as a garniture with braized meats, and can be added to all kinds of forced meats and to stuffing for turkeys, capons, geese, and chickens. Confectioners use chestnuts to a large extent. They rarely keep through the season. All first-class grocers keep them in a preserved state.

SOUP-PUREE OF CHESTNUTS.

No. 488.—Roast six dozen large chestnuts, and then put them in boiling water to peel off the inner skin. Put them in the saucepan, with enough broth to cover them. Cover the pan and let them cook slowly until tender, and then rub them through a fine sieve. Put them back in the saucepan and add one gallon of thickened chicken or veal broth. Set it on the fire and stir it with a wooden spoon until it boils. Then add a glass of Madeira wine and season to taste. Set it on the side of the fire to boil slowly for half an hour and then skim it well. Then strain it through a fine sieve, after which put it back in a saucepan to keep warm. When ready to serve it add a piece of butter and a garniture of asparagus tops.

SOUP-CREAM OF CHESTNUTS, HUNTER'S STYLE.

No. 489.—Prepare the Chestnuts as in No. 488. Put them in a saucepan with a piece of butter and moisten with enough broth to cook them. Then rub them through a fine sieve. Put this puree in a saucepan with one gallon of thickened game broth. Mix it well, stirring it until it boils, and season it to taste. Let it boil slowly for twenty minutes and then take off the grease. Strain it into another saucepan through a fine sieve. When ready to serve put six ounces of butter and six ounces of puree of partridge (diluted with the yolks of six raw eggs, and a pint of cream), into another saucepan and then pour the puree in slowly while stirring it. Care must be taken not to let it boil or else it will curdle.

SOUP GARBURE WITH CHESTNUTS, POLIGNAC.

No. 490.—Peel three dozen large Chestnuts, then pour over them some boiling water to peel off the inner skin. Line the bottom of a saucepan with thin slices of fat pork, put on top of this three pounds of veal trimmings. Add three raw onions, in which stick six cloves, then add three carrots, a faggot of parsley garnished with celery, in which tie two bay leaves and a few grains of pepper. Lay the Chestnuts over this and cover the whole with thin slices of fat pork. Moisten this with good broth, to cover it, and let it simmer until well cooked. Then take out the Chestnuts and split each one in half. Then put in a deep baking dish a layer of thin slices of toasted bread, then a layer of the Chestnuts, and keep on alternating this way until the dish is full. Strain the broth that the Chestnuts were cooked in, and pour some over it and set it in an oven to gratinate. Serve with a soup tureen of good consomme.

PUREE OF CHESTNUTS.

No. 491.—Peel two pounds of Chestnuts, and pour over them some lightly salted boiling water, to peel off the inner skin. Then put them in a saucepan with a piece of butter, and toss them over the fire a few minutes. Then moisten them with a glass of white wine and some broth. Cover the saucepan and let them cook until tender. Then take them all out and pound them through a colander, and rub them through a fine sieve. Put the puree in a saucepan to keep warm, and before serving add a piece of butter and a soup-spoonful of meat glaze. This may be served as a garniture. When served as a vegetable, garnish the puree with sausages *chipolata*.

GLAZED CHESTNUTS.

No. 492.—Roast two pounds of Chestnuts; peel them and remove the inner skin. Put them in a frying-pan with half a pint of water and two ounces of sugar. Let them boil until the moisture is reduced and the chestnuts are nicely glazed. Add the juice of a lemon, and toss them over well. Then roll them lightly in powdered sugar.

Article XLIX.

French *Chiche.*   **CHICK PEA, OR EGYPTIAN PEA.**   German *Chich.*

No. 493.—The Chick Pea is a hardy annual plant, originally from the south of Europe. The stem is about three feet high, erect and branching. The pods are about an inch long, three-quarters of an inch wide, and are somewhat rhomboidal in shape, being inflated or bladder-like, and containing three globular, wrinkled, pea-like seeds. The peas, though not very digestible, are employed for soup in purees, and are sometimes roasted and ground and mixed with the common variety of coffee.

CULTURE.

No. 494.—Sow in April, in the same manner as garden peas. The drills should be three feet apart, and the seed sown an inch and a half deep. Keep the ground free from weeds, and harvest before the complete maturity of the seeds.

RED CHICK PEA.

No. 495.—This is a variety with red or brownish-red seeds.

WHITE CHICK PEA.

No. 496.—Similar to the common variety in size, but has white seeds.

YELLOW CHICK PEA.

No. 497—This variety has yellow seeds, and is much used.

ARTICLE L.

French — *Gesse.* **CHICKLING WITCH, OR SPANISH LENTIL.** **German** — *Gesse.*

No. 498.—This is principally cultivated for its seeds, the flour from which is mixed with wheat flour or rye, and made into bread. The seeds are irregularly shaped and of a dun or brownish color, having a pleasant flavor. They are sown at the same time and in the same manner as the taller kinds of garden peas.

ARTICLE LI.

CHICCORY, OR SUCCORY.

Chiccoree. *Cigorien.*

No. 499.—Chiccory is extensively used by Germans as a substitute for coffee, and large quantities of the prepared root are annually exported to this country for a similar purpose. It is also prepared in this country now.

CULTURE.

No. 500.—Chiccory is cultivated the same as carrots. In the fall the roots should be taken up and cut in small pieces and put where they will dry. Dry them the same as you would dry apples. When required for use it should be roasted and ground like coffee.

ARTICLE LII.

CHINESE SPINACH.

Amarante. *Amaranth.*

No. 501.—This is a hardy annual plant, originally from China. The stems are three feet high, having many branches that are prolific with green leaves variegated with red. They are long and sharply pointed. The leaves are used in the same manner as spinach and resemble it in taste. Sow them in April in good garden soil, and they will yield abundantly during most of the summer.

ARTICLE LIII.

CHINESE YAM, OR POTATO.

French — Igname. *German* — Yam-wurzel.

No. 502.—This is a most valuable esculent, little known in this country. It grows rapidly and has creeping habits. The flowers, which are white and grow in clusters, have a cinnamon fragrance. The root is of a pale russet color, oblong, regularly rounded, and globe shaped, being largest at the lower end. The flesh is remarkably white and very mucillaginous in its good state. When boiled or roasted they possess a rice-like taste. They are quite farinaceous and nutritive, being much whiter and finer grained than our potatoes.

ARTICLE LIV.

CHIVES, OR WELSH ONION.

Cive ou Civette. *Hohllauch.*

No. 503.—The Welsh Onion is a hardy perennial, said to have originated in Siberia. It is quite distinct from the common onion as it forms no bulbs, but produces numerous elongated, angular tunicated stems, not unlike scullions or the smaller variety of leeks. The young stems and leaves are used during winter and spring as salad.

COMMON OR RED WELSH ONION.

No. 504.—The skin or pellicle is of a reddish-brown color, changing to a silvery white about the base of the leaves. The plant is about a foot high and is hardy and early.

WHITE WELSH ONION.

No. 505.—This is a sub-variety of the common red onion. The skin is rose-white and changes to silver-white at the upper portion of the stem. The leaves are longer, deeper in color, firmer and less liable to wither and decay than the common variety. The upper part of the stem is considered better and more tender, and has a milder flavor than other varieties, though it is less productive.

ARTICLE LV.

French
Ciboulette.

COMMON CHIVES.

German
Schnittlauch.

No. 506.—The Chive is a hardy, bulbous-rooted perennial plant. The leaves, which are produced in tufts, are seven or eight inches long, erect and cylindrical in shape. The young leaves are the parts of the plant used, and to keep them in a fresh and tender condition the plants should be frequently shorn to the ground. They possess the flavor peculiar to the onion family, and are principally used as an ingredient in soups and spring salads. For omelets the Chive is considered almost indispensable. (See omelet with herbs.)

CULTURE.

No. 507.—As the plant seldom, if ever, produces seeds, it is always propagated by a division of the roots or bulbs. The bulbs are planted in May, two or three together, in rows 15 inches apart, and covered three inches deep. They require little attention, and increase rapidly. If not cut to excess, a plant will continue for years.

ARTICLE LVI.

CHUFA, OR EARTH NUT.

Glan de terre. *Erdnus.*

No. 508.—This is a perennial plant that originated in the south of Europe. The roots are long and fibrous, and produce at their extremities numerous oblong, jointed, pale brown tubers, about the size of a filbert. The flesh of the tubers is tender, having a yellowish color, and a pleasant, sweet, nut-like flavor. When the tubers are dried they taste somewhat like almonds, and keep a long time. When dried and pulverized, they impart to water the color and richness of milk. They are eaten raw or roasted.

CULTURE.

No. 509.—They succeed well in California. Plant the tubers in April, two inches deep, in drills two feet apart. They will be ready for harvesting in October.

ARTICLE LVII.

CICELY SWEET, OR SWEET-SCENTED CHERVIL.

French — *Cerfeuil odorant.*
German — *Spanish Kerbel.*

No. 510.—This is a hardy perennial plant that is not cultivated to any extent. It is aromatic, but is seldom used for seasoning.

ARTICLE LVIII.

CINNAMON.

Cannelle.   *Zimmet.*

No. 511.—The tree which produces the Cinnamon is supposed to have come originally from the Island of Ceylon, and is called the Cinnamon tree, or Kerandoe, by the natives there. The leaves are similar to the bay leaves, and have the same flavor as the tree. The Cinnamon is the second peeling of the tree and is thin and smooth. It is of a yellowish red color, and has an agreeable, sweet and piquant flavor. It is largely used by pastry cooks and confectioners and for various culinary purposes, both in sticks and ground. Cinnamon is also cultivated in Tonquin, but only in the King's domain. Cinnamon flavor mixes, and tastes better, with preparations made with milk than any other flavor.

ARTICLE LIX.

CLARY.

Sclarée.   *Scharlei.*

No. 512.—The leaves of this plant are sometimes used for flavoring certain soups. They impart a strong peculiar flavor, agreeable to some but unpleasant to most persons. It has some of the properties of common sage, and is occasionally sold and used as a substitute for it. It is rarely cultivated.

ARTICLE LX.

French — Champignon.   **CLAVARIA (a variety of Mushrooms).**   **German** — Champignon.

No. 513.—There are several varieties of this fungus, all of which are edible and many are indigenous to our woods, being found in damp, shady places. For its preparation see Mushrooms.

ARTICLE LXI.

CLOVES.

Gerofle.   Nelken.

No. 514.—Cloves are principally used for culinary purposes, and also by confectioners and distillers. As their flavor is very strong they should always be used in moderation. In the Indies they make a jelly of the green fruit, which is exported in large quantities to this country. It is highly esteemed there and very expensive here.

ARTICLE LXII.

COCOA.

Coco ou Cocoa.   Cacao.

No. 515.—Cocoa is the fruit of the Cocoa tree, which grows in abundance in South America. The tree is about the size of a chestnut tree, and produces ribbed pods, which contain from 25 to 50 seeds, which resemble ground almonds, and are covered with a dry pelicule. They have a bitter taste. There are several different varieties, namely, those of Caracas, of Ceylon, of Berbiche, of Saint Madelaine, and of Saint Domingo islands. They all differ in size and flavor. The best are those from Caracas, being lightly flattened and resembling our broad beans. The next best are those from St. Madelaine and Berbiche. It is less flattened than the Caracas variety, and its pelicule is covered with a fine, ash-colored powder. The other varieties are much more bitter and oily, and are mostly used to make the Cocoa Butter. The germ of the Cocoa is always at the thick end, while in our almonds it is at the small end. The Cocoa of Caracas, St. Madelaine and Berbiche, mixed in equal quantities, makes the best quality of chocolate. This mixture gives an unctuous, oleaginous matter which chocolate should always possess. If chocolate is made simply from the Caracas Cocoa it will be too dry, while that made from the others alone would be too oily and bitter. Hence, the combination mentioned is necessary. After the Caracas beans are picked they are buried in the ground for four or six weeks, which causes them to lose some of their bitter taste. Care must be taken or they will have an exceedingly moisty flavor. The Caracas Cocoa, mixed with the others, always makes the best chocolate.

The cocoa, broma and chocolate we drink are made from Cocoa. When made into chocolate, it is ground into a paste and mixed with sugar, etc. There are several grades, some for eating, some for candies and creams, and some for beverages. Cocoa and broma are more healthful as a breakfast beverage than chocolate, as the latter is too rich.

GROUND COCOA.

No. 516.—Dilute two table-spoonfuls of ground Cocoa, with two spoonfuls of water. Then put it in a small saucepan and moisten it with three cupfuls of boiling milk or water. Stir it well and let it boil five minutes. Then sweeten it to taste.

SHELL COCOA.

No. 517.—Put two ounces of half-broken Cocoa in a saucepan with one quart of boiling water. Let it boil slowly for half an hour, or until half of the moisture is reduced. Add a little milk if desired and sweeten to taste. This is preferred by people whose stomachs are delicate.

BROMA.

No. 518.—This is made the same as Cocoa.

CHOCA.

No. 519.—Take a cup of chocolate, a cup of coffee and a cup of cream, and mix them well together. This makes a delicious beverage.

PLAIN CHOCOLATE.

No. 520.—Scrape or break two ounces of Chocolate in small pieces. Put it in a saucepan with two table-spoonfuls of boiling water, stirring it until it is melted. Then add two cupfuls of hot boiled milk. Sweeten to taste. As soon as it commences to boil, take it off of the fire and serve.

POT CHOCOLATE.

No. 521.—The best Chocolate is made in a pot expressly made for this purpose, in which there is a silver whisk. Put four cupfuls of milk or water in a chocolate pot. (Or put one ounce of Chocolate to one cup of milk.) When the milk boils add the fine grated Chocolate. When the Chocolate is melted and well mixed, set it on the side of the fire for ten minutes to keep warm. Then take the whisk between the palms of both hands and make it revolve backwards and forwards briskly until the Chocolate is whipped to a froth. Then serve.

CHOCOLATE, WITH EGGS OR CREAM.

No. 522.—Grate four ounces of Chocolate, and put it in a saucepan with four soup-spoonfuls of boiling water, and stir it until it is melted. While stirring it, add in slowly five cupfuls of boiling milk. Let it boil up once, then sweeten it to taste, and set it on the side of the fire to keep warm. Have ready the whites of four eggs, whipped to a stiff froth. Add half of this quantity to the Chocolate, mixing it well. Sweeten the remaining half of the eggs with powdered sugar. Serve the Chocolate in cups, with a spoonful of the sweetened egg froth on top.

NOTE.—Chocolate can be made as above, with cream instead of eggs. Add the cream when the Chocolate is ready to serve, having it whipped to a froth and flavored with vanilla.

Stir it well when you put it in, so the hot Chocolate will warm it, without letting it boil.

NOTE.—Chocolate can be made with water or milk, or with both, mixed in equal quantities. This is merely a matter of taste, as some prefer it with water and others with milk or cream. When sweetened Chocolate is used, no sugar, or very little, should be added, as the delicate flavor is destroyed when too sweet. Sweeten plain Chocolate to taste. Never keep Chocolate on the fire boiling.

ADULTERATED CHOCOLATE.

No. 523.—Chocolate is often adulterated by unprincipled manufacturers, which makes it a most vile compound instead of the nutritious beverage intended. They use small, common Cocoa, first extracting the Cocoa butter, and then mix with the remaining Cocoa a quantity of grilled sweet almonds. They also use the refuse of coarse brown sugar in place of pure sugar, and as a substitute for vanilla they use common storax, which is the sawdust of the Tonqua tree; but persons experienced in flavor will detect the difference immediately. Impure Chocolate is also adulterated with butter, potato flour, starch, and other heterogeneous substances.

Article LXIII.

French   **COFFEE.**   **German**
Café.   *Kaffee.*

No. 524.—Coffee is produced on a small bushy tree. The flowers are odorous, and the fruit jelly-like, having two seeds. Coffee is said to have originated in Arabia, but is now cultivated in different parts of the world. The Arabian historian, Ahmet Effendi, wrote that Coffee was first used in Arabia in the fifteenth century. The Egyptians prepare a drink with Coffee which the Arabs call Kawa. Coffee was introduced in France by the Venetians in 1657, after which its use became universal. There are five principal varieties of Coffee. The Mocha is considered the best, and is divided in three classes—namely, the Baouri, which is the best and is hardly ever obtainable in this country, as it is reserved for the highest classes in Arabia and Turkey; the Saki and the Salabi. The Coffee from Martinique, Java, Rio and Guadaloupe, is considered next best in quality. The grades from Santa Domingo, Costa Rica, and all other kinds, are of inferior quality. Coffee is now in use all over the civilized world, and is largely adulterated with the chiccory root, especially when ground. For this reason Coffee should always be procured in beans and ground when required. It will keep its flavor better in this way. Adulterated Coffee was first used in 1808, during the campaign of Napoleon. The dealers, seeing the large profit that could be made by combining chiccory with Coffee, adopted it, and even claimed that chiccory improved Coffee, which is not so. Most of the ground Coffee now prepared and sold by unscrupulous dealers is adulterated with chiccory, ground peas and common Coffee beans. Coffee beans are roasted in Coffee roasters that can be purchased from dealers. It is better to buy Coffee beans in their green state as their quality can then be better distinguished than when roasted. The interior of the Coffee roaster is round, and the beans when being turned in the receptacle will roll over and over, and thus get evenly roasted on the surface of the hot roller. Commence to roast the Coffee over a slow fire, so it will be gradually and thoroughly browned, which will take place in about forty-five minutes. When it is browned take it out of the roaster and spread it on a blanket. It will then emit an agreeable odor. Turn it occasionally to cool it, and when cold put it in jars corked tight and grind it when needed. The Mocha Coffee has the best flavor, and is generally mixed with Java or Rio. This makes the best black Coffee. The Coffee from Martinique and Costa Rica, when mixed, is the best to use when milk is added. Coffee when ground is made by infusion. French and American coffee pots are so well known that no description of them is necessary. Either can be used. Coffee should always be made fresh, and care should be taken to have the water to the boiling point before it is poured over the Coffee. Coffee should not remain long in tin pots, as it contains an ingredient that combines with tin or iron, and imparts a disagreeable flavor when it lays for any length of time. For this reason when large quantities are made at a time it should be kept in earthen jars. When Coffee is left over, after a meal, always put it in an earthen jar to use the following day.

Coffee is now made as it was years ago. The Orientals do not strain it. They boil it with the sugar in and serve it in cups, suspended below a punctured shell, called fitzyanes. Coffee made and served in this manner does not excite the nerves as when made in the French or American styles, but the latter modes are considered the best. When using a French coffee pot the boiling water has to drain through the ground Coffee and runs clear immediately. Hence it is unnecessary to clarify it. When it is boiled in a saucepan and clarified with eggs or other substances, it loses much of its strength and flavor. Some physicians advance the theory that Coffee is injurious to health, but this is a fallacy, when it is used in moderation. A certain gourmet of advanced years, yet in robust health, was in the habit of imbibing a cup of Coffee after every meal. One evening while at dinner in the Palace Hotel with his friend, a well-known physician, the latter remarked casually that Coffee was a slow poison, and urged the gourmet to discontinue its use.

"Well," remarked the gourmet, with a sly twinkle in his eye, "I agree with you on that point, but I must say that it is terrible slow, for I have been using it continuously for the past seventy years, and am still alive and well." The doctor then subsided.

REMARKS ON MIXING COFFEE.

No. 525.—Coffee is easy to make, but must be made with care. The principal point is not to have your Coffee beans ground or roasted too long before using, and to always use good Coffee. To one pound of Mocha add two pounds of Java, or use one pound of Mocha, one pound of Java, and one pound of Costa Rica or Rio. These mixtures make the best Coffee. Coffee is made best in the so-called French coffee pots, which are made for large or small quantities. When boiling Coffee, the aroma evaporates to a considerable extent, which does not occur in French coffee pots. Ground Coffee should never be boiled when it can be done otherwise. Always use boiled milk or warm cream with Coffee, as cold milk injures the taste of the Coffee. Black Coffee, or *cafe noir*, is always taken after dinner, and should be made stronger than breakfast Coffee. It is served with brandy, kirschwasser or rum, which is put in the Coffee, or first burnt with sugar, as may be desired. It is called brulo. It facilitates digestion and excites the faculties of the mind.

COFFEE FOR FAMILY USE.

No. 526.—To make ordinary breakfast Coffee, use four ounces of ground Coffee to one quart of boiling water. When using the French coffee pot, put the Coffee in the upper vessel with the strainer over it. Pour a little of the boiling water over it slowly, and in five minutes pour over the rest of the water until it is all in the bottom. Keep the pot in a warm place, not letting the Coffee boil. Take about three cupfuls of the Coffee out of the bottom and strain it through the top again. Repeat this once more, as it makes the Coffee stronger and then it will be ready for use.

When making Black Coffee for after dinner, use more Coffee or less water to make it strong.

BOILED COFFEE, No. 1.

No. 527.—When no French coffee pot is used, the Coffee must be boiled in a saucepan and strained through a double thickness of flannel. When making Coffee in large quantities in a saucepan, put five pounds of ground Coffee in a saucepan, two fresh raw eggs, and a cupful of cold water. Mix it all well together with a wooden spoon, and then pour in, slowly at first, five gallons of boiling water, stirring it at the same time. Then set it on a brisk fire, and as the Coffee rises to the top press it down with a spoon. Let it boil up once, and then set it on the side of the fire to keep warm, not letting it boil. Drop half a cupful of cold water over the top, in drops, and the Coffee will settle immediately. Do this, if in a hurry, otherwise it will settle naturally in five or ten minutes. Strain it all through a double thickness of flannel, and it is ready for use.

BOILED COFFEE, No 2.

No. 528.—When using a boiler (in which there is a faucet three inches from the bottom, with a fine strainer inside), and the Coffee is made as in No. 1, it need not be strained through flannel. Set it on the side of the fire to keep the Coffee warm, and put a piece of iron under the boiler to keep it a distance away from the fire. Then sprinkle half a cupful of cold water over the top, put the cover on tight, and in ten minutes run the Coffee out until it runs clear. Then you will pour it back in the boiler. After this it will all run perfectly clear if not allowed to boil.

COFFEE, GERMAN STYLE.

No. 529.—Mix one quart of made Coffee and one quart of boiled milk, and boil them together. This will impart a pleasant flavor to the Coffee.

ESSENCE OF COFFEE, FOR CREAMS.

No. 530.—Mix half a pound of Mocha and half a pound of Java, and pour over it a pint of boiling water. Cover the saucepan tight and let it stand in a warm place for ten minutes. Then strain it through a French coffee pot, pouring it through the strainer twice again. When cold put the Coffee in bottles, and use it as needed.

COFFEE ICE.

No. 531.—Take a small cup of Coffee and put it in a tumbler with the same quantity of water and a lump of ice. Sweeten it a little. This makes a delightful, refreshing summer beverage, which will be greatly appreciated at a light luncheon.

Article LXIV.

COLT'S-FOOT, COMMON.

French *Tussilage.* **German** *Hufflattich.*

No. 532.—This is a hardy, herbaceous perennial plant. The leaves are small, radical, roundish and heart-shaped, and from five to seven inches in diameter. The plants blossom in February or March, before the appearance of the leaves, and often while the ground is frozen and covered with snow. The leaves are the parts of the plant used, and are generally cut in July and September. In drying, spread them singly in an airy, shaded situation, but do not expose them to the sun. They are beneficial in cases of colds and pulmonary complaints.

CULTURE.

No. 533.—Colt's Foot thrives best in rich, moist soil. It may be propagated from seeds, but is generally cultivated by dividing its long, creeping roots.

ARTICLE LXV.

French
Coriandre.

CORIANDER.

German
Koriander.

No. 534.—Coriander is a hardy, annual, aromatic plant, that is cultivated for its seeds, which have an agreeable taste, and are used by confectioners and distillers, and by druggists to disguise the taste of medicine. When young, the leaves are used the same as chervil.

CULTURE.

No. 535.—Sow them early in spring. When gathering them for the seeds, care should be taken not to bruise the stems or leaves, as when bruised they have a disagreeable odor, which is imparted to the seeds. They should be gathered on a dry day.

ARTICLE LXVI.

CORN POPPY, OR COQUELICOT.

Coquelicot.   *Die Kornrose.*

No. 536.—This is a red flower, which grows wild in corn fields. The petals are separated and spread out to dry when they are gathered. Separate them if they adhere to each other. When well dried, put them in a dark, dry place. They are used for diet drinks (tisanes.)

Article LXVII.

French — Mâche. **CORN SALAD, OR LAMB LETTUCE.** **German** — Lämmersalat.

No. 537.—This small salad is used during winter and spring as a substitute for lettuce. It is also prepared and cooked the same as spinach. The Corn Salad that grows natural is better than that which is cultivated. It is used in salads, and when mixed with beets and celery it improves it as a breakfast salad.

CULTURE.

No. 538.—Sow the seed during August or September, in shallow drills about one foot apart. If the soil is dry it should be pressed firmly over the seed in order to secure prompt germination. Cover them with straw upon the approach of severely cold weather. The plants will also do well if grown in spring, and, like most salad plants, are greatly improved if grown in very rich soil. The ground can scarcely be made too rich for them. In warm weather the plants will mature in from four to six weeks.

CORN SALAD.

No. 539.—Wash the Salad in plenty of cold water. Then drain it and put it on a salad dish and season it with salt, pepper, oil and vinegar. Parsley or chives, chopped fine, may be added if desired.

CORN SALAD, WITH BEETS.

No. 540.—Prepare the Salad the same as in No. 539. Add some cold boiled sliced beets. Handle it carefully. This is a good breakfast Salad.

CORN SALAD, WITH CELERY.

No. 541.—Cut the celery in a small Julienne, and prepare as in No. 539. Endives or watercress can also be added.

ARTICLE LXVIII.

French   CORN.   German
Mais.   *Mais, or Korn.*

No. 542.—The garden variety of Corn for table use, is distinct from the field Corn variety. It is much relished in this country, especially so when used in its fresh state. When dried, it is cracked and ground into hominy, of which there are several kinds, which are much used for breakfast, either boiled or fried. It is ground into meal (white and yellow), which is used for making bread and cakes. It is delicious when used as a mush with milk or cream. Corn starch is made from Corn, and is much used for custards, cream and various other pastry preparations. It is also a healthy nourishment for invalids and infants, and may be used for all preparations for which arrow root is used.

CULTURE.

No. 543.—A rich, warm, alluvial soil is best, and before planting it should be as deeply and thoroughly worked as possible. Cultivate it deeply and thoroughly as soon as the plants appear, and then every few days until it tassels. Thorough cultivation and warm rich soil are the key notes to success.

EARLY MARBLEHEAD.

No. 544.—This is the best and earliest sweet corn, and is of excellent quality. The stalks are short, having many suckers from the root. The ears are long, but of medium width, with only a few husks. The cob is red and the kernels are small, broad and shallow, of a white color, sometimes tinged with red. They must be cooked quickly in boiling water, because the red cob will color the grain if it is allowed to simmer over a slow fire, or allowed to remain in the water after being cooked.

DOLLY DUTTON.

No. 545.—The stalks are very short, with but few suckers. The ears are small and straight and well covered with husks. This is the smallest kind in cultivation.

EXTRA EARLY ADAMS.

No. 546.—Nearly as early as the Dolly Dutton, but inferior in quality. Will succeed in the South where others fail. The stalks are very short, with no suckers. It bears a single, very full, round short ear. It is well covered with husks, and the kernels are white and smooth.

EARLY MINNESOTA.

No. 547.—This is later than the Adams best. An old and popular variety. The stalks are short and not suckering. bearing one or two ears well covered with husks. Ears long, and pointed. Kernels very broad, sweet and tender. It does not shrink much in drying.

EARLY RED NARAGANSETT.

No 548.—One of the best red varieties of sugar corn grown. The kernels are much shriveled, and exceedingly sweet and tender. It is esteemed as one of the very best table varieties.

CROSBY'S EXTRA EARLY.

No 549.—A most excellent variety, with ears of large size and medium length; sweet, rich, and delicate.

RUSSELL'S EARLY PROLIFIC SUGAR.

No 550.—This comes into use a few days after the Crosby, and is of excellent quality. It is very productive, and one of the best kinds for family use.

EARLY SWEET SUGAR.

No. 551.—The ears are of good size, tender, and sugary. The plant is productive, hearty, and quite early.

MOORE'S EARLY CONCORD SWEET.

No. 552.—This has large, full ears. The quality is unexceptionable. It is valuable as an intermediate variety.

BLACK MEXICAN.

No. 553.—Although the ripe grain is black or bluish-black, the corn, when in condition for the table, cooks remarkably white, and is surpassed by none in tenderness.

EXCELSIOR.

No. 554.—This is the best quality of the second early sorts, and the best for general crop. Stalks medium, bearing from three to six small curved ears, which are filled out to the end with broad, white kernels, that cook exceedingly sweet and tender.

AMBER CREAM.

No. 555.—The stalk is very vigorous. It is very productive, having large ears and long kernels. It is deep, rich, and sugary, varying in color from light red to white.

TRIUMPH.

No. 556.—The stalks are large, with large ears of fine quality. It is the earliest of the very large sorts and is highly esteemed for canning purposes.

EGYPTIAN SWEET.

No. 557.—A variety noted for its productiveness; the stalks having from two to four ears each. It is peculiarly adapted for canning, and in consequence of its sweetness and tenderness, its superiority is noticeable.

MAMMOTH SWEET.

No. 558.—This variety produces the largest ears of any sort, a single ear weighing from two to three pounds. The quality is excellent, sweet, tender, and delicious. For family use it cannot be excelled.

STOWELL'S EVERGREEN SWEET.

No. 559.—This variety is intermediate in its season, and if planted at the same time as the early kinds, will keep the table supplied until October. It is hardy and productive, very tender and sugary.

BURLINGTON EARLY ADAMS.

No. 560.—An excellent early field variety, and often used for the table, particularly in the South. Ears eight inches long, with twelve or fourteen rows. The kernels are white and rounded, somewhat deeper than broad, and indented at the outer end, which is whiter and less transparent than the inner.

EARLY CANADA.

No. 561.—A very early, yellow variety, much grown in Canada, and good for localities where the seasons are short, or where first planting has failed.

LACKAWAXEN.

No. 562.—This is a white flint, eight-rowed variety, with very large and deep grains. There are usually two ears to a stalk. It completes its growth in ninety-five days, and is considered very prolific.

EARLY WHITE FLINT.

No. 563.—This is an excellent, productive variety, with ears of good size, pearly white, and of a beautiful appearance. Much used for making hominy.

LARGE RED BLAZED, EIGHT-ROWED.

No. 564.—An excellent variety for field culture, with large ears, well filled out at the top and end. Its color is yellow, splashed with red at the point.

EARLY GOLDEN DENT.

No. 565.—This is a variety as early as the flint sorts, and is highly recommended for general use. The stalks are of medium size, with very broad leaves. The ears are short and are always filled to the point. The cob is small, and the kernels are long and yellow. It makes a good meal.

CHESTER COUNTY MAMMOTH.

No. 566.—A large, late variety, very popular in Pennsylvania. A sure and hardy cropper, but will not mature well in the extreme Northern States. It is one of the best of the Dent varieties. The stalk is large, bearing one or two very large ears. Kernels narrow, very long, and deep yellow. Cob very small.

BLUNT'S PROLIFIC.

No. 567.—This is one of the most prolific varieties grown. The ears are short and well shaped, averaging three, and frequently running as high as eight to a stalk. The kernel is white, of the general form of the Dent variety, but harder, and makes an extra quality of pure, white meal. It is not early, and will not do well at the extreme North.

RICE CORN, FOR PARCHING.

No. 568.—This is a very handsome variety, that is exceedingly prolific, and is used entirely for parching, being superior to all others for this purpose. The ears are short and the kernels are long, pointed and white, resembling rice in appearance.

BOILED GREEN CORN.

No. 569.—Take the husks off of the Corn, break off the stem, remove all the threads and the upper end. Put them to boil in boiling water, lightly salted, and let them boil until tender. Serve in a napkin with butter, separately.

NOTE.—When the Corn is to be kept for some little time after it is cooked, it is always best to add some boiled milk to the water.

CORN, WITH MILK OR CREAM.

No. 570.—When the Corn is boiled as in No. 569, cut the Corn from the ear, put it into a saucepan, moistened with milk or cream, season with salt and pepper, and when the moisture is nearly reduced, add a piece of butter, tossing it over well until the butter is melted. Then serve it.

STEWED GREEN CORN.

No. 571.—Cut the grains from six ears of Corn, put them into a saucepan with a quart of boiling water and cook for twenty minutes. Then drain off most of the water and add half a pint of milk. Season with salt and pepper and add an ounce of butter, with which mix a teaspoonful of flour. Stir the Corn until the butter is dissolved, and let it simmer for fifteen minutes.

CORN, WITH BEANS.

No. 572.—When the Corn is boiled as in No. 569, cut it from the ears and add one-half or quarter of its quantity of string beans, cut in diamond shape, or green flageolet beans, cooked separately. Season with salt and pepper, moisten with a little milk or cream, and when thoroughly warmed add a piece of butter.

SUCCOTASH.

No. 573.—Succotash is made with Corn and small Lima beans, using two parts of Corn to one part of beans. Cut the grain off of one dozen ears of Corn, and shell the beans. Put them in a saucepan with sufficient boiling water to cover them, add a little salt and cook them until they are tender. Then drain off half of the moisture and add the same quantity of boiled milk. Knead a spoonful of flour in a piece of butter and add it with the milk. Let it all simmer for twenty minutes, stirring it occasionally, so that the mixture will not adhere to the bottom of the saucepan. Season it with salt and pepper.

NOTE.—Green flageolet or string beans may be used instead of Lima beans, the string beans should be cut in pieces, one inch long.

CORN, WITH TOMATOES.

No. 574.—Cut the grains from one dozen ears of Corn and put them into a saucepan with an equal quantity of peeled tomatoes cut into square pieces. Let them cook until the tomatoes are well cooked and the moisture nearly reduced. Season them with salt and pepper, and before serving add a piece of butter.

CORN FRITTERS.

Fo. 575.—Cut the grains from six ears of Corn and put them into a saucepan, moistening them with a little cream, and season with salt, pepper and a pinch of sugar. Let it all simmer until reduced of its moisture, then set it off of the fire to cool. Make a batter with two spoonfuls of flour, milk and eggs—not too thin. Add it to the Corn, mixing it well. Have in a frying pan some hot lard. Then fill a soup-spoon with the Corn batter and drop it into the lard (not too much at a time). Fry them until nicely browned on both sides, drain them on a napkin and serve them with fried parsley to garnish.

NOTE.—When using a batter like that used in Queen fritters, it will make the fritters more delicious.

GREEN CORN CAKES.

No. 576.—Grate the corn from one dozen ears and put it into a bowl, adding one pint of milk, four ounces of melted butter and six raw eggs. Mix the whole well together. Season to taste and add flour enough to make a light batter. Bake the same as you would buckwheat or Corn cake.

CANNED CORN, HOW TO PREPARE.

No. 577.—Canned corn may be had of all grocers the whole year round. Open the can, put the corn into a saucepan and moisten it with milk or cream. Season with salt and pepper, and add a piece of butter, tossing it well over until the butter is melted. Serve hot.

NOTE.—Any of the preparations given above for green corn, may also be made of canned corn.

ROASTED CORN.

No. 578.—Turn back the husk, pick out the silk threads, re-cover the ear with the husk, and roast it in the hot ashes of a wood fire. Serve it with butter, salt and pepper. An excellent and easy mode of cooking corn for campers.

SOUP—CREAM OF CORN.

No. 579.—Cut the grains from one dozen good-sized ears of corn. Put them into a saucepan to cook, with three pints of boiling water, one onion, a faggot of celery, and a leek. Season with salt, pepper, nutmeg, and a pinch of sugar. When the corn is cooked add two quarts of cream sauce. Let it simmer for fifteen minutes, then remove the onion and faggot, add a piece of butter, and serve hot.

NOTE.—The soup, when prepared as above, may be rubbed through a fine sieve, then put back into a saucepan, to keep warm, and before serving add half a pint of cream, into which dilute the yolks of six raw eggs. Put into a soup tureen some fine chopped parsley or chives, and on this pour the soup.

CORN CHOWDER.

No. 580.—Cut one pound of fat pork in small pieces, and put them in a saucepan. When they are nicely fried remove the pieces and put four finely sliced onions in the hot fat. When they are fried, add one gallon of hot water, letting it boil until the onions are thoroughly cooked, when you will rub it through a fine sieve. Then peel one dozen potatoes, slice them fine, and cut the same quantity of green corn from the cob. Put them in a saucepan, in layers, sprinkle each layer lightly with flour, and season with salt and pepper. Then pour the above strained broth over the layers, cover the saucepan and set on the fire to boil for thirty minutes. By this time the corn and potatoes should be cooked. Then add one quart of boiled milk, a piece of butter and some crackers, split in half and soaked in cold water. Put the cover on the saucepan and cook the chowder ten minutes longer.

HULLED CORN.

No. 581.—Hulled corn can be procured from dealers, and is best during the fall and winter. Its attractiveness lays in its snowy whiteness. Put the quantity desired into a saucepan, with milk to cover, set it on the fire and season it lightly, with salt only. Let it simmer slowly. Care must be taken not to let it scorch, and when it is cooked add a good sized piece of butter. Serve separately with a pitcher of cream and a bowl of sugar.

BOILED COARSE HOMINY.

No. 582.—Soak the Hominy in cold water over night, and in the morning drain off the water and put the Hominy into a saucepan with fresh water. Let it cook slowly, and occasionally stir it with a wooden spoon. Season it with salt, and when cooked drain it in a colander. Then put it back into the saucepan and season it with salt and white pepper, and add a good sized piece of butter. Then stir the Hominy with a wooden spoon until the butter is melted, and moisten it with a little hot milk or cream.

NOTE.—This Hominy may be served as a dinner vegetable, or with cream and sugar.

FINE HOMINY.

No. 583.—Fine Hominy is mostly used for breakfast and luncheon, and a pot of cream ought always to be served with it.

Soak two pounds of Hominy over night, and when it is ready to cook, have in a saucepan six quarts of boiling water, lightly salted, into which put the Hominy slowly, while stirring it with a wooden spoon. Let it boil slowly, occasionally stirring it from the bottom, until it is well cooked, and when cooked it should be similar to mush. If found too thick, add a little more hot water or milk, and serve with butter, cream and sugar.

FRIED HOMINY.

No. 584.—Cook the Hominy as in No. 583, only have it thicker. When it is well cooked put it into square, buttered pans, about two inches thick, and set it aside to get cold. When cold, cut the Hominy in slices and dip them into beaten eggs, diluted with a little milk. Then flour them and fry them in clarified butter. It is occasionally served with roast wild ducks.

HOMINY CROQUETTES.

No. 585.—Put into a saucepan one pound of hot boiled Hominy. Stir it off the fire until nearly cold, and be very careful to have no lumps. Add a piece of butter, sweeten to taste, and add the yolks of four raw eggs. Have the whole well mixed, then roll them on the table into croquettes, then dip into beaten eggs and then into fresh bread crumbs. Shape them nicely and fry in hot lard.

BAKED HOMINY.

No. 586.—Put into a saucepan one pound of hot-boiled Hominy, stirring it until nearly cold. Then add two ounces of butter and the yolks of six raw eggs. When the whole is well mixed, add in slowly half a pint of cold milk and sweeten it to taste. Then beat the whites of four eggs into a stiff froth, and mix the froth gently into the Hominy. Then put it into deep, buttered dishes, and bake gently until nicely browned.

CORN MEAL.

No. 587.—Corn Meal is finely ground corn, it is also called Indian Meal. There are two kinds of Corn Meal, the white and the yellow. The best variety of white Corn Meal is made from Blunt's prolific corn, and the best variety of the yellow is made from the Golden Dent variety. Mush is generally made from the latter kind. Corn Meal is also used for making a great variety of bread and cakes, which will be fully described in the Book on Pastry. It is also used for making gruels, soups, etc., for infants and invalids, as it is considered very nutritious and healthful.

BOILED MUSH.

No. 588.—Have in a saucepan four quarts of boiling water. Season it with a spoonful of salt. Pour into the water slowly three pounds of the Corn Meal, stirring it slowly with a wooden spoon until it thickens. Then set it on the side of the fire to cook slowly, occasionally stirring it well up until it is well cooked. When cooked, serve it with fresh butter, cream or milk.

NOTE.—This can be made of yellow or white Meal; the yellow is, however, generally preferred.

FRIED MUSH.

No. 589.—Prepare a Mush as in No. 588, and when it is cooked add a piece of butter and mix it well. Then pour the Mush into a buttered, square pan, about two inches thick. Cover this with a buttered paper, so as to prevent the Mush from having a crust, and when cold cut it into slices a quarter of an inch thick. Then dip the slices into beaten eggs, and after flouring them, fry them in clarified butter. Drain, and serve them on a napkin.

CORN MEAL GRUEL.

No. 590.—Have in a saucepan two quarts of boiling water, and while the water boils drop into it half a pound of Corn Meal, stirring it with a wooden spoon until it boils steadily. Then set it on the side of the fire to boil slowly for one hour. Season it with a little salt. A little wheat flour may be added, while cooking, and it may also be sweetened with a pinch of sugar and a little nutmeg. This may be served as it is, or may be strained and may be cooked with milk or broth.

POULAINTA, OR CORN MEAL WITH CHEESE.

No. 591.—Poulainta is an Italian preparation, which is nourishing and healthful, and is used by the Italians as we use corn meal mush. Put two quarts of water in a saucepan, and when it boils add salt and a piece of butter. Then put the Corn Meal in slowly, stirring it all the time (so it will not get lumpy), until it commences to thicken. Then set it on the side of the fire to cook slowly, stirring it up from the bottom occasionally. When it is cooked add half a pound of grated Parmesan cheese, and a piece of butter, mix it well together. Serve in a large dish, with a beef gravy reduced with Tomato sauce and flavored with the essence of dry mushrooms. Serve a tureen of consomme with it.

POULAINTA, WITH GAME.

No. 592.—Prepare the Poulainta as in No. 591, and when it is cooked put it on a large dish, making a hollow space in the center. (Prepare, separately, two dozen reed birds.) Put the birds in a frying-pan with a piece of butter, toss them over the fire, and when nearly cooked add some fine herbs, and then cook them thoroughly. Put the birds in the center of the Poulainta. Put a few spoonfuls of gravy in the pan, let it boil up once, and then pour it over the birds.

CRUSTS OF POULAINTA, MILANAISE STYLE.

No. 593.—Cook one pound of yellow Corn Meal in six pints of water, the same as in No. 591. Keep it stiff, and when cooked add six ounces of butter and four ounces of grated Parmesan cheese. Mix it all well and put it in a buttered tin pan, about two inches deep. When it is cold, turn the mush out of the pan and cut it with a round cutter into pieces, about the size of a dollar in circumference. With a smaller cutter make an impression on the top of each piece, and then fry them in hot lard. When nicely colored drain them. Then take the cover off of each, and hollow out the center, not breaking the crust, and set them in the oven to dry.

Put the yolks of five raw eggs in a saucepan, dilute them with half a pint of cream. Add one-quarter of a pound of Gruyere or American cheese, cut in small, thin pieces, and a pinch of nutmeg. Set it on the fire and stir it with a small whisk until the cheese is melted. Then add one-quarter of a pound of grated cheese, and keep stirring it until melted. Do not let it boil. Fill the crusts with the preparation and serve them hot.

NOTE.— For other (Poulaintas) Corn Meal Farina see Article Farina.

CORN GRIDDLE CAKES—COMMON CORN CAKES.

No. 594.—Put into a bowl one quart of sour or buttermilk, one tablespoonful of soda, a little salt, and add enough flour to make a nice batter. Bake immediately.

BATTER CAKES.

No. 595.—To one quart of milk add enough white Corn Meal, with one handful of wheat flour, to make a light batter. Put with this four spoonfuls of yeast and a little salt, and when it is all well mixed gather it together and cover it with a cloth, so as to let it raise over night. In the morning add one ounce of melted butter and a teaspoonful of soda, dissolved in hot water. Mix well together and then bake.

FLANNEL CAKES.

No. 596.—To one quart of milk add enough Corn Meal to make a light batter. Put with this four spoonfuls of yeast and a little salt. When it is well mixed cover it with a cloth to raise it over night. In the morning add an ounce of melted butter and four well beaten eggs. Mix them well together and then bake.

FLAP JACKS, OR TRIMMED LACE.

No. 597.—Put into a bowl one pound of Corn flour. Make a hollow in the center and add one ounce of melted butter and two spoonfuls of molasses or brown sugar. With this put one quart of hot milk, mix it together, and cover it with a cloth and let it stand in a warm temperature overnight. In the morning add the yolks of four raw eggs, four ounces of wheat flour and a little salt. Mix them well up, and if the batter should be too thick add a little cold milk. Then add in, gently, the whites of the eggs (beaten to a stiff froth), and bake.

CORN STARCH.

No. 598.—Corn Starch is the fecula of Corn, and is used for all the purposes for which arrow root is used in cooking. It is also much preferable to arrow root for alimentary purposes. It is used in creams, custards, blanc mange, and a numberless variety of cakes and fritters. It is also delicious for thickening certain soups and sauces, instead of flour, as it keeps them clear and transparent. Though many preparations made with Corn Starch are not as succulent as when made in their original styles, especially will this be found to be the case with creams, blanc mange, etc. It often happens that when articles are made of Corn Starch which are too stiff, or which are not well cooked, they retain a starchy taste. It is very nutritious for infants and invalids, when boiled in milk or made into custards. The recipes will be found in their respective places in the Books on Soups, Sauces and Pastries.

ARTICLE LXIX.

COUCH GRASS.

French — Chiendent.
German — Queckengrass.

No. 599.—Couch Grass is a medicinal plant, of which there are several varieties. The root is the portion of the plant used in tisanes (diet drinks) and other decoctions.

Culture same as other pot herbs. See Article V.

ARTICLE LXX.

COS LETTUCE, OR ROMAINE.

Romaine. Bind Salat, or Forellen Salat.

No. 600.—The Romaine, or Cos Lettuce, of which there are several varieties, is one of the most crisp and refreshing salads grown. (See article on Lettuce.) Its leaves are long, narrow and of a dark green color. It stands the heat well, and should be tied up to blanch a week or ten days before cutting. It is used as a salad the same as ordinary lettuce, and is also boiled and prepared in the same way as spinach. It is braised and stuffed the same as lettuce.

ARTICLE LXXI.

COSTMARY, OR ALECOST.

French — *Tanaisie Barbodine.*
German — *Frauenmünze.*

No. 601.—Costmary is a hardy perennial plant with a creeping root, and an erect, branching stem from two to three feet in height. The radical leaves, which are produced on long footstalks, are oval, serrated and of a grayish color. Those of the stalks are smaller than the radical ones but similar in form. The plant has a soft, agreeable odor, and is sometimes used as a pot herb for flavoring soups. The leaves are used in salads and also for flavoring ale or beer.

CULTURE.

No. 602.—Costmary may be cultivated in almost any soil. It is generally propagated by dividing the roots, which increase rapidly. It should be planted in spring or autumn. Set them two feet apart in each direction.

ARTICLE LXXII.

CRANBERRY.

Canneberge.
Moosbeere.

No. 603.—The Cranberry is a trailing shrub, which grows wild in swampy meadows and on the borders of inland lakes. It can be improved, however, by planting in any moist soil that is thoroughly manured with decayed manure. When cultivated in this way the berries will be larger and of better flavor, and the yield will be more abundant. The berries are round, of a reddish color, and have an aciduous flavor. There are several varieties. The bell-shaped is the largest, having a dark-red color. The cherry variety comes both large and small, the large kind being preferred. The color is dark-red, and it is considered next in excellence to the bell-shaped. The oval or egg-shaped Cranberry comes large and small also. It is a good variety, but not as profitable as the others.

CULTURE.

No. 604.—Procure the plants with their natural earth and plant them early in spring, four feet apart, in moist sandy soil, well manured.

CRANBERRY SAUCE.

No. 605.—Pick one pound of Cranberries and wash them in cold water. Put them in a copper basin with a glassful of water and cook them over a brisk fire. Sweeten with sugar stirred in with a wooden spoon until they are like a marmalade. Then strain them through a fine sieve and put them in an earthen jar. The sauce is used with turkey and for tarts and pies. If Cranberries are cooked in tin basins they will not keep their rich red color.

ARTICLE LXXIII.

French   **CRESS, OR PEPPER GRASS.**   **German**
Cress m.   *Pillenfarn.*

No. 606.—Cress, or Pepper Grass, is a pungent salad, and is mostly used in mixing with other salads. Mixed with fine herbs it has a piquant, agreeable taste, and it should always be used when young and freshly plucked. It gives a most agreeable taste to all green salads.

CULTURE.

No. 607.—The seed should be sown in drills about eighteen inches apart on very rich ground, and the plants well cultivated. Keep off insects by dusting with Pyrethrum powder. It may be planted very early. Continue sowing every week, as it matures very rapidly and runs to seed.

The fine curled Cress is very superior, and will bear cutting several times. The Perennial American resembles the water Cress, and may be cut several times.

The Garden Broad Leaved has a mild flavor and is generally used in soups.

ARTICLE LXXIV.

French　　　　　　**GARDEN CRESS.**　　　　　　**German**
Cresson alénois des jardins.　　　　　　　　　　　*Kresse.*

No. 608.—This is one of the best plants in cultivation for herbs, and can be easily raised in pots or boxes. It runs quickly into seed and withers as soon as plucked, so for this reason it is rarely found in the markets. It is an excellent ingredient for salads, having a mild, piquant taste. The leaves should never be chopped, but are plucked or served in bunches. The leaves when laid between buttered sandwiches and eaten with eggs, make a relish highly esteemed by epicures.

ARTICLE LXXV.

WATER CRESS.

Cresson de Fontaine.　　　　　　　　　　　*Brunnen-Kresse.*

No. 609.—The Water Cress is a hardy, perennial, aquatic plant, growing abundantly along the margins of running streams, ditches and ponds. It is very easily introduced by planting it along the margins of ponds and streams where it does not already grow, and will increase both by the spreading of the roots and seeding.

It has a particularly pleasant, pungent taste, and is agreeable to nearly every one. It is also one of the most delicious small salads.

CULTURE.

No. 610.—The seeds should be sown and lightly covered in gravelly, murky lands, along the border of small, rapid streams. They will need no subsequent culture, as in favorable conditions they increase very rapidly by self-sowing of seed and extension of roots. Good beds should be fenced in to keep animals from trampling on them, and should also be kept clear of wild herbs.

ITS USE.

No. 611.—It is eaten as a morning salad, and should only be used when fresh. It should be washed well in cold water and then drained. (Care must be taken not to bruise or press it.) Then add a little vinegar, salt and pepper. It is also mixed with other green salads, and is largely used for garnishing roast chickens, steaks, etc. It can also be cooked and prepared the same as spinach.

ARTICLE LXXVI.

French
Concombre.

CUCUMBER.

German
Gurke.

No. 612.—There are many varieties of Cucumbers. They are eaten raw and are also cooked in various ways. When used in salads they should be sliced very fine and sprinkled with salt to drain them of the water, otherwise they are apt to cause indigestion. It is a vegetable that can be grown to perfection by any one who controls a few square yards of soil which is fully exposed to the sun—the fruit being so very much better when gathered from the vine than when procured in the market. Some varieties are used for cooking purposes and some for pickling, and are then called pickles, or gherkins.

CULTURE.

No. 613.—The plants are tender, and planting should be delayed until settled warm weather or ample facilities are provided to protect them from frost and during cold storms. Form low, flat hills, six feet apart each way, of rich soil, by mixing in a quantity of thoroughly decomposed manure, stirring the soil to a depth of sixteen inches or more. Scatter one seed every inch along the rows, and cover them one inch deep, pressing the soil over them. As soon as the plants are up they will be liable to attack by the striped cucumber beetle. These may be kept off by frequent dusting with air-slacked lime. Care should be taken not to use too much lime, for if too strong it will kill the vines. When the plants are well established, thin to three plants to each hill. In gathering, pick all the fruit before it begins to ripen, as the vines will cease setting fruit as soon as any seed commences to mature. In gathering for pickles cut the stem instead of pulling the fruit off, and be careful not to mar the fruit in any way, for if the skin is broken the pickles will not keep.

EARLY WHITE SPINE.

No. 614.—A favorite market variety, of medium size, with deep green flesh, crisp and of fine flavor.

EXTRA LARGE WHITE SPINE.

No. 615.—This is a larger variety of dark-green color, largely used for forcing.

BOSTON PICKLING.

No. 616.—A variety largely used, very productive, and of superior quality.

EARLY FRAME.

No. 617.—An old and popular variety of medium size, straight and handsome, and excellent for pickling when young.

EARLY CLUSTER.

No. 618.—A much esteemed early sort, growing in clusters and extremely productive.

GREEN PROLIFIC.

No. 619.—This is one of the best for pickling. Its characteristics are its very uniform growth (hardly ever yielding Cucumbers too large for pickling) and its immense productiveness.

EARLY RUSSIAN.

No. 620.—This is the earliest variety of fruit produced, and is small, hardy and productive.

LONG GREEN.

No. 621.—A fine long fruit of excellent quality, of a dark-green color, firm and crisp.

Talby's Hybrid, the Long Green Turkey, and the Short Green, are considered excellent varieties for family use.

ENGLISH FRAME OR FORCING VARIETIES.

No. 622.—These are almost exclusively raised for self-gratification, and are grown in hot-houses. Sow them in small pots in January, February or March, in a hot-bed or hot-house, and when grown to three leaves plant them out in previously prepared hills of loose rich soil in the center of the sash. Keep a temperature of sixty-five degrees at night, to seventy or eighty degrees with sun heat. When grown under glass artificial impregnation of the flowers is necessary, by the usual method of using a camel's-hair pencil, or if not a hive of bees should be kept, if Cucumbers are grown on a large scale in green-houses. When grown in the open air there is no need of this, as the insects and winds effect impregnation. The following selections include some of the leading English varieties:

Berkshire Champion,	Duke of Edinburgh,
Blue Gown,	Cuthill's Black Spine,
Carter's Champion,	Invincible,
Improved Lion House,	Master's Prolific,
Dale's Conqueror,	Long Green,
Telegraph,	Prince Albert.
Marquis of Lorne,	Monroe's Rabley,
Lord Kenyon's Favorite,	Walker's Rumblers.

CUCUMBERS, WITH CREAM SAUCE.

No. 623.—Pare half a dozen Cucumbers, slice them in half and scoop out the seeds. Then cut them in scallops, all the same size, and put them into a bowl with cold water, a little salt and some vinegar. Half an hour after this drain off the water and dry them on a napkin. Then put them into a flat saucepan with a piece of butter, and season them with salt, pepper, nutmeg and a pinch of sugar. Cover the saucepan and set it on a moderate fire. Let them cook slowly until they are tender, then drain off the butter and add four spoonfuls of Cream sauce. Toss the whole together gently, and dish them up with a little fine chopped parsley over them.

CUCUMBERS, POULETTE.

No. 624.—Prepare the Cucumbers the same way as in No. 623, but instead of Cream sauce add Allemande sauce. Before serving, add the juice of half a lemon. Dish them up nicely, and have pieces of bread cut into fancy shapes fried, then glaze them to garnish around the dish.

CUCUMBERS, DUCHESSE.

No. 625.—Pare half a dozen Cucumbers, then cut them into quarters and scoop out the seed. Parboil them for two minutes in water lightly salted, to which add a little vinegar. Then immerse them in cold water and dry them on a towel, after which, put them in a flat saucepan with a little clarified butter. Season them with salt, pepper, nutmeg and a pinch of sugar, and put them on a brisk fire and fry them lightly on both sides (not letting the butter get browned). Then take them out with a small skimmer, without breaking them, and dish them up. Prepare separately a reduced

Supreme sauce, in which add two spoonfuls of grated Parmesan cheese, and pour it over the cucumbers. Then serve.

CUCUMBERS, SPANISH STYLE.

No. 626.—Pare half a dozen Cucumbers. Slice them in halves and scoop out the seeds. Then cut the Cucumbers in scollops and parboil them for two minutes. Then immerse them in cold water. Dry them on a napkin and put them into a buttered flat saucepan, and season them with salt, pepper and a pinch of sugar. Then put on the lid and let them simmer until the moisture is reduced; after which add two spoonfuls of veal gravy and one of Espagnole sauce. Let them cook until tender, then dish them up, straining the gravy through a fine sieve into another saucepan. Reduce it to its proper consistency. Then take it off of the fire, and add a piece of butter and some fine chopped parsley, while stirring it until the butter is melted. Then pour it over the Cucumbers, and serve.

STUFFED CUCUMBERS, SPANISH STYLE.

No. 627.—Pare one dozen Cucumbers, slice them in halves, scoop out the seeds, and parboil the Cucumbers for two minutes. Immerse them in cold water and drain them on a napkin. Stuff them with a forced meat, made of the breasts of chickens, into which add some cooked fine herbs. Arrange the Cucumbers in neat order in a deep, flat saucepan, lined with thin slices of fat pork. Then moisten them with a clear Espagnole sauce or veal gravy, and cover each Cucumber with a thin slice of fat pork. Put the lid on the saucepan and set it into the oven to cook, basting them occasionally. When they are nicely glazed, dish them up and serve them with a reduced Madeira wine sauce.

STUFFED CUCUMBERS, ITALIAN STYLE.

No. 628.—Prepare one dozen Cucumbers as in No. 627. Stuff them with a forced meat of roast chicken, into which add some fine chopped fresh mushrooms, and the same quantity of boiled smoked beef tongue. Sprinkle fresh bread crumbs over each one, and arrange them in a buttered baking pan with a few drops of olive oil on each one. Then bake them in a moderate oven, and when they are nicely browned dish them up with a white or brown Italian sauce.

STUFFED CUCUMBERS, TURKISH STYLE.

No. 629.—Prepare one dozen Cucumbers as in No. 627. Chop fine half a pound of cold, braized lamb, to which add a quarter of a pound of fine chopped beef suet, some cooked fine herbs, and three spoonfuls of rice, cooked in broth. Season with salt, nutmeg, and a pinch of red pepper. Mix it well together over the fire, while adding the yolks of three raw eggs. Stuff the Cucumbers with this stuffing and sprinkle fresh bread crumbs over them. Then arrange them in a buttered baking pan, with a piece of butter over each one, and bake them in a moderate oven until nicely browned. Then dish them up with a reduced, plain Tomato sauce.

SCOLLOPED CUCUMBERS, FOR GARNITURE.

No. 630.—Pare one dozen Cucumbers, slice them in half and cut out the seeds. Then parboil them for two minutes, immerse them in cold water, and dry them on a napkin. Put into a flat saucepan two spoonfuls of clarified butter, add the Cucumbers, and season them with salt, pepper, and a pinch of sugar. Cover the saucepan and let them simmer until cooked, without letting them get browned. Then drain off the butter and add the juice of one lemon, with some fine chopped parsley. Use as needed, as soon as they are cooked.

SCOLLOPED CUCUMBERS, FOR GARNITURE WITH SAUCE.

No. 631.—Prepare the Cucumbers in the same way as in No. 630, and fry them lightly in clarified butter, then drain off the butter and add two spoonfuls of white broth, and reduce it on a brisk fire to a glaze. Then add, as may be needed, a few spoonfuls of Cream, Allemande, or Espagnole sauce.

NOTE.—For large garnitures the stuffed Cucumbers are used, alternated with other vegetables.

PUREE OF CUCUMBER.

No. 632.—Prepare one dozen Cucumbers in the same manner as in No. 630. Then put them in a saucepan with a piece of butter, and season with salt, pepper, a pinch of sugar, a faggot of parsley garnished with a sprig of thyme, a few cloves, and a slice of raw, lean ham. Then put on the lid and let them simmer to reduce the moisture, after which add four spoonfuls of Cream or Allemande sauce, and let it cook for fifteen minutes. Then take out the faggot and rub the Cucumbers through a fine sieve. Return the puree into a flat saucepan, and add a glass of cream to it. Reduce this to its proper consistency while stirring it with a wooden spoon. Before serving, add a piece of butter.

SOUP—CREAM OF CUCUMBER, QUEEN STYLE.

No. 633.—Pare one and a half dozen medium sized fresh Cucumbers, slice them in half and take out the seeds. Then cut them in scollops and parboil them for two minutes, after which drain them. Then put them into a saucepan with a piece of butter and set them on a brisk fire. When the moisture is reduced add one quart of white broth to them, with a faggot of parsley well garnished. Season them with salt, pepper, nutmeg and a little fine sugar. When they are cooked, add two quarts of Cream sauce, and let them cook slowly for ten minutes. Then take out the faggot and rub the soup through a fine sieve; then return it to the saucepan and keep it warm in a hot water bath. Before serving add half a pound of butter in small pieces, and stir briskly with a whisk until the butter is melted; then add some fine chopped chives.

PUREE OF CUCUMBERS, PATTI STYLE.

No. 634.—Prepare one and a half dozen Cucumbers as in No. 633, and when they are parboiled drain them dry. Then put them into a saucepan with a piece of butter and season with salt, pepper, nutmeg and a pinch of sugar. Toss them over a brisk fire for a few minutes, then add a pint of chicken broth. Reduce it and then add one gallon of thickened chicken or veal broth and let it cook slowly for half an hour. Skim it well and then rub the soup through a fine sieve. Return the puree to the saucepan and keep it warm on the fire. Before serving add a piece of butter and a pint of cream, into which dilute the yolks of six raw eggs. Mix the whole well together (not letting it boil). Serve with a garniture of small scolloped Cucumbers, nicely glazed.

CUCUMBERS, WITH PUREE OF CHICKENS.

No. 635.—Prepare the Cucumbers as in No. 634, and when they have been tossed over the fire, add to them one quart of light Cream sauce and let them cook slowly until tender. Season them highly and add half their quantity of a puree of chicken diluted with chicken broth, enough to give it its proper consistency. Then rub it through a fine sieve, return it to the saucepan and keep it warm in a hot water bath. When ready to serve add a piece of butter, stirring it well until the butter is melted. Serve with small balls made with a forced meat of chicken previously poached in broth.

CUCUMBERS FOR RELISH.

No. 636.—Pare the Cucumbers and cut them in thin slices. Serve them in relish dishes with a piece of ice on top of them to keep them cool.

Peeled raw tomatoes, thinly sliced, may be used with them.

NOTE.—In using Cucumbers as a plain relish only the young and freshest kinds should be used.

CUCUMBER SALAD, FRENCH STYLE.

No. 637.—Pare one dozen Cucumbers—(when small, slice them; when large, split them in half)—scoop out the seed and slice them fine. Then put them into an earthen bowl. Sprinkle them with salt and mix them well together. Set them in a cool place for one hour; after which drain off the water, pressing the Cucumbers gently. Season with pepper, oil, vinegar, and salt if needed, and add a little fine chopped parsley. Mix well together, and serve in a salad bowl.

CUCUMBER SALAD, SPANISH STYLE.

No. 638.—Prepare the Cucumbers the same as in No. 637, and when dressing them, add some sliced green bell peppers and some sliced peeled tomatoes.

CUCUMBER SALAD, GERMAN STYLE.

No. 639.—After the Cucumbers are pared, cut and sliced as in No. 637, add, when ready to serve, some sliced green onions, and season them with salt, pepper, oil and vinegar, and add a little fine chopped parsley, and mix the whole well together.

NOTE.—A light Mayonnaise dressing may be added if desired.

PRESERVED CUCUMBERS.

No. 640.—Pare two dozen Cucumbers, cutting each one into four or five pieces, and trim so as to have them of uniform size. Take out the seed, and as you prepare them, put them into a bowl of cold water, lightly salted and acidulated. Then put on the fire a copper basin with one gallon of water. Into this put the Cucumbers when the water is boiling, and when they are half-cooked take the basin off of the fire, and half an hour later take out the Cucumbers. Drain them on a cloth. Then place them in quart cans, into which add cold boiled water lightly salted, so as to cover them. Solder on the covers and boil the cans in a hot water bath for one hour.

PICKLED CUCUMBERS (PICKLES OR GHERKINS).

No. 641.—Select small and nicely shaped Cucumbers without any specks. Put them into a barrel of the size you intend filling. Put a layer of salt on each layer of Cucumbers, and add cold water enough to cover them. Then cover them with a round board, on top of which place some heavy weight to press the Cucumbers down. Keep them in a cool place for six weeks, and occasionally stir them from the bottom.

When ready to put them up, drain off the brine and throw away any of the Cucumbers that may have become softened. Put the good Cucumbers into fresh cold water over night. Drain the quantity you need and put them into a copper basin, lined with cabbage leaves. Pour over them, so as to cover, wine or cider vinegar. Then cover with cabbage leaves, and set the basin on the fire to boil. After which, set them on the side of the fire and let them boil slowly, until the Cucumbers become firm. After this, take them off of the fire, and when they are cold put them into jars or other vessels, with a sprig of tarragon in each jar. (These Cucumbers may be put up with other pickled vegetables, such as cauliflower, beans, peppers and onions, each prepared separately, and arranged in jars, etc.) Pour vinegar over them and cork them up well.

PICKLED CUCUMBERS.

No. 642.—Pare half a dozen Cucumbers, cut them in half and scoop out the seeds. Then cut them in slices half an inch thick and trim so as to have them all equal in size. Put them into an earthen bowl. Sprinkle them with a quarter of a pound of salt, and let them stand for ten hours, turning them over occasionally. Then draw off the water and put them in jars with an ounce of pepper corn and four bay leaves. Cover them with vinegar. Cork them tightly and set them in a cool place.

PICKLED CUCUMBERS—MIXED PICKLES.

No. 643.—Put into a small barrel two pounds of small, white onions, two pounds of small, round green peppers, and two hundred small Cucumbers. Make a strong brine, and pour it, boiling hot, over the Cucumbers. Two days after this, drain them and pour a new, cold brine over them. On the following day drain off this brine and boil it, adding a little salt to it, skim the brine well and pour it over the pickles. Two days after drain the pickles and put them into fresh water, rinsing them well. Then put them in jars and cover them with boiled wine or cider vinegar, adding a small piece of alum to the vinegar.

NOTE.—Cucumbers may be pickled in spiced vinegar in the same way as the above, only in boiling the vinegar it is necessary to put into a cloth bag one ounce of cloves and one of allspice, and to boil this with the vinegar.

ARTICLE LXXVII.

French **CUCKOO-FLOWER CRESS.** **German**
Cresson Elegant des prés. *Kuckuksblume.*

No. 644.—This is a hardy, perennial plant, that is grown in the Northern and Southern States. The stem is about fifteen inches high, being erect and smooth. The leaves are deeply divided and have a warm, pungent taste, such as is always noticeable in the Cress family. They are used when young as a salad, the same as other cresses. Medicinally it has the reputation of being highly anti-scorbutic, and it also aids digestion. There are four varieties: the white flowering, the purple flowering, the double white flowering, and the double purple flowering. The last two varieties are propagated by a division of the roots. The single varieties are propagated from seed, which is sown in April, in shallow drills, one foot apart. The roots may be divided in spring or autumn.

ARTICLE LXXVIII.

CUMIN.
Cumin. *Kümmel.*

No. 645.—Cumin, though a native of Egypt, may be successfully grown in the Southern or Middle States. The plant is cultivated for its seed, which is carminative and is used the same as caraway and coriander, and for flavoring a liqueur called Kümmel. It is a tender, annual plant. Its seeds are long and furrowed, and of a pale brownish color. It requires a light, warm, loamy soil. Sow in May in drills fourteen inches apart and half an inch deep. When the plants are well up trim them to three inches apart in the lines.

ARTICLE LXXIX.

CURRY.
Kari. *Kari.*

No. 646.—Curry is a preparation made of spices that come from East India. It comes both as a powder and a paste. There are many spurious imitations made here that are composed of ground red and black pepper, curcuma, cloves, nutmeg and ginger, and which are far inferior in quality to the genuine article; in fact, they hardly resemble it. Preparations in which Curry is a component part should always be accompanied by a dish of rice.

Article LXXX.

French
Pisse en lit.

DANDELION.

German
Löwenzahn.

No. 647.—Those who only know the Dandelion as the persistent weed in pastures and lawns (which is gathered for salads when young and green), know no more of its real value than one who has only seen the poisonous wild parsnip or carrot knows of the value of those vegetables. The improved variety makes it one of the earliest and best greens in cultivation. It is a hardy perennial plant, resembling the endive, and affords one of the best and most healthful of spring salads.

CULTURE.

No. 648.—When cultivated the seeds should be sown in May or June, in drills half an inch deep and twelve inches apart. The plants will be ready for use the following spring. It is also extensively grown for its roots. For this purpose it is sown in September and cultivated well during the fall, and in the following season the roots will be fit to dig up in October. The roots, after being dried, constitute an article of commercial importance, being extensively employed as a substitute for, or mixed with coffee.

LARGE LEAVED DANDELION (CULTIVATED).

No. 649.—When cultivated its leaves are fully double the size of the common Dandelion. It is a great improvement over the common variety, and when blanched it can be prepared in every way, the same as the endive.

DANDELION SALAD.

No. 650.—Prepare the same as endive salad, No. 703. It is a healthful breakfast salad.

DANDELION BROTH.

No. 651.—Dandelion boiled in water is a refreshing diet drink when cold.

Article LXXXI.

French *Aneth*.   **DILL.**   German *Dill*.

No. 652.—Dill is a hardy biennial plant, and is cultivated for its seeds, which have an aromatic odor and a warm pungent taste. It is a corrective for flatulence and colic in infants, and is added to pickled cucumbers to heighten their flavor. The leaves are sometimes used to flavor soups and sauces, and the seeds for flavoring pickles.

CULTURE.

No. 653.—Sow early in spring and keep clear of weeds.

Article LXXXII.

DIET DRINKS (Tisanes).

Tisane.   *Diät Getränke.*

No. 654.—It is the duty of every chief cook to know how to compound and prepare diet drinks, juleps and apozems. Diet drinks, or tisanes, are made for sick persons, to be taken as a refreshment. They should be prepared in such a manner that the taste will be agreeable to the patient. In making diet drinks it is best to use earthen pots. They should not be allowed to draw more than half an hour or they will get too strong and bitter. When flowers, leaves or herbs are used, diet drinks are made by infusion; when roots are used, they are boiled.

The following are the principal plants, roots, flowers, herbs and seeds from which diet drinks are made:

Basil, Sweet,
Barley (heads or crowns),
Beets (white),
Borage,
Brier leaves,
*Catechu,
Centaury,
Chamomile,
Chervil,
Colt's-foot (flowers),
Colt's-foot (roots),
*Comfrey (roots),
Coriander (seeds),
Corn Poppy,
*Corsican Sea Moss,
*Crow's-foot,
Elder Tree (flower buds),
Endive,
Fennel, Sweet,
*Gentian Root,
Hollyhock,
Horseradish,
*Iceland Moss,
Juniper Berries

Lettuce,
*Lichen,
Lime Tree or Linden Tree,
Mallow (flowers),
Malt,
Marsh Mallow,
*Marsh Trefoil,
Marjoram, Sweet,
Mint,
Mullen.
Oak (common wall Germander),
*Orange (blossoms),
*Orange (leaves),
Parsley (roots),
*Pomegranate (roots.)
Rosemary,
Sage,
Sorrel,
Thyme,
Venus hair,
*Violet (flowers),
Water Cress,
*White Archangel Nettle.

* See description of these in the glossary.

DECOCTION OF MALT.

No. 655.—Malt is barley or other grain steeped in water till it germinates, and then dried in a kiln, thus evolving the saccharine principle. The decoction of malt makes an emollient diet drink of agreeable taste, which is nourishing to a small degree.

HERB JUICE.

No. 656.—Herb juice is made by combining a variety of herbs and vegetables, such as the endive, water cress, lettuce, chervil, sorrel and white beet. Use equal parts of the herbs or vegetables desired and pound them in a mortar into a fine, homogeneous paste. Then press out or extract the juice. Mix four or five ounces of it in a cup of veal or chicken broth and drink it before breakfast. A spoonful of lime syrup may be added to it. This is a drink that will cleanse the system well.

ICELAND MOSS, OR LICHEN DIET DRINK.

No. 657.—Put one ounce of Iceland Moss or Lichen into one pound of water, to macerate for twelve hours. Then drain off the water and put the Moss to boil in three pounds of fresh water, letting it boil until one-third of the quantity of water is reduced. Then strain it through a napkin and add one ounce of marsh mallow syrup. This is an emollient drink, and is frequently used for complaints relative to the chest or breast, and for affections of the larynx. It would be advisable to dilute this with one-third of its quantity of cow's milk, if the stomach can stand it.

COLT'S-FOOT DIET DRINK.

No. 658.—Put half an ounce of Colt's-foot roots in a pint of water, and let it boil a few minutes. Then take it from the fire and add two pinches of Colt's-foot flower. It should be taken at regular intervals. It may be mixed with wine instead of water, if taken at dinner.

AN ANTI-BILIOUS DIET DRINK.

No. 659.—Take half a handful of barley heads having long beards or arms, and put them in a pint of water. Let it boil awhile and then add two rennet apples, peeled and cut in quarters. Then strain it through a napkin and add four ounces of vinegar syrup and the juice of two lemons. It is then ready for use.

AN EMOLLIENT DIET DRINK.

No. 660.—Put a handful of mallow flowers and two ounces of Canadian venus-hair in a pint of boiling water and let it steep. Then strain it and add one ounce of ground gum arabic and two ounces of clarified honey. It is then ready for use.

A PECTORAL DIET DRINK.

No. 661.—Take two ounces of dates, two ounces of jujube and two ounces of dried currants. Put them in a pint of water to boil. When boiled strain them through a towel and add one ounce of gum or marsh mallow syrup. It is then ready for use.

Another pectoral diet drink can be made as follows: Make a decoction of rennet apples, after which add to it equal proportions of violet flowers, colt's-foot, mallow and mullen. Sweeten it with honey and strain it through a fine hair sieve. It is then ready for use.

APOZEMS.

No. 662.—Apozems are concentrated tisanes with medicinal and pharmaceutic preparation, and should be made by infusion or decoction. The ingredients should be macerated or ground to a powder, as the case may be. Apozems used for cleansing the system have sarsaparilla or burdock as a basis. The stiptic, diuretic, purgative and the febrifuge Apozems should be made only from a physician's prescription, as should any others that are intended for internal use. They can be made with convenience to use as lotions, gargles or injections. The method of cooking them and the mode of application must be thoroughly understood.

NOTE.—Use the apothecaries' weight in weighing mixtures.

A DIURETIC OR APERIENT APOZEM.

No. 663.—Take four drams of wild horseradish, and two drams of crushed juniper berries. Put them in a pot. Pour twelve ounces of boiling water over them and cover the pot tight. In a few minutes strain it through a piece of flannel and let it stand. When it is cold add a pint of white wine, in which you have dissolved two ounces of vinegar, honey and syrup of squills mixed in equal quantities. This Apozem is used in cases of gravel or when the flow of urine is embarrassed. Take three wine glasses full in the morning before breakfast.

A VERMIFUGE APOZEM.

No. 664.—Take one ounce of Corsican sea moss and one ounce of Artemesia syrup and put them in eight ounces of boiling water to steep. This Apozem is appropriate for children having worms. Grown persons who have the solitary worm use a decoction of pomegranate roots, which is an efficient remedy.

AN ANTI-SCORBUTIC APOZEM.

No. 665.—Take a handful of menyanthes leaves, one of sorrel leaves and one of horseradish roots. Put them in four pounds of water and boil it until the quantity of water is reduced one-half. This is an excellent remedy in cases of scurvy.

AN ASTRINGENT APOZEM.

No. 666.—Take two drams of catechu and two drams of comfrey roots. Boil them in one quart of water, and when reduced to one-quarter of its volume, strain it and add two ounces of quince syrup. Take half a cupful at a time.

A STOMACHIC APOZEM.

No. 667.—Take one ounce of gentian root, cut in small pieces and boil it in a pint of water. Then add two ounces of the end butts of oak (small germander) and two ounces of the following mixture, equally proportioned: Centaury, fumitory, marsh trefoil, and hop seed. Let it all steep for two hours, and then drain it through a towel without pressing it. Take half a glassful every hour.

A PURGATIVE APOZEM.

No. 668.—Take two ounces of senna leaves, one ounce of Glauber's salt, one dram of anise seed, one dram of coriander seed, one ounce of chervil leaves, and one ounce of burnet leaves. Add to this mixture one sliced lemon. Put it all in an earthen bowl, with two pounds of cold water, and let it macerate for twenty-four hours, stirring it occasionally. Strain it through a towel with light pressure, and then filter it. This is an agreeable and efficient purgative.

A GERMAN APOZEM, OR WHITE DECOCTION.

No. 669.—Pound in a mortar two ounces of bread crumbs and two drams of calcine crow's-foot until thoroughly pulverized. Boil one ounce of white cube sugar in a quart of water for twenty-five minutes, and then add to it one ounce of orange flower water and the pulverized bread crumbs and crows-foot. Strain it all through a fine sieve, with pressure. Take half a glassful every other hour. Shake the mixture well before taking. This is an excellent corrective of diarrhœa.

Article LXXXIII.

French — EGG PLANT. — **German**
Aubergine. — *Eierpflanze.*

No. 670.—The Egg Plant is a tender, annual plant, that originated in South America. When well grown and properly cooked, it is a delicious table vegetable. Its fruit resembles a large egg in shape. There are two varieties, the white and the violet.

CULTURE.

No. 671.—The seed germinates slowly and should be started in strong heat, for in this, as in all tropical plants, it is of importance to secure a rapid and continuous growth from the first, the plants never recovering from a check received when young. When the plants have formed two rough leaves, transplant them to four inches apart, keep the bed closed and very warm, shaded from the direct rays of the sun, and giving them an abundance of water until the ground is warm and all danger, not only from frost but from cold nights, is past. Then harden off the plants by gradual exposure to the sun and air, and decrease the supply of water. Then carefully transplant them into warm, rich soil, setting the plants two and one-half feet apart. If needed shade the young plants and protect them from the potatoe bug, which is very fond of them, and if not prevented will soon destroy the young plants.

EARLY LONG PURPLE.

No. 672.—This is one of the earliest and most productive varieties. The fruit is long and of a dark, rich, purple color, of fine quality.

BLACK PEKIN.

No. 673.—Nearly as early as the above, and as large as the New York purple. It is very prolific and desirable for market. The fruit is nearly round, the skin is smooth, black and glossy; and the flesh is white, fine grained and delicate.

LARGE NEW YORK PURPLE.

No. 674.—This is large and round, and of excellent quality, and is highly esteemed in the Eastern market.

IMPROVED LARGE PURPLE.

No. 675.—This is the best in cultivation, being early, a sure crop, and of fine quality. The plants are large and vigorous, with light green leaves. The fruit is very large and oval-shaped, a deep purple in color, with an occasional dash of green about the stem. The flesh is white, tender and superior in quality.

GUADALOUPE STRIPED.

No. 676. The fruit is nearly oval in shape, and the skin white and variegated with purple, being very ornamental.

ORNAMENTAL VARIETIES.

No. 677.—There are three kinds which are not eatable, but are very ornamental in gardens—namely, the scarlet, the tomato-shaped and the white-fruited. The fruit of the scarlet is about the size of a hen's egg, of a whitish color, which changes to yellow and afterwards to a brilliant scarlet. The tomato-shaped is of a bright red color. The white-fruited is egg-shaped and very ornamental.

EGG PLANT, FRIED (FRENCH STYLE).

No. 678.—Peel and slice two Egg Plants. Sprinkle fine salt over each slice, and then replace them in shape again. Press them gently and set them aside for half an hour. Then drain off the water, dry them, dip them in beaten eggs, then in flour, and fry them in hot lard. Season with salt and serve them on a napkin.

EGG PLANT, BREADED AND FRIED (AMERICAN STYLE).

No. 679.—Prepare the Egg Plants as in No. 678. Season them with salt and pepper, dip them in beaten eggs, and then in raspings of bread. Fry them in hot lard, drain them, and serve them on a napkin.

EGG PLANT, LYONNAISE.

No. 680.—Peel four Egg Plants and cut them in quarters. Parboil them for fifteen minutes in water lightly salted, drain them and trim and cut them in scollops. Put them in a flat saucepan with a piece of butter, season with salt and pepper, and fry them to a nice, bright color. Before serving add a little finely chopped parsley.

EGG PLANT WITH CHEESE, NEAPOLITAN STYLE.

No. 681.—Peel and slice three Egg Plants, sprinkle a little salt between each slice, and replace them in shape again. After half an hour press them dry, then fry them in olive oil and drain them on a napkin. Season them with salt and pepper and arrange them in a buttered baking dish, with a little grated Parmesan cheese between each slice. Sprinkle fresh bread crumbs and grated cheese, over the top, moisten them with a few drops of olive oil, wipe the borders of the dish, and bake them in a moderate oven.

EGG PLANT, WITH CREAM AND CHEESE.

No. 682.—Prepare the Egg Plant as in No. 680. Fry them in clarified butter and place them in a baking dish, with a reduced cream sauce, in which add four ounces of grated Parmesan cheese, sprinkle fresh bread crumbs over the top, and a piece of butter divided into small pieces, and bake in an oven.

PUREE OF EGG PLANT.

No. 683.—Cut three Egg Plants into halves and fry them in hot lard. Then drain them on a napkin with the cut side on the bottom. When cold peel them, cut them into small pieces, put them in a saucepan with a piece of butter and let them simmer until the moisture is reduced. Season with salt, pepper and nutmeg. Add four spoonfuls of Allemande or Cream sauce, and when well mixed rub it through a fine sieve. Before serving add a piece of butter.

STUFFED EGG PLANT, AMERICAN STYLE.

No. 684.—Cut four Egg Plants into halves lengthwise, and with a knife cut around the inner part, close to the skin, without detaching it. Fry them in hot lard and drain them on a linen towel, the side which is cut being downward. Then scoop out the middle part so as to leave only the shell. When they are all prepared chop finely that which you scoop out of the Egg Plant. Put in a saucepan two fine chopped onions with a piece of butter. Fry them lightly and add the chopped Egg Plant with four ounces of fine chopped mushrooms. Reduce the moisture, then add four spoonfuls of Espagnole sauce, one handful of fresh bread crumbs and a little fine chopped parsley. Season with salt, pepper and nutmeg. Stir them well together, adding in slowly the yolks of five raw eggs. When well mixed fill the shell of the Egg Plant, arrange them together in a buttered pan, sprinkle bread crumbs over them, put a piece of butter in each and bake them in a slow oven. Serve with a brown Italian sauce.

STUFFED EGG PLANT, BRAZILIAN STYLE.

No. 685.—Prepare the Egg Plant the same as No. 683. Add to the stuffing four soup-spoonfuls of fine chopped capers, with two teaspoonfuls of anchovie paste. Serve with a reduced Espagnole sauce.

STUFFED EGG PLANT, TURKISH STYLE.

No. 686.—Prepare the Egg Plant as in No. 683. Cook in white broth a quarter of a pound of rice. When well cooked and dry, chop two onions fine and put them in a saucepan with three spoonfuls of olive oil. Fry them lightly, and then add one clove of fine chopped garlic, the chopped Egg Plant, and the same quantity of roast mutton cut into small pieces. Let it simmer slowly and then add the rice. Season it with salt and a pinch of red pepper, and add four spoonfuls of Tomato sauce and some fine chopped parsley. Mix all well together and set it aside to get cold. Then stuff the Egg Plant with this preparation and sprinkle fresh bread crumbs over each. Arrange them in a buttered pan, with a few drops of olive oil over each, bake them in a moderate oven, and serve with a reduced Tomato sauce.

STUFFED EGG PLANT, PARISIAN STYLE.

No. 687.—Prepare three Egg Plants as in No. 683. Stuff them with the following preparation: chop three white onions fine, put them in a saucepan with a piece of butter and fry them lightly. Add the Egg Plant, which you cut into small, square pieces, also the breast of two roast chickens, same quantity of roast pork, and a quarter of a pound of marrow. Let it simmer for twenty minutes, and then add one handful of fresh bread crumbs. Season it with salt, pepper and nutmeg, and then add the yolks of four raw eggs. Mix the whole well together, adding some fine chopped parsley. Having filled the Egg Plants with the stuffing, sprinkle fresh bread crumbs over them, with a piece of butter on each. Bake them in an oven and serve with a reduced Madeira wine sauce.

EGG PLANTS, FOR GARNITURE.

No. 688.—Use small Egg Plants, and stuff them as in Nos. 683, 684, 685, and 686. For entrees of broiled meats use the puree as in No. 682, to which you may add a reduced Madeira wine sauce in place of Allemande sauce, as may be required.

EGG PLANT SALAD.

No. 689.—Peel two middle sized Egg Plants, cut them in slices a quarter of an inch thick, sprinkle each slice with a little salt, and put them together again. After half an hour press them gently, to extract the moisture. Then dry them on a napkin. Fry them lightly in clarified butter, then drain them on a napkin. When cold cut them in small pieces, put them in a salad bowl, with some scolloped pickled sturgeon, a spoonful of grated horse-radish mixed with mustard, a clove of fine chopped garlic, a little fine chopped parsley, and a handful of water cress. Season them with salt, pepper, olive oil, and vinegar. Mix the whole well together, then arrange them properly, and garnish them with stoned olives and hard boiled eggs cut into quarters.

ARTICLE LXXXIV.

French   **EGYPTIAN CUCUMBER.**   **German**
Concombre Egyptien.   *Egyptische Gurke.*

No. 690.—This is a tender annual plant, that is seldom cultivated in this country. The fruit is small, oblong, and very hairy, and is eaten either raw or cooked. In Egypt, a refreshing and agreeable beverage is made from the bulbs. Its culture is the same as that of cucumbers or melons.

ARTICLE LXXXV.

ELDERBERRIES.
Graine de Surreau.   *Hollunderbeere.*

No. 691.—The Elderberry tree is found in all parts of this country, the flowery buds and fruit being used. The flowery buds are used for diet drinks. Pick them in bunches in the morning, before the rising of the sun, put them in a wooden tub and cover it with a blanket. When the heat will have expanded them, pick off the flowers, spread them out on a table, and when perfectly dry, put them in boxes, and keep them in a dry, dark place. The berries when ripe are used for making and coloring red wine.

ELDERBERRY CATSUP.

No. 692.—Pick two quarts of ripe Elderberries, put them in an earthen jar and pour two quarts of boiled wine vinegar over them. After three days drain them and put the liquid in a saucepan, adding two spoonfuls of sugar, half an ounce of pepper corn, a teaspoonful of ginger, a teaspoonful of ground mace, and a soup spoonful of Anchovie paste. Let it boil for half an hour, stirring it occasionally, and then pour it over the berries again. Cover it when cold, and after three days strain it through a towel, then put it in bottles and cork them well.

ARTICLE LXXXVI.

French — *Aunée.*
ELECAMPANE.
German — *Alantwurzel.*

No. 693.—Is a hardy, herbaceous, perennial plant, growing spontaneously in moist places and in the vicinity of gardens where it has once been cultivated. The stem is from three to five feet high, thick and strong, branching towards the top. The leaves are from nine inches to one foot in length, oval-toothed on the margin, and downy below. The flower resembles a small sunflower, and is general propagated by dividing the roots, but may be grown from seeds, which are sown just after ripening. Elecampane is cultivated for its roots, which are carminative, sudorific, tonic, and alleviating in pulmonary diseases. They are in perfection when of two years' growth.

ARTICLE LXXXVII.

Chicorée ou Scarole.
ENDIVE, OR CHICOREE.
Endive, or Cichorie.

No. 694.—The Endive, in its natural state, is very bitter, but when properly blanched its leaves make a fine salad, and coming as it does, after the Lettuce, it is very useful for autumn and winter salad. There are two special kinds, of which there are ten different varieties. The Wild Chicoree, known as the Dandelion, is mostly eaten in salad when young and tender. The cultivated Endive (broad leaf) is used as a vegetable, and is prepared the same as spinach.

CULTURE.

No. 695.—It may be grown at any season of the year, but is generally used late in the fall. Sow the seed during June or July, in drills fourteen inches apart, and when well up thin the plants to one foot apart. When nearly full grown tie the outer leaves together over the centre, in order to blanch the heart of the plant. They will usually be fit for the table in ten days, and will continue in condition for use for about one week, so that the tieing up should be done every few days, in order to secure a succession.

FRENCH MOSS.

No. 696.—Is beautifully curled, and when well developed appears like a tuft of moss.

BROAD-LEAVED BATAVIAN.

No. 697.—This is the chicoree (scarole) of the French kind, and is chiefly used for cooking, but, when the outer leaves are gathered and tied at the top, the whole plant will blanch nicely and make an excellent salad for the table.

GREEN CURLED.

No. 698.—Is the hardiest variety, with beautifully curled dark green leaves, which blanch white and are very crisp and tender.

ENDIVES, WITH CREAM SAUCE.

No. 699.—Select six young and tender heads of Endives. Trim off the three outer hard layers of green leaves, trim the edges of the others, cut off the roots and wash the heads in plenty of cold water. Separate the leaves, as there are liable to be small worms in them, and then drain them. Have some lightly salted boiling water in a saucepan. Put in the Endives, let them cook until tender and then immerse them in cold water. Then drain them and press them dry between the palms of the hands. Chop them fine on a chopping board. Then put four ounces of butter in a saucepan, and when it is melted add the chopped Endives, stirring them well over a brisk fire for a few minutes. Season them with salt, pepper and nutmeg, and add four spoonfuls of Cream sauce. When it is all well mixed and thoroughly warmed, serve it with small pieces of toasted bread around the dish.

ENDIVES, GERMAN STYLE.

No. 700.—Prepare the Endives as in No. 699. Add two spoonfuls of flour when the butter is melted, and let them cook to a light brown while stirring well. Then add the Endives. Season with salt, pepper and nutmeg, and while mixing it all well together add a pint of cream or milk. Then serve it.

ENDIVES WITH POACHED EGGS.

No. 701.—Prepare the Endives as in No. 699. Add Allemande sauce in place of Cream sauce, and garnish with poached eggs, having a few drops of meat glaze on each egg.

ENDIVES WITH VEAL GRAVY.

No. 702.—When the Endives are prepared as in No. 699, chop them coarsely. Then put four ounces of butter in a saucepan, and when it is melted add two spoonfuls of flour. Cook it to a light brown while stirring it, add them and the Endives. Season them with salt, pepper and nutmeg. Mix them well, and add in slowly a pint of veal gravy. Add a piece of butter before serving.

PUREE OF ENDIVES.

No. 703.—Prepare and cook the Endives as in No. 699. Then chop them fine. Put them in a saucepan with a piece of butter, and season with salt, pepper and nutmeg. Stir it well over a brisk fire and add four spoonfuls of reduced Allemande or Cream sauce. Then rub the puree through a fine sieve and put it back in the saucepan to warm thoroughly. Then add a spoonful of half-glaze and a piece of butter, and serve it.

ENDIVE SALAD, FRENCH STYLE.

No. 704.—Wash and trim the endives carefully, separate the leaves, drain them and put them in a salad bowl. Rub a clove of garlic on two pieces of bread crust about the size of a dollar (this is called chapon). Add them to the salad and season with salt, pepper, vinegar and olive oil, and mix it all gently together.

NOTE.—Dress the salad only when ready to serve.

ENDIVE SALAD, GERMAN STYLE.

No. 705.—Prepare the Endives as in No. 704. Season it with salt, pepper, vinegar and olive oil, and add some fine chopped parsley or chives, and half as much fine sliced boiled new potatoes as there is salad. Mix it all gently together and garnish it with pickled beets and hard boiled eggs cut in halves.

ENDIVE SALAD, AMERICAN STYLE.

No. 706.—Trim and carefully wash the Endives, separate the leaves and put them on a napkin to absorb the moisture. Then put them in a salad bowl, season them with salt, pepper, olive oil and vinegar, and add some fine chopped tarragon and chervil. Put two fine chopped shallots in a towel and dip them in boiling water for one minute. Then immerse them in cold water, wring them dry and put them in the salad, mixing it gently together.

Arrange it properly, placing on the top some fine sliced green bell peppers. Garnish it with hard-boiled eggs cut into quarters.

SOUP—CREAM OF ENDIVE WITH POACHED EGGS.

No. 707.—Prepare one gallon of thickened chicken or veal broth. Trim and wash eight Endives carefully, and boil them in water lightly salted. When boiled immerse them in cold water, then drain them and press them dry. Chop them in small pieces, put them in a saucepan with a piece of butter, and season with salt, pepper, nutmeg. and a pinch of sugar. Put them on a brisk fire and stir them well until the moisture is reduced. Then pour in the chicken broth slowly, and let it boil for twenty minutes. Then skim it and rub it through a fine sieve, and put it back in the saucepan to keep warm. Before serving it dilute eight raw eggs in a pint of cream, and add it to the soup, with six ounces of butter. Stir it all well until the butter is melted. Serve separately a dish of poached eggs in broth.

ENDIVES PRESERVED IN CANS.

No. 708.—Select four dozen Endives, trim off the outer green leaves, and wash the remainder in plenty of cold water. Parboil them until tender, then immerse them in cold water, drain them and press them dry. Then chop them coarsely, and put them in a saucepan with a piece of butter. Set the pan on a brisk fire, stirring well until all of the moisture is reduced. Then put them in an earthen jar to get cold. When cold put them in quart tin cans, solder on the covers, and boil the cans in a hot water bath for two hours.

Article LXXXVIII.

| French | FARINA. | German |
| Farina. | | Farina. |

No. 709.—Farina is made from wheat or corn and is largely sold under the name of Semoule, which, however, is a different article. Farina was the first and principal food of the ancient Romans. It is used in soups, puddings and other pastry preparations. When it is cooked in milk and sweetened it makes an agreeable diet for invalids. It also makes a nice gruel when made with milk, water or broth.

FARINA (POLENTA) OF CORN MEAL, PIEMONTAISE.

No. 710.—Put three quarts of water in a saucepan, and when it boils add a little salt and a piece of butter. Then drop in slowly two pounds of corn meal Farina, while stirring it. When it commences to thicken set it on the side of the fire to cook slowly for twenty-five minutes, stirring it up from the bottom occasionally. When it is cooked take it off of the fire and add six ounces of butter and six ounces of grated Parmesan cheese, mixing it all well together. Then put it in Charlotte moulds, that are buttered with clarified butter, and keep them warm until ready for use, when you will turn them out and sprinkle grated Parmesan cheese over them. Serve them with a reduced beef gravy, in which put some essence of mushrooms.

NOTE.—Broth may be used instead of water. If cooked this way serve a tureen of game consomme with them.

FARINA (POLENTA) OF CORN MEAL ON SKIVERS.

No. 711.—Cook the Farina the same as in No. 710, but keep it firmer. When cooked take it off of the fire and add a piece of butter and some grated Parmesan cheese. Then pour it in a buttered pan, having it about one-quarter of an inch thick, put a buttered paper cover over it, and set it on ice to get cold. Cut out as many pieces as possible, the size of a twenty-five cent piece, with a round cutter. Then cut some Swiss cheese in thin slices, and with the same cutter cut out the same number of pieces as you have of the Farina. Take a four inch wooden skiver and place on it a ring of the Farina and then a ring of cheese, alternating in this way until three inches are covered. Then roll them in fresh bread crumbs, dip them in beaten eggs and then bread them again. Mould them neatly and fry them in hot lard. When nicely browned drain them and replace the wooden skiver with a silver one. Serve them on a napkin.

FARINA CRUSTS (POLENTA) OF CORN MEAL, ITALIAN STYLE.

No. 712.—Cook the Farina as in No. 710, but keep it firmer. When it is cooked, add four ounces of butter and six ounces of grated Parmesan cheese, and mix them well together. Then put it in one dozen small, round buttered Charlotte moulds. Smooth the tops evenly, cover them with a buttered paper and set them in a cool place. When they are cold turn them out. Remove the paper cover, roll them in fresh bread crumbs, and dip them in beaten eggs. Then bread them again and shape them nicely. Make a light impression on the top of each with a small cutter. Then fry them in hot lard, and when nicely browned, drain them. After this, take off the small cover and scoop out the center, (taking care not to break the shell), and fill them with the following preparation:

Put the yolks of five raw eggs in a saucepan, add a pinch of nutmeg, and dilute it all with half a pint of cream. Add to it one pound of grated Parmesan cheese. Set it on a moderate fire and stir it until the cheese is melted. (Do not let it boil.) It should have the consistency of a sauce.

When filled, serve them hot.

FARINA CRUSTS OR STANDS, OF CORN MEAL, FOR HOT OR COLD SIDE DISHES.

No. 713.—These crusts or stands are made either with bread, rice or Farina. Those made with Farina are better than those with rice, for hot dishes, as they are not so heavy, and are better than those made with bread, as the Farina does not absorb the moisture as quick as the bread when they lay for any length of time. Cook the Farina in water, lightly salted, keeping it firm. When it is cooked put it in a buttered mould as near the size of the crust as possible, that you intend making. Smooth the surface, cover it with a buttered paper, cover and put on this a wooden cover with a weight on top to press the Farina down solid in the mould. Lay it aside to get cold and hard. Then take it out of the mould, and with a small sharp knife cut it into any shape desired. Dip it in beaten eggs and then in fresh bread crumbs or raspings of bread, and fry it in hot lard until nicely browned. Then drain it and keep it for use.

FARINA TARTLETS OF CORN MEAL.

No. 714.—Cook the Farina as in No. 710, and keep it firm. Butter some small Tartlet moulds with clarified butter and set them in a cool place to let the butter get cold. Put the Farina into the moulds with a table knife, leaving a space in the center for filling. Fill the center with grated Parmesan cheese and smooth off the top. Then set them in a cool place, and when they are cold take them out of the moulds. Bread them in a mixture of half bread crumbs and half grated Parmesan cheese. Then dip them in beaten eggs and bread them again with the same mixture. Shape them well, then fry them in hot lard until nicely browned. Then drain them, dish them up on a napkin and serve them hot.

FARINA QUENELLES, OR BALLS, OF CORN MEAL.

No. 715.—These are made nearly the same as Tartlets, except that Gruyere cheese is used instead of Parmesan cheese. When they are cold dip them in beaten eggs and fry them in hot lard. They may be used as a garniture or served the same as Tartlets.

FRIED FARINA (POLENTA) OF CORN MEAL, RAMEQUIN.

No. 716.—Cook one pound of Farina as in No. 710. When it is cooked take it off of the fire, add three ounces of butter divided into small pieces, and four ounces of grated Parmesan cheese. Season it with salt, pepper, nutmeg and a pinch of sugar, and mix it well together. Moisten the pan slightly with cold water and drop a soup-spoonful of the Polenta into it so it will spread out a little, and continue doing this until the bottom of the pan is well covered, keeping each cake separate. Put some grated Parmesan cheese in the center of each, or a small piece of Gruyere cheese. Now cover each piece with a thin layer of the Polenta and set the pan aside, so the cakes will get cold. With a cutter about the size of a dollar cut out the cakes to a round shape. Take them out of the pan, dip them in beaten eggs and then in bread crumbs. Put a little clarified butter in a frying pan, and when it is warm add the Ramequin (not putting too many in the pan at a time), and fry them on both sides to a nice brown. Serve them on a napkin with fried parsley as a garniture.

FARINA (POLENTA) FOR GARNITURES.

No. 717.—When the Polenta is cooked as in No. 710, put it in small round buttered Charlotte moulds and keep them warm. Then turn them out and use them for large garnitures. They are especially appropriate for Italian dinners. Those prepared as in Nos. 713, 714, 715 and 716 can also be used as garnitures.

FARINA GRUEL.

No. 718.—Boil one pint of water, milk or broth, and when boiling drop in it four soup-spoonfuls of Farina, stirring it well. Let it cook slowly for twenty-five minutes. Sweeten or season to taste.

ARTICLE LXXXIX.

French
Fécule.

FECULA.

German
Fecula.

No. 719.—Fecula is the nutritious part of wheat, starch, farina or potatoes. It is used in sauces and soups, being devoid of flavor, and is nutritious, healthful and light. It can be used for every purpose that arrow root is used for. In cooking Fecula for invalids, it should be first diluted in cold water and then put in boiling milk, broth or water. About two spoonfuls is sufficient for a pint of liquid. Stir it well when putting it in. Let it cook for about twenty minutes, and then season or sweeten it as may be desired.

ARTICLE XC.

French
Fenouil.

SWEET FENNEL.

German
Fenchel.

No. 720.—Sweet Fennel is a hardy, perennial, aromatic plant, of which there are several varieties. The common, or bitter fennel, has strong, deep, fleshy roots, and the seeds have a brownish color and a bitter taste similar to the leaves. Sweet Fennel seeds are used by confectioners and distillers, and the leaves are used for flavoring soups and sauces. The seeds resemble anise seeds.

CULTURE.

No. 721.—Fennel is cultivated the same as anise. Italian Fennel is quite distinct from the common variety, and is cultivated annually. The flowers are produced in umbels, as in the other species. The seeds are yellowish in color, slender, slightly curved, and have a pleasant anise like taste. When the stems have attained a sufficient size, they should be earthed up, the same as celery, to blanch. If properly treated the stems will be white, crisp and tender in about three weeks. When blanched they lose their bitter taste and are excellent for salads, possessing a sweet, pleasant, aromatic taste, and may be served the same way as plain celery for a relish.

STEWED FENNEL.

No. 722.—Wash the Fennel in plenty of cold water and trim off the hard leaves. Parboil them for five minutes, then immerse them in cold water, and trim them evenly. Then cook them the same as celery, in No. 462. Pour over them some Butter, Allemande or Espagnole sauce.

ARTICLE XCI.

FLAVORS, ESSENCES, AND EXTRACTS.

French *Essence.* German *Extrakt.*

No. 723.—Flavors, essences and extracts, are used by confectioners and pastry cooks, and for various culinary purposes, to impart an agreeable aroma, and are purchased in liquid form. The best quality should always be procured. Aromatic herbs and plants are used in making coffee, tea, wine, juleps, and many other drinks. The concentrated essence of meat, game, fish, or vegetables, when added to sauces and other culinary preparations gives a splendid flavor and is greatly relished.

ESSENCE OF VEGETABLES.

No. 724.—Put in a saucepan four pounds of rump of beef, a shin of veal cut in pieces, one hen, ten carrots, eight onions, five turnips, two heads of lettuce, two heads of celery, a faggot of chervil, and half a dozen cloves. Pour one gallon of broth over this and let it boil. Skim it well and let it cook slowly until well done. Then strain the broth, and if not strong enough reduce it to one quart.

ARTICLE XCII.

FLOUR.

Farine. *Mehl.*

No. 725.—Flour is the finely ground meal of wheat or any other grain, and has many grades and varieties. It is much used for alimentary purposes, and the best should always be procured. The flour used in making bread is of a different quality than that of which pastry is made. Flour when dried in the oven and lightly colored or cooked with butter to a light brown, gives a better flavor to sauces. It also makes a healthful soup and is more digestible than when used raw.

REPÉRE.

No. 726.—Repére is flour mixed with the white of eggs into a paste, and is used to make crusts stands, or any borders adhere to a dish.

ARTICLE XCIII.

French — *Garbure.*
GARBURE.
German — *Garbür.*

No. 727.—Garbure is an old and popular soup in Gascony, France. It is composed principally of vegetables, the basis always being gratinated. For its preparation see the Book on Soups.

ARTICLE XCIV.

Ail.
GARLIC.
Knoblauch.

No. 728.—Garlic is a bulbous rooted plant, having a strong, penetrating odor. The bulb is composed of many smaller bulbs called cloves. It is not popular with Americans, although used considerably in Europe and in the Southern States. It should be used with moderation, as the breath of persons who eat Garlic is very offensive. It is used in many preparations, but can be omitted and replaced by using shallots or onions, when desired. Garlic, when used in salad, should be rubbed on a crust of bread (called chapon). When used for stews, etc., and left whole, its flavor will not be strong and penetrating as when mashed or chopped, and gives the preparation an appetizing and agreeable taste, especially in mutton stews.

CULTURE.

No. 729.—Prepare the ground the same as for onions. Plant the bulbs in drills eight inches apart, and four inches apart in rows, and cover them two inches deep. When the leaves turn yellow, take up the bulbs and dry them as you would do with onions.

GARLIC BUTTER OR GASCONY BUTTER.

No. 730.—Boil one dozen cloves of Garlic for ten minutes. Then drain them and pound them in a mortar with half a pound of butter. Add a little nutmeg and a pinch of red pepper, and when well mixed, rub it through a fine sieve and keep it in a cool place.

CHAPON FOR SALAD DRESSING.

No. 731.—This is principally used when dressing endives or dandelion for salad, but may be used in all green salads to give it a Garlic flavor. Cut a crust of bread the size of half a dollar, rub it with the clove of Garlic and mix it in with the salad.

PUREE OF GARLIC.

No. 732.—Peel one dozen Garlic bulbs and parboil them in plenty of water lightly salted, until they are cooked. Then drain them and put them in a saucepan with a piece of butter. Set it on a brisk fire to reduce the moisture. Season with salt and a pinch of red pepper and rub them through a fine sieve. Put the puree in a saucepan and add a few spoonfuls of reduced Espagnole sauce. Before serving, add a piece of butter.

NOTE.—This puree should only be made when ordered specially.

ARTICLE XCV.

French   **GHERKIN.**   **German**
Achars ou Cornichon.   *Essiggurke, or Pfeffergurke.*

No. 733.—The Gherkin is a native of the West Indies and is not a cucumber proper, but is a little rough, prickly fruit of comparatively small size, with a regular oval formation. It grows on a pretty vine, having leaves similar to the watermelon, and is principally grown for pickling. It is seldom used at the table in its raw state. In America small cucumbers are used, and when pickled are called Gherkins. See Cucumbers, Article LXXVI.

ARTICLE XCVI.

GINGER.

Gingembre.   *Ingwer.*

No. 734.—Ginger is an aromatic plant, a native of Hindostan, and is cultivated in all parts of India and China. The root is the portion in which the virtues of the plant reside. After the roots are gathered and cleansed they are scalded in boiling water, to prevent germination, and are then rapidly dried. This is the ordinary black ginger, most of which comes from Calcutta, and is called East India Ginger. In Jamaica another variety is prepared by selecting the best roots, depriving them of their epidermis and drying them carefully in the sun. This is the highly valued white Ginger, generally called Jamaica Ginger. A preserve is made from Ginger by selecting the young roots, depriving them of their cortical covering and boiling them in syrup. This is imported from the East and West Indies, and from China. When good it is translucent and tender. The odor of Ginger is aromatic and penetrating, the taste spicy, pungent, hot, and biting. These properties gradually diminish and are ultimately lost by exposure. It is used by pastry cooks, and confectioners, in putting up spiced preserves and fruits. Pieces of Ginger that are light and friable, worm-eaten or very fibrous, should be rejected. Ginger is often adulterated with rice-starch, flour-ginger, brick dust, chalk, capsicum, and mustard. Ginger is a grateful stimulant and carminative, and is often given in dyspepsia, flatulent colic, and the feeble state of the alimentary canal attendant upon atonic gout.

Article XCVII.

French
Concombre des Propféttes.

GLOBE CUCUMBER.

German
Kugelgurke.

No. 735.—The Globe Cucumber is a tender annual plant and is said to have originated in Arabia. The fruit is round and small, being thickly set with rigid bristles. In its green state it is generally pickled and can be prepared the same as ordinary cucumbers. Globe Cucumbers are not generally preferred to the ordinary kind.

Article XCVIII.

GOOSEFOOT, OR WHITE QUINOA,

Anserine.
Kiebekraut.

No. 736.—Is an annual plant propagated from seeds, and is from the southern part of the United States. There are three varieties: The white, the red, and the black. The white seed is preferred. The stem is five feet high with pale green leaves. The flowers have a whitish color and are produced in clusters. The seeds are small, of a yellowish-white color, resembling the millet. The leaves are used the same as greens. The seeds are used the same as common wheat, and for medicinal purposes.

CULTURE.

No. 737.—If grown in good soil the plant will produce an abundance of foliage. Sow it in May, in drills four feet apart, and as it grows, thin out gradually a foot apart in the rows.

ARTICLE XCIX.

French   **GRAHAM FLOUR.**   **German**
Graham Farine.   *Graham Mehl.*

No. 738.—Graham Flour is taken from the name of Sylvester Graham, a lecturer on dietetics, and is merely unbolted wheat. It is used in making bread, pastry and gruels, which will be described in the book on Pastry.

GRAHAM GRIDDLE CAKES.

No. 739.—Put one pound of Indian meal in a bowl and add one pint of warm water and two quarts of cold milk. Mix with this one pound of Graham Flour to make a light batter. Then add one ounce of dissolved compressed yeast and a large spoonful of molasses. Mix it well together, cover it with a towel and let it rest over night. In the morning add a handful of white flour, a little salt, a spoonful of melted butter, a pinch of soda, and a little water, if necessary, to make a light batter. Cook it the same as Buckwheat Cakes, No. 268.

ARTICLE C.

HERBS.

Herbe.   *Kräuter.*

No. 740.—No garden is complete without a few Herbs for culinary or medicinal purposes, and care should be taken to harvest them properly. This should be done on a dry day, just before they come into full bloom. They should then be dried and packed away closely.

CULTURE.

No. 741.—Sow them in spring in shallow drills, one foot apart, and when well up thin out or transplant them to a proper distance apart.

FINE HERBS FOR CULINARY PURPOSES.

COOKED FINE HERBS.

No. 742.—Chop one white onion finely, or use half an onion and half a shallot, as may be required. Put them in a saucepan with a piece of butter, cover the pan, and let them cook slowly, (not letting them get browned.) When they are cooked, add some finely-chopped parsley and some finely-chopped mushrooms (truffles if needed), and let them cook until the moisture is reduced. Then add a spoonful of veal glaze and put it away in an earthen bowl for future use.

FINE HERBS RAW.

No. 743.—These comprise parsley, chives, fennel, tarragon, chervil, shallots and onions being used separately or mixed, as may be required.

DUXELLE.

No. 744.—Prepare Duxelle the same as you would cooked fine herbs, and when cooked add two spoonfuls of reduced Allemande sauce. For a brown Duxelle use a reduced Espagnole sauce.

FINE HERB SAUCE.

No. 745.—Chop one large onion finely and put it in a saucepan with a piece of butter. Fry it lightly, and then add a handful of finely chopped fresh mushrooms. Cover the saucepan and let them cook until the moisture is reduced. Then add a pint of Allemande or Espagnole sauce, letting it boil slowly for twenty minutes. Then skim it and add some finely chopped parsley.

DRY HERBS.

No. 746.—These are Herbs that have been cut and dried. Some are used whole, while with others only the leaves or flowers are used. They are used to aromatize certain culinary dishes, and also for medicinal purposes. When pulverized they are used as spices. The kinds mostly used, which should always be kept on hand, are as follows: Basil Sweet, Bene, Borage, Burnet, Caraway Seed, Catnip, Cicely Sweet, Dill Seed, Sweet Fennel, Sweet Marjoram, Summer Savory, Sage, Thyme, etc.

ARTICLE CI.

French   **HOLLYHOCK, OR ROSE MALLOW.**   **German**
Roses Trémiere.   *Rosenpappel.*

No. 747.—Remove the flower from the stem before they are developed, then dry them thoroughly and put them in boxes in a dry place, free from dirt. Use them for for diet drinks (tisanes) as in Article LXXXII.

ARTICLE CII.

HOOSUNG, OR OOSUNG.
Oosung.   *Adsung.*

No. 748.—This is a lettuce-like plant from China, which is not cultivated much in this country, but is well known on the Pacific Coast. The succulent stem is the part used. This is divested of the outer rind, then boiled in water lightly salted and dressed with Butter or Hollandaise sauce. It may also be used in soups and sauces the same as okra. The cultivation is the same as that of lettuce.

ARTICLE CIII.

HOPS.
Houplon.   *Hopfen.*

No. 749.—Hops are considered a native product of this country, and are found in all parts of the United States. The roots are perennial, but the stems are annual. The bearing and fertile flowers are produced on separate plants, the former being very numerous, and panipulated. The fertile flowers are generally cemented together, or form a collection of small scales which are more or less covered with a fine yellow powder called Lupalin. The plant is principally cultivated for its flowers, which are largely used by manufacturers of malt liquors. The young shoots are cut in the spring, and used for culinary purposes, when they are five or six inches high. They are eaten as a salad, or are prepared the same as asparagus, which they somewhat resemble in taste. They are recommended by physicians for persons having nervous debility.

BOILED HOPS WITH SAUCE.

No. 750.—Cook the stems the same as asparagus, and serve them with Cream or Hollandaise sauce. They are good to use on "fast" days, and when cold they are mixed with other vegetables for salad.

STEWED HOPS, WITH SAUCE.

No. 751.—Take some young stems and cut them in pieces about one inch long, all of equal size. Then peel them and as you prepare them put them in cold acidulated water. Put a saucepan, containing some light salted water, on the fire. Add a little vinegar and when it boils add the Hops. When they are cooked drain them and then dry them on a napkin. Then put them in a saucepan with a piece of butter and season with salt, pepper, nutmeg and a pinch of sugar. Toss them over the fire and when warmed add a few spoonfuls of Allemande sauce. Before serving add a piece of butter, the juice of one lemon and some finely chopped parsley, tossing them well over until the butter is melted. Garnish it with small pieces of toast.

FRIED HOPS.

No. 752.—When the Hops are prepared as in No. 751, drain them and then dry them on a napkin. Then parboil them for five minutes, after which immerse them in cold water and dry them on a napkin. Then put them in an earthen bowl, add the juice of a lemon, and season them with salt and pepper. Set them aside for awhile, and when ready for use drain them, flour them lightly and put them in a frying batter. Take them out of the batter one at a time, put them in the frying pan in hot lard and fry them. When cooked drain them, season with salt and pepper, and serve them on a napkin.

NOTE.—They should be fried in a frying pan (not too many at a time), the same as oyster plants. They may be fried by simply dipping them in beaten eggs and then rolling them in flour.

ARTICLE CIV.

HOARHOUND.

Marrube. *Andorn.*

No. 753.—Hoarhound is a perennial herb with a strong aromatic odor and a bitter, pungent taste. It is a tonic and enters largely into the composition of cough syrups and lozenges, being principally used by confectioners and for medicinal purposes.

CULTURE.

No. 754.—It will thrive in any soil, but will be stronger if grown in light, poor soil.

ARTICLE CV.

HORSE-RADISH.

Raifort. *Meerettij.*

No. 755.—Horse-radish is a plant having a root of a pungent taste, which when grated is much used as a condiment. There are two varieties, the wild and the cultivated. The latter kind is the best, attaining a large brown colored root, the flesh of which is white. It has a burning spicy taste, and is used both raw and cooked. It is grated and served as a relish, or in sauces, and is also very agreeable to eat with boiled beef.

CULTURE.

No. 756.—The best method of growing Horse-radish is from the little roots, four or five inches in length, and not from the crowns. The small roots will produce good radish fit for use in one season's growth. Plant a set with the small end down, where the slanting cut is, and so that the top will be two inches under the soil. It can remain in the ground until very late in the autumn, and can be bedded, or a portion can remain in the ground until spring. A dozen roots will furnish all that will be needed for family use for a life time, as it constantly increases, and the only danger is that it will spread too fast and become troublesome. It is best, therefore, to plant it in some corner of the garden where it can grow without injuring other plants.

HORSE-RADISH FOR A RELISH.

No. 757.—Scrape and grate the roots, put them into an earthen bowl and moisten them with a little wine vinegar. It is best to prepare it fresh every day. It creates an appetite, and is excellent with boiled beef. If it is to be kept for use, put up in tightly-corked bottles.

HORSE-RADISH SAUCE.

No. 758.—Scrape and grate one root. Have in a saucepan one pint of Cream sauce, and when it boils add the Horse-radish, cover the pan and let it simmer on the side of the fire for fifteen minutes. Then rub it through a fine sieve into a saucepan, and add a piece of butter and a piece of meat glaze.

HORSE-RADISH SAUCE WITH APPLES.

No. 759.—Scrape and grate one root and chop it finely. Put one pint of Apple sauce in a saucepan. Then add the Horse-radish and reduce the sauce to one-quarter of its quantity on the fire. Then rub it through a fine sieve into an earthen bowl. Add the juice of one orange to it, and serve it cold.

HORSE-RADISH SAUCE, WITH CREAM.

No. 760.—Scrape and grate one root, chop it finely and put it into an earthen bowl, with the same quantity of bread crumbs. Add three spoonfuls of cream and one of sour cream, a teaspoonful of powdered sugar, a little vinegar and some salt. Mix them all well together.

NOTE.—Make it one hour before using it and serve it with hot or cold roasted meat.

HORSE-RADISH BUTTER.

No. 761.—Scrape and grate one root, put it into a mortar with half a pound of butter, and pound it into a paste. Then rub it through a fine sieve and keep it in a cool place for use.

HORSE-RADISH VINEGAR.

No. 762.—Grate half a pound of Horse-radish and put it into an earthen jar, with two ounces of sugar. Pour two quarts of wine or cider vinegar over it, and cover the jar tightly. In ten days strain it and filter it, then put it in bottles and cork them well.

ARTICLE CVI.

HYSSOP.

Hysope. *Isop.*

No. 763.—Hyssop is a hardy perennial plant, having an aromatic flavor and a warm, pungent taste. It is a stimulant and expectorant, and is used in asthma and chronic catarrh. The flowering summits and leaves, when dried, are the parts used for making tea, etc.

CULTURE.

No. 764.—Sow them in a dry, sandy soil, and thin them out to eight inches apart.

ARTICLE CVII.

INDIAN STAR ANISE SEED.

Anis Etoilé ou Badiane. *Sternanis.*

No. 765.—The tree from which this seed is procured grows in the Phillipine Islands and in China. The natives call it Pausi-Pansi. The seeds give an agreeable taste to alimentary compounds and are much used in the West India chocolates. The oil has the same properties as that of anise seed, but is more subtile and penetrating. The Chinese eat the seeds as a relish after their repasts, and the natives of India make a liquor from them called Anise-Arak, which is largely exported to Holland, where it is also highly esteemed.

ARTICLE CVIII.

JAPAN PEA.

Pois Japonais. *Japan Erbse.*

No. 766.—The Japan Pea is a native of Japan and the East Indies. The plant is strong and erect, with numerous spreading branches. The seed pods are small and downy, and grow abundantly in clusters over the entire plant. The seeds are small and round, and when ripe are of a creamy yellowish color. The seeds are the only part of the plant eaten, and when young are tender and delicate. The ripe seeds are soaked in water, the same as our common dry white beans are. They then become quite soft and tender, and have a pleasant nutty and oily flavor. There is a variety with green seeds, which is considered superior to the yellow seeded. They thrive best in the Southern States in this country. Prepare and cook them the same as our common peas.

CULTURE.

No. 767.—The plant is raised from seed and requires the entire season for its development. Sow the seeds as soon as the ground is warm, in drills twenty inches apart, and drop the seeds twelve inches apart in the drills, covering them with three-fourths of an inch of soil.

ARTICLE CIX.

JASMINE.

French
Jasmin.

German
Jasmin.

No. 768.—The flowers of the Jasmine are use by pastry cooks and confectioners for flavoring purposes. They are dried and put into bottles with spirits of wine.

ARTICLE CX.

JUNIPER.

Genièvre.

Wachholderbeere.

No. 769.—The Juniper berry is the fruit of the Juniper tree. It is used for seasoning sour kraut and in cooking ham. It is also used by distillers for certain liquors.

ARTICLE CXI.

KALE, OR BORECOLE.

Chou-vert.

Blätter-Kohl.

No. 770.—Kale or Borecole are general terms applied to those classes of cabbages which do not form heads. Some of the varieties are the most tender and delicate, of any of the cabbage species. They are hardy, and improve when exposed to a light frost.

CULTURE.

No. 771.—They may be sown as late as December in the Northern States. They will grow out during the winter in the South, without protection, and are treated like the winter cabbages. If they are cut when slightly frozen, thaw them out in cold water before boiling them.

TALL GREEN CURLED SCOTCH.

No. 772.—This is a hardy variety, which is improved by a moderate frost. It is about two feet high, with an abundance of dark green curled leaves. It stands the winter in the Middle States without any protection.

GERMAN DWARF, PURPLE.

No. 773.—This is a dwarf compact plant, composed of a mass of large, finely frilled leaves, of a deep purple color. It is tender and of excellent quality.

GERMAN DWARF, GREEN.

No. 774.—This is a smooth leaved sort that is very popular in the South, where if sown in the fall it needs no protection, growing vigorously all the winter. It is not equal to the other varieties for use in the North.

DWARF ERFURT.

No. 775.—This is a fine curled variety of a yellowish green color, that grows very close to the ground.

COTTAGER'S.

No. 776.—A valuable variety of excellent flavor. It grows about one foot high, and the leaves are of a rich green color, curled and feathered to the ground.

KALE, WITH CREAM.

No. 777.—Wash and trim three heads of Kale. Boil them in water, lightly salted, until tender, then immerse them in cold water, drain and press them dry. Then chop them finely and put them into a saucepan with a piece of butter. Season with salt, pepper and nutmeg, add a little cream, reduce it to its proper consistency, and serve it.

KALE FOR GREENS, WITH SALT PORK OR BACON.

No. 778.—Kale is much used for greens with salt pork, bacon or any other salt meats. Cook the greens with the meats or separately, chop them coarsely and serve them with the meats.

NOTE.—The Kale can also be used, when stewed, in any way that cabbage is used.

ARTICLE CXII.

French *Lavande.*

LAVENDER.

German *Lavendel.*

No. 779.—This is a hardy perennial, aromatic plant, common to the south of Europe. The flower yields an oil used in medicine and perfumery. The Spike-Lavender yields a coarser oil that is used in the arts and for the distillation of Lavender Water, or is dried and used to perfume linen. The flowers should be picked before they are fully expanded, and dried quickly. They are also distilled, and so is the oil from the flower, bearing its name.

ARTICLE CXIII.

LEEK.

Poireau. *Lauch.*

No. 780.—The Leek is a hardy biennial plant of the Onion family. It is, however, without a proper bulb, having, in the place of this a cylindrical body of succulent leaves, which are eatable. The small bulb is oblong and tunicated, the lower blanched portion being the part eaten. By some people it is preferred to the onion, when young. It is used principally for flavoring and as an ingredient in soups.

CULTURE.

No. 781.—Dig the trenches eight inches deep and make the soil, at the bottom, rich and fine. Sow the seeds early in spring and cover them lightly with earth. Thin them to six inches apart, and when the plants are twelve inches high gather the leaves together and fill the trench so as to blanch the lower part of the plants. Store them in the cellar or out of doors (as you would celery), before severe weather commences.

LONDON FLAG.

No. 782.—This variety is more generally cultivated in this country than in any other. It is hardy and of good quality.

LITTLE MONTAGNE.

No. 783.—This is one of the smallest of the Leek species. The stems are short and slender.

PROLIFEROUS LEEK.

No. 784.—This is a vigorous variety of the common Leek. The bulb will remain sound several weeks after they have ripened.

YELLOW POITON.

No. 785.—The blanched portion of the stem is of a yellowish white color, and is more tender than that of any other variety, and of a remarkably large size.

LARGE ROUEN.

No. 786.—The stem is rather short, with very thick dark green leaves. It is considered one of the good kinds.

SOUP PUREE OF LEEKS, VIENNOISE.

No. 787.—Slice fine the white part of one dozen good sized Leeks, and put them into a saucepan, with a piece of butter. Fry them lightly (not long enough to get browned), and then add one or two quarts of broth. When they are well cooked add three quarts of thickened chicken or veal broth. Season with salt, pepper, nutmeg, and a pinch of sugar, and add a faggot of parsley garnished. Let it cook slowly for twenty-five minutes. Then take out the faggot, skim off the grease, rub the soup through a fine sieve, and put it back in the saucepan to keep warm. Before serving add one pint of cream, in which dilute the yolks of eight raw eggs and a piece of butter. Stir it until the butter is melted. Then add some fine chopped chives, and serve it with fried bread crumbs separately.

Article CXIV.

French
Lentilles.

LENTIL, OR LENS.

German
Linse.

No. 788.—This is a hardy annual plant, with an erect and angular branching stem, one foot and a half high. The pods are somewhat quadrangular, and enclose one or two lens-like seeds, the size and color varying in different varieties. The Lentil is a vegetable of the greatest antiquity, and was much esteemed in olden times by those making long journeys. The seeds are used and prepared the same as beans, and for soups and purees, they are prepared the same as dried peas.

CULTURE.

No. 789.—Sow the seeds in May, in drills the same as green peas. They succeed best in dry, warm, light soil.

COMMON LENTIL.

No. 790.—This variety is considered superior to the large Lentil. The seeds are much smaller and are greatly esteemed.

GREEN LENTIL.

No. 791.—This somewhat resembles the small Lentil, the principal distinction being in the color, which is green, spotted and marbled with black.

LARGE LENTIL.

No. 792.—The seed is white or cream colored. It is one of the most productive of all varieties, though inferior in quality.

SMALL LENTIL.

No. 793.—This is rather a late variety, of a close branching habit, being very prolific, and a variety much used by the French.

LENTILS, MAITRE D'HOTEL.

No. 794.—Wash one quart of Lentils in lukewarm water and put them into a saucepan with three quarts of water, a little salt, two onions, two carrots and a faggot of celery. Put them on the fire to boil, skim them and let them boil slowly until tender. Then drain off the moisture, take out the carrots, onions and celery, and add six ounces of butter and some fine chopped parsley, and season it to taste. Toss them in the pan well together, adding a few spoonfuls of the broth, if needed.

FRICASSEE OF LENTILS.

No. 795.—Prepare and cook the Lentils as in No. 794, and when tender drain them. Put into a saucepan one chopped onion, with four ounces of butter, and a spoonful of flour. Let it cook slowly until nicely browned. Then add some of the broth of the Lentils, to make a light sauce. Let it boil for fifteen minutes, and then add the Lentils. Season them with salt and pepper, and let them simmer for fifteen minutes; then serve.

PUREE OF LENTILS FOR GARNITURE, CONDE.

No. 796.—When the Lentils are cooked, as in No. 794, take out the carrots, onions, and celery. Then drain them and rub them through a fine sieve. Put the Puree in a flat saucepan and add four spoonfuls of Espagnole sauce. Reduce it to its consistency, and before serving add a piece of butter.

SOUP, PUREE OF LENTILS.

No. 797.—Cook two quarts of Lentils, as in No. 794, adding half broth to the water. When thoroughly cooked take out the carrots, onions, and celery, and rub it through a fine sieve. If too thick add the quantity of broth necessary. Put it back in the saucepan, stirring it until it boils. Then set it on the side of the fire to boil slowly for twenty-five minutes. Before serving skim it well, add a piece of butter and serve with small fried bread crumbs. A ham bone, or piece of salt pork, may be boiled with the soup.

SOUP, PUREE OF LENTILS, CONTE.

No. 798.—Wash two quarts of Lentils and put them in a saucepan with one gallon of water. When it boils skim it. Then add two onions (in which stick six cloves), a faggot of parsley garnished with celery, and two carrots. Season with salt, put on the cover and let it boil slowly until tender. Then take out the faggot of parsley and the carrots and onions, and rub the soup through a fine sieve. Put it back into the saucepan and add game broth to make it of the desired consistency. Set it on the fire, stirring it with a wooden spoon until it boils. Then let it boil slowly for half an hour. Skim it well. Prepare separately four heads of braized celery, and when cooked cut them into scallops, adding them to the soup, when it is ready to serve.

PUREE OF LENTILS, HUNTERS' STYLE.

No. 799.—Prepare the soup as in No. 798, adding a piece of bacon while cooking the soup. When it is done take out the bacon and the vegetables, and rub the soup through a fine sieve. Make separately a game broth of quails or partridges. Dilute the puree with this broth, letting it boil slowly for half an hour. Skim it well and add the breasts of the birds, cut into small square pieces, and serve with small fried bread crumbs.

ARTICLE CXV.

French **LETTUCE.** **German**
Laitue. *Lattichsalat.*

No. 800.—Lettuce is a hardy annual plant of Asiatic origin, and is always grown from seed. It may be had at all seasons of the year, but its quality is not always the same. There is no vegetable more generally used than Lettuce, yet few people know how appetizing it is when brought to the table fresh and in an unwilted condition. It ranks as one of the best green salads, and is much used with chicken and other salads. Lettuce is also used as a vegetable prepared the same as spinach, and when stuffed, and is used as a garniture for soups and meats. There are a number of varieties of Lettuce.

CULTURE.

No. 801.—The quality of Lettuce depends largely upon rapid and vigorous growth, and to secure that we need very rich, mellow soil, frequent surface cultivation, and an abundant supply of water. For the earliest crop sow the seed under glass, in March, and thin out the plants to prevent crowding. If you intend to mature the plants under glass, keep the beds quite close, and water it frequently and abundantly with liquid manure, and keep it well shaded during sunny days. If the plants are to be set in the open ground, give them all the air possible, without freezing them, and harden them off by full exposure and the withdrawal of water before transplanting. The plants should be set out as soon as a warm spot can be made very rich and mellow. When they are set out, sow the seeds in drills, fourteen inches apart, and thin them out, as wanted for the table, until they stand eighteen inches apart. Hoe them frequently, and water them when dry. The Cos varieties should be tied up about ten days before using, in order to blanch the inner leaves.

EARLY TENNIS BALL.

No. 802.—This is the best variety of head Lettuce for growing under glass, being very hardy and having thick, crisp, and tender leaves. It forms a compact head under glass, but when in the open air, unless planted very early, it is liable to be loose and open.

BLACK SEEDED SIMPSON.

No. 803.—The leaves of this variety are very large and form a compact mass, rather than a distinct head. They are of superior quality, being thin and tender, and of a light green color. Their color prevents any wilting of the plant being noticed, and as a consequence, it is a popular market variety.

SIMPSON EARLY CURLED.

No. 804.—This is one of the best early varieties for family use. All of the leaves tend to produce a large loose head. The leaves are dark green, beautifully crimped, and are tender and crisp.

EARLY BOSTON CURLED.

No. 805.—This variety has numerous large dark green leaves, that grow close together, the edges being deeply frilled, so that the whole plant forms a round mass, closely resembling a bunch of moss.

EARLY PRIZE HEAD (FERRY'S).

No. 806.—This is the best Lettuce known. It forms a mammoth hardy plant, of which even the outer leaves are crisp and tender, remaining so throughout the season. It is slow to run up to seed. Its flavor is delicious, and it is much used in soups, etc.

HANSON.

No. 807.—This is a very fine heading variety, of large size, and stands the sun better than any other sort. The heads are large, solid, sweet, tender, and crisp throughout, and are devoid of any bitter taste.

DEACON.

No. 808.—This plant is small, having very thick and smooth dark green leaves, which are crisp and tender.

EARLY CURLED SILESIA.

No. 809.—An early variety of very strong growth, which does not form a head, but is the best kind for cutting and bunching when young. The leaves are large and wrinkled and of a light yellow color. It resembles the Cos varieties in quality.

FRANKFORT HEAD.

No. 810.—A dark green curled variety with close round heads, which when opened are finely blanched and very crisp. It remains in head a long time.

LARGE DRUMHEAD.

No. 811.—The head is remarkably large and compact, though somewhat flattened. It is crisp and tender and one of the finest summer varieties. Its color is pale green without and white in the center.

PHILADELPHIA BUTTER.

No. 812.—This is a very early variety, desirable for forcing and for early planting out of doors, but it does not stand the sun well. It is medium in size, having a compact head, the leaves being smooth and thick and of a bluish-green color.

BROWN DUTCH.

No. 813.—This is an old and hardy variety, and always forms a large, solid head, which is somewhat coarse looking. The leaves are large and thick, of a deep green color outside, but beautifully blanched within. They are exceedingly sweet, tender, and of good flavor.

GREEN FRINGED.

No. 814.—An ornamental variety of exceeding beauty, but inferior in quality. The inside of the leaves is white, the edges a light green, delicately fringed and crimped. Its handsome appearance makes it well worthy of cultivation for table decoration alone.

WHITE PARIS COS.

No. 815.—This is a large hardy variety, which takes long in running to seed, and is considered by many to be far better than the other varieties. The heads are long and upright, with oblong leaves, that are tender, brittle, and highly flavored.

SALAMANDER.

No. 816.—This is the best variety for summer use, forming large, compact heads. It is light green in color outside, and white inside. Its great advantage is that it will stand drought and heat, and will remain longer in heads than the other varieties.

LETTUCE BRAIZED, SPANISH STYLE.

No. 817.—Select one dozen solid heads of Lettuce and trim off the outer leaves. Wash the Lettuce in plenty of cold water and then drain them. Parboil them for five minutes, then immerse them in cold water. After this press each head in the hand well, arrange them on a napkin and trim them. Next line a deep flat saucepan with thin slices of fat pork, on which you will put the heads of Lettuce side by side. Season with salt, pepper and nutmeg, and add a faggot of parsley garnished with two bay leaves, a sprig of thyme and two onions having three cloves stuck in each. Cover each head of Lettuce with slices of fat pork and moisten them with stock broth. Cover the saucepan and let this boil once and then set it on the side of the fire to cook slowly until done. Then drain them on a sieve and sponge off the grease with a napkin. Then put them in a saucepan with three spoonfuls of half glaze, and set them in the oven. When glazed serve them with a reduced Espagnole sauce.

LETTUCE BRAIZED, GERMAN STYLE.

No. 818.—Prepare the Lettuce as in No. 817, and when cooked drain them on a napkin and sponge off the grease. Then dish them up and pour over them some Allemande sauce, reduced with cream.

STUFFED LETTUCE.

No. 819.—Prepare one dozen heads of Lettuce as in No. 817, and when parboiled immerse them in cold water, then press them in the hands and dry them. Put them on a towel on the table, spread out the leaves of each head and season with salt, pepper, and nutmeg. Add in the middle of each head some forced meat of veal (Godiveau) flavored with cooked fine herbs. Put the Lettuce in shape again, trim them and arrange them in a deep flat saucepan, lined with thin slices of fat pork. Moisten them with veal gravy, then let them boil, after which cover the saucepan and set it in the oven. Sprinkle them with the gravy occasionally, so they will glaze nicely. When cooked dish them up, strain off the gravy, take off the grease, and serve the gravy with them.

LETTUCE STUFFED AND FRIED.

No. 820.—Prepare the Lettuce the same as in No. 819, and when cooked drain them on a sieve, and sponge off the grease with a napkin. Then bread them and dip them in beaten eggs, and then bread them again in fresh bread crumbs. Fry them in hot lard and serve them on a napkin, with a garniture of fried parsley.

LETTUCE WITH CREAM.

No. 821.—Trim off the outer leaves of one dozen heads of Lettuce and wash the heads in cold water several times. Then put them in a saucepan, with boiling water lightly salted, and let them cook for ten minutes on a brisk fire. Then immerse them in cold water, drain them in a colander and press them dry in the hands. Then chop them fine. Put six ounces of butter in a saucepan, and when melted add two spoonfuls of flour, and let it cook to a light brown. Then add the Lettuce, stirring it in well, and season with salt, pepper, and nutmeg. Add in slowly a pint of cream and let it cook for ten minutes. Before serving, garnish it with hard boiled eggs, cut in quarters, and with toasted bread, cut in fancy shapes.

LETTUCE, WITH GRAVY.

No. 822.—Proceed the same as in No. 821, but in place of cream add some veal gravy or a good broth. Garnish with poached eggs or toast.

LETTUCE FOR GARNITURE.

No. 823.—When Lettuce is to be used for garnishing joints or large entrées, use the braized or stuffed Lettuce as in Nos. 817,

818, 819 and 820. When it is used for garnishing small entrées and broiled meats, use Lettuce with cream or gravy, as in Nos. 821 and 822. When it is used as a salad garniture select the inner leaves and steep them in cold water until ready for use. Keep the hearts to place on the top of the salad, or cut them in fine shreds and garnish around the dish, alternating with eggs.

LETTUCE SALADS.

No. 824.—Trim off the outer leaves of the Lettuce, wash the heads in cold water, trim the leaves, and then drain them on a salad strainer. Before using, drain them on a napkin, being careful not to press the leaves. Put them in a salad bowl and season with salt, pepper, sweet oil and vinegar.

NOTE.—Dress the salad only when ready for use. Germans generally add some sliced young onions and a mustard dressing. This is made by mashing the yolk of a hard boiled egg in a salad bowl, diluting it with oil and vinegar, and adding mustard. Then mix it well together and season with salt and pepper. Pour this mixture over the Lettuce, and mix it well with a wooden spoon and fork in a careful manner. Americans, especially in New England, dress the salad with sugar, vinegar, and cream. In the South they use oil, vinegar, salt, and pepper, or with a Mayonnaise dressing, and garnished with hard boiled eggs. The French add some fine chopped chervil and tarragon, and occasionally a clove of garlic, chopped fine, or some garlic rubbed on a crust of bread (Chapon). The Spaniards and Mexicans add some fine sliced green peppers, with sliced green onions. The English use a dressing made with the yolks of hard boiled eggs, diluted with oil, vinegar, and the juice of onions or shallots, and seasoned with salt and pepper. For a family dinner dish up the salad plain, with hard boiled eggs separately, or as a garniture. It requires an expert to dress a salad well. When ready for the salad the hostess should dress it, or if one of the company is noted as a good salad dresser, she should request him to dress it.

LETTUCE WITH CONSOMME (GARBURE).

GRATINATED CRUSTS WITH LETTUCE.

No. 825.—Trim one dozen heads of Lettuce, wash them well in cold water and then parboil them for ten minutes. Then immerse them in cold water and press them dry in the hands. Arrange the leaves nicely and tie them so they will keep their shape. Now prepare a deep, flat saucepan lined with thin slices of fat pork, some trimmings of veal, four sliced carrots and one sliced onion. Then put the Lettuce in and add a faggot of parsley garnished with one bay leaf and three cloves. Cover it all with thin slices of fat pork and moisten with enough broth to cover it. Set it on the fire to boil. Then cover the saucepan and set it on one side to cook slowly until tender. Then take them out carefully, place them on a clean board, take off the strings and cut them in two or three parts, lengthwise. Put in a deep baking dish some thin slices of toasted bread, then a layer of Lettuce, and continue this way until the dish is full. Season with salt and pepper. Then strain off the gravy that they were cooked in, and pour it over the Lettuce and toast to cover it. Then set the dish in an oven to cook slowly until nicely browned. Before serving, take off the grease and serve with a soup tureen of consomme.

LETTUCE WATER FOR INVALIDS.

No. 826.—Wash and clean three heads of Lettuce, and soak them in one quart of boiling water for one hour. Then strain it through a napkin. Season with a little sugar, and take a cupful one hour before each meal for several days. It is recommended for those whose stomachs are deranged and also for those afflicted with nervousness.

PRESERVED LETTUCE WHOLE.

No 827.—Select three dozen fresh picked heads of Lettuce and trim off the outer leaves. Wash them well in cold water, and then parboil them for ten minutes in water lightly salted. Then immerse them in cold water and dry them on a napkin. Then arrange them in a flat saucepan and moisten them with enough broth to cover them. Let them cook until tender, and then drain them on a napkin. Cut out the stalks, and then cut the heads of Lettuce in half, lengthwise, laying the tops over in the middle close together; so they will not curl outward. Then put them in square quart tin cans, the same way that you would arrange asparagus. Cover them with water lightly salted, solder on the covers and boil the tin cans in a hot water bath for two hours.

PRESERVED LETTUCE, IN CANS.

No. 828.—Prepare them as endives are prepared. See Article LXXXVII, No. 828.

LETTUCE WHEN USED IN VEGETABLE SOUPS.

No. 829.—Use the green tender leaves and wash them well to keep them green. Then cut them in shreds or with a cutter and put them in boiling water to cook for a few minutes. After this immerse them in cold water, then drain them and put them in soup when ready to serve.

ARTICLE CXVI.

| French | LICORICE. | German |
| Réglisse. | | Süshols-Bärenzuker. |

No. 830.—Licorice is a hardy perennial plant, the root of which abounds with a sweet juice, and is much used in demulcent compositions. It has fleshy, creeping roots, which, when undisturbed, attain great length and penetrate deep into the earth. The roots are the only part of the plant used, and are used by porter brewers and confectioners and for medicinal purposes. The sweet, mucilaginous juice, which is extracted from the roots by boiling, is much esteemed as an emollient for coughs and colds.

CULTURE.

No. 831.—It is propagated by planting slips of the roots, four or six inches long, that have two or three buds. Plant them in March, as soon as the ground can be worked, eighteen inches apart in rows that are three feet apart, covering them with three inches of earth. Every year late in autumn, when the sap has gone down and the leaves turned yellow, cut the old stem down with a pruning knife to a level with the ground. At this time the creeping stems are forked up and cut off close to the main stems. They are then preserved in sand for future planting. The roots will be ready for taking up three years after planting. This should be done towards winter, when the sap goes down in the roots. A trench three feet deep should then be dug around the roots, so they can be extracted without injury to them. They are then kept in sand until used.

ARTICLE CXVII.

| | LIMA BEANS. | |
| Féve | | Bohne. |

No. 832.—The Lima Bean is one of the latest and most tender of garden beans. The stem is about ten feet high, and the leaves are smooth, shiny and narrow, yet comparatively long. The pods are about four inches long and an inch and a quarter broad, being flattened in shape, and containing from three to five beans. They are green and wrinkled when young, and of a yellowish color when

ripe. The pods are tough and parchment-like in all stages of their growth, and are never eaten. The Beans when either green or ripe, are universally esteemed for their peculiar flavor and excellence. If gathered when suitable for use in their green state, and dried in the pods, they can be preserved during the winter. When required for use, they should be shelled, then soaked for a short time in clear water, and cooked the same as green beans. When they are treated in this manner, they will be found to be nearly as tender and well flavored as when freshly plucked from the plants. The Lima Bean seldom perfects its crop in the Northern States, as only a small portion of the pods attain a good size, being destroyed by early frost.

CULTURE.

No. 833.—Commence planting when the weather is settled and the soil is warm and in good working condition. Procure a number of poles six feet in length and set them out three feet apart each way. Plant five or six Beans in each hill, covering them with one inch of soil and being careful to set each Bean with its germ downward. After they have grown for awhile and before they begin to run, pull up the weakest and leave but three of the most vigorous plants in each hill. As they increase in height they should be tied to the poles with a soft, fibrous material. When they have ascended to the tops of the poles the ends should be pinched off. The ends of all branches that rise above that height should also be treated in the same way. This prevents them from running into vines and tends to make them blossom earlier and bear sooner and more abundantly. When cultivated near the Sieva, the varieties readily hybridize and the Lima Bean rapidly degenerates. Plants grown in the Southern States are healthy and vigorous and produce large Beans of excellent quality.

GREEN LIMA BEANS.

No. 834.—This is a sub-variety of the common Lima Bean, differing from it principally, in the pea-green color of the seed. It will remain longer on the plant without becoming hard, and is considered more tender than other kinds.

MOTTLED LIMA BEANS.

No. 835.—This is also a sub-variety of the common Lima Bean. The seeds are of a dull white, or greenish-white color, mottled or clouded with purple.

NOTE.—For the prepartion of Lima Beans, See Article on Beans.

ARTICLE CXVIII.

French
Till-ul.
LIME TREE, OR LINDEN TREE.
German
Die Lind.

No. 836.—The Lime, or Linden Tree, bears a fruit allied to the lemon, but smaller and more intensely sour. It is a handsome tree and is found in all warm climates. It has panicles of light yellow flowers and large cordate leaves. The flowering buds should be picked before the rising of the sun. They should then be peeled and dried and kept in a clean, cool place, free from dust. They are used for tisanes.

ARTICLE CXIX.

LOVAGE.

Angelique a feuille-d'ache. *Lieb stöckel.*

No. 837.—Lovage is a hardy perennial plant having a hollow, branching stem six or seven feet high. It has smooth, deep green, glossy leaves, that somewhat resemble those of celery. The roots are large and fleshy, having a dark-brown color without and being yellowish within. Both the roots and seeds are used. The roots are sliced and dried and are used by confectioners in that state. They are also used in medicine as an aromatic stimulant.

CULTURE.

No. 838.—Lovage requires a deep, rich, moist soil, and should be sown in August, or immediately after ripening. When the young plants have grown three inches, transplant them three feet apart in each direction. When they are well established they will require but little care and will continue for years.

ARTICLE CXX.

LUPINE.

Lupin. *Wolfsbohne*

No. 839.—Lupine is a leguminous plant, having a strong, erect, branching habit. It is not cultivated for food, but the white and yellow Lupine are grown for their farinaceous seeds. The pods are straight and hairy, about three inches long, and contain five or six large, white, flattened seeds, having a slightly bitter taste. They are said to possess important medicinal qualities. The yellow Lupine, which is a native of Sicily, is a hardy annual plant, resembling the white species. They are both grown in some parts of this country, and when in their green state they are cut up and ploughed under the soil as a fertilizer. Plant them in poor, dry soil.

Article CXXI.

French
Macis.

MACE.

German
Muskatenbluthe.

No. 840.—Mace is the second coat, or aril, which covers the nutmeg; a thin and membranaceous substance, of an oleaginous nature and yellowish color, being in flakes, divided into many ramifications. It has an agreeable aromatic taste, not being as bitter as the nutmeg. It is much used for culinary purposes, in pastry and in distilling liquors, and can be obtained in flakes or ground.

NOTE.—See Nutmeg Article.

Article CXXII.

MADRAS RADISH.

Radis (Madras).   *Retdij (Madras).*

No. 841.—The Madras Radish is generally cultivated for its pods, which are sometimes twelve inches in length. They are solid, crisp, and tender, and when young they are used for pickling, and for salads, being much superior to the common radish. The roots are sometimes eaten whole when they are young and tender, but they soon become fibrous, strongly flavored and unfit for use. When the Madras Radish is cultivated for its pods, sow it in drills that are two feet apart, and thin the plants to nine inches apart in the drills.

Article CXXIII.

French
Mauve.

MALLOW—CURLED LEAVED.

German
Malve.

No. 842.—Mallow is an annual plant that was introduced from Europe, and which grows spontaneously in gardens when once cultivated. The stems are frequently more than six feet in height. The leaves, which are of a rich green color, are nearly five inches in diameter and are smooth, lobed and beautifully frilled or curled on the borders. No part of the plant is considered suitable for food, but the beautiful leaves are used for garnishing desserts. Sow the seeds about the first of May, covering them with one inch of soil. The plant requires much space.

Article CXXIV.

MARANTA, OR ARROW-ROOT PLANT.

Arrow-root. *Arrow-mehl.*

No. 843.—This is a genus of plants found in tropical America, and some species also in India. They have tuberous roots containing a large amount of starch, and from one species arrow-root is obtained. The Indians are said to employ the roots of this species in extracting the poison of arrows, whence the name. The fecula obtained is called Arrow-Root. The root of this plant is perennial, tuberous, fleshy, horizontal and scaly, and is a foot or more in length, having numerous long, white fibres. It sends forth several tuberous jointed, curved, white stoles, the points of which sometimes rise above the ground and become new plants. Several stems proceed annually from the same root, being branched and slender, and about four inches high. The Arrow-Root plant is a native of the West Indies, where it is largely cultivated, and its cultivation is also carried on in the East Indies, Africa and the Southern States. That from the Bermuda Islands is most esteemed, Jamaica furnishing the next best quality. The plant is propagated early, by cutting off the roots. Arrow-Root is adulterated with flour from other roots, such as the Curcuma and the Tacca Oceanica from the Sandwich Islands. Potato flour is also used. Arrow-Root when ground, is a light, white powder, devoid of taste or odor. It has a firm feeling when pressed between the fingers, and produces a faint crackling sound when rubbed. It is a pure starch, corresponding in its chemical properties with that of corn starch or potato starch. When purchased it should be free from any unpleasant flavor, as it is liable to get musty. Keep it in a dry place.

PREPARTION OF ITS FLOUR.

No. 844.—The flour is prepared in the following manner: The roots are dug up when a year old, then washed and pounded into a pulp, which is thrown into water to separate the amylacteous from the fibrous portion. The fibres are removed with the hands, which leaves the starch suspended in the water, to which it gives a milky color. The milky fluid is strained through a coarse towel, and is allowed to stand that the flour may settle. The flour is then washed with fresh water and is dried afterwards in the sun.

ITS USE.

No. 845.—Arrow-Root is nutritious and demulcent, and affords a light and easily digested article of diet for the sick and convalescent. It is peculiarly suited, from its demulcent properties, to those afflicted with complaints of the bowels and diseases of the urinary passages. It is much used as food, for infants after weaning or when the mother's milk is insufficient. It is prepared by dissolving it in hot water with which it forms a pearly gelatinous solution, and if sufficiently thick it forms a jelly-like mass when cool. A tablespoonful will contribute sufficient consistence to a pint of water. It should first be made into a paste with a little cold water and the boiling water should then be added, with brisk agitation. The preparation may be rendered more palatable by adding lemon juice and sugar, or, in extreme sickness, by adding wine and spices. It is usually prepared with milk when taken by children.

ARTICLE CXXV.

MARJORAM.

French
Marjolaine.

German
Marjoram.

No. 846.—Marjoram is a perennial aromatic plant, somewhat hardy, but not hardy enough to endure the winter in the North. When the plants are in bloom they are cut and dried and are used for flavoring salted meat and venison soup. They are also ground and used in flavoring stuffings, etc.

CULTURE.

No. 847.—Sow the seeds as early as possible and thin out the plants to ten inches apart. It is also propagated by dividing the roots either in spring or autumn.

SWEET MARJORAM.

No. 848.—Sweet Marjoram is always treated as an annual in the Northern States. The plant grows low, having a branching stem and rounded leaves. This variety is said to have come from Portugal, and is mostly used for culinary purposes. It is highly aromatic, and is used in its green and dried state.

COMMON MARJORAM.

No. 849.—This variety is perennial and is more hardy than the Sweet Marjoram. It is used in the same manner as the sweet variety.

POT MARJORAM.

No. 850.—This variety is a native of Sicily. Its leaves are oval and comparatively smooth. It produces small purple flowers in spikes. It is used in the same way as the other varieties are, but is inferior to the Sweet Marjoram.

WINTER SWEET MARJORAM.

No. 851.—This is a perennial variety somewhat hardy and resembling the Sweet Marjoram, being next in quality to it. The plants should be cut when just coming into bloom and dried well in the shade.

ARTICLE CXXVI.

French	MARSH MALLOW.	German
Guimauve.		*Sammetpappel.*

No. 852.—This is a plant that is common in marshes near the sea shore. The flowers are used for diet drinks (tisanes), and should

Article CXXVII.

French
Mélilot.

MELILOT.

German
Mellilot.

No. 853.—This is a plant having yellow flowers, of a peculiar odor and flavor, resembling the Tonqua bean. It is put in a faggot when roasting or stewing rabbits or hares, to impart an agreeable flavor. It is also used in dairies to color cheese.

Article CXXVIII.

MINT.

Menthe.   *Garten Münze.*

No. 854.—Mint is a hardy perennial aromatic plant, producing, by distillation, a highly odoriferous and pungent essential oil. It is generally cultivated in gardens, but grows naturally near brooks and in rich, moist soil. It is used in making sauces for flavoring, for medicinal purposes, for flavoring drinks, and by confectioners. The common or plain leaved variety is the best for general use. The Spear-Mint is inferior for culinary purposes, but is prettier for garnishing, on account of the curled foliage.

CULTURE.

No. 855.—It is propagated best by a division of the roots, which readily establish themselves wherever planted. In cultivating from seed, sow under glass and transplant them when the leaves are formed.

MINT SAUCE, AMERICAN STYLE.

No. 856.—Pick one handful of green Mint leaves, wash them clean, dry them on a napkin and cut them fine. Put half a pint of good wine vinegar and half a pint of water in a bowl, and sweeten it to taste with light brown sugar. Then add the Mint and a little salt and pepper and mix the whole well together. Let it stand for fifteen minutes before using. This sauce is much used in this country and is greatly esteemed with roasted spring lamb.

MINT SAUCE, FRENCH STYLE.

No. 857.—Prepare it the same as in the American style, using warm lamb or beef gravy instead of water.

ARTICLE CVXXIX.

French	**MOREL.**	German
Morille.		*Morchel.*

No. 858.—In its natural state the Morel is found growing in orchards, in damp woods, and in moist pastures. There are several varieties, all of which are edible. It is about four inches in height and is distinguished by its white cylindrical hollow, and solid smooth stem. Its cap is spherical and hollow, and of a dark brown or gravy color. It adheres to the stem by its base, and is deeply pitted over the entire surface. It is in perfection early in the season, but should not be gathered after a rain or while it is wet with dew. If gathered when dry it may be preserved many months. The Morel is much used in its dry or fresh state, to heighten the flavor of stews and gravies. This mushroom is to be obtained from Italian warehouses and is the best variety in use in its dried state.

MORELS, POULETTE.

No. 859.—Wash the Morels in tepid water, trim them and then cut the large ones in quarters. Parboil them for five minutes, then immerse them in cold water and afterwards drain them on a napkin. Then put them in a saucepan with a piece of butter, one small onion and a faggot of parsley, garnished, and season them with salt, pepper, and nutmeg. Toss them over a brisk fire, then add four spoonfuls of Allemande or Cream sauce, and let them cook slowly for fifteen minutes. Then take out the onion and the faggot, add a piece of butter and the juice of one lemon, and toss the whole over the fire well. Then serve.

MORELS, SPANISH STYLE.

No. 860.—Prepare them the same as in No. 859, using Espagnole sauce instead of Allemande or Cream sauce, and finish it by adding a small piece of Anchovie butter.

MORELS ON SKIVERS.

No. 861.—When the Morels are cleaned and parboiled, as in No. 859, cut them in quarters, put them in an earthen bowl, and season them with salt, pepper, and nutmeg. Pour some clarified butter over them, and mix them well. Then put them on wooden skivers, dip them in fresh bread crumbs, and broil them on a slow fire. Cut ten slices of bacon in small pieces, fry them nicely, and dish them on a platter with the broiled Morels on top, having put the Morels on silver skivers before serving them.

MORELS FRIED.

No. 862.—When the Morels are cleaned and parboiled, as in No. 859, cut them in halves, put them in a saucepan, moisten them with broth and let them cook until reduced to a light glaze. Then season them with salt, pepper, and nutmeg, take them out of the saucepan, flour them, and then fry them in hot lard. Add to the light glaze, two spoonfuls of mutton gravy, a piece of butter, the juice of half a lemon, and some fine chopped parsley. Pour this sauce over the Morels and then serve.

MORELS, WITH GRATINATED CRUST.

No. 863.—When the Morels are washed and parboiled as in No. 859, cut them in scollops. Then put them in a saucepan with a piece of butter, one onion and a faggot of parsley garnished. Toss them over a brisk fire and sprinkle them with a little flour while tossing them. Then moisten them with white broth, let them cook slowly for fifteen minutes, then take out the onion and faggot of parsley and season with salt, pepper and nutmeg. Dilute the yolks of four raw eggs in a glass of cream and pour it over the Morels off of the fire, tossing them well together. Then serve them with gratinated crusts, the same as mushrooms.

MORELS FOR GARNITURE.

No. 864.—Prepare them as in Nos. 859 and 860 with Allemande, Espagnole or Cream sauce.

MORELS STUFFED.

No. 865.—Wash clean and trim them as in No. 859, parboil them for fifteen minutes, then immerse them in cold water and drain them on a napkin. Chop the trimmings and stems fine and put them in a saucepan with a piece of butter and two fine chopped shallots. Put the cover on the pan and let them cook slowly until the moisture is reduced. Then put them on a plate to get cold and add some cooked forced meat of chicken or veal and some fine chopped parsley. Stuff the Morels with this preparation, sprinkle fresh bread crumbs over them, arrange them in a flat saucepan lined with thin slices of fat pork, and put a small piece of butter on each. Moisten them with broth and set them in the oven to cook slowly until nicely browned. Serve them with a reduced Madeira wine sauce, to which add a little fine chopped parsley.

Article CXXX.

French   **MULLEN, OR MULLEIN.**   German
Mol-ne ou Bouillon blanc.   *Wollkrout.*

No. 866.—Mullen is a field plant. Its leaves and flowers have been employed as remedial agents. They have a slight odor and a mucilaginous, bitterish, feeble taste. Mullen leaves are demulcent and emollient, and are said to possess anodyne properties, which render them useful in pectoral complaints. A strained infusion of the flowers is used in mild catarrhs and in diarrhœa. It will be found advantageous to moisten the leaves previous to boiling them. Pick the flowers before they expand, dry them in the shade, mixing and turning them occasionally to have them perfectly dry. Keep them in boxes in a cool dry place, and use them in diet drinks (tisanes), as in Article LXXXII.

Article CXXXI.

MUSHROOMS.

Champignon ou Mousseron.   *Champignon, or Ertshwamm.*

No. 867.—The Mushroom is one of a large class of cryptogamic plants of the natural order of *Fungi*. The name is sometimes popularly restricted to such species as are used for food. It is a cellular plant, having generally a more or less rounded thallus supported upon a stalk, and having seeds upon the under surface or gills. They are numerous, being found in all parts of the world, and are usually of very rapid growth, often springing up and coming to maturity in a single day. Many species are used for food in different parts of the world, while other species are poisonous. Many varieties abound in the pastures and woods in all the States, and may be gathered wild and enjoyed by those who have not the means of raising them artificially. They are gathered in all the different stages of their growth, and are used boiled, stewed, stuffed or broiled, and when dried are used for flavoring. The current belief is that, while many fungi are virulently poisonous, others, including the common Mushroom, are free from poison, and may be eaten in any quantity. The fear of poison deters many from making any use of this savory and nourishing but treacherous vegetable, and if they are afraid to eat them it is a matter of considerable importance to have the real standing of fungi as food stuffs made clear. According to recent investigations the question seems to be, not how to distinguish the poisonous from harmless species, but how to treat Mushrooms of every sort in such a way as to remove or neutralize the poison which they contain, with the precaution of using this class of food stuffs at all times with moderation. It has been ascertained that repeated washing with cold water removes most of the poison of Mushrooms, and that boiling dissolves out the rest. The water in which Mushrooms are boiled, however, is always poisonous, more so even than raw Mushrooms. Dried Mushrooms have been found to be dangerous for twenty days, and also the water in which such Mushrooms had been boiled. They are not really safe until after four months' drying. Therefore, treat all Mushrooms as poisonous; carefully throw out all the water in which they have been washed; cook them well, and never eat them in large quantities. The fact that all Mushrooms are more or less poisonous should be no bar to their use as food, proper care being taken in the cooking and eating. The detection of poisonous Mushrooms is a matter of deep consideration. The surest method of detecting them, and a precaution that should always be taken, is to put a silver coin or a solid silver spoon in the water in which Mushrooms are cooked. If the silver assumes a bluish or black color it may be assured that one or perhaps all of the Mushrooms are poisonous, and they should be thrown away.

CULTURE.

No. 868.—There can be no doubt but what all of the edible kinds would finally submit to and probably improve by cultivation, though as yet but a single species has been generally introduced into the garden. The common Mushroom is the only kind cultivated, and can be grown in cellars, sheds, on shelves in the open air, or in caves free from iron or coal. Beds of the required width and length are made of fermenting horse manure, at a temperature of about seventy degrees, being eighteen inches deep. Plant the broken pieces of spawn in this bed, six inches apart, covering the whole with two inches of light soil, and protecting it from cold or severe rains. The Mushrooms will appear in about six weeks. Irrigate only when the bed is quite dry, with soft or lukewarm water. The best of all situations, when available, in which to grow Mushrooms, are underground caves, such as supply the Paris markets with such vast quantities.

THE COMMON MUSHROOM.

No. 869.—When the common Mushroom first appears it has a white color, is of a roundish button-like form, and apparently rests on the surface of the ground. When fully developed the stem is solid and two inches in height, and its cap measures from one to four inches in diameter, changing to a brownish color when old and becoming tough and fleshy. It is readily distinguished when of medium size, by its fine pink or flesh-colored gills and pleasant odor. When old, the gills become of a chocolate color and it is then liable to be confounded with other kinds of a dubious quality. However, the species which resemble it most is slimy to the touch and is devoid of its fine odor, having rather a disagreeable smell. The noxious kinds always grow in woods or on the margin of woods, while the wholesome Mushroom springs up chiefly in open pastures, and should be gathered only in such places when young and tender. The Mushroom produces no real seed, but instead of it has a white fibrous substance in broken threads, called spawn, which is preserved in horse manure, being pressed in the shape of bricks. It will preserve its vitality for years when prepared in this manner.

AGARICUS COMATUS MUSHROOM.

No. 870.—This is an excellent variety that is found in abundance in stumps of trees in pastures, appearing in spring and autumn. It is much used in catsup, but should only be used when young.

SWEET OR DELICIOUS MUSHROOM.

No. 871.—This is a variety of medium size, having a yellowish color ringed with orange on the top. It somewhat resembles a deleterious species, but is readily distinguished from it, as when it is cut when fresh the juice is quite red and afterwards turns green, while the juice of the noxious kind is white and unchangeable. It is found in the fall of the year, growing under fir or pine tr·es.

THE ST. GEORGE MUSHROOM.

No. 872.—This is a variety that attains a weight of four or five pounds in California, but is not as delicate as the common Mushroom. Those grown in Europe are superior to the common Mushroom in flavor and are more digestible. It grows in rings in pastures or in thickets under trees, and reappears for successive years on the same spot.

BLEWIT'S BLUE HATS.

No. 873.—This is a favorite species, and is sold largely in the markets. It has a soft, moist, smooth pileus, with a solid bulbous stem, tinted with light blue. The gills are of a dingy white color, and rounded towards the stem. It should only be gathered in dry weather, as it absorbs moisture readily, and thereby is injured in flavor and rendered more liable to decay.

AGARICUS PRIMULAS.

No. 874.—This variety is found only in spring, and grows in rings on the borders of woodlands, at which time an abundance of its spawn can be obtained. It may be preserved by transplanting it into bricks of loam and horse manure, in which it will keep for several months, the same as the spawn of common Mushrooms. This variety is used both in its fresh and dried state. It is preserved by being cut into quarters, and then dried in the air for several days, when it is strung up and kept for future use.

THE FAIRY KING.

No. 875.—This Mushroom is found growing in rings, and has a pileus of a brownish ochre color, which changes to a paler cast as it grows, until it gradually fades into a rich, creamish yellow color. It is of excellent flavor, and is valuable for domestic use, owing to the facility with which it is dried, and its extensive dissemination. It may be kept for years without losing its aroma or flavor.

NOTE.—The Boletus, Clavaria, and Morel varieties of Mushrooms will be found under their respective headings.

HOW TO CLEAN AND PREPARE MUSHROOMS.

No. 876.—Mushrooms should be used as soon as they are gathered. Put the solid ones in one pan, and those that are hollow in another, having two quarts of acidulated water in each pan. Wash them well, then trim them and put them in separate pans again, that contain acidulated water. Let them soak for a while until ready to use them. The small, solid button Mushrooms will resemble the cultivated French Mushrooms when cooked, and may be used for sauces and small garnitures. Cut off the stems of the hollow ones before washing them. The heads are used for stuffing, and are also broiled. The tops of the solid ones should be cut in crescent-like grooves, to give them a fancy appearance. The trimmings are chopped fine, and are used with fine herbs.

COOKED MUSHROOMS, FOR GENERAL PURPOSES.

No. 877.—When the Mushrooms are washed and cleaned as in No. 876, select a saucepan that is not too large for the quantity of Mushrooms to be cooked. Put two pounds of fresh Mushrooms in the saucepan and add four ounces of butter, a quarter of a glassful of cold water, and the juice of two lemons. Cover the saucepan, put it on a brisk fire, and when the Mushrooms have boiled for two or three minutes, pour them into an earthen jar. When they are cold cover them with a buttered paper cover and keep them in a cool place. They may be used for any kind of sauces or garnitures. The juice is added to sauces to reduce them.

NOTE.—When cooking large quantities of Mushrooms, put the saucepan on the fire and add them when the liquid boils. A wine-glassful of water will be sufficient for five pounds of Mushrooms.

MUSHROOMS, WITH ALLEMANDE SAUCE.

No. 878.—Reduce some Allemande sauce with some Mushroom gravy and then add the Mushrooms. If they are small leave them whole; if large, cut off the stems and slice them as desired.

MUSHROOMS, WITH ESPAGNOLE SAUCE.

No. 879.—Reduce some Espagnole sauce with some Madeira wine and Mushroom gravy, and then add the Mushrooms as in No. 878.

MUSHROOMS ON TOAST (SAUTÉ).

No. 880.—Put a small piece of butter in an omelet pan, and when it is warm add a handful of Mushrooms and toss them over the fire until thoroughly warmed. Then add a little salt and pepper, two spoonfuls of Mushroom juice, a little lemon juice and some fine chopped parsley. Serve it all hot on pieces of thin buttered toast.

PUREE OF MUSHROOMS.

No. 881.—Wash and clean two pounds of Mushrooms as in No. 876, and put them in a saucepan with a piece of butter and the juice of half a lemon. Set the saucepan on a brisk fire, stirring its contents occasionally, until the moisture is well reduced. Then put them in a mortar and pound them fine, and return them to the saucepan. Then add five spoonfuls of Allemande or Cream sauce, season it with salt, pepper and nutmeg, and let it simmer slowly for fifteen minutes. Then rub it through a fine sieve, and put it in a flat saucepan, reducing it with half a cup of cream. Before serving, add a piece of butter.

NOTE.—Half a pound of cooked forced meat of chicken may be added, instead of the Allemande or Cream sauce. Keep the puree in a cool place, and when ready for use, add a piece of butter and bring it almost to the boiling point, stirring it all continually.

BROILED MUSHROOMS ON TOAST, MAITRE D'HOTEL.

No. 882.—Wash and clean two dozen large Mushrooms, cut off the stems and dry them on a napkin. Put them in an earthen bowl with two or three spoonfuls of sweet oil, a little salt and the juice of one lemon. Half an hour before using them cover them with a buttered paper cover and let them macerate. Broil them on a fire that is not too brisk and serve them on a hot plate on pieces of hot buttered toast, with the bottoms of the Mushrooms upwards. Mix a little fine chopped parsley and a few drops of lemon juice with a piece of butter and put some of the mixture on each Mushroom.

BROILED MUSHROOMS, BORDELAISE.

No. 883.—Prepare two dozen Mushrooms as in No. 882, and put them in an earthen bowl with three spoonfuls of sweet oil, a little salt and a few grains of pepper. Cover them with a buttered paper cover and set them in a cool place for one hour to macerate before using them. Broil them nicely and put them on a hot plate. Prepare the following mixture separately in a saucepan: Mix two spoonfuls of sweet oil, a small piece of garlic chopped fine, and some chopped parsley and chervil. Warm this thoroughly and pour it over the Mushrooms, then squeeze the juice of one lemon over them and serve them hot.

MUSHROOMS, PROVINCIAL.

No. 884.—Prepare two dozen large Mushrooms as in No. 882, slice them and put them in an earthen bowl with two spoonfuls of sweet oil, a little salt, a few grains of pepper and two mashed cloves of garlic. Cover them with a buttered paper cover and set them in a cool place to macerate for an hour before using. When ready to use them, put one spoonful of sweet oil in an omelet pan, then chop the mashed garlic finely and add it to the warmed sweet oil. Then put the Mushrooms in and toss them over the fire until thoroughly warmed. Add a little fine chopped parsley and the juice of half a lemon, and serve the Mushrooms on toast.

MUSHROOMS, PIEMONTAISE.

No. 885.—Wash and clean half a pound of Mushrooms, then slice them and put them in an omelet pan with a piece of butter and toss them over a brisk fire. When they are cooked add two spoonfuls of Allemande sauce, a few drops of meat glaze, a little fine chopped parsley, the juice of half a lemon and a piece of butter. Toss them over the fire until the butter is melted and then serve them hot.

USE OF TRIMMINGS AND PEELINGS.

No. 886.—When the trimmings, peelings and stems of the Mushrooms are carefully washed, dry them well and chop them fine. Then put a piece of butter and some fine chopped shallots in a saucepan. Cover the pan and let them simmer slowly on a slow fire until cooked. Then add the chopped Mushrooms and let it cook until the moisture is reduced. After this put them in a bowl and use them with fine herbs, in Italian sauce or with baked fish.

STUFFED MUSHROOMS, WITH FINE HERBS.

No. 887.—Select two dozen large Mushrooms and cut off the stems close to the top, then wash them and drain them on a napkin. Put two fine chopped shallots in a saucepan, fry them lightly and then add two handfuls of fine chopped Mushrooms and cook them slowly. When the moisture is nearly reduced, add three spoonfuls of Allemande sauce reduced, and a little fine chopped parsley. In a little while put this to one side to get cool, and when cold stuff the selected Mushrooms with the mixture. Put them in a buttered pan, sprinkle fresh bread crumbs over them, and put a few drops of sweet oil on top of each one. Then bake them in a moderate oven and serve them with a reduced Madeira wine sauce.

STUFFED MUSHROOMS, ITALIAN STYLE.

No. 888.—Select two dozen large Mushrooms, and cut off the stems close to the top, then wash them in acidulated water and drain them on a napkin. Put two fine chopped shallots and a piece of butter in a saucepan, and fry them lightly. Then add two handfuls of fine chopped Mushrooms, cover the pan and let them cook until the moisture is reduced. Then add one handful of fresh bread crumbs, season with salt, pepper, and nutmeg, and add a little fine chopped parsley and two spoonfuls of Allemande or Cream sauce. Mix it all well together, then take it off of the fire, add the yolks of three raw eggs, and set it aside to get cold. Then stuff the selected Mushrooms with this mixture, sprinkle fresh bread crumbs over them, arrange them in a buttered baking pan, and put a few drops of sweet oil on each Mushroom. Then bake them in a moderate oven and serve them with a brown Italian sauce.

MUSHROOMS FOR GARNITURE.

No. 889.—Use the solid, round, button-like Mushrooms for garnishing. Leave them whole, or if quite large use only the head. Keep them white, and groove the heads in crescent shapes, as it gives them a finer appearance. Dress them in bands, alternating with other vegetable garnitures. Stuffed Mushrooms are used for large garnitures, the same as stuffed tomatoes or peppers.

MUSHROOMS WITH GRATINATED CRUSTS.

No. 890.—Select one pound of small, solid Mushrooms, cut off the stems, and then cook them. Put them in a saucepan with a piece of butter, the juice of half a lemon, a spoonful of water and a faggot of parsley garnished with a clove of garlic. Season them with salt and pepper. Toss them over a brisk fire, and when well cooked and the moisture is reduced, take out the faggot and add four spoonfuls of Allemande or Cream sauce. Have some crusts ready, and fill them with this mixture. Put two cooked Mushrooms, having the tops grooved in crescent shape, on top of each crust and moisten the tops with a few drops of meat glaze, and serve them hot. The crusts mentioned above, are made as follows: Cut some bread in pieces four inches long, two inches wide, and one and a half inches thick. Trim the sides in a nice shape and hollow out the centre of each piece, leaving the edges one-quarter of an inch thick. Then fry them in clarified butter, after which drain them and put them in an oven to dry. When ready, fill the centre with the Mushrooms. French rolls will answer the same purpose when prepared as follows: Cut them in half, scoop out the centre, butter them and set them in the oven to dry.

MUSHROOMS BAKED IN SHELLS.

No. 891.—Prepare the Mushrooms the same as in No. 890, and when the sauce is well reduced, fill some buttered silver shells with the Mushrooms. Then sprinkle fresh bread crumbs over the top and put a small piece of butter on each. Bake them until they are nicely browned and serve the shells on a plate with a napkin. The Mushrooms may also be prepared and baked with a reduced brown or white Italian sauce, or with a reduced Allemande sauce with essence of Mushrooms.

MUSHROOMS, POULETTE.

No. 892.—Clean and wash one pound of Mushrooms. Put them in a saucepan with a small piece of butter, the juice of one lemon, and two spoonfuls of water. Cover the saucepan, put it on a brisk fire, and let the Mushrooms cook until they commence to boil. While this is cooking dilute two spoonfuls of flour in some cold water, strain it through a fine sieve, and, when the Mushrooms commence to boil, add the gravy to it to thicken it. Then let the Mushrooms cook slowly for five minutes, when you will add a glassful of cream diluted with the yolks of four raw eggs and a piece of butter. Toss them all well together off of the fire, and serve them as soon as they are ready with a little fine chopped parsley over them.

MUSHROOMS WITH CREAM SAUCE, AMERICAN STYLE.

No. 893.—When the Mushrooms are prepared and cooked as in No. 876, put them in a saucepan with a piece of butter. Season with salt and pepper, and add some Cream sauce with some of the Mushroom gravy. Let them simmer for fifteen minutes, and then serve the Mushrooms on toast.

ESSENCE OF FRESH MUSHROOMS.

No. 894.—Wash half a pound of fresh Mushrooms, or the same quantity of trimmings. Put them in a saucepan with a piece of butter, the juice of one lemon and two soup-spoonfuls of white broth. Cover the pan and set it on a brisk fire to cook for five minutes. Then strain the gravy through a napkin, and use it as needed.

SOYA SAUCE.

No. 895.—Soya Sauce can be procured from all first-class grocers, and is used principally as a dressing for fish. In case of necessity, prepare it as follows, using fresh field Mushrooms, if possible, although any kind will do. Use about three pounds of small Mushrooms, and some trimmings, if any are on hand. Wash them well and put them in layers in an earthen jar. Sprinkle each layer with a little salt. Cover the jar and set it in a cool place for twelve hours. Then draw off all of the liquid and strain it through a napkin into a saucepan. Let it boil until it is reduced to one-quarter of its quantity, and then add a glassful of port wine, a little red pepper, and spices of all kinds in equal quantities. Let it boil again until reduced as before, then strain the liquid, put it in bottles and cork them tightly. Then cook them in a hot water bath for five minutes, and when cold it is ready for use.

MUSHROOM CATCHUP.

No. 896.—Take six pounds of Mushrooms and put them in an earthen bowl in layers, sprinkling each layer with salt. Set it in a cool dry place for six hours, mixing them well, and mashing or breaking them in small pieces at the same time. Then cover them with a towel for three days, stirring them occasionally. Then drain off the juice and put it into an earthen jar. To each quart of juice add half an ounce of ginger, half an ounce of allspice, a teaspoonful of Cayenne pepper, and half a tea-spoonful of ground mace. Cover the jar tight and set it in a saucepan with cold water, and set it on the fire to boil, keeping it at the boiling point for six hours, adding boiling water as it reduces. Then pour the Catchup in a saucepan, let it boil slowly for half an hour, skimming it well, and then put it in an earthen bowl and keep it in a cool place. When it is cold and clear, pour off the liquid, without disturbing the sediment, and put it in tightly-corked bottles.

MUSHROOMS, BORDELAISE.

FOR BOLETUS, OR CEPES.

No. 897.—Imported Boletus, or Cepes, are much superior to those grown here, and are packed in oil in tin cans.

Put one dozen Cepes in an omelette pan with two spoonfuls of sweet oil. When thoroughly warmed, drain off the oil and add some finely chopped garlic and parsley. Toss them over the fire a couple of times, season with salt and pepper, add a spoonful of half glaze, and serve them hot.

When fresh Cepes are used, they should be cleaned without washing them. Toss them over the fire in a pan with some sweet oil, and when they are cooked drain them, and then put them in the pan again with a spoonful of sweet oil, and finish as the others.

MUSHROOMS, PROVINCIAL.

FOR BOLETUS, OR CEPES.

No. 898.—Clean and slice one dozen fresh Cepes and put them in a flat saucepan with a piece of butter, some finely chopped onions and a faggot of parsley garnished with one bay leaf and two cloves of garlic. Toss them over a brisk fire, and when the moisture is reduced, add two spoonfuls of Espagnole sauce and one of Tomato sauce. Season with salt and pepper, let them cook about five minutes, and then take out the faggot. Before serving, add a spoonful of Anchovie butter, the juice of half a lemon, and a little finely chopped parsley. Toss them well over the fire until the butter is melted, and serve them with small pieces of toast around the dish.

When canned Cepes are used, drain off the oil and proceed as above.

MUSHROOMS, POLONAISE.

FOR BOLETUS OR CEPES.

No. 899.—Clean and slice one dozen Cepes, put them in a small flat saucepan with a little finely chopped onion and toss them over a brisk fire until the moisture is reduced. Then season them with salt and a pinch of red pepper, add three spoonfuls of Cream sauce and toss them well together. Put them in a buttered baking dish, sprinkle fresh bread crumbs over the top, add a little clarified butter, and then bake them in an oven.

MUSHROOMS, WITH CREAM.

FOR BOLETUS, OR CEPES.

No. 900.—Clean one dozen Cepes, cut them in halves and put them in a small flat saucepan with a piece of butter. Toss them over a brisk fire until the moisture is reduced, then season with salt and a pinch of pepper, and add a faggot of parsley garnished with fennel. Moisten them with a cupful of cream and let them cook slowly for fifteen minutes. Then remove the faggot and put the Cepes on a dish.

Mix some finely chopped fennel or parsley with a piece of butter, stirring it until the butter is melted, and then pour it over the Cepes and serve them.

If large quantities of Cepes are cooked it will be best to add a light Cream sauce.

MUSHROOM TARTLETS, WITH CREAM.

No. 901.—Butter and flour two dozen tartlet moulds, and put in a thin layer of puff paste.

Slice some Mushrooms or Cepes finely, and put them in a frying pan with a piece of butter and a few finely chopped shallots. Toss them over a brisk fire for a few minutes, season them with salt and pepper, and add a little finely chopped parsley. Fill the tartlet moulds with the Mushrooms, then put them in the oven to cook, and when nearly done take them out.

Beat the whites of two eggs into a froth, and add six spoonfuls of cold reduced Cream sauce to it. Have it ready when you take the tartlets from the oven, and pour a little over each one. Put them in the oven again, and when they are nicely browned take them out of the moulds and serve them on a napkin.

MUSHROOMS IN SHELLS, RUSSIAN STYLE.

No. 902.—Put a piece of butter and a little finely chopped onion in a saucepan and fry them lightly. Then add one pound of Mushrooms (previously washed and trimmed). Season with salt and pepper, moisten them with some lightly thickened veal gravy, and let them cook for five minutes. Add a little finely chopped parsley and the juice of half a lemon, and put them in small silver baking shells. Sprinkle fresh bread crumbs over them, and put a piece of butter on top of each one. Let them bake in an oven, and when they are nicely browned, serve them hot in the shells on a napkin.

DRY MUSHROOMS.

No. 903.—Dry Mushrooms should always be kept on hand. The best are to be obtained from Italian warehouses. Keep them in a dry place in covered jars. They are used for flavoring meats and sauces, and are also used in preparing macaroni.

MUSHROOMS PRESERVED IN CANS.

No. 904.—When preserving Mushrooms only fresh and solid ones should be used. Use the hollow ones for other purposes.

Select the quantity of Mushrooms desired, trim them, wash them in cold acidulated water and then drain them. Put them in a saucepan, and to every three pounds add the juice of one lemon, a wine-glassful of water and a pinch of salt. Cover the saucepan, set it on a brisk fire and let the Mushrooms cook for five minutes. Then put them in an earthen bowl, and when they are cold drain off the moisture.

Put the Mushrooms in pint tin cans and add enough of the juice to cover them. Then solder on the covers and boil the cans in a hot water bath for two hours.

MUSHROOMS PRESERVED IN JARS.

No. 905.—Cook the Mushrooms the same as in No. 876 (adding a little more butter than usual), let them get cold and then put them in glass jars holding one quart and cover them air tight. Then boil them for one hour and a half in a hot water bath. Much depends upon the quality of the Mushrooms, and they should be prepared as soon as possible after they are plucked.

MUSHROOM TRIMMINGS, PRESERVED FOR FINE HERBS.

No. 906.—Take the trimmings of Mushrooms, wash them carefully, chop them finely, then put them in a towel and press out all of the moisture. Take a sufficient quantity of shallots to equal one-eighth of the amount of Mushroom trimmings, chop them finely and press them in a towel. Mix the trimmings and shallots, and put them in a saucepan with a piece of butter. Set it on the fire for ten minutes, stirring it occasionally with a wooden spoon, then set it aside to get cold. Then put the mixture in pint tin cans or glass jars, seal them hermetically and boil them in a hot water bath for one hour.

MUSHROOMS PRESERVED.

FOR BOLETUS, OR CEPES.

No. 907.—Select Cepes all of the same size, peel and wash them and dry them on a towel. Arrange them in layers in pint tin cans, season each layer with salt, and put one clove of garlic in each can. Put sufficient of the best olive oil in each can to cover them. Then solder on the covers and boil the cans in a hot water bath for one hour and a half.

ARTICLE CXXXII.

French *Melon Muscat.* **MUSK MELON.** **German** *Melon.*

No. 908.—This is a delicious species of melon; so called on account of its musky fragrance. Owing to the great facility with which the various kinds intermix or hybridize, the varieties are not only numerous, but are constantly increasing. Familiar names of different varieties are changed annually, as new kinds with superior recommendations spring up, and are offered as welcome substitutes for the old kinds.

CULTURE.

No. 909.—Cultivate them as you would cucumbers, except that the hills should be six feet apart, but avoid planting them near cucumbers, as they will mix with and injure the quality of the melons; this, and heavy rains at the time of ripening, will destroy the flavor of the finest stock. Rich earth for the young plants is far better than manure, but if the latter must be used, see that it is well rotted. If the plants grow very rank, more and finer fruit will be secured by pinching off the ends of the shoots when about three feet long. Cantaloupes are cultivated in the same manner.

BEECH WOOD MELON.

No. 910.—The melon is nearly spherical, but is somewhat longer than broad. The skin is of a greenish yellow color, thickly and regularly netted. The flesh is green, being sugary, and of excellent flavor.

CHRISTIANA.

No. 911.—This variety is small and roundish, and matures early. Its skin is of a yellowish green color, the flesh is yellow, sweet, and juicy, and of good quality.

CITRON.

No. 912.—This is a medium sized melon, nearly round, but flattened slightly at the ends, being deeply and thoroughly ribbed. The skin is green, and thickly netted, but when fully matured it becomes tinged with yellow. The flesh is thick, green, and juicy, having a rich sugary flavor. It is a hardy abundant bearer, uniform in quality, and is much used in the Southern States.

HARDY RIDGE.

No. 913.—A productive variety, having small fruit, which is strongly ribbed and has irregular warts all over its surface. The skin is of a dull yellow color. The flesh is about an inch deep, of a bright orange-red color, and is sweet and well flavored.

LARGE RIBBED NETTED.

No. 914.—The melon is large, oval, and strongly ribbed, and is hardy and productive when planted in good soil. The skin is thickly netted and yellow in color. The flesh is of a salmon-yellow color, remarkably thick and sweet, but is not finely grained.

NUTMEG.

No. 915.—The fruit is oval and regularly ribbed, and when fully ripened is very delicious, being ranked as one of the best kinds. The skin is of a pale green color, thickly netted, though somewhat thin. The flesh is light green, rich, sweet, juicy, and highly perfumed.

PINE APPLE.

No. 916.—This variety is small and nearly round, having ribs that are but faintly defined and at times not being noticeable. The skin is thin and of an olive-green color, being more or less netted. The flesh is green, juicy, sweet, and highly flavored. This kind is easily grown and is very productive.

SKILLMAN'S FINE NETTED.

No. 917.—This is one of the earliest sorts, somewhat resembling the pine apple. It is firm and almost round, being slightly flattened at the ends. The flesh is green, juicy, sugary, and excellent.

VICTORY OF BATH.

No. 918.—The fruit is egg shaped and faintly ribbed, being rounded at the blossom end, and slightly contracted toward the stem. The skin is thin and green, clouded with yellow, and sparsely covered with fine net marks. The flesh is green.

WHITE JAPAN.

No. 919.—This is a roundish, medium sized or small melon, which ripens early, is very desirable and quite productive. The skin is very thin and of a cream-white color, the flesh being remarkably sweet and finely flavored.

MUSK MELON FOR RELISHES.

No. 920.—Musk melons, like all the different varieties of melons, are served as a relish, or for dessert. They should be kept in a cool place about an hour before serving them. Cut the melon in half, remove the seeds, slice it in ordinary pieces, and serve them on a napkin. Either sugar or pepper and salt can be used with them.

PICKLED MELONS (MANGOES).

No. 921.—The small young and green citron, or cantaloupe melons, can be used. Cut out a small piece of the melon, wedge-shaped, so it can be replaced nicely, scoop out the seeds, replace the plug, and put the melons in the jar or barrel that you intend to fill. Make a brine, using one pound and a quarter of salt to a gallon of water, and boil it. Then pour it boiling hot over the melons, cover the barrel, and in three days drain off the brine, take the melons out of the barrel and stuff them the same as pickled stuffed bell peppers. Then put them in jars, pour some cold boiled wine or cider vinegar over them, to cover, put a small piece of alum in each jar, and cover them tightly.

PRESERVED MELONS, SPICED.

No. 922.—Musk, citron or cantaloupe melons can be used. Cut the melons in quarters, take out the seeds and remove the tenderest part of the flesh. Then peel off the rinds and cut up about five pounds of the melon in scollops. Put six pounds of sugar in a basin, to which add five pints of vinegar. Make it boil, and pour it boiling hot over the melons which you have put in a jar. Drain off the syrup the next day, then boil it and skim it, and pour it boiling hot over the melons. Repeat this every day for five days. On the sixth day boil the syrup again, adding to it one ounce of white ginger, a small stick of cinnamon, six cloves, and the melons. Let it boil slowly for fifteen minutes, skim it clear, and then take it off of the fire to get cool. When cold put them in glass jars and cover them tightly.

PRESERVED MELONS IN SYRUP.

No. 923.—Cut the melons in quarters, take out the seeds, and peel off the rinds. Parboil them for three minutes, then immerse them in cold water and drain them. Put them in an earthen bowl. Make a syrup, using three pounds of loaf sugar to one and a quarter pounds of water. Set it on the fire to boil, skim it well and then pour it boiling hot over the melons. Cover them with a paper cover and set them aside for twenty-four hours. Drain off the syrup next day and let it boil, adding some more sugar, and then let it boil to a thread. Set it aside to get cold and then pour it over the melons again. Boil it over again next day to the same degree, skimming it well, and pour it over the melons when boiling hot. Boil it the next day to a thick thread, skimming it well; then add in the melons and let the syrup boil up twice. On the following day boil the syrup again to the same degree, then add the melons and let them simmer slowly for five minutes. When well skimmed put the melons in glass jars, and when they are cold cover them tightly.

NOTE.—The juice of a lemon, or a little wine vinegar, can be added to the syrup when cooking it to heighten the flavor.

ARTICLE CXXXIII.

French	MUSTARD.	German
Moutarde.		*Senf.*

No. 924.—There are five kinds of Mustard, the plant and the seed having a pungent taste. A condiment is made from the ground seeds, which are also used as remedial agents, being useful externally in cataplasms, and internally as a diuretic and irritant. The rough leaves of the White Mustard plant, when young and undeveloped, make a pungent salad when mixed with water cress. They are also cooked and prepared the same as spinach. The Black Mustard seed makes the most piquant Mustard for table purposes.

CULTURE.

No. 925.—Sow the seeds thickly in rows and cut the plants when they are about two inches high. For a crop of seeds sow in April, in drills one foot apart, and thin the plants out moderately when they are about three inches high. For use during winter it may be sown at intervals in boxes, in the green house or in frames.

WHITE MUSTARD.

No. 926.—The White Mustard plant is a hardy annual that grows in gardens and fields, having thin stems that attain a height of about three feet. The leaves are large and of a rich deep green color. When it is grown in gardens for salad or greens sow it as early as the ground will admit, in drills ten inches apart. Remove the weeds and water it well in dry weather. Cut the plants when in seed leaf, as when they become developed they get strong and ill-flavored.

CHINESE OR PEKIN MUSTARD.

No. 927.—This is a hardy annual that grows about four feet high, and has large leaves, which are used in salad and are also prepared the same as spinach.

CURLED MUSTARD.

No. 928.—This plant is small, with greenish yellow leaves of medium size, that are finely cut on the borders and beautifully curled. They have a pleasant taste when used in salads. The seeds resemble those of the Black Mustard.

CUT LEAVED MUSTARD.

No. 929.—The leaves, when young, make an excellent salad when mixed with water cress.

BLACK MUSTARD.

No. 930.—This is a hardy annual that grows in great abundance. The young plants, cut to the ground, are used the same as spinach, or in salads. The common table Mustard is made from the seeds of this variety.

CHARLOCK MUSTARD.

No. 931.—This is a wild field plant and is used for greens or salad and has a peculiar pleasant taste.

MUSTARD FLOUR MIXED FOR TABLE USE.

No. 932.—Americans generally prefer Mustard flour mixed with vinegar or plain with water. Epicures prefer it mixed with hot water and white wine, or with new wine and vinegar. French Mustard can be obtained from all first-class grocers. There are several varieties, some of which are flavored with tarragon, anchovies or fine herbs, etc.

NOTE.—Never use a metallic spoon in mustard as it forms verdigris when left to stand in the Mustard pot, and may render it poisonous.

ANCHOVIE MUSTARD.

No. 933.—Trim one dozen of salted anchovies, pound them in a mortar into a fine paste, and rub the paste through a fine sieve. Then put it back in the mortar and add half a pound of Mustard flour diluted with white wine. Mix it all well together and put it in small bottles and cork them tightly.

RAVIGOTE MUSTARD.

No. 934.—Pick half a pound of the leaves of burnet, tarragon, chervil, and garden cress. Dip them in boiling water for a minute, then immerse them in cold water, and afterwards put them in a towel and press out all of the moisture. Pound it finely in a mortar, adding a clove of garlic if that flavor is desired. Then rub it through a fine sieve and put it back in the mortar. Add half a pound of Mustard flour diluted with water, and mix the whole well together. Then put it in small bottles and cork them tightly.

MUSTARD SAUCE FOR DEVILED MEATS.

No. 935.—Put half a pound of Mustard flour in a bowl and add a pinch of red pepper, a little salt, and four soup-spoonfuls of Worcestershire sauce. Dilute this with wine vinegar to the consistency of a sauce. Put it in bottles for future use.

Article CXXXIV.

French   NASTURTIUM.   **German**
Capucine.   *Indishe Kresse.*

No. 936.—This is a climbing plant, which, though generally treated as an annual, is a tender perennial. It has peltate leaves and spurred flowers of a vivid yellow or orange color, and strong odor. The fleshy fruits have a warm, pungent flavor, like the cress, and are pickled and used the same as capers. The small green ones are preferred and are used in sauces and with salads. The young shoots are eaten as a salad, while the richly colored flowers make a handsome garniture for salads.

CULTURE.

No. 937.—When they are cultivated for their flowers or seeds they should be planted in poor, light soil. The drills are made three feet apart, and the young plants should be thinned out to six inches apart. The young crop is supported by staking or bushing, the same as peas, and requires much attention. See that they are properly attached to the stakes, and keep the ground free from weeds.

SMALL NASTURTIUM.

No. 938.—This is a dwarf variety, the stem rarely measuring more than two feet in length. The flowers are yellow and the pods are small, being preferred to the others for pickling. It yields abundantly.

TALL NASTURTIUM.

No. 939.—This variety is very ornamental for covering arbors, having a stem from six to eight feet high. Sow it in rich made soil to have luxuriant foliage. It has large yellow flowers, with the upper petals slightly streaked and marked with purple.

DARK FLOWERING.

No. 940.—This variety is similar to the Tall Nasturtium, except that the flowers are of a dark brown color.

NASTURTIUM SEED BUDS, PICKLED.

No. 941.—Pick the quantity of seed buds desired, and put them in bottles. Boil some good wine vinegar, and when it is cold pour it over the seed buds in the bottles, and add a sprig of tarragon. They are used the same as capers.

ARTICLE CXXXV.

French NETTLE. **German**
Ortie.   *Nessel.*

No. 942.—The common Nettle is a hardy, herbaceous perennial, which grows naturally and in abundance by the wayside, but it is seldom seen where people have not been at work; hence it is considered a sort of domestic plant. The stem is erect and branching, while the leaves are heart-shaped at the base, toothed on the borders, and thickly set with small, stinging hair-like bristles. The common Nettle produces a large proportion of fiber, which is used in making ropes, cordage, sewing thread, and white linen cloth of superior quality. Like many other common plants the superior merit of these troublesome weeds has been greatly overlooked. Early in April the tops will furnish tender leaves that are used as a pot herb for soups, or are prepared the same as spinach. The cultivated

Nettle is used most, being propagated from roots that are planted either in pots or in the forcing house. They will soon send up an abundance of tender tops. They may be blanched by covering them with other pots. If planted close to a flue in the vineyard they will produce excellent Nettle-kale or Nettle-spinach in January or February.

ARTICLE CXXXVI.

French   **NEW ZEALAND SPINACH.**   **German**
Epinart (Belle dame).   *Spinat.*

No. 943.—This Spinach is quite distinct from the common garden Spinach, varying essentially in its general habit. It is a hardy annual plant, and is more productive than the average of spinaceous plants. The leaves are of a fine green color, large, broad, thick and fleshy. The leaves are the parts of the plant eaten, being gathered as they are developed, leaving the ends of the young shoots uninjured. If not cut to excess the plant will yield abundantly until destroyed by frost. The leaves retain their fresh, succulent character after they are fully grown, and even under the influence of the heat and draught. It is prepared the same as common garden Spinach for table use.

ARTICLE CXXXVII.

NUTMEG.

Muscade (Noix).   *Muskatennus.*

No. 944.—The Nutmeg tree is about thirty feet high, with numerous branches, and an aspect somewhat resembling that of the orange tree. The leaves stand alternately on short foot stalks, and are oblong-oval, pointed, entire, undulated, bright green and somewhat glossy on their upper surface, whitish beneath, and of an aromatic taste. The flowers are male and female on different trees. The former are disposed in axillary, peduncled, solitary clusters, and the latter are single, solitary, and axillary, Both are minute and of a pale yellowish color. The fruit which appears on the tree mingled with the flowers, is round or oval; of the size of a small peach, smooth, at first pale green, but yellow when ripe, and marked with a longitudinal furrow. The external covering, which is at first thick and fleshy, and abounds in an austere, astringent juice, afterwards becomes dry and coriaceous, and, separating into two valves from the apex, discloses a scarlet, reticulated membrane, commonly called mace, closely investing a thin, brown, shining shell, which contains the kernel or Nutmeg. It is a native of the Moluccas and other neighboring islands, and abounds in the Banda Islands, whence the chief supplies of Nutmegs were long derived. Numerous varieties are cultivated in Sumatra, Java, Penang, Ceylon, and other parts of the East Indies, and have been introduced into the Isles of France and Bourbon, Cayenne, and several of the West India islands. The Penang Nutmegs are distinguished by not being limed. When Nutmeg is cut or broken it presents a yellowish surface, varied with a reddish brown, branching, irregular veins, which give to it a marbled appearance. These dark veins abound in oily matter, upon which the medicinal properties depend. The odor of Nutmeg is delightfully fragrant, the taste warm, aromatic, and grateful. Its virtues are extracted by alcohol and ether. The largest Nutmegs are the most expensive. They should be rejected when very light, with a feeble taste and smell, worm eaten, musty, or marked with black veins. Nutmeg has considerable narcotic power, and when taken in doses of from two to three drams will produce stupor and delirium, and dangerous if not fatal consequences. It is frequently used as an agreeable addition to farinaceous articles of diet, and to various kinds of drink in cases of languid appetite and delicate stomach. It is usually given in substance, and is brought by grating to the state of a powder. Its pleasant flavor makes it invaluable in cookery for seasoning. Nutmeg should always be purchased entire, as when it is ground it soon loses its strength. To ascertain if they are fresh stick a pin in one, and if the pin is oily when you withdraw it the Nutmeg is fresh. When dry they are of no use.

Article CXXXVIII.

French *Petits Chêne.*   OAK, COMMON WALL GERMANDER.   **German** *Baumgamander.*

No. 945.—The Oak Germander is a small perennial European plant, the leaves and tops of which have an agreeable aromatic odor, diminished by drying, and a bitter, somewhat astringent, aromatic, durable taste. They have been used as a corroborant in uterine, rheumatic, gouty, and scrofulous affections, and intermittent fevers. Pick the flowers, remove the petals, and dry them. For their preparation see Diet Drinks, Article LXXXII.

Article CXXXIX.

French **OATS.** **German**
Farine D'Avoine. *Hafermehl.*

No. 946.—The common white Oat is specifically distinguished by its loose panicle, its two-seeded glumes, and its smooth seeds, one of which is awned. It is cultivated all over the world chiefly for horses, but the grain is very nourishing and is largely consumed as food in Great Britain and other countries. A decoction is said to possess decided diuretic properties, and to be useful in dropsy. The seeds deprived of their husks are sometimes called groats. As a food coarsely ground Oat meal is usually preferred to the fine meal. Oat meal is very slightly, but not unpleasantly, bitter, and yields most of its nutritive matter readily to boiling water. Gruel made from Oat meal affords a nutritious and easily digested aliment. It is generally administered after brisk cathartics to render them easier and more efficient in their action.

BLACK CHAMPION.

No. 947.—This new Oat possesses great merit. Its tillering properties are remarkable. The heads, or panicles, are long and very spreading, averaging sixty or seventy spikelets, from twelve to eighteen inches in length, with two large grains to each spinkelet. The kernels are extra large, plump and heavy, black and glossy; are without awns, while the husk is thin and soft. The straw is from three to six feet long, stiff and elastic, does not lodge, and so far seems to be rust-proof. Only half the quantity of seed should be sown, compared with other sorts.

AMERICAN TRIUMPH.

No. 948.—This variety has many excellent qualities. Its average height when standing in the field is six feet, yet the straw is so strong and firm that it holds up well, without lodging. The tall, luxuriant heads are filled with plump, heavy grains.

RUSSIAN WHITE OATS.

No. 949.—This grain is very productive, a single grain giving sixteen stalks in many instances. It is generally free from rust, and is well adapted for general use.

GRUEL.

No. 950.—Gruel is prepared in different ways with oat meal flour, and with the grain. Use fresh flour only, as it is liable to have a sour taste, if not kept in a dry, warm place. When using flour the gruel is prepared with water, milk or broth, then sweetened with sugar or honey, and flavored with the juice of a lemon. When making gruel from the whole grains steep them in cold water over night, then drain them and let them cook slowly in water or milk, and when cooked strain the gruel through a towel with pressure, and sweeten to taste.

OAT MEAL GRUEL.

No. 951.—Oat meal gruel may be prepared by boiling an ounce of meal with three pints of water to a quart, straining the decoction, allowing it to stand until it cools, and then pouring off the clear liquor from the sediment. Sugar and lemon juice may be added to improve its flavor; raisins are not unfrequently boiled with the meal and water for the same purpose.

SCOTCH OAT MEAL GRUEL.

No. 952.—Soak one pound of Oat meal over night, then strain the liquid through a towel, with pressure, to extract as much of the farinaceous matter as will go through. Put one quart of water in a saucepan, and when it boils add a little salt and the liquid extracted from the Oat meal. Let it boil down until it thickens, and serve it hot, or allow it to cool to a jelly-like mass, and serve it with cream and powdered sugar.

OAT MEAL PORRIDGE.

No. 953.—Boil two quarts of water in a sauce pan, season it with salt, and drop in slowly one pound of Oat meal while stirring it with a wooden spoon. Let it boil slowly for a few minutes, then set it on the side of the fire to boil slowly for three quarters of an hour, stirring it up occasionally from the bottom. A little milk and butter may be added before serving, or serve it with a pitcher of cream, some sugar and butter.

CREAM OF OAT MEAL.

No. 954.—Put two quarts of milk in a sauce pan, and when it boils add six ounces of Oat meal flour diluted with cold milk, stirring it well. Then let it boil slowly and add a stick of cinnamon, the peel of a lemon, a few coriander seeds, a pinch of salt and one of mace. Cover the saucepan and let it cook slowly for twenty minutes. Then strain it through a fine sieve, and put it back in the saucepan to keep warm, not allowing it to boil. Add some powdered sugar to sweeten it, stirring until the sugar is melted. Serve it in small cups.

ARTICLE CXL.

OKRA, OR GUMBO.

French Gumbo.
German Ocher.

No. 955.—Okra is an annual plant from the West Indies and South America, and is largely raised in the Southern States. It is cultivated for its green seed pods, which are used in soups and served as a vegetable. The pods when young and tender should be cut in sections, strung on twine and hung up in the shade to cure (the same way as dried fruit). In this condition the Okra can be used for soup at any time.

CULTURE.

No. 956.—Sow the seed thinly in dry, warm soil, in shallow drills two feet apart. Cover the seeds lightly, and after the plants are up thin them out to nine inches apart. Hoe frequently and draw a little earth to the stems as they continue to grow. Gather the pods when quite green and about an inch and a half long.

DWARF GREEN.

No. 957.—The earliest and best variety for the Northern or Eastern States.

LONG GREEN.

No. 958.—Long, pale green and ribbed.

FALL, OR GIANT (WHITE PODDED).

No. 959.—It yields abundantly, especially in the Southern States, and is similar to the dwarf plant with the exception of being larger in size.

STEWED OKRA, PLAIN.

No. 960.—Cut the stems from fifty Okra, and put them into a saucepan with boiling water to cover. Season with salt and cook them on a brisk fire until they are tender. Then drain them and dish them up, pouring over them a little melted butter, with which add the juice of a lemon and some salt and pepper.

STEWED OKRA, WITH TOMATOES.

No. 961.—Cut the stems from two dozen Okra, put them into a saucepan with one dozen peeled tomatoes cut in quarters, and moisten with two soup-spoonfuls of water. Add a piece of butter and season with salt and pepper. Let them simmer for half an hour.

NOTE.—When cooked they may be baked by being put in a buttered deep baking dish and sprinkled over with fresh bread crumbs. Wipe the border, put a piece of butter on top, divided in small parts, and bake in a moderate oven.

OKRA STEWED WITH FINE HERBS.

No. 962.—Cut off both ends of some Okra, wash them in cold water and then put them into a saucepan with a pint of boiling water and a little salt. Let them boil on a brisk fire, and when tender drain off some of the liquid, add a piece of butter and season with salt, pepper and a little fine chopped parsley.

OKRA SALAD.

No. 963.—When the Okra is boiled as in No. 960 drain them, and when cold slice them and add a few finely sliced green peppers, vinegar, oil and a few chopped chives.

OKRA FOR GARNITURE.

No. 964.—When used for garniture in stews, add the Okra when the meats are nearly cooked. Leave the smaller pods whole and cut the larger ones in half.

OKRA FOR SOUP.

No. 965.—Cut the Okra in slices an eighth of an inch thick and add them to the soup fifteen minutes before serving. Let it boil slowly.

DRY OKRA, ITS USE.

No. 966.—Dry Okra is used for soup when the green variety is not to be had. Wash it in cold water and let it soak for an hour, then proceed as above, care being taken to have only a good quality or the Okra will taste like hay. When the best quality of canned Okra can be had it will be found far superior to the dry, and it needs only to be added to the soup a few minutes before serving.

OKRA, OR GUMBO SOUP, WITH CHICKEN.

No. 967.—Cut two tender chickens into small pieces, about three quarters of an inch thick, and put them in a saucepan with a piece of butter. Fry them lightly and then add two medium-sized onions, chopped finely, with half their quantity of lean, raw ham, cut the same way. Cook them for a few minutes, then moisten with a gallon of chicken or veal broth. When it boils skim off the grease and add a faggot of parsley garnished with celery and a leek. Season with salt and pepper, add two green peppers cut into small slices and set it on the side of the fire to boil slowly. When the chicken is half cooked add one dozen of peeled tomatoes cut in quarters (or if they are large into six parts), with four ounces of Carolina rice and about fifty sliced Okra. When they are cooked skim the soup, take out the faggot, and serve. When properly cooked the broth will be found to have a mucilaginous consistency.

ARTICLE CXLI.

French ONIONS. **German**
Oignon. *Zwiebeln.*

No. 968.—The Onion is a half-hardy biennial plant. The roots and leaves, however, are annual, as they usually perish during the first year. The bulbs, for which the plant is generally cultivated, are biennial, and differ to a considerable extent in their size, form, and color. It contains considerable nutriment and has valuable medicinal qualities. The disagreeable odor it imparts to the breath may be avoided in a great measure by thorough cooking, or by eating a few leaves of parsley. Much depends upon the climate and soil as well as the quality of seed, which exerts a great influence on the crop, and to this end great care should be exercised in selecting the seed. The white Onion is much sweeter than the red. Onions are used more than any other vegetable for culinary purposes.

PREPARATION OF THE SOIL.

No. 969.—A good crop of Onions can be raised in any soil which will produce a full crop of corn, unless it be stiff clay, very light sand or gravel, or certain varieties of muck or swamp land. There is no crop in which the quality of the manure used is of greater importance than in this. If it is too rank it is quite sure to make soft Onions, with many scullions. It should be fermented during the previous summer to kill the wheat seeds. All refuse of the previous crop should be removed, the manure spread evenly, and the ground plowed a moderate depth, in order to thoroughly mix the manure with the soil. Cultivate as early in the spring as the ground will permit. It is impossible to cultivate the crop economically unless the rows are perfectly straight, and to secure this, stretch a line along one side, fourteen feet from the edge, and make a distinct mark as a guide. Then having made a wooden marker something like a giant rake (with five teeth about a foot long, and fourteen inches apart), make four more marks by carefully drawing it with the outside tooth in the line and the head at right angles to the perfectly straight mark made by the line. Continue to work around this line until on the third passage of the marker you reach the side of the field where you began. Measure fifteen feet two inches from the last row, stretch the line again and mark around in the same way. This is much better than to stretch a line along one side. Sow the seed as soon as the ground is ready, which can be done best by a hand seed drill.

CULTURE.

No. 970.—As soon as the Onions are up so they can be seen the length of the rows, hoe them by just skimming the ground between the rows. A few days after give them the second hoeing. This time hoe close up to the plants. After this weeding must commence, which should be done thoroughly and carefully, stirring the earth around the plants in order to destroy any weeds that have just started and cannot be seen. In about two weeks they will require another hoeing and weeding, similar to the last, and two weeks later another if necessary. If the work is carefully done the crop will need no further attention until ready to gather. Then, as soon as the tops die and fall, the crop should be gathered by pulling four rows and laying them in one row (the tops all one way), and then forming a similar row with the tops in the opposite direction. If the weather is fine they will require no attention, while curing, but if not they will need to be stirred, by simply moving them slightly along the row. When the tops are perfectly dry cut them off half an inch from the bulb and throw each pair of rows together, forming windrows about nine feet apart. After a few days of bright weather they will be fit to store away.

HOW TO KEEP ONIONS THROUGH THE WINTER.

No. 971.—It is essential for the preservation of Onions to keep them dry, to have thorough ventilation, and to keep them free from frost. One of the most popular methods of keeping Onions is to spread straw to the depth of fifteen inches on a dry floor and upon this spread the Onions ten inches deep and cover them with one foot of straw. They will then keep in fine condition for months. Upon the approach of cold weather close the doors and windows, keeping the temperature just above the freezing point. With proper care they can be kept sound until spring.

REMARKS ON SMALL ONIONS.

No. 972.—It is difficult to grow Onions from seed in certain localities, while from sets good Onions are grown quite early. The sets are little Onions grown up the previous year and taken up when as large as peas. When set out in the spring they very soon form good large Onions. There are two kinds of Onions that are not grown from seed, the Potato and the Top Onion. The Potato Onion grows in clusters under the ground. These little bulbs are planted in the spring and produce large Onions. The large Onions are planted the next spring and produce the clusters. The Top Onion produces the small clusters on the top of the stem, where the seed is produced in the common varieties. These small Onions are planted in the spring and the result is full grown Onions; the large ones with a year's growth produce the clusters.

EARLY RED GLOBE.

No. 973.—This variety is globe-shaped and very handsome in appearance. The skin has a deep red color, and the flesh is mild and tender.

EXTRA EARLY RED.

No. 974.—A medium-sized flat variety, producing abundantly and very desirable for early use. It is uniform in shape, of moderate size and is strongly flavored.

LARGE RED WETHERFIELD.

No. 975.—This is a standard and favorite variety in the East and is excellent for exportation. It is very productive, generally of large size and keeps well. It is almost round, being a little flattened. The skin is of a purplish red color and the flavor is strong.

LARGE YELLOW DUTCH.

No. 876.—One of the oldest and best known varieties. It is mild and well flavored, having white, finely grained flesh.

YELLOW DANVERS.

No. 977.—This is a fine globular variety of medium size. The skin is of a yellowish-brown color, and the flesh is white with a mild flavor.

WHITE PORTUGAL, SILVER SKIN.

No. 978.—This is a large, flat and mild flavored Onion, that is much esteemed for pickling, and keeps better than any of the white Onions.

WHITE SILVER SKIN, FOR PICKLING.

No. 979.—This is a large Onion, and is preferred to any other kind for pickling. It is handsome in appearance.

WHITE GLOBE.

No. 980.—This variety yields abundantly, producing handsome globe-shaped bulbs. The flesh is firm, finely grained and of mild flavor.

LARGE MEXICAN.

No. 981.—This variety attains a diameter of six inches, and weighs from three to four pounds. It is usually eaten raw, having white, coarsely-grained flesh of mild flavor. The skin is generally white, and sometimes of a light reddish color.

EARLY NEOPOLITAN MARZAJOLA.

No. 982.—A beautiful white-skinned flat variety, and a good keeper. If it is sown in February or March, a crop will mature early in the season.

GIANT ROCCA.

No. 983.—This variety is well adapted for culinary purposes, having a mild flavor, tender flesh and a light brown skin. It produces large globular Onions from seed the first season, but to attain its largest growth, the smallest bulbs should be set out the next spring, when they will continue increasing in size instead of producing seed.

GIANT WHITE ITALIAN TRIPOLI.

No. 984.—This is a large, beautiful, pure white flat variety, that will produce large Onions from seed, but to attain their largest size the small bulbs should be set out the following spring. The flavor is mild and excellent.

NEW QUEEN.

No. 985.—This variety grows quickly and keeps well. If sown in February, it will produce Onions two inches in diameter early in summer. If sown in July, they will be ready to pull out in autumn, and will be sound and fit for use until the following autumn. If sown thickly, they will mature perfectly hard. They are particularly valuable for pickling.

RED, YELLOW OR WHITE BOTTOM SETS.

No. 986.—The sets are produced by sowing the seed very thickly in the spring, without thinning them out; they mature when about one inch up. Their use is precisely the same as the Top Onions—to set them out in the spring instead of sowing seed. The seed of the White Silver Skin or the White Portugal varieties, is used for the White Set. They do not keep as well as the others, but produce small white Onions early in the season.

ENGLISH MULTIPLIER.

No. 987.—Esteemed by many as the best variety for early use. It is large in size, of a mild, sweet sugary flavor, very early and a large producer. The large Onions produce several small Onions in clusters around the bulb, growing mostly on the top of the ground.

POTATO ONION.

No. 988.—This variety produces a quantity of young bulbs on the root, which should only be planted in spring, six inches apart, in rows that are eighteen inches wide, under one inch of soil. The English Multiplier should be planted in the same way. The large bulbs produce small Onions and the small bulbs large ones.

PLAIN BOILED ONIONS.

No. 989.—Peel two dozen medium-sized Onions, cut off the roots and stems and be careful not to injure the skin. Put them in a saucepan, cover them with water, add a little salt and a piece of butter, cover the saucepan, set it on a brisk fire and when they are tender strain off the water and serve them with melted butter.

BOILED ONIONS, WITH BUTTER OR CREAM SAUCE.

No. 990.—Boil the Onions in the same manner as in No. 989, and when tender drain off the water and add three spoonfuls of Butter or Cream sauce. Let them simmer for five minutes and then serve.

FRIED ONIONS.

No. 991.—Peel three or four Onions, cut off the roots and stems slice them crosswise and with the finger detach the rings. Season with salt, flour them and mix them well together. Put them in a colander and shake off the superfluous flour. Then fry them in hot lard, and when they are nicely colored, drain them on a napkin and serve.

SMOTHERED ONIONS.

No. 992.—Peel half a dozen Onions, cut them in halves, trim off the ends, slice them finely and put them in a saucepan with a piece of butter. Cover the saucepan and put them on a slow fire to simmer (stirring them occasionally) and when lightly colored drain off the butter and serve them as needed.

GLAZED ONIONS.

No. 993.—Peel two dozen small white Onions of equal size, and be careful not to cut the tops or roots too much, or they will come apart when they are being cooked. Put them in a flat saucepan with a piece of butter, season with salt and sprinkle them with a little powdered sugar. Moisten them, to cover, with broth (or water), put them on a brisk fire and when the moisture is half reduced, set them in a moderate oven, occasionally shaking them over. When the moisture is reduced to a glaze roll the Onions in it so as to glaze them evenly, and use them as needed.

NOTE.—When they are to be served with a sauce, dish up the Onions when they are cooked and glazed, and a ld to the glaze two soup-spoonfuls of Espagnole sauce, and one of gravy. Then let it boil slowly, skim off the grease, reduce it to its consistency and pour it over the Onions.

STUFFED ONIONS.

No. 994.—Take half a dozen white Onions of equal size, peel them carefully, but do no not cut the end parts too deep. Parboil them for ten minutes in water lightly salted; to which add a piece of butter. Drain them, and then dry them on a napkin. When cool scoop out the center of each Onion and fill them with a forced meat of veal of chicken, into which add some cooked fine herbs. Arrange the Onions in a buttered flat saucepan, close together, and season them with salt and a little sugar. Cover each Onion with a thin slice of fat pork, moisten them with broth, and set them on the fire. When it boils put on the cover and set the pan in a moderate oven. When cooked dish them up, strain the gravy in another saucepan and skim off the grease. Add three spoonfuls of Espagnole sauce to reduce it to its consistency, and serve it on the dish with the Onions.

STUFFED ONIONS, AMERICAN STYLE.

No. 995.—Prepare the Onions in the same manner as in No. 994, and when they are drained and cooled, scoop out the center of each one, which you will chop finely, and add enough of fresh bread crumbs to give a nice consistency. Also add two tablespoonfuls of fresh mushrooms finely chopped, two tablespoonfuls of cooked fine herbs, reduced with a little Espagnole sauce, and a little fine chopped parsley, and season with salt and pepper. Mix the whole well together and stuff the Onions with it. Arrange them in a buttered flat saucepan, sprinkle some bread crumbs over them, and put a small piece of butter on top of each one. Then bake them in a moderate oven until nicely browned.

PUREÉ OF ONIONS (BROWN SOUBISE).

No. 996.—Peel one dozen large red Onions, cut them in halves, trim off the ends and slice them fine. Then parboil them for two minutes, immerse them in cold water and drain them dry. Then put them in a saucepan with a piece of butter, and fry them to a light brown, stirring them occasionally with a wooden spoon. Then drain off the butter and moisten them with broth enough to have them well covered. When the broth is reduced add a pint of Espagnole sauce and let it cook for ten minutes. Then rub it through a fine sieve and put the puree in a saucepan. Season it to taste.

PUREE OF ONIONS (WHITE SOUBISE).

No. 997.—Peel one dozen large white Onions, cut them in halves, trim off the ends, slice them finely, and parboil them for two minutes. Then immerse them in cold water, drain them and dry them well on a towel. Then put them in a well buttered saucepan and season with salt, nutmeg, a little sugar, and a pinch of red pepper. Cover them with a buttered white paper. Then cover the saucepan and set it in a slow oven to have the Onions well cooked (being careful not to let them get colored). When they are cooked tender put them in another saucepan with a quart of Cream sauce (be very careful, as they often get a little browned on the bottom). Mix them well together and rub the puree through a fine sieve. Then put it back in the saucepan to keep warm, and before serving add a piece of butter.

BROWN ONION SAUCE.

No. 998.—Prepare two or three Onions in the same manner as in No. 992, and when they are cooked drain off the butter, add four spoonfuls of Espagnole sauce, and let it cook for ten minutes.

NOTE.—If this sauce is wanted in a hurry prepare them as follows: Toss the Onions lightly in butter until nicely browned. Then drain off the butter, add the sauce and let them simmer for fifteen minutes.

WHITE ONION SAUCE.

No. 999.—When the soubise is to be used for sauce, prepare it in the same manner as in No. 997, and add a little chicken broth with a few drops of glaze to thin it out a little more.

BROWN ONION SAUCE—PIQUANT.

No. 1000.—Chop six Red Onions finely, put them in a saucepan with a piece of butter and fry them lightly. Then add a wine-glassful of vinegar and let it reduce to one third. Then add one spoonful of mustard flour, mix it well, and then, while stirring, add in slowly three spoonfuls of veal gravy and four of Espagnole sauce. Let it boil slowly for twenty-five minutes, season with salt and pepper, rub it through a fine sieve, and keep it warm for use.

ONIONS FOR GARNITURE.

No. 1001.—Onions for garniture are prepared in various ways. The small white or button Onion is used most. When they are peeled, parboil them for five minutes and drain them on a napkin. Then put them in a flat saucepan with a piece of butter, a pinch of sugar and a little salt, and moisten them to cover with white broth. Set them in a moderate oven to glaze, tossing them over occasionally, so they will glaze evenly. These Onions are used with stews, beef *a la mode*, and for mixed vegetable garnitures. For large garnitures the stuffed Onions may be used. For chops or small entrees the white or brown puree of Onions soubise is used. Small Onions, when plainly boiled and tossed over the fire (with the addition of a little Cream or Allemande sauce), may also be used.

SMALL ONIONS BAKED FOR GARNITURE, SPANISH STYLE.

No. 1002.—Select two dozen small white Onions of equal size. Put them in a pan and bake them without peeling. When they are three-quarters done, peel and put them in a flat saucepan with half a wine-glassful of vinegar. Reduce this, and add a teaspoonful of mustard flour. Toss them over the fire for a few minutes, and add three spoonfuls of veal gravy and six of Espagnole sauce. Let them simmer slowly until cooked.

ONION GRAVY.

No. 1003.—Cut four Onions in halves and slice them finely. Then put them in a saucepan with a piece of butter, fry them lightly and add a pint of veal gravy. Season with salt and pepper, and when it is reduced to one-third, skim off the grease and strain the gravy through a towel.

ONION GRAVY WITH SAGE.

No. 1004.—Chop three Onions finely with one dozen green sage leaves, and put them in a saucepan with a piece of butter. Cover the saucepan, and let them simmer slowly. When the Onions are nearly cooked (without being browned), add one pint of veal gravy, and when it is reduced to one-third skim off the grease and strain the gravy through a towel.

NOTE.—These gravies are used as an essence that is frequently added to the gravy of Roast Fowl or Game.

ONION JUICE.

No. 1005.—Peel the Onion and grate it with pressure on a grater into an earthern bowl, or slice the Onion finely, put it in a towel, and press the juice into an earthen bowl. This is used in making green salads, and is preferred by many who do not like raw Onions.

ONIONS CHOPPED, FOR FINE HERBS, ETC.

No. 1006.—Onions should never be chopped (as would be implied by the term *chop*), but should be finely cut with a knife. When the Onions are peeled, cut them in halves, take one part and slice it finely without detaching the pieces; then slice it the same way crosswise; then cut straight down. In this way you can make the pieces of any desired size, and will always have them uniform and perfectly square. If chopped Onions are to be kept for some time, dip them in boiling water for one minute, then immerse them in cold water, drain them on a towel, and wring the moisture from them. In this manner, the Onions will remain white. If treated differently, they will soon turn black.

NEW GREEN ONIONS FOR RELISH.

No. 1007.—Remove the outer skin, trim off the tops, wash them in cold water, then drain and serve them plain, or slice them. Season with salt, pepper, vinegar and oil. Serve them in relish dishes, the same as cucumbers.

ONION PEELINGS, THEIR USE.

No. 1008.—The Red Onion peeling is used for coloring Easter eggs. Wash the eggs clean and dry them with a towel, being careful not to crack them. Put them in a saucepan with plenty of the onion peeling, add cold water to cover them, and set them on the fire to boil slowly for ten minutes. Then take them off of the fire, and when cold, take them out. Wipe them with a towel, on which put a few drops of oil, and it will give them a glossy appearance.

ONION SOUP.

No. 1009.—Peel and trim the ends of three medium sized Onions, cut them in halves, and slice them finely. Then put them in a saucepan with a piece of butter, and fry them to a light brown color. Then add two soup-spoonfuls of flour, and let it cook for five minutes, while stirring it, and add in slowly three pints of hot broth or water. Season with salt and pepper, and let it boil slowly for twenty minutes. Have ready in a soup tureen, half a dozen small pieces of toasted bread. Lay a thin slice of fresh butter on each piece, pour the soup into the tureen and cover it, to keep it hot. Serve with it a plate of grated Gruyere or Parmesan cheese.

NOTE.—The Flour may be omitted and the thin layers of butter on the toast may be substituted by thin layers of Gruyere (Swiss) Cheese.

ONION SOUP, STANISLAUS STYLE.

No. 1010.—Butter the crusts of three or four French rolls, and set them in an oven to get crisp. Cut off the end parts of four medium sized white Onions, peel them, cut them in halves and slice them finely. Then put them in a saucepan with a piece of butter, and fry them lightly, stirring them well to have them all nicely browned. Then add three pints of hot water, season it with salt and pepper, and also add the bread crusts. Cover the saucepan, and when it boils, set it in a moderate oven for half an hour; then serve.

ONION SOUP, WITH MILK.

No. 1011.—Chop five medium sized Onions finely and put them in a saucepan with a piece of butter. Let them cook slowly until lightly colored. Then add one glassful of hot water and let them cook for fifteen minutes, after which rub them through a fine sieve and put the puree back in a saucepan with three pints of boiling milk. Set it on the fire, stir it until it boils, and season with salt and pepper. Put in a soup tureen some small pieces of toasted bread, pour the soup over it, cover the tureen and serve it hot.

NOTE.—If the soup is to be sweetened with sugar omit the salt and pepper; use half milk and half cream and butter the toast lightly.

SOUP-PUREE OF ONIONS, BAVARIAN STYLE.

No. 1012.—Peel six large white Onions, slice them finely, parboil them for two minutes, immerse them in cold water and dry them on a towel. Then put them in a saucepan with a piece of butter and let them simmer until they are tender (not letting them get browned). Then drain off the butter, add a pint of Cream sauce and season with salt, a little sugar and a pinch of red pepper. Mix the whole well together and rub it through a fine sieve. Put it back into the saucepan and add two quarts of thickened chicken or veal broth. Set it on the fire, stir it until it boils and then let it cook slowly for twenty minutes. Skim it well, and before serving add a piece of butter and a large glassful of cream, in which dilute the yolks of six raw eggs. Stir it well until the butter is melted, and be careful not to let it boil again. Serve it with a small plate of fried bread crumbs.

SOUP-PUREE OF ONIONS, BRETONNE STYLE.

No. 1013.—Peel six large red Onions and slice them finely. Put them in a saucepan with a piece of butter, and let them cook slowly until they are nicely browned. Then add a pint of beef broth and reduce it to a glaze, after which add three quarts of broth, in which you have cooked a quarter of a pound of split peas. Season with salt and pepper, and cook it slowly for fifteen minutes. Then skim it well, rub it through a fine sieve and put it back in the saucepan to keep warm. If necessary, add a little more broth. Before serving, add a piece of butter, mix it well, and serve with it some small fried bread crumbs on a plate.

ONION CUSTARD FOR GARNITURE OF SOUPS.

No. 1014.—Put in an earthen bowl half a pint of puree of white Onions (soubise), for the preparation of which see No. 997. Dilute this with four spoonfuls of cream, and add two raw eggs and the yolks of ten raw eggs. Season with salt, pepper, and a pinch of nutmeg. Mix the whole well together, and strain it through a fine sieve. Butter some small fancy shaped tartlet moulds and fill them with this preparation. Then place the moulds in a pan containing hot water (being careful not to let any of the water get into the moulds). Set them in a moderate oven to cook, but do not let them get browned. When they are cooked, turn them out of the moulds and let them get cold. Use them as required and directed in the Book on Soups.

ONION SOUP, GARBURE.

No. 1015.—Cut the ends off of one dozen medium sized white Onions, peel them and slice them in pieces one-eighth of an inch thick. Put them in a flat saucepan with some clarified butter and fry them to a light brown color. Put in a deep baking dish a layer of thin slices of toasted bread and on this a layer of Onions, seasoning them with salt and pepper. Then put another layer of toast with Onions on it, continuing in this way until the dish is full. Moisten it with broth and set it in the oven to gratinate. Serve with this a soup tureen of good beef broth.

NOTE.—Care must be taken not to let the Onions get burnt or scorched, or they will give the garbure a bitter taste.

PICKLED ONIONS.

No. 1016.—Peel as many small white Onions as you desire to pickle, having them as equal in size as possible (when peeling them be very careful not to cut into them). Put them into a strong brine for four or five days, then drain them and pour cold water over them to refresh them. Then parboil them for ten minutes and immerse them in cold water, after which dry them on a towel. Pick the pieces that are likely to come off carefully from the Onions. Then put the Onions in glass jars, with a few pepper-corns and some blades of mace, and fill the bottles (so as to cover the Onions) with boiled wine or cider vinegar. When cold cork them tightly.

NOTE.—In boiling the vinegar add half a pound of sugar to each gallon.

PICKLED ONIONS (ANOTHER WAY).

No. 1017.—Peel as many small white Onions as you desire to pickle, having them as equal in size as possible (be careful not to cut into them while peeling). Parboil them in plenty of water for five minutes, then immerse them in cold water, after which drain and dry them on a towel. Remove the pieces that are likely to come off and put the Onions in an earthen bowl. Cover them with cold boiled white wine vinegar, and on the following day drain off the vinegar and put the Onions in glass jars, with a little salt and one bay leaf in each jar. Then boil the vinegar that you drained from the Onions, skim it well, and when it is cold pour it over them, to cover, and hermetically seal the jars. Keep them in a cool place.

ONION VINEGAR.

No. 1018.—Peel and slice finely ten large white fresh Onions, put them in an earthen jar and add a soup-spoonful of salt and one of sugar. Boil two quarts of wine vinegar and pour it over the Onions while it is hot. Cover and set them away, and at the expiration of two weeks strain and filter the vinegar. Then pour it into bottles, adding a small sprig of tarragon to each bottle. Cork the bottles tightly and keep them in a cool place.

ARTICLE CXLII.

French   **ORACH OR MOUNTAIN SPINACH.**   **German**
Arroche.   *Orrach.*

No. 1019.—Orach is a hardy annual plant. The leaves are variously shaped, somewhat oblong, comparatively thin and slightly aciduous to the taste. They are prepared for the table in the same way as spinach or sorrel, and are generally mixed with sorrel when used in soups or purees, to reduce the acidity. Orach is best when grown in a rich, deep and moist soil, and is cultivated in the same manner as spinach.

GREEN ORACH.

No. 1020.—This variety grows low and has leaves of a dark green color, broad, wrinkled, slightly toothed and bluntly pointed.

LURID ORACH.

No. 1021.—The leaves are of a pale, purple color tinged with dark green, being slightly wrinkled, pointed and toothed on the borders toward the base, which forms two acute angles.

PURPLE ORACH.

No. 1022.—The leaves have a dull, dark purple color and are more wrinkled and deeper toothed than the other sorts. They change to a green color when boiled.

RED ORACH.

No. 1023.—The leaves are oblong heart-shaped, somewhat wrinkled and slightly toothed on the margin. Its upper surface is of a very dark dingy purple color. They change to green when boiled.

RED STALKED GREEN ORACH.

No. 1024.—The leaves are dark green, tinged with a dull brown, are wrinkled and toothed, somewhat curled and of a tall growth.

RED STALKED WHITE ORACH.

No. 1025.—This variety is of a dwarfish growth, with heart-shaped leaves of a yellowish green tinged with brown, the margins being stained with purple.

WHITE ORACH.

No. 1026.—White Orach is of comparatively low growth. The leaves are pale green or yellowish green in color, wrinkled, with long tapering points, plainly toothed towards the base which forms two acute angles.

ARTICLE CXLIII.

French
Iris, or Fleur de Lis.

ORRIS, OR IRIS ROOT.

German
Irris.

No. 1027.—This is a genus of bulbous or tuberous rooted plants, the roots of which have an agreeable odor, resembling that of violets. The best variety comes from Florence, Italy. It is easily distinguished by its large white roots. As it will keep long and retains its flavor, it is substituted for the violet, which loses its flavor in a short time. The root, when ground into a flour, is extensively used by pastry cooks for various preparations.

ARTICLE CXLIV.

OXALIS (TUBEROUS ROOTED WOOD SORREL).

Oxalis.   *Oxalis.*

No. 1028.—This is a perennial plant that is cultivated in Mexico and the Southern part of the Pacific Coast. The stalk is one foot in height, with smooth and branching leaves, four together. The leaflets are wedge-shaped, of a pale yellowish-green color, the upper surface being marked by two brownish lines. The flowers are of a carmine rose color, stained with green at the base of the petals. The roots are fusiform, from three to four inches long and an inch and a half in diameter. They are white and fleshy, and are surmounted with numerous small scales or bulbs, which serve for propagation. The roots are boiled and served with Cream or Butter sauce. The young leaves and flowers, which have a pleasant acid taste, are used as salad.

CULTURE.

No. 1029.—The plant succeeds best in rich, warm, mellow soil. Plant them in May, six inches apart in drills that are fifteen inches wide. Let them remain in the ground until in danger of freezing, or until November. Pack them in dry sand and keep them in the cellar for winter use.

Article CXLV.

French — *Pak Choi.*
PAK-CHOI.
German — *Pakchoi.*

No. 1030.—Pak-Choi is an annual plant, a native of China. The root leaves are oval, regular, smooth and deep green, with long, naked, fleshy, white stems, somewhat similar to those of the Swiss-chard or leaf beets. The leaves are eaten boiled, like Cabbage, but are much more tender and of a more agreeable flavor. It is sown in April in hills or drills, and should be thinned out to twelve inches apart.

Article CXLVI.

PALMATE-LEAVED RHUBARB.
Rhubarbe des Moines. *Rhubarber.*

No. 1031.—This species is readily distinguished by its deeply divided or palmate leaves, and is the variety from which the dried root chiefly used in medicine, is obtained. The roots are thick and succulent, with a brownish skin and light yellow flesh, streaked or variegated with red. The Rhubarb from Turkey is generally preferred, but its superiority is, to a great degree, attributable to the manner in which it is dried. Like the Pie Rhubarb, it requires a deep, rich soil, and will not be ready for taking up until five years old.

Article CXLVII.

PALM CABBAGE.
Choux Palmiste. *Palm Kohl.*

No. 1032.—This variety of Cabbage is very popular in Holland, but in this country it is only grown in gardens. When young it is very tender, and is prepared the same as other green cabbage. The plant grows to a height of three feet. The leaves are straight, and of a dark green color, with strong ribs resembling those of palm leaves, from which it takes its name.

Article CXLVIII.

| French | PARSLEY. | German |
| Persil. | | Petersilie. |

No. 1033.—Parsley is one of the most useful vegetables. Its leaves are used in cookery for garnishing and flavoring purposes, and its roots are used in medicine as an aperient. It is a native of Sardinia, but flourishes in almost every part of the world. It is an umbelliferous plant having a biennial root, with an annual, round, furrowed, jointed, erect, branching stem, about two feet in height. All parts of the plant contain a volatile oil, to which it owes its odor and mainly its taste. It excites the appetite and accelerates digestion. There are six varieties.

CULTURE.

No. 1034.—The seed is slow in germinating, and should be sown early in spring, in rich, mellow soil. When the plants are two inches high transplant them. The oftener they are transplanted and cut back the finer and more perfect the leaves will be. Handsome foliage is formed when the plants are well grown.

FINE TRIPLED CURLED.

No. 1035.—This is a fine dwarfish curled variety, which, when well grown, resembles a tuft of finely curled moss. It is hardy and slow in running to seed, but is liable to degenerate, as it constantly tends to increase in size and to become less curled.

CARTER'S FERN LEAVED.

No. 1036.—A variety of beautiful form and color, which is well adapted for garnishing. It is an ornamental garden plant.

PLAIN PARSLEY.

No. 1037.—This kind is hardier than the curled varieties; is good for flavoring, but has plain leaves.

HAMBURG, OR TURNIP-ROOTED.

No. 1038.—This is a fleshy, rooted variety, the roots of which are used for flavoring soups.

FAGGOT OF PARSLEY.

No. 1039.—A faggot of Parsley generally consists of a bunch of green Parsley, in the center of which a bay leaf, a sprig of thyme, and a few grains of cloves are put, the bunch being tied together with a string. It is used for flavoring soups, stews, etc. The edges should always be nicely trimmed. Celery and leeks are sometimes added to the faggot.

CHOPPED PARSLEY.

No. 1040.—Take fresh Parsley leaves, wash them in cold water and dry them on a towel. Chop them finely on a clean board, then put the Parsley in a towel and wring out all of the moisture. Then put it in a bowl and keep it ready for use. When chopped Parsley is used for sauces it should be dipped in boiling water for a minute, then immersed in cold water and wrung dry in a towel. By doing this it will retain its green color.

FRIED PARSLEY FOR GARNISHING.

No. 1041.—Pick and wash a bunch of Parsley and dry it in a towel. Have some hot lard or grease in a frying-pan on the fire, and put the Parsley into it. As soon as it is crisp, take it out and drain it on a napkin. Care must be taken to have the lard or grease very hot, as one minute is sufficient to fry the Parsley, which, if fried longer, will turn to a dark brown color. If the Parsley is not fresh, it will assume the same color.

PARSLEY FOR GARNISHING.

No. 1042.—Take one bunch of curled Parsley, wash it in cold water, drain it and put it in a bowl with a piece of ice. When Parsley remains in water too long, it acquires a bad odor. When garnishing dishes, which are to be covered and have to remain for some time before serving, it is best to use fried Parsley. Fresh Parsley is best as a garniture for cold dishes of meat. Parsley stems are cut two inches long and put into croquettes, when made in pear-shape, to imitate pear stems.

ARTICLE CXLIX.

French
Panais.

PARSNIPS.

German
Pastinake.

No. 1043.—The Parsnip is a hardy biennial plant that is much cultivated in this country. The roots are considered healthful and are esteemed for their delicate and pleasant flavor. They are used as a vegetable and as an ingredient in soups.

CULTURE.

No. 1044.—Parsnips succeed best in a deep, free, rich soil. That which has been heavily manured for a previous crop should be selected. Sow them in drills from fifteen to eighteen inches apart, as early in spring as the ground can be found in fair working condition. When the plants are about two inches high thin them out to six or eight inches apart. The roots are hardy and improve by remaining in the ground through the winter.

LONG SMOOTH YELLOW.

No. 1045.—The roots are oblong, ending somewhat abruptly with a small top root. It grows mostly below the surface, has a very smooth clear skin, and is easily distinguished by the leaves arising from a cavity on the top or crown of the root.

LONG WHITE DUTCH.

No. 1046.—The roots are very long, white, smooth, tender, sugary, and most excellently flavored, being very hardy, and will keep through the winter without protection.

THE STUDENT.

No. 1047.—A finely flavored variety, especially for table use.

SHORT ROUND FRENCH.

No. 1048.—One of the earliest varieties.

PARSNIPS, WITH BUTTER SAUCE.

No. 1049.—Scrape the Parsnips well, then cut them in pieces two inches long and slice them not too thin. Put them in a pan with cold acidulated water. Have in a saucepan on the fire some boiling water. Add to it a little vinegar and salt, the Parsnips and a piece of butter, and cook them on a brisk fire until tender; then drain them and return them to the saucepan. Add Butter sauce, season with salt and pepper, toss them well together and serve.

FRIED PARSNIPS.

No. 1050.—Prepare the Parsnips in the same manner as in No. 1049, and when they are cooked drain them and put them in a bowl. Season them and add a little fine chopped parsley or chervil and the juice of two lemons. When ready for use dip them in a light batter and fry them in hot lard. Serve them on a napkin and garnish them with fried parsley.

NOTE.—When Parsnips are to be cooked and kept for a day or two add a white thickening when the water boils, and when the Parsnips are cooked, pour them into a pan or an earthern jar and cover it with a buttered paper cover. Use them as needed.

MASHED PARSNIPS.

No. 1051.—Scrape and wash the Parsnips, cut them in small pieces, boil them in water lightly salted, add a piece of butter, and when they are cooked drain them. Remove the fibrous parts and rub the Parsnips through a fine colander. Put them back in the saucepan, add a piece of butter and a little cream, season with salt and pepper, and warm them thoroughly while stirring.

PARSNIP FRITTERS.

No. 1052.—Prepare the Parsnips as in No. 1051, and when rubbed through the colander set them aside to cool, and to each pound of mashed Parsnips add eight well beaten raw eggs. Mix the eggs and Parsnips well together and add flour enough to make the whole into a light batter. Fry them in hot lard and serve them on a napkin.

ARTICLE CL.

French	PATIENCE.	German
Patience.		*Gartenampfer.*

No 1053.—A hardy perennial plant, not cultivated much in this country. When fully developed it is from four to five feet high. The leaves, which are large, long and broad pointed, are more succulent and tender, and attain a much larger size, when the flowering shoots are cut off as they make their appearance. The plant is hardy, and if cut over regularly will continue healthy and productive for a few years. The leaves are used the same as spinach, and are put forth quite early in spring. They should be used when young and tender and mixed with sorrel. Patience Dock is much used by the Swedes, prepared in this manner, and is much esteemed in their country.

ARTICLE CLI.

French   PEA-NUT.   **German**
Arachis.   *Erdnus.*

No. 1054.—The Pea-nut is an annual plant, a native of Central America and Africa. The stem, when full grown, is about fourteen inches in height. The leaves are primate, with four leaflets, and a leafy, emarginate appendage at the base of the petals. The fruit or pod is of an oblong form, often contracted at the middle, but sometimes of bottle form, reticulated, and of a yellowish color. The kernels, of which the pod contains from one to three, are oblong, quite white, and are enclosed in a thin brown skin or pellicule. A remarkable peculiarity of this plant is that the lower blossoms alone produce the fruit. After the decay of the petals the ovaries insinuate themselves into the ground, beneath which at a depth of several inches, the fruit is afterwards perfected. They are eaten roasted, and are used by confectioners, and for culinary purposes as a substitute for almonds.

CULTURE.

No. 1055.—The Pea-nut succeeds well only in warm climates. Plant them as early as the weather becomes suitable, in a warm, light, loamy soil, deeply ploughed and pulverized, in rows a foot apart. In planting, the Pea-nut should be unbroken in the pod, and as soon as the flower appears the vines are earthed up from time to time, so as to keep them chiefly within the ground.

AFRICAN PEA-NUT.

No. 1056.—A comparatively small, smooth, and regularly formed sort. The shell is thin, usually enclosing two kernels.

WILMINGTON PEA-NUT.

No. 1057.—Similar to the African. The pods, however, are longer, and the shell thicker and paler. They enclose two or three kernels. They are cultivated largely in the Southern States.

TENNESSEE PEA-NUT.

No. 1058.—The pods are large, thick, and irregular in form, and usually contain two kernels. This variety is less esteemed than the others.

Article CLII.

French		German
Pois.	**PEAS.**	*Erbsen.*

No. 1059.—The Pea is a hardy annual plant, and its cultivation is almost universal. The green Pea is a delicious vegetable, and is highly esteemed for its flavor and taste. To have them in perfection they must be plucked before they mature, and should be shelled and cooked as soon after as possible, as they lose much of their tenderness and flavor if kept for any length of time. The fact that those brought from a distance seldom reach the markets in their perfect state is an objection to their use, which, coupled with the knowledge that when they are closely packed they become intensely overheated and are rendered devoid of taste and unwholesome, deters many from using this popular vegetable. When sent from a distance they should be packed in open baskets (not in boxes, barrels or sacks), and laid in layers two inches deep, alternating with layers of clean straw. There are hundreds of varieties, but they differ very little from each other. New kinds are introduced annually, each claiming to be superior sorts, but the locality has a great deal to do with their quality. The field Peas can be used in their dry state for purees and soups, but they are not as easily digested as the other kinds.

CULTURE.

No. 1060.—Peas come earliest to maturity in light rich soil. For a general crop a deep loam or a soil strongly inclining to clay is best. For an early crop decomposed leaves or leaf mold should be used, or, if the soil is very poor, stronger manure may be used. For general crops a good dressing should be applied, and for the dwarf growing kinds the soil cannot be too rich. When grown as a market crop Peas are never staked, and are sown in single rows two or three inches deep and from two to three feet apart, according to variety or the strength of the soil. When grown in small quantities for private use, they are generally sown in double rows six or eight inches apart, and the tall varieties are staked up with brush. For an early crop sow them in February, March or April, according to latitude, as soon as the ground can be worked. Make repeated sowings every two weeks in succession. After the first of June, sowing should be discontinued until the middle of August, when a good crop may sometimes be secured by sowing an early sort.

EXTRA EARLY SORTS.

THE AMERICAN WONDER.

No. 1061.—A highly improved variety, with stout branching vines that grow early, about nine inches high, and are covered with long well filled pods. The Peas are of the best quality.

KENTISH INVICTA.

No. 1062.—A round blue Pea, about two feet in height, with straight, well filled pods. It is the earliest of the blue sorts, and is superior in flavor to any of the white varieties.

LAXTON'S ALPHA.

No. 1063.—This is the earliest wrinkled Pea known, and is about three feet in height. The seeds are indented and wrinkled, of a light blue color and delicious flavor. A good variety.

EARLY TOM THUMB.

No. 1064.—The seeds are small and round, but are not always of good quality.

BLUE PETER.

No. 1065.—One of the best of the dwarf varieties, and a great producer. The seeds are large, blue, round and somewhat wrinkled.

EXTRA EARLY.

No. 1066.—This variety furnishes Peas as early as any variety. The Peas are large and the pods continue bearing for ten days.

EARLY SORTS.

LITTLE GEM.

No. 1067.—A desirable dwarf, green, wrinkled variety, about fifteen inches high. In its green state, the Peas are large and sweet.

PREMIUM GREEN.

No. 1068.—This resembles the Little Gem, but has heavier and more prolific vines and larger pods. They fully equal the later sorts in quality.

M'LEAN ADVANCER.

No. 1069.—A green wrinkled variety, nearly three feet high, with long, broad pods, which are well filled. Their flavor is excellent and they are considered by many to be the best of their season.

CARTER'S LITTLE WONDER.

No. 1070.—This is a sweet, wrinkled Pea about two feet in height, being very early and having a delicious flavor.

EARLY PHILADELPHIA.

No. 1071.—A variety that is in demand in the vicinity of Philadelphia. It is prolific and of very good flavor.

DWARF CHAMPION.

No. 1072.—A prolific variety of good quality and flavor. The Peas are white, shriveled and indented.

LATE SORTS.

CHAMPION OF ENGLAND.

No. 1073.—This is one of the best flavored Peas, being equal to any in quality and more in demand than other varieties. It is very productive, and from four to five feet in height. The seeds are shriveled and of a whitish green color.

LARGE BLUE IMPERIAL.

No. 1074.—One of the best summer varieties, a good bearer, very strong, and about three feet high. The pods are large, long, pointed and somewhat flat, and contain about ten large, blue, flattened Peas.

LARGE WHITE MARROWFAT.

No. 1075.—This is a prolific bearer, of strong growth, and is about five feet in height. It is cultivated more extensively for summer crop than any other variety. The pods are large, round, light colored, and well filled, with large, blue, slightly flattened Peas.

DWARF MARROWFAT.

No. 1076.—This variety is earlier than the White Marrowfat, but is similar to it in character and appearance, except in its dwarf growth. It will not require bushing.

LARGE BLACK-EYED MARROWFAT.

No. 1077.—A prolific and excellent mammoth variety, about five feet in height, with large, full pods.

YORKSHIRE HERO.

No. 1078.—The vines are stout and about two feet high, bearing at the top a number of broad pods filled with large Peas, which keep in season a long time, and do not become hard. They are of fine quality and are preferred over all others by those who like a marrow-like Pea.

EDIBLE PODDED SORTS.

DWARF GRAY SUGAR.

No. 1079.—This is an early, prolific variety, and grows about two feet in height. The pods are broad, flat and crooked, containing about six Peas, of a dark brown color, that are large, shriveled, and indented.

TALL SUGAR.

No. 1080.—This variety grows about five feet in height, is very sweet and tender. The pods and Peas are eaten.

FIELD SORTS.

No. 1081.—Of the many Field Sorts the Golden Wine, the Crown, the Parisian Blue, the Creepers, the Common White, and the Common Blue, are perhaps the best varieties in cultivation. In their dry state they are used in soups, purees, etc.

GREEN PEAS, ENGLISH STYLE.

No. 1082.—Have two gallons of boiling water in a saucepan on a brisk fire, and add to it five pounds of shelled green Peas, a faggot of parsley garnished with a head of lettuce, and a few green onions, and season it with a little salt. Let them boil until tender, then drain them, take out the faggot and dish up the Peas, with a piece of butter in the middle and a piece on top.

NOTE.—A sprig of mint may be added with the faggot, or some finely chopped mint may be sprinkled over the Peas. This is merely a matter a taste.

GREEN PEAS, PARISIAN STYLE.

No. 1083.—Put into a saucepan five pounds of green Peas, one quart of water and six ounces of butter. Put the pan on a brisk fire, add a faggot of parsley garnished with a head of lettuce and a few green onions. Toss them over occasionally, and when cooked add four ounces of butter, into which mix two spoonfuls of flour. Toss the Peas well over until the butter is melted, then let them cook fifteen minutes longer, and season with salt, pepper and a little sugar. Should the Peas become too thick add a little hot water.

GREEN PEAS, FAMILY STYLE.

No. 1084.—Put into a saucepan four ounces of butter, and when it is melted, add two spoonfuls of flour. Mix them well together, stirring with a wooden spoon, and let it cook slowly until lightly colored. Then add five pounds of Peas, and in two or three minutes add one quart of boiling water. Season with salt, pepper and a pinch of sugar, and add a faggot of parsley garnished with a head of lettuce. When the Peas are cooked, take out the faggot and add one cupful of cream into which dilute the yolks of three raw eggs. Toss them well together, not letting them cook any more.

GREEN PEAS WITH CREAM, SHARON STYLE.

No. 1085.—Peas cooked in this style must be served as soon as cooked or they will lose their delicacy.

Put into a saucepan two pounds of fresh young Peas, a tumbler of cold water, a piece of butter and a head of lettuce, into which tie a sprig of green thyme. Cover the saucepan, put them on a brisk fire and toss them over occasionally. When they are cooked take out the lettuce, season with salt, pepper, and a pinch of sugar, and add a cup of double cream, into which dilute the yolks of two raw eggs. Toss them well together off of the fire, and serve with small pieces of toasted bread around the dish.

GREEN PEAS WITH BACON.

No. 1086.—Cut into small square pieces a quarter of a pound of lean bacon (previously parboiled for two minutes), and put them into a saucepan. Add three pounds of green Peas and moisten with a quart of boiling broth. Set the pan on a brisk fire, add a faggot of parsley garnished with green onions and a head of lettuce, and season with salt, pepper and a pinch of sugar. When thoroughly cooked, take out the faggot, and dish them up with braised lettuce around the dish.

GREEN PEAS FOR GARNITURE.

No. 1087.—When the Peas are cooked, as in No. 1082, immerse them in cold water, then drain them and set them aside, covering them with a napkin until ready to use. When ready to use them, put them into a saucepan with a piece of butter, and season with salt, pepper, and a pinch of sugar. Toss them over the fire until thoroughly warmed, and when serving add some fine chopped parsley.

NOTE.—Cream, Allemande, or Espagnole sauce may be added if desired.

PUREE OF GREEN PEAS, FOR GARNITURE.

No. 1088.—Cook two pounds of Green Peas as in No. 1082. When cooked drain them and put them into a saucepan with four spoonfuls of Cream sauce; season with salt, pepper and a pinch of sugar. Mix them well together and rub them through a fine sieve. Put the puree back into the saucepan to keep warm and before serving add a piece of Butter.

NOTE.—When the puree is rubbed through a fine sieve, put it in a flat saucepan, add half a pint of cream, and set the pan on a brisk fire to reduce the puree to its proper consistency. Before serving, add a piece of butter. This puree will be found more succulent than the foregoing.

SOUP—PUREE OF GREEN PEAS.

No. 1089.—Put into a saucepan two gallons of water with a little salt, and when it boils add five pounds of fresh Peas, a faggot of parsley garnished with a few green onions, and a head of lettuce. As soon as the Peas are tender, remove the faggot, drain them and rub them through a fine sieve. Put the puree in a saucepan and add three quarts of lightly thickened chicken or veal broth. Set it on the fire and stir it until it boils; then let it boil slowly for twenty minutes and season with salt, pepper and a pinch of sugar. Before serving add half a pound of butter, divided into small pieces, and stir it well until the butter is melted. Serve small fried bread crumbs with it.

SOUP—PUREE OF GREEN PEAS, ST. GERMAIN.

No. 1090.—Cook the Peas as in No. 1089. When tender drain them, take out the faggot, put the puree back into the saucepan and add two quarts of Cream sauce, diluted with chicken broth to its consistency. Season with salt, pepper and a pinch of sugar. Rub it through a fine sieve, put it back into the saucepan and keep it warm in a hot water bath. Before serving add a piece of butter and stir it well until the butter is melted. This soup should have a bright, green color (if necessary use green color of spinach. Serve with small balls of forced meat of chicken, poached in broth.

NOTE.—In making this soup two and a half pounds of Peas, and two and a half pounds of green asparagus tops may be used.

SOUP—PUREE OF SPLIT PEAS.

No. 1091.—Carefully sort three pounds of yellow dried Peas, wash them well, let them soak for five hours in cold water, and then drain them. Put them into a saucepan with three quarts of cold water, or use half water and half broth. Add a faggot of parsley garnished with one leek and some celery, two onions with four cloves in each, two carrots, and a piece of parboiled salt pork, or bacon. Cover the saucepan, let them cook slowly until thoroughly done, and then take out the faggot, carrots, onions, and pork or bacon. Add some plain broth to give the puree its proper consistency, and season with salt and pepper. Then rub it through a fine sieve and put it back in the saucepan, stirring it well until it boils. Then let it simmer slowly for half an hour and add a piece of butter. Before serving, cut the pork or bacon in small pieces, fry them crisp, drain them, mix some small fried bread crumbs with them, and put them in the soup, or serve them on a plate, as may be desired.

SOUP—PUREE OF SPLIT PEAS, WITH JULIENNE SOUP, CONDE.

No. 1092.—This soup is a puree of split Peas, into which half of its quantity of Julienne soup is added.

SOUP—PUREE OF DRIED GREEN PEAS, GERMAN STYLE.

No. 1093.—Pick and wash four pounds of the Peas, put them into a saucepan and boil them in three quarts of water or broth. Garnish with a faggot of vegetables tied together, season with salt, and let them cook slowly until tender. Then remove the faggot, and add broth enough to bring the soup to its proper consistency. Rub it through a fine sieve, return it to the saucepan, and set it on the fire to boil for twenty minutes, then skim it well and add a piece of butter and two handfuls of boiled rice. A ham-bone or piece of pork may be cooked with the soup if desired.

PRESERVED GREEN PEAS.

No. 1094.—Have the Peas freshly plucked and shelled, and uniform in size. Put them into boiling water, lightly salted, and when they are three-quarters cooked, drain them. Then dry them on a towel, and when they are cold, put them into quart tin cans. Cover the Peas in the cans with cold boiled water, adding to each can a little salt and a pinch of carbonate of soda. Cover the cans hermetically, and boil them in a hot water bath for two hours.

ARTICLE CLIII.

French *Pouliot.*
PENNYROYAL.
German *Polei.*

No. 1095.—Pennyroyal possesses a warm, pungent, aromatic taste, and is used exclusively for medical purposes. An infusion of the leaves is stimulating, sudorific, tonic and beneficial in colds and chills. It is a small, branching, annual plant, common to gravelly localities and abounding towards autumn in dry fields, where crops of wheat or rye have been recently harvested.

ARTICLE CLIV.

Poivre et Piment.
PEPPER.
Pfeffer.

No. 1096.—There are many varieties of Pepper, both annual and perennial, the latter being of a shrubby or woody character, and as it is a tropical plant, it is tender. The annual varieties can be grown in the Middle and Southern States successfully.

The annual, or common garden Pepper, is a native of India.

Pepper is used more than any other spice. There are three kinds in use—the White, Black, and Red. It facilitates digestion and corrects flatulency. In warm countries it is used in great quantities, but for good cooking it should be used with moderation, and persons of nervous debility should abstain from using any. For persons living on plain food, and having out-of-door work, it imparts vitality, and is very beneficial. There are also a large variety of Peppers eaten and prepared in their green state, and put up like pickles. The large Bell Peppers are stuffed and used as a vegetable, and are also excellent for pickling, and when sliced are much esteemed in salads, in connection with tomatoes and cucumbers.

CULTURE.

No. 1097.—Sow in hot beds early in April, and transplant to the open ground when the weather is favorable. They should be planted in warm, mellow soil, in rows eighteen inches apart, or they may be sown in the open ground, when danger of frost is past, and the soil is warm and the weather settled.

CHILI.

No. 1098.—This variety has sharply conical pods of a brilliant scarlet color, which are exceedingly pungent when ripe. They are principally used in making Pepper sauce. The plants should be started early in hot beds.

LONG RED CAYENNE.

No. 1099.—This kind has a long, slim, pointed pod, and when ripe, is of a bright red color. The flavor is strong and pungent.

LARGE SQUASH.

No. 1100.—The fruit is large, flat and tomato-shaped, more or less ribbed, with a smooth and glossy skin. The flesh is mild, thick-meated and pleasant to the taste, although it possesses more pungency than many of the other varieties.

GOLDEN DAWN.

No. 1101.—This kind resembles the Large Bell in size and shape, and has a beautiful golden yellow color. The flavor is pleasant and delicate.

LARGE BELL.

No. 1102.—A large sort of square form, tapering to a point. It is an early variety, less pungent than most kinds, and is thick and hard. It is suitable for filling with cabbage, etc.

SWEET MOUNTAIN.

No. 1103.—This is similar to the Bell Pepper in shape and color, but is large and milder in flavor.

CRANBERRY.

No. 1104.—The fruit resembles the cranberry in appearance, and is a good variety for pickling.

GROSSUM.

No. 1105.—A large French variety of irregular shape, which is good for mangoes.

CHERRY, OR LITTLE GEM.

No. 1106.—The fruit or berries are of a globular form, about the size of a large red currant, and of a brilliant scarlet hue. They are produced in the greatest profusion, and will be found useful in the preparation of pepper sauces, and when pickled as soon as plucked. To prepare them for use in their dry state, it is only necessary to cut the plants close to the roots when the fruit is ripe. String the berries and hang them up in a warm, dry room. They will retain their piquancy for years. The plant is so beautiful that when grown in pots it will always prove ornamental; the glossy, coral red of the numerous pods presenting a fine contrast to the deep green foliage surrounding them.

CHILI PEPPERS PRESERVED IN VINEGAR.

No. 1107.—Select small Chili Peppers, all of the same size, cut the ends and put the Peppers into pint bottles. Fill them to cover with wine vinegar, cork the bottles tightly, and in six weeks the Peppers will be ready for use.

CHILI PEPPER VINEGAR.

No. 1108.—Put into a demijohn a quarter of an ounce of dried marigolds, one clove of garlic, three shallots, a few grains of pepper, four cloves, and one and a half pounds of Chili Peppers, from which cut off the ends. Then add one gallon of wine vinegar and cork the demijohn tightly. Six weeks after strain the vinegar through a filter and put it into bottles.

PEPPER VINEGAR.

No. 1109.—Cut one dozen bell Peppers and half a dozen long green Peppers in slices, and put them in a jar with half a dozen pepper-corns. Boil six pints of vinegar, to which add two ounces of sugar, and as soon as it boils pour it over the Peppers. When it is cool cover the pot and set it away for two weeks; then strain the vinegar through a filter, put it in bottles and cork them tightly.

PRESERVED PICKLED BELL PEPPERS.

No. 1110.—Take one hundred fresh green pods, slice them down on one side, cut off the stems, take out the seeds, and put them in a small barrel, or earthen jar. Cover them with cold brine. Ten hours after this drain off the brine, add the same quantity of fresh brine, and let it stand in a cool place. The following day drain them on a towel for half an hour, and then put them into glass jars. Boil the quantity of wine vinegar required to cover them, and when the vinegar is cold pour it over the Peppers and cover them tight. Six weeks after being put into the jars they will be ready for use. They are much esteemed by epicures.

PRESERVED STUFFED PICKLED BELL PEPPERS.

No. 1111.—Cut the stems from one hundred Bell Peppers, then slice the tops without detaching them, scoop out the seeds, and put them in a brine of the same kind as in No. 1110, then drain them. Cut the white part of three heads of cabbage into small, fine shreds, parboil them for five minutes, then immerse them in cold water, and drain them dry. Then season with a little salt. Stuff the Peppers with the cabbage, covering it with the undetached slices of the Peppers. Arrange them in jars and pour over them, to cover, some cold boiled vinegar. Cover them tightly, and in two months they will be ready for use.

PICKLED STUFFED BELL PEPPERS, SHARON STYLE.

No. 1112.—Prepare the Peppers in the same manner as in No. 1111. Cut the tender parts of two heads of cabbage into fine shreds, parboil them for five minutes and drain them in a colander. Then put the cabbage in an earthen bowl, and add to it four ounces of white mustard seed, two ounces of celery seed, and four soup-spoonfuls of grated horse-radish. Season with a little salt, and mix the whole well together. Stuff the Peppers with this preparation and in the center of each place a small onion or a pickle. Tie the cover on with a string, arrange them nicely in jars, and pour over them cold boiled vinegar to cover them. Hermetically seal the jars.

HOW TO MAKE RED PEPPER.

No. 1113.—The pods of the cherry Peppers will furnish a quality of Cayenne Pepper superior to that ordinarily sold. The larger and milder kinds are powdered in the same manner and make a wholesome and pleasant quality of Pepper, sufficiently pungent for ordinary use.

BROILED BELL PEPPERS.

No. 1114.—Dip the Peppers in boiling water and then peel them. Broil them on a slow fire and serve them on toast, with a little melted butter, into which add a little fine chopped parsley.

STUFFED BELL PEPPERS, AMERICAN STYLE.

No. 1115.—Select one dozen nicely shaped Bell Peppers, slice off the tops and scoop out the seeds. Chop two onions finely and put them into a saucepan with a piece of butter. Fry them lightly and then add a handful of fine chopped mushrooms. Cover the saucepan, and when the moisture is reduced add four spoonfuls of reduced Allemande sauce, a handful of fresh bread crumbs, and season with salt, pepper, and a pinch of nutmeg. Mix them well together, then take the saucepan off of the fire and add the yolks of two raw eggs and some finely chopped parsley, and stir them well together. Stuff the Peppers and arrange them in a buttered baking pan. Sprinkle fresh bread crumbs over them, put a piece of butter on each one, then bake them in a moderate oven, and when nicely browned serve them on a dish with a teaspoonful of veal gravy over each one.

STUFFED BELL PEPPERS, FRENCH STYLE.

No. 1116.—Prepare the Peppers as in No. 1115, then prepare a forced-meat of veal (Godiveau), to which add some cooked fine herbs. Cover each with a thin slice of fat pork, and then arrange them on a flat saucepan. Moisten them with veal gravy, then cover them with a buttered paper and bake them slowly until they are nicely glazed. Dish them up with a reduced Espagnole sauce.

STUFFED BELL PEPPERS, BRAZILIAN STYLE.

No. 1117.—Prepare one dozen Peppers as in No. 1115. Chop one onion finely and put it into a saucepan with a piece of butter.

Put on the cover and let it simmer. When the onion is half cooked add half its quantity of finely chopped mushrooms and the same quantity of green Peppers. Let this simmer until the moisture is reduced. Then add four spoonfuls of Allemande sauce and a handful of fresh bread crumbs. Season with salt and nutmeg, and add some finely chopped parsley and a small pinch of garlic. Mix them well together while adding the yolks of two raw eggs. Then stuff the Peppers, covering each one with a thin slice of fat pork. Arrange them in a buttered flat sauce pan, bake them in a moderate oven and serve them with a brown Italian sauce.

GREEN PEPPERS, FOR GARNITURE.

No. 1118.—For large garnitures the stuffed Peppers described in Nos. 1115, 1116 and 1117, are used, alternated with stuffed tomatoes or mushrooms. For boiled meats use them as in No. 1114.

PEPPERS FOR RELISHES.

No. 1119.—Trim the stems off, and if the Peppers are large cut them in four or six pieces. Remove the seeds and then serve them on a relish dish, garnished with radishes. When pickled Peppers are used, first dry them in a napkin and then slice them, adding a little oil, vinegar and salt. The large bell Peppers are broiled first, then peeled and sliced and seasoned with oil, vinegar, pepper and salt.

TO MAKE WHITE PEPPER.

No. 1120.—Soak some pepper-corns in cold water until the skin is tender, then peel and dry them and grind them in a coffee mill.

ARTICLE CLV.

PEPPERMINT.

Menth Poivrée. *Pfeffermünze.*

No. 1121.—Peppermint is a hardy perennial plant introduced into this country from Europe. It grows naturally and abundantly along the banks of small streams and in rich wet localities. When once established, it spreads rapidly, and will remain for a long period. The stems are smooth, erect, four-sided, and from two to three feet in height. The leaves have an agreeable odor and a peculiarly warm pleasant flavor. The plant is principally used for distillation, being cultivated for this purpose, and will bear from four to five years by proper attention. The best quality of oil is produced during the first year.

ARTICLE CLVI.

PE TSAI.

French — *Choux Pitsai.*
German — *Chinesichen Kohl.*

No. 1122.—This is an annual plant, a native of China. The leaves are of an oval form, rounded at the ends, somewhat blistered on the surface, and at the center are collected into a long and rather compact tuft or head. The plant, when well grown and ready for use, resembles a head of Cos lettuce, and will weigh six or seven pounds. It is used like common cabbage, being sweet, mildly flavored, and easy to digest. The young plants are also boiled like spinach.

ARTICLE CLVII.

PICKLES.

Cornichon. *Essiggurken.*

No. 1123 —Small cucumbers are best for pickling, and for this purpose they must be plucked young, when they attain the proper size. The fruit should not be permitted to ripen on the vines, for if allowed to do so the plants become much less productive. See Pickled Cucumbers, Nos. 641 and 642.

MIXED PICKLES.

No. 1124.—Are composed of young cucumbers, cauliflower, peppers, string beans and onions. The mode of pickling them has been described. When ready for pickling put them into glass jars with a few juniper berries. Dilute some mustard flour with vinegar, season it with a pinch of red pepper and pour it over them, to cover. Then seal the jar hermetically.

CHOW CHOW (HOME MADE).

No. 1125.—Select five dozen small cucumbers, of from one to one and a half inches in length; four dozen small, white peeled onions, half a dozen small green peppers, and the flower buds of two tender cauliflowers, separated into small pieces. Put them into a strong brine for two days, then drain them in a colander and pour lukewarm water over them to rinse them. Parboil the onions for five minutes, then immerse them in cold water, and when refreshed drain them also into the colander. When dry, put the onions, cucumbers, peppers and cauliflowers in a copper basin. Dilute in a pint of lukewarm water eight ounces of mustard flour, to which add a teaspoonful of cayenne pepper and three ounces of tumeric. To this add enough of either cider or wine vinegar to cover the vegetables. Then set them on the fire and let them simmer until tender (if desired a little sugar may be added while cooking). When tender take them off of the fire, put them in an earthen bowl, and when they are cold put them in wide-mouthed bottles and cork tightly.

Article CLVIII.

French
Picridium.

PICRIDIUM.

German
Picridium.

No. 1126.—A hardy biennial plant, from the southern part of Europe. The stem is eighteen inches high, and the leaves about eight inches long, irregular in form and generally broad at the ends, heart-shaped and clasping at the base. The leaves have a pleasant agreeable odor, and while young and tender are mixed with salads. Sow the seed in May in drills a foot apart and half an inch in depth. The plants, when allowed to run to seed, produce but little foliage. Nip off the flowering shoot as soon as it makes its appearance.

Article CLIX.

Sachet.

POKE, OR PIGEON BERRY.

Poke.

No. 1127.—A hardy, herbaceous perennial plant, common by the roadside in waste places, and springing up spontaneously on newly burned pine lands. It has a branching, purplish stem, and large oval-pointed entire leaves. The fruit consists of a flat, purple, juicy berry, which is sometimes used as a purple dye. The annual phytolacca is less vigorous and stocky. Sow the seeds in April, in drills, fifteen inches apart. The young shoots are boiled and served the same as sea kale. In taste it is similar to asparagus.

The roots are used for medicinal purposes, and when taken internally act as a violent emetic.

POKE STALKS, WITH BUTTER SAUCE.

No. 1128.—When the stalks are two inches high, and show only a tuft of leaves at the top, gather them. (They are unfit for use when larger or older.) Scrape the stalks and put them in cold, acidulated water. Tie them in bundles (the same as asparagus), put them in a saucepan of boiling water, and let them cook until tender. Serve them on a napkin with Butter or Hollandaise sauce, separate.

ARTICLE CLX.

French	POPPY.	German
Pavot.		Mohnsamen.

No. 1129.—A hardy annual plant, growing naturally in various parts of this country. It is cultivated for its seeds, which give an oil of very agreeable flavor, that is used for domestic purposes (in place of olive oil), by druggists and for fine art painting. The seeds are also used for bird food, and for this purpose are known as marrow seed.

CULTURE.

No. 1130.—Sow the seeds in April or May, in rows two feet apart. It is cultivated easily and can be grown successfully in the Middle or Southern States.

ARTICLE CLXI.

PORTUGAL CABBAGE.

Choux Portugais. *Portugal Kohl.*

No. 1131.—A variety of Cabbage quite distinct from the common head sorts. The stalk is short and thick; the outer leaves are large, roundish, of a dark bluish-green color, wrinkled on the surface and slightly undulating on the borders. The midrib of the leaf is large, thick, nearly white, and branches into veins. It forms a loose head and when full grown is nearly two feet high. Different parts of the Cabbage are used for culinary purposes. The ribs of the outer and large leaves, when boiled, somewhat resemble the sea-kale, both in texture and flavor. The heart, or middle, of the plant is, however, the best for use, as it is delicate and agreeably flavored, being without any of the coarseness often found in the common Cabbage. It is cultivated in the same manner as the common Cabbage. See Cabbage, Article XXX.

Article CLXII.

French *Pomme de terre.* **POTATOES.** **German** *Kartoffeln.*

No. 1132.—The Potato is an esculent and farinaceous plant, and a native of South America. In its wild, natural state, the tuber rarely exceeds an inch in diameter, and is comparatively unpalatable, but owing to cultivation they have greatly increased both in size and variety. There are over two hundred varieties, some of which are far superior to others, much depending on the culture and the soil in which they are grown. They are considered the most important of all the esculent roots, and a valuable article of human subsistence. The Potato is a healthful and nourishing vegetable, being agreeable to most all constitutions. It can be obtained throughout the year, and may be prepared without much trouble. The Potato is also used for other preparations. The Potato flour (fecula) is used by invalids and confectioners, and is mixed into the preparations of the common sorts of chocolate. The Potato blossom is used in making paint, and the leaves when dried are used by tobacconists.

CULTURE.

No. 1133.—The soil best suited for the Potato is of the drier and lighter description; pasture land or new land with the turf freshly turned, producing the most abundant as well as the most certain crop. When grown in land of a stiff clayish texture, or in wet soils, they are not only extremely liable to disease, but the quality is also very inferior. If the soil is good but little manure will be required. In highly enriched soil the plants appear to be more liable to disease than when grown in soil that is naturally good. The best fertilizers are those of a dry or absorbent nature, such as plaster lime, superphosphate of lime, and bone dust. For wet soil these are particularly beneficial, as they not only promote growth, but prevent disease. The Potato is propagated from tubers, which are either divided into sets, or planted entire. Whichever practice may be adopted, experience has proven that plants from well ripened tubers are not only more healthful and more productive, but actually come to perfection earlier than those produced from immature sets. Potatoes are usually planted either in hills or ridges, the former method being the most common in this country. If planted in hills they should be made three feet apart, on light warm soil. They require covering nearly four inches deep, but in cold, wet situations two and a half inches will be sufficient. Cultivation should be commenced as soon as the young shoots are fairly above the surface, and as the season advances gather the earth gradually about the hills or long drills, adding a little at each successive hoeing for the support of the growing plants, and to encourage the development of the rich roots, for it is at the extremity of the roots that the tubers are found. After the appearance of the blossoms cultivation should be discontinued, and no further attention will be required until ' the time for harvesting. The season of maturity of the earlier sorts will be indicated by the decay of the plants. The later sorts will continue their growth until checked by frost, previous to which time they will not be ready for harvesting. New Potatoes may be had in the Southern States and in California in February and March, and in the Northern States as early as May or June, when the weather is practicable.

The table should be supplied from day to day directly from the field or garden, as the tubers rapidly deteriorate after being taken from the ground, especially if exposed to a warm, light atmosphere, or when kept in a warm, dry cellar. In the preservation of potatoes it is of the first importance that they be excluded from light (if this is neglected they become injured). Fermentation is also an important evil to be guarded against, as it changes the whole substance of the Potato. Of the many old and new varieties that claim public favor the following are selected:

EARLY MAYFLOWER.

No. 1134.—Ripens very early, and in quality is claimed to be equal to the Snowflake. It is, in fact, a cross between the Snowflake and Peachblow. The tubers are of medium size and run very uniform, being slightly flattened, oval shaped, and of a light lemon color. The skin is well covered with very fine netting, and has very few eyes. The flesh is white and solid. It cooks evenly and thoroughly, without falling to pieces, and has no hard core, so common to other sorts.

WALL'S ORANGE.

No. 1135.—Unsurpassed as a table variety. Its color is very distinct, being of a decided orange hue, from which it derives its name. It is unequaled in quality and productiveness, and one of the strongest growers.

JUMBO.

No. 1136.—This is one of the largest growing Potatoes in cultivation, being at least one-third larger than the Peerless. It seems to be entirely free from rot and is one of the very best keepers. The tubers are nearly round, the skin white, the eyes small and sunken and the flesh white and of excellent flavor. Either baked or boiled they are dry and mealy.

CHAMPION OF AMERICA.

No. 1137.—The tubers are flesh-colored and the eyes carmine, small and even with the surface. It grows to an immense size on strong ground, producing tubers as heavy as three pounds in weight. It is a tremendous yielder, one of the best of keepers, and is not to be excelled for cooking purposes.

ROCHESTER FAVORITE.

No. 1138.—A late variety that is white, oval-oblong and very uniform in size. An immense yielder and a handsome variety, excellent for table use.

SAINT PATRICK.

No. 1139.—A handsome, smooth and regular variety, with very few and shallow eyes. A large yielder and of the best quality; excellent either baked or broiled being dry and mealy.

BEAUTY OF HEBRON.

No. 1140.—One of the best early sorts with white skin and flesh. A good keeper, excellent for table use, either baked or boiled.

EARLY ROSE.

No. 1141.—The leading variety for earliness, quality and productiveness.

WHITE ROSE.

No. 1142.—A second early variety of medium size, very uniform and finely formed, with white skin slightly russeted.

LATE ROSE.

No. 1143.—The best of the late varieties.

PEERLESS.

No. 1144.—A favorite variety for general use.

SNOWFLAKE.

No. 1145.—A variety of medium earliness and unsurpassed for mealiness and delicacy of flavor.

EARLY TELEPHONE.

No. 1146.—One of the best yielders, producing from one planted tuber as many as thirty or forty of good quality.

VERMONT CHAMPION.

No. 1147.—Grows to an immense size; of fine shape and a good yielder.

PEACH BLOW.

No. 1148. This variety is well known, as it is planted in immense quantities all over the country. It is very productive and ripens about the same time as the Burbank. The tubers are of medium size, oval-oblong, and very handsomely formed. A good keeper, and one of the very best for transportation.

MAMMOTH PEARL.

No. 1149.—The skin is white, the tubers medium in size, and the eyes are quite even with the surface. An excellent variety for table use, being exceedingly floury and well flavored.

EARLY GEM.

No. 1150.—One of the best early Potatoes, of medium size, oval-oblong in form and very smooth. The eyes are shallow and few in number. It cooks well and has white and exceedingly mealy flesh.

CARTER.

No. 1151.—A medium sized, round, flattened white Potato, and one of the finest varieties, with numerous deeply sunk eyes. The flesh is white, remarkably dry, farinaceous and well-flavored.

BUCKEYE.

No. 1152.—A handsome round Potato, with a little bright pink at the bottom of the eyes. It is grown to a considerable extent in the Western States. It cooks dry and light, and is well flavored when grown for early use. When grown for a late crop, in rich ground, many of the tubers are liable to be hollow in consequence of their rapid growth, thus impairing their value for table use.

CALIFORNIA RED.

No. 1153.—A bright red Potato, having tubers that vary in form from long to nearly round. One of the most productive of all the varieties, but its liability to disease accounts for it not being generally cultivated.

BOILED POTATOES.

No. 1154.—Wash the Potatoes in cold water and remove all the small particles attached to them. Then put them into a saucepan with water to cover, add a little salt, put on the cover and set them on a brisk fire to bring them to a boil. Then set them on the side of the fire to let them boil moderately. As soon as they are done drain off the water, replace the cover tightly and set the Potatoes on the stove again for five minutes to dry them. If the Potatoes are good the flesh will be dry, white and mealy. Serve them in a napkin.

NOTE.—Do not let Potatoes boil too quick, nor let them remain in the water after they have been boiled.

BOILED PEELED POTATOES.

No. 1155.—Peel the Potatoes and wash them in cold water (have them as near alike in size as possible). Put them into a saucepan, three-quarters full of cold water, add a little salt, put on the cover and boil them as in No. 1154. When done drain off the water and cover the Potatoes with a napkin. Then put on the cover, set them back on the stove, and when dried serve them in a napkin or with melted butter.

BOILED NEW POTATOES.

No. 1156.—New Potatoes need not be peeled. Wash them in cold water, then rub them with a coarse towel and the skin will come off. Put them into a saucepan three-quarters full of cold water, add a little salt and boil them as in No. 1154. When done drain them and serve with melted butter or Cream sauce over them.

BOILED POTATOES, GERMAN STYLE.

No. 1157.—Boil two dozen peeled Potatoes, and when they are done dish them up with the following preparation over them: Put into a frying pan two ounces of butter and one finely chopped onion. Fry the onion to a light brown color and add a little fresh bread crumbs. Toss this over a brisk fire, and when browned pour it over the Potatoes.

STEAMED POTATOES.

No. 1158.—Steamed Potatoes are preferred by some to boiled Potatoes, and those that are not of the best quality will be found better when steamed than boiled. Have a small boiler three-quarters full of water. When the water boils set on top of this boiler another one with perforated holes in the bottom, and into this put the Potatoes; adding a little salt to them. Cover them tightly with a perforated cover. When the steam comes through freely the Potatoes will be done. Serve them in the same way as boiled Potatoes. Where vegetables are cooked by steam power, perforated baskets are made to fit the boilers, and in this case the faucets must be left open so that no water can accumulate in the boiler.

STEWED POTATOES, AMERICAN STYLE.

No. 1159.—Take one dozen boiled Potatoes and peel them (when of medium size cut them in halves, and when large cut them into quarters). Then slice them in pieces all alike a quarter of an inch thick, and put them into a saucepan with half a cup of hot milk and a small piece of butter, and season with salt, pepper and a pinch of nutmeg. Let them simmer until the milk is nearly reduced, then add four spoonfuls of Butter sauce and let them cook about four minutes longer. Then add a piece of butter, some finely chopped parsley, and toss them well together off of the fire until the butter is melted.

STEWED POTATOES, MAITRE D'HOTEL.

No. 1160.—Prepare the Potatoes as in No. 1159. Then put them into a saucepan with a cup full of white broth and set it on a brisk fire. Season with salt and pepper, and when the broth is nearly reduced add four ounces of butter, some finely chopped parsley and the juice of one lemon. Toss them well together until the butter is melted, and serve.

STEWED POTATOES, EPICUREAN STYLE.

No. 1161.—Take two dozen small, new Potatoes, cut them in slices a quarter of an inch thick, put them into a flat saucepan and moisten them with broth to cover. Season with salt and pepper, put the cover on the saucepan and set it on a brisk fire. When the broth is nearly reduced the Potatoes should be cooked. Then add a piece of butter, some finely chopped parsley, and the juice of one lemon. Toss them well together off of the fire until the butter is melted, and then serve. When old potatoes are used, cut them first in halves, and then into slices of an equal size.

BAKED STEWED POTATOES, WITH CREAM, CHADWICK STYLE.

No. 1162.—Boil one dozen new Potatoes, cut them into pieces a quarter of an inch long and an eighth of an inch thick. Put them into a saucepan with two spoonfuls of cream, and season them with salt, a pinch of red pepper and a pinch of nutmeg. When the cream is reduced, add four spoonfuls of Cream sauce and toss them well together. Then put them into a buttered baking dish and bake them in an oven until nicely browned. Wipe the border of the dish in which the Potatoes have been baked and serve them on a dish with a napkin.

STEWED POTATOES, BRETONNE STYLE.

No. 1163.—Put into a saucepan two finely sliced onions, with a piece of butter, and fry them lightly. Then add two soup-spoonfuls of flour, and let them cook for five minutes while stirring them with a wooden spoon. Then add in slowly, half a pint of broth and a soup-spoonful of wine vinegar. Let this simmer slowly until the onions are well cooked, then add one and a half dozen of sliced and boiled new Potatoes. Season with salt and pepper, and when thoroughly warmed serve them.

STEWED POTATOES, HANOVERIAN STYLE.

No. 1164.—Pare four dozen small new Potatoes, put them into a saucepan and moisten them with broth to cover. Boil them on a brisk fire, and when cooked add four ounces of butter, a little salt, and some finely chopped parsley. Toss them well together off of the fire until the butter is melted, and serve.

STEWED POTATOES, WITH MUSTARD SAUCE.

No. 1165.—Cut into small pieces four ounces of raw ham, and put it into a saucepan with a piece of butter. Fry it lightly, and add two soup-spoonfuls of flour. Let it cook for five minutes while stirring it with a wooden spoon. Dilute this with broth enough to make a light sauce, and season with salt and pepper. Then put with this, two spoonfuls of wine vinegar, a faggot of parsley, garnished with a sprig of thyme and one bay leaf. Let it boil slowly for twenty minutes, then skim it clear, and take out the faggot. Then add two soup-spoonfuls of French mustard, and when well mixed add one dozen cold boiled sliced Potatoes, and when thoroughly warmed, serve.

STEWED POTATOES, WITH BACON.

No. 1166.—Put into a saucepan a quarter of a pound of bacon cut into slices about an inch long. Fry it lightly. Then add to it two soup-spoonfuls of flour and cook it to a light brown while stirring it with a wooden spoon. Dilute this with half a pint of broth, and when it boils add one dozen sliced Potatoes and a faggot of parsley garnished with a sprig of thyme and one bay leaf. Season with salt and pepper and let it simmer slowly for twenty minutes, when the Potatoes must be cooked. Take out the faggot and serve.

HASHED POTATOES, WITH CREAM.

No. 1167.—Hashed Potatoes are not chopped; they are boiled Potatoes, thinly sliced and then cut into small squares. Cut half a dozen boiled Potatoes as above and put them into a saucepan with a cup of cream. Set them on a brisk fire and when the moisture is half reduced, season with salt, pepper, a pinch of nutmeg (if desired) and a piece of butter. Toss them well together off of the fire until the butter is melted. When serving sprinkle a little finely chopped parsley over them.

NOTE.—A spoonful of Cream sauce may be added. If this is done, moisten with less cream in the first place.

HASHED POTATOES, BROWNED.

No. 1168.—Prepare the Potatoes as in No. 1167, moisten them with two spoonfuls of cream and season with salt and pepper. When the moisture is nearly reduced add a piece of butter and a spoonful of Cream sauce. Mix them well together. Put into an omelet pan a small piece of butter, and when melted add the Potatoes, letting them brown slowly. Gather the Potatoes and shape them nicely in the pan like an omelet. Then turn them on to a dish and serve.

BAKED HASHED POTATOES, WITH CREAM.

No. 1169.—Prepare the Potatoes as in No. 1167, and when the cream is nearly reduced, add two spoonfuls of Cream sauce and season with salt, pepper and a pinch of nutmeg. Toss them well together, put them into a buttered baking dish, sprinkle fresh bread crumbs over them and put a piece of butter on top. Wipe off the borders and place them in an oven to bake to a nice brown.

BAKED POTATOES WITH SALT HERRINGS, BERLIN STYLE.

No. 1170. Boil one dozen peeled Potatoes, cut them in slices and season with salt. Then select three fine pickled herrings, wash, skin and bone them. Then cut them into scollops and soak them in milk.

Slice two white onions finely, and put them into a saucepan with a piece of butter. Fry them slowly, not letting them get browned, and then add two soup-spoonfuls of flour. Let it cook a few minutes while stirring it, and dilute it with cream or boiled milk, so as to have a thick sauce. Season with salt, pepper and nutmeg, add a few drops of meat glaze, and cook it slowly for twenty minutes. Then rub it through a fine sieve.

Butter a deep baking dish, put a layer of the sliced Potatoes in it. Cover them with the sauce and add a layer of the scolloped herring. Alternate thus until the dish is full, and have the top layer of Potatoes. Cover them with the sauce, and over this sprinkle some fresh bread crumbs, adding some small pieces of butter over the top. Wipe off the borders and bake it slowly for twenty minutes.

BAKED POTATOES, CARLSRUHE STYLE.

No. 1171.—These are prepared the same as those in No. 1170, except that the herrings should be omitted, using scollops of smoked lamb or pig's tongue, and sliced breakfast sausages instead.

BAKED POTATOES WITH ANCHOVIES.

No. 1172.—Peel, boil and slice one dozen Potatoes and season them with salt. Wash half a pound of Anchovies and remove the skin and bones. Cut six hard-boiled eggs in quarters. Then butter a deep baking dish thickly, place a layer of the sliced Potatoes in the bottom and moisten it with sour cream. On this put a layer of the eggs and Anchovy, alternating in this way until the dish is full. Have a layer of Potatoes on top, moisten it with sour cream, and sprinkle raspings of bread on top, with a small piece of butter. Wipe off the borders and bake it for fifteen minutes.

BOILED POTATOES, ITALIAN STYLE.

No. 1173.—Chop one large, white onion finely, put it into a saucepan with a piece of butter and fry it lightly. Then add two soup-spoonfuls of flour and let it cook for five minutes while stirring it. Dilute this with a pint of cream to make a thick Cream sauce, cooking it slowly for ten minutes. Then add two spoonfuls of finely cut, lean ham, two spoonfuls of grated Parmesan cheese and the yolks of four hard boiled eggs chopped fine, and season with salt and pepper. Slice from two to three dozen boiled new Potatoes, and put a layer of them in a deep-buttered baking dish. Cover them with the sauce and proceed in this way until the dish is full. Sprinkle fresh bread crumbs on top, adding some small pieces of butter. Wipe off the borders and bake it in a moderate oven for twenty-five minutes.

NOTE.—Anchovies or finely sliced smoked sausages may be laid between the layers of Potatoes if desired.

POTATOES TOSSED IN BUTTER (SAUTÉ.)

No. 1174.—Slice half a dozen boiled Potatoes and put them into a frying pan with two spoonfuls of clarified butter. Season with salt and pepper and toss them over a brisk fire until nicely browned. Before serving, add some finely chopped parsley.

POTATOES, LYONNAISE.

No. 1175.—Cut an onion in half, trim off the ends, and slice it finely. Put it into a frying pan with two spoonfuls of clarified butter, and fry it lightly. Then add half a dozen sliced boiled Potatoes and season with salt and pepper. Then toss them over the fire until nicely browned, and before serving add a little finely chopped parsley.

POTATOES TOSSED, (SAUTÉ) ITALIAN STYLE.

No. 1176.—Prepare half a dozen sliced boiled new Potatoes as in No. 1175, using sweet oil instead of butter, and in place of onions use finely chopped shallots. When the Potatoes are nicely browned, add a little finely chopped parsley and two spoonfuls of well reduced veal broth. Toss them well over the fire and serve hot.

POTATOES SAUTÉ, HOLLANDAISE.

No. 1177.—Cut half a dozen boiled Potatoes into quarters and trim them. Then put them into a frying pan with some clarified butter or goose grease. Fry them slowly, and when they are nicely browned drain off the butter or goose grease, and add the juice of one lemon and some fine chopped parsley.

BROILED POTATOES.

No. 1178.—Slice half a dozen cold boiled Potatoes in pieces half an inch thick, and season them with salt and pepper. Then dip them into clarified butter, and arrange them on a double broiler. Broil them on both sides over a slow fire, and when they are done dish them up with a piece of butter. A little finely chopped parsley, and a few drops of lemon juice may be mixed with the butter.

BAKED POTATOES.

No. 1179.—Wash two dozen Potatoes and have them as nearly equal in size as possible. Put them on a pan and place it in the oven to bake. Turn them occasionally, and when done serve them in a napkin, with some fresh butter separate.

BAKED NEW POTATOES.

No. 1180.—Wash and clean two dozen new Potatoes in the same manner as for boiling. Put them into a flat saucepan with a piece of butter, and put it in the oven to bake. Toss them over occasionally, and when done add a little salt (care must be taken not to let the butter get burnt). When roasting them with a loin of veal or lamb, add the Potatoes when the meat is about three-quarters done. They may be served as a vegetable or used for garnishing.

MASHED POTATOES.

No. 1181.—To have good mashed Potatoes, only white and mealy ones should be used. New Potatoes, or those that are watery, should not be used. Boil or steam the Potatoes. When boiled drain off the water and set them on the fire again to dry. Then pound them through a fine colander while they are hot, and add salt, white pepper and a piece of butter. Work them well with a wooden spoon, and add some boiled milk slowly, so as to have them of the proper consistency. When they are to be kept for a little time, cover the surface with some butter or milk, which will prevent their getting dry before using. They should be light, white, and creamy.

BAKED MASHED POTATOES.

No. 1182.—Prepare the Potatoes as in No. 1181, adding a little less milk. Put them in a buttered baking dish, and arrange them in shape nicely with a knife. Baste them with the yolk of a raw egg diluted in milk, wipe the borders, and then bake them.

BAKED MASHED POTATOES WITH SPINACH, FRANKFURT STYLE.

No. 1183.—When the Potatoes are prepared, as in No. 1182, add a quarter of their quantity of finely chopped cooked spinach, and season with salt, pepper and nutmeg. Mix them well together and put them into a buttered baking dish. Sprinkle some fresh bread crumbs and a piece of butter over the top, and bake them slowly.

BAKED MASHED POTATOES WITH HAM, BUCKEYE STYLE.

No. 1184.—Prepare the Potatoes as in No. 1182. Put into a saucepan a piece of butter, two finely chopped shallots and a quarter of a pound of finely chopped ham. Toss them lightly over the fire and add them to the Potatoes, with a little finely chopped parsley. Mix them well together, put them into a buttered baking dish, and finish as in No. 1183.

POTATO CROQUETTES.

No. 1185.—Boil one dozen peeled Potatoes. When done, drain them and pound them through a fine colander, add a piece of butter and season with salt, pepper and nutmeg. Mix them well together while adding the yolks of four raw eggs. Put this preparation on a floured table and form them into any Croquette shapes desired. Then dip them in beaten eggs and bread them in raspings of bread or fresh bread crumbs. Fry them in hot lard, then drain them and dish them up in a napkin, with fried parsley to garnish on each end.

POTATOES, DUCHESSE.

No. 1186.—Prepare the Potatoes as in No. 1185, adding a little boiled milk while mixing them. Put the preparation on a floured table and roll it into cork shapes three inches long

Then flatten them with a knife to one inch in thickness, and arrange them in a buttered and floured pan. Impress any design desired on the top of each, and baste them with a brush dipped in milk diluted with the yolk of one raw egg. Ten minutes before using bake them in a hot oven to a nice brown, and then dish them up in a napkin or as a garniture with fish.

POTATOES STUFFED, SURPRISE.

No. 1187.—Prepare the Potatoes as in No. 1185. Put the preparation on a floured table, divide it into parts, and roll them into balls about two inches in diameter. Then flatten them out and fill the center of each one with a puree of green peas, or artichokes. Gather up the sides to keep the puree in the center, and roll the Potatoes into the shape of pears (care must be taken to have them well closed and smooth). Set them on a floured pan, fry them in hot lard, and handle them very carefully. Drain them on a napkin, and in dishing them place into the small end of each, a green stem of parsley to imitate a pear stem.

POTATO BALLS, AMERICAN STYLE.

No. 1188.—Prepare the Potatoes as in No. 1186. Then put the preparation on a floured table, roll it out into balls, then flatten them a little and flour them lightly. Put a little clarified butter in a frying pan, and when it is warm add the Potato cakes. Fry them on a slow fire, and when browned on both sides dish them up. Serve them for breakfast or lunch.

POTATO BALLS, MARGOT STYLE.

No. 1189. — Prepare the Potatoes as in No. 1185. Add an equal quantity of finely chopped braised veal, beef or lamb. Season with salt and pepper, and add a little finely chopped parsley and some finely chopped onions, lightly fried in butter. Mix them well together and roll them into balls. Then flatten them a little, dip them into some beaten eggs, flour them, and fry them in hot lard. Serve them on a napkin, with fried parsley to garnish.

POTATOES, CONVENT, OR PELERINE STYLE.

No. 1190.—Slice four medium sized white onions, detach all the circles, and put them into a flat saucepan with a piece of butter. Fry them to a light color (care being taken not to let the butter burn), then add six sliced boiled Potatoes. Toss them over a brisk fire until thoroughly warmed, and then add a cup of boiled cream and a pinch of sugar. Season with salt and pepper and let them simmer for fifteen minutes. Then add four ounces of butter, with some finely chopped parsley, toss them well over until the butter is melted, and then serve. The best new Potatoes should be used in order to properly appreciate this delicious dish.

POTATOES, DAUPHINE.

No. 1191.—Bake one dozen Potatoes, scoop out the center, and while they are hot rub them through a sieve. Then prepare them the same as in No. 1185. Roll them out on a floured table into pieces two inches long and one inch thick. Roll the ends to a point, and with a knife put any design that may be desired upon them. Place them into a buttered baking dish and baste them with a small brush dipped into a little milk diluted with the yolk of one raw egg. Bake them in a hot oven for five minutes, and when ready, serve.

FRIED POTATOES, SARATOGA CHIPS.

No. 1192.—Peel and wash the Potatoes, and slice them finely with a knife or cutter made for this purpose. Keep them in cold water, and when ready to fry, drain them. Then throw them into hot lard and let them fry crisp. Drain them on a napkin, season them with a little salt, and serve them hot. Fried Potatoes of any kind should be served as soon as fried, and must always be hot when served.

FRIED POTATOES, LONG BRANCH STYLE.

No. 1193.—Use large Potatoes which have no core. Peel and wash them, and cut them with a cutter made expressly for this purpose (sometimes called shoo-fly). They will resemble macaroni stems. Keep them in cold water until ready for frying, then drain them and fry them in a deep frying pan, with plenty of lard. When fried, drain them on a napkin to absorb the grease, and add a little salt. One Potato cut in this style will make as large a dish full as three in any other way. All fried Potatoes should be served on napkins.

FRIED POTATOES, FRENCH STYLE.

No. 1194.—When the Potatoes are peeled, slice them about a quarter of an inch thick, then cut them into sticks of about the same thickness. Fry them as in No. 1192.

FRIED POTATOES, JULIENNE STYLE.

No. 1195.—The Potatoes are cut as in No. 1194, but much finer, and fried as in No. 1192.

FRIED POTATOES, PARISIAN STYLE.

No. 1196.—With a spoon cutter made for the purpose, cut out of two dozen peeled Potatoes, some round pieces about the size of a large marble. Keep them in cold water until ready for use. Then fry them in hot lard until three-quarters done, and drain them on a napkin. Then put them into a flat saucepan with a piece of butter and finish cooking them. Then add a little salt and some finely chopped parsley, toss them well over, drain off the butter, and serve them.

POTATOES, BRABANT STYLE.

No. 1197.—Scoop the Potatoes as in No. 1196, then boil or steam them until they are three-quarters done. Then put them into a flat saucepan with a piece of butter and fry them lightly until nicely cooked and colored. Then drain off the butter and add four spoonfuls of white Soubise sauce, toss them well over, add a little salt, and serve them immediately.

POTATOES, CHATEAUBRIAND.

No. 1198.—Prepare the Potatoes as in No. 1197, and when they are nicely browned drain off the butter and add a piece of fresh butter, a little finely chopped parsley, some salt, the juice of half a lemon and a few drops of meat glaze. Toss them well over the fire and serve. They are also served with a double tenderloin steak, which bears the same name.

POTATOES SOUFFLÉ (PUFFED).

No. 1199.—Peel half a dozen medium sized Potatoes, slice them about one-sixteenth of an inch in thickness. Fry them in lard that is not too hot, and when they are soft drain them and put them into another pan with hot lard. Turn them with a skimmer constantly, and when they are nicely browned, drain them on a napkin, add a little salt, and serve them in a napkin.

POTATO PUREE, JACKSON STYLE.

No. 1200.—Bake two dozen Potatoes, scoop out the center and pound them through a fine colander. Add a piece of butter, season with salt and pepper, moisten with veal broth, and, when well mixed, dish them up with boneless sardines over them.

POTATO CAKE.

No. 1201.—Prepare the Potatoes as in No. 1185, but instead of seasoning with salt, add some powdered sugar to sweeten, and some vanila or lemon flavor. When the preparation is cool add the white of five eggs beaten to a froth. Then put it into a buttered mould, sprinkle the top with some bread crumbs and bake in an oven.

POTATOES FOR GARNITURE.

No. 1202.—The boiled new Potatoes, or the Parisian when boiled, are served as a garniture for fish. The Croquettes, Duchesse, Surprise, Dauphine, Parisian, Chateaubriand, and Pureé, are served with entrées and joints, or for large garniture for fish.

The Sauté, Lyonnaise, Chateaubriand, mashed and fried potatoes, are served with broiled meats.

POTATO FLOUR (FÉCULE).

No. 1203.—This can be obtained from all first-class grocers, and is used the same as arrowroot for invalids, and also in making griddle cakes, soups, custards, etc. Should necessity require it, the following recipe will be found very useful for making it in small quantities.

Peel and wash one dozen white farinaceous Potatoes, and rub them through a fine hair sieve into a basin of cold water, keeping the Potato always moist with water. Then set the basin aside to settle for two hours, after which drain the water off slowly, leaving the Potato flour in the bottom of the basin. If the flour is to be kept it must be dried.

POTATO BALLS FOR SOUPS (QUENELLES).

No. 1204.—Bake half a dozen Potatoes, and when done cut them in halves, scoop out the centre and rub them, while hot, through a sieve. Then put the puree in a pan with a piece of butter and half a cupful of cream. Season with salt, pepper, and nutmeg. Put the saucepan on a brisk fire and stir the puree well with a wooden spoon until it becomes a paste (the same as a Panade). Then take it off of the fire, and when it is a little cold add the yolks of four or five raw eggs and the whites of two eggs beaten to a froth, and mix them gently. Poach a little of this preparation, to see that it has the proper consistency, and if found satisfactory, roll the mixture on a floured table into small balls (Quenelles), and poach them in white broth, lightly salted. Serve them in soup as required.

SOUP—PUREE OF POTATOES, WITH CREAM, PARMENTIER.

No. 1205.—Pare one dozen medium sized Potatoes, cut them in slices and put them in a pan with cold water. Slice the white part of three leeks and two onions finely, put them in a saucepan with a piece of butter and fry them lightly. Then add three quarts of white broth, and when it boils, drain the water off the Potatoes and add them to the Soup with a faggot of parsley garnished with celery, and a few pepper-corns. Season with salt, let it boil slowly until the Potatoes are cooked, skim it well, take out the faggot and rub the soup through a fine sieve. Put it back in the saucepan, set it on the fire to boil slowly, and add a little broth if necessary, stirring it until it boils; after fifteen minutes, skim it well and set it on the side of the fire to keep warm. Before serving, add six ounces of butter divided into small pieces, and half a pint of cream diluted with the yolks of six raw eggs. Mix it well until the butter is melted. Put it into a soup-tureen with a little finely chopped chervil, and serve some small fried bread crumbs separate.

SOUP—PUREE OF POTATOES, JACKSON STYLE.

No. 1206.—Take two onions, one stalk of celery, and the white part of two leeks. Slice them finely, put them in a saucepan with a piece of butter, and fry them lightly. Then add two quarts of beef broth, and when it boils add one dozen medium sized sliced Potatoes, a faggot of parsley, garnished with a sprig of thyme and a few pepper-corns. Season with salt, cover the saucepan, and let it boil slowly until the Potatoes are thoroughly cooked. Then take out the faggot, rub the soup through a fine sieve and put it back into the saucepan, add three pints of thickened chicken or veal broth, and stir it until it boils. Season to taste, let it boil slowly for fifteen minutes, skim it well, and set it in a hot water bath to keep warm. Before serving add a large piece of butter and a glass of cream. Serve a plate of small fried bread crumbs separate.

NOTE.—With the soups described in Nos. 1205 and 1206, finely chopped chives, chervil, or parsley is generally added. A garniture of green peas, green asparagus tops, or Potato balls (as described in No. 1204) may also be added.

POTATOES FOR BORDERS.

No. 1207.—Pare two dozen Potatoes and then boil or steam them. When done pound them through a colander, add a piece of butter and season with salt, pepper and nutmeg. Mix them well together with a wooden spoon, and moisten them with a cup of milk. Then add the yolks of five raw eggs, mixing them well with the Potatoes. butter the border moulds with clarified butter, fill them carefully with the Potatoes, smooth the tops, and put them in the oven to bake for fifteen minutes. Then take them out of the oven and let them cool for fifteen minutes. Then pass the blade of a knife between the Potatoes and the mould, turn the borders on a dish and remove the mould carefully. Then brush the borders with the yolk of an egg, diluted with a few drops of water. Put them back in the oven for a few minutes to get brown, and fill the center with the preparation intended for the border, which will be described hereafter.

NOTE.—They may also be made by sprinkling the moulds with bread crumbs after they are buttered. When prepared in this manner, bake them for twenty minutes and they will be ready to serve. When making the Potato borders by hand prepare the Potatoes as above, then put them on a floured table and shape them in rolls long enough to border the dish. Have the border about two inches thick. Cut a carrot diagonally, dip it in flour and then make an impression in the border with it, or various different designs can be impressed on the top. In this way the borders can be made more attractive than when made in mould. Brush the borders with the yolks of eggs diluted with a little water, wipe the edges clean and set them in the oven for a few minutes to get nicely colored.

POTATO CRUSTS.

No. 1208.—Prepare the Potatoes as in No. 1185. Then put them into a buttered square tin pan (having them an inch and a half thick), smooth the top evenly and cover it with a buttered paper. Then set them aside to cool. When cold turn them out on the table, and with a round cutter (the size of a dollar) cut them out. Roll them in fresh bread crumbs, then dip them in beaten eggs and bread them again. Form them nicely, and with a cutter (the size of a twenty-five cent piece) make an impression on the tops to mark the cover. Fry them in hot lard, and when nicely colored drain them, and in a few minutes remove the cover and scoop out the center, being careful not to injure the shell. Then fill them with the desired garniture, after which they take their name.

NOTE.—Potatoes in this style are often called Timbals and Patés.

POTATO SALAD.

No. 1209.—Boil some Potatoes, slice them finely and fill a soup plate with them. Add some sweet oil, vinegar, salt, pepper, a few small sliced green onions and three spoonfuls of hot water. Then mix them all together and serve it in a salad bowl.

POTATO SALAD, WITH ANCHOVIES OR HERRINGS.

No. 1210.—Prepare the Potatoes as in No. 1209, and add boned anchovies or herrings cut into small pieces. Season with salt, pepper, two spoonfuls of capers and finely sliced green onions. Arrange them in a salad bowl and garnish with pickled beets.

POTATO SALAD, WITH TRUFFLES.

No. 1211.—Cut the Potatoes with a round cutter about one inch and a quarter in diameter. Slice them finely and put them into a salad bowl with sliced truffles that have been cooked in Madeira wine. Cover the bowl and set it aside for one hour. Then season with salt, pepper, oil and vinegar, arrange it properly and garnish with water cress.

POTATO SALAD, BENNETT STYLE.

No. 1212.—Cut the Potatoes as in No. 1211, and put them in a salad bowl with four or six finely sliced gherkins. Rub the yolks of two hard boiled eggs through a fine sieve, put them in a bowl and add a tea-spoonful of mustard flour and one of anchovic paste, some salt, pepper and finely chopped chervil. Dilute this with oil and vinegar, mix them well and then add the Potatoes. Arrange them nicely in a salad bowl and garnish with hard boiled eggs cut in halves, and some sliced truffles that have been cooked in Madeira wine.

POTATO SALAD, WITH ASPIC JELLY, CHARTREUSE.

No. 1213.—Boil two dozen firm, solid Potatoes; those that are mealy will not do for this recipe. They must be thoroughly cooked and then cooled. Then trim them into pieces about one or one-half of an inch thick, and after this cut them with a round column cutter, obtaining as many perfect pieces as possible. Put them on a napkin. Have some broken ice in a pan and put the mould in it that you intend filling. Line the mould with a coating of Aspic jelly and decorate the bottom with the whites of hard boiled eggs and some capers and olives in the shape of a rosette. Then dip the small round pieces of Potato in Aspic jelly and arrange them nicely around the inside of the mould close together, to form a solid wall. (They may be alternated with sliced beets or gherkins.) When this is done, line the inside again with Aspic jelly to fill up the interstices.

Now cut some hard boiled eggs in fine slices, place them in the bottom of the mould over the rosette, and put over this a few thin slices of beef tongue and some capers. Pour a little Aspic jelly over it to keep it firm.

Cut some cold boiled Potatoes in thin square pieces and put them in a salad bowl. Add to it one-quarter of its quantity of boned sardines, cut in small pieces, and a few capers. Now make a Mayonnaise dressing with Aspic jelly (see Book on Sauces). Season it highly. Mix it with the Potatoes quickly, before the dressing becomes hard, and put the mixture in the mould to fill it. Then smooth off the surface evenly and keep the mould in a cool place until ready to use it. When ready to serve it, dip the mould in lukewarm water, dry it with a napkin, turn it over on a dish and remove the mould carefully.

NOTE.—This can be garnished with a variety of vegetables, and its success depends altogether upon the care taken in preparing it. It may be filled with mixed vegetables, but they must be dried thoroughly before using. Care must be taken in making the Aspic Mayonnaise, which should be seasoned well. Only fresh and tender vegetables should be used.

ARTICLE CLXIII.

French   **PUMPKIN.**   **German**
Potiron gourge ou Citrouille.   *Kurbis.*

No. 1214.—The Pumpkin is now rarely used as a vegetable, having been superseded by the squash, which being finer grained and more highly flavored, is more acceptable. The Pumpkin, however, retains its popularity when prepared for use in pies. Some varieties grow to an immense size, and when dry are cut into the shape of buckets, baskets, and a variety of ornamental things.

CULTURE.

No. 1215.—Pumpkins are generally raised on cultivated ground, between hills of corn or potatoes, but they may be raised profitably in fields by themselves.

LARGE YELLOW.

No. 1216.—This grows to a large size, and is well adapted for cooking purposes. It is irregular in shape and size, being depressed and flattened at the ends; others are round or elongated. It has a deep, rich, yellow color, is finely grained, and has an excellent flavor.

CUSHAN.

No. 1217.—This is a great favorite in the Southern States, but is too tender for general cultivation in a Northern climate. It is very productive, grows to a large size, and somewhat resembles the winter crooked-neck squash. It is of a light cream color, sometimes streaked with green, and the flesh is of a salmon color.

SWEET SUGAR PUMPKIN.

No. 1218.—This is a good cooking variety, being unsurpassed for use in pies. It grows to an immense size, often weighing over a hundred pounds. It is oblong in shape, having a mottled light green and yellow skin, with thick, sweet, tender, yellow flesh, and large seeds.

NANTUCKET.

No. 1219.—This is small or medium in size, and somewhat oblong or bell-shaped. The thick, deep green skin is faintly ribbed, and more or less covered with prominent wart-like excrescences. The flesh is thick, yellow, finely grained, and has an excellent flavor.

PUMPKIN DIET DRINK (TISANE).

No. 1220.—Put four ounces of dried Pumpkin seeds in an earthen jar, and pour a pint of boiling water over them. Let it steep for twenty minutes and then take half a cupful at a time. It will be found beneficial for strangury and kindred complaints.

NOTE.—Parsley roots well washed, scraped and cut into small pieces, will do for the same purpose.

BAKED PUMPKIN, VERMONT STYLE.

No. 1221.—Cut a ripe Pumpkin in quarters, take out the seeds, pare off the rind and then cut it in slices half an inch thick. Put it in a buttered baking dish, moisten it with four spoonfuls of water, and set it in a moderate oven to bake. When cooked butter each piece and serve them hot.

MASHED PUMPKIN.

No. 1222. Cut a ripe pumpkin in halves, take out the seeds, pare off the rind and then cut it into scallops. Put it in a saucepan with enough boiling water to cover it, and let it boil until tender. Then drain it and pound it through a fine colander. Put it back in the saucepan, add a piece of butter, season with salt and pepper, and, when thoroughly warm, serve it.

SOUP—CREAM OF PUMPKINS.

No. 1223.—Cut a ripe Pumpkin into quarters, take out the seeds, pare off the rind and then cut it into small pieces. Boil them in lightly salted water, and when done drain them in a colander. Then put them in a saucepan with a piece of butter, season with salt, pepper, sugar and nutmeg and let them simmer for ten minutes, stirring them occasionally. Then add three quarts of thickened chicken or veal broth, and when it boils add a faggot of parsley garnished with celery, onions and leeks. Let it boil slowly for half an hour, then skim it well, remove the faggot and rub the soup through a fine sieve. Then put the puree in a saucepan to keep it warm, and when ready to serve it, add a piece of butter and a pint of cream, diluted with the yolks of six raw eggs. Mix them well together until the butter is melted. Serve with some small fried bread crumbs on a separate plate.

ARTICLE CLXIV.

French — *Pourpier.*   **PURSLAIN.**   **German** — *Portulak.*

No. 1224.—Purslain is a hardy annual plant, the cultivated varieties of which are an improvement over the common Purslain. The stem is tender and succulent, and is usually about one foot in length. The leaves are fleshy, broad and round, tapering at the ends. The plant may be cut for use when about five inches high, and is pickled, or may be boiled the same way as spinach.

COMMON PURSLAIN.

No. 1225.—This kind grows abundantly in gardens and cultivated fields. The green and the golden Purslain are improved sub-varieties, and though considered more succulent than the common Purslain, they will hardly repay one for the trouble of cultivating them, the difference in quality being very slight. The common variety is the kind in general use. Sow it in shallow drills, at any time from April to July. It thrives well in any soil.

ARTICLE CLXV.

RADISH.

Radis.   *Rettig.*

No. 1226.—The Radish is cultivated for its roots, which should always be eaten in their raw state when quite young, as they are apt to be pithy and tough when full grown. The young leaves are used as a small salad, and the green seed pods for pickling. The roots are served as a relish with salt, butter and bread.

CULTURE.

No. 1227.—A warm, sandy loam, made rich and light by well rotted manure, with a liberal dressing of salt, will keep them free from worms. Sow the seed in twelve inch drills as early as the ground can be worked, once in two weeks for a succession of crops. Thin them to two inches apart as soon as the raw leaves appear. Radishes must have plenty of room and should be grown quickly or they will invariably be tough and wormy.

SPRING AND SUMMER RADISHES.

No. 1228.—These varieties are all comparatively hardy, and may be sown in open ground, early in spring, when the soil is in good working condition.

OBLONG BROWN.

No. 1229.—The oblong brown Radish has a pear-shaped bulb, with an elongated top root, and does not grow particularly large. The flesh is white, hard and piquant in taste.

OLIVE-SHAPED SCARLET.

No. 1230.—The bulb is an inch and a half deep, three-fourths of an inch in diameter, oblong and somewhat in the form of an olive. The skin is of a fine scarlet color, and the flesh is rose colored, tender and excellent.

SCARLET TURNIP-ROOTED.

No. 1231.—The bulb is spherical and measures an inch in diameter in perfection. The skin is of a deep scarlet color, and the flesh is crisp and tender.

LONG SCARLET.

No. 1232.—This variety is largely cultivated. The root is long, a considerable portion of it growing above the ground. The skin is of a pink color, and the flesh is white, crisp and of good flavor, though less pungent than the scarlet turnip-rooted.

LONG WHITE.

No. 1233.—The root is long and slender, similar to the long scarlet. The skin is white, but becomes tinged with green when exposed to the light. The flesh is white, crisp and mild, and forms a nice contrast when served with the red varieties

LONG WHITE, PURPLE TOP.

No. 1234.—This is a sub-variety of the long white; the portion of the root above ground being tinged with purple.

SMALL YELLOW TURNIP-ROOTED.

No. 1235.—The root is similar to that of the scarlet turnip rooted. The skin is smooth and yellow, and the flesh is white, crisp, finely grained and rather pungent.

WHITE CROOKED.

No. 1236.—The root is very long, being sometimes over twelve inches in length, and an inch in diameter, nearly cylindrical, often irregular, and sometimes assuming a spiral or cork-screw shape. The skin is white and smooth, and the flesh is white and pungent, but not as fine as many of the other varieties.

YELLOW TURNIP-ROOTED.

No. 1237.—The bulb is nearly spherical, but tapers slightly towards the top root, which is slender. It grows large, but should be eaten when young and about an inch in diameter. The skin is of a yellowish-brown color, and the flesh is white, crisp and mild.

LONG SALMON.

No. 1238.—This is similar to the scarlet variety and appears about the same time.

LONG PURPLE.

No. 1239.—The root is long, considerable of it growing above the ground. The skin is deep purple in color, and the flesh is white, and of good flavor. If the seeds are sown in drills, the same as mustard, they will bring forth large green leaves, which can be used in small salads.

EARLY BLACK..

No. 1240.—The bulb is nearly spherical, but tapers slightly, being similar to the gray turnip-rooted. The skin is rough, wrinkled, and of a dull black color, and the flesh is white, solid and piquant in flavor.

EARLY LONG PURPLE.

No. 1241.—This is a small and early sub-variety of the long purple.

EARLY SCARLET TURNIP-ROOTED.

No. 1242.—The bulb is spherical, though flattened slightly, and often bursts longitudinally before attaining its full size. The skin is of a deep scarlet color, and the flesh is rose colored, crisp, mild and pleasant.

EARLY WHITE TURNIP-ROOTED.

No. 1243.—This is an excellent variety, similar in form to the scarlet-rooted, but smaller. The skin and flesh is white.

GRAY OLIVE-SHAPED.

No. 1244.—This is similar to the scarlet olive-shaped. The skin is gray and the flesh is white, crisp and well flavored.

GRAY TURNIP-ROOTED.

No. 1245.—This is generally round, though sometimes irregular in shape. It grows large and becomes hollow, and therefore should be eaten when young. The skin is mottled with greenish-brown, and is often marked with transverse white lines. The flesh is mild and of a greenish-white color, but not very solid.

AUTUMN AND WINTER RADISHES.

No. 1246.—These varieties may be sown from the middle of July to the middle of August. The soil should be made light and pliable and should be watered well in dry weather. Radishes may be obtained in September and October direct from the garden. For winter use the roots should be harvested before the ground freezes, and should be packed in earth or sand, out of danger from frost. They should be immersed in cold water before being used. They are served as salad, the same as the spring or summer varieties.

LARGE PURPLE WINTER.

No. 1247.—This is a sub-variety of the black Spanish, and resembles it in shape and character. The skin at first is black, but when washed assumes a beautiful purple color.

BLACK SPANISH.

No. 1248.—The bulb is pear-shaped, having a long top root, which at first is slender and somewhat cylindrical in form, it swells, however, as it advances in age, and finally attains a large size, being sometimes ten inches in length and four inches in diameter. It is one of the latest and hardiest varieties, being excellent for winter use. The skin is rough and nearly black, and the flesh is white, solid and pungent.

LONG BLACK WINTER.

No. 1249.—A small sub-variety of the black Spanish. The root is long and tapering.

LONG-LEAVED WHITE CHINESE.

No. 1250.—The root is of fusi-form, about five inches long and an inch in diameter. The skin is white and of fine texture, and the flesh is white, crisp, finely grained and pungent.

ROSE COLORED CHINESE.

No. 1251.—The bulb is somewhat cylindrical and terminates in a long slender top root. The skin is fine and of a light rose color, and the flesh is firm and piquant.

WINTER SPANISH.

No, 1252.—This variety succeeds best in light sandy soil. The roots are somewhat fusi-form, though sharply conical at the base. They sometimes measure eight inches in length, and three inches in diameter. The skin is white and wrinkled, being tinged with purple when exposed to the sun. The flesh is white, solid and pungent, though it is milder than that of the black Spanish.

CALIFORNIA MAMMOTH WHITE WINTER.

No. 1253.—A mammoth white-fleshed winter Radish of excellent quality.

RED RADISHES, FOR RELISHES.

No. 1254.—Radishes can be obtained in the Southern and Pacific States all the year round in the open air, and may also be obtained all the year in the Northern States when grown in hot-houses. Use only those that are solid, cut off the green top leaves, leaving only the small ones attached. Then scrape or slice the Radishes and put them in relish dishes on finely cracked ice or in cold water.

BLACK RADISHES FOR RELISHES.

No. 1255.—Peel them and slice them finely. Sprinkle salt over them one hour before serving, then press out the moisture and serve them in small relish dishes.

RADISHES FOR GARNITURE

No. 1256.—Radishes are largely used for garnishing salads, being cut into shapes resembling flowers. The black Radishes are used in green salads.

THE OIL RADISH.

No. 1257.—This is a variety of the common Radish, principally cultivated for its seeds, which yield an oil. It is superior to the rape seed oil and is more difficult to extract. It is cultivated extensively in China and the Southern States. The plant produces more seed pods than the common Radish.

ARTICLE CLXVI.

French RAMPION. **German**
Raiponce. *Die Rapunzel.*

No. 1258.—The Rampion is a biennial plant, the wild variety being known as the Primrose. The leaves are long, narrow and pointed. The roots are white, of fusi-form, and fleshy, somewhat resembling the turnip. Both the leaves and roots have a pleasant, nut-like flavor, and are generally eaten raw as a salad, when young.

CULTURE.

No. 1259.—The best roots are obtained from a rich, loamy soil, that is not exposed to the direct rays of the sun. Sow the seeds in

April, in shallow drills that are ten inches apart, and when they are well up thin them to four inches apart in the rows. When the plant runs to seed the roots become fibrous, strongly flavored, and unfit for use.

Article CLXVII.

RAMPION, OR GERMAN OR EVENING PRIMROSE.

French — *Primevère.*
German — *Schlüsselblume.*

No. 1260.—This is a hardy biennial plant that grows abundantly on the roadsides in this country. The roots, which are the only parts used, are, when full grown, about ten inches long, of fusiform, and have strong fibres. The whitish, thick outer skin peels off readily, and should always be removed. It has a nutty flavor when eaten raw, and is inferior to the true Rampion, being slightly pungent in taste. They are used in salads when young, and are prepared in the same manner as the oyster plant, when full grown.

RAMPION SALAD.

No. 1261.—When prepared as a salad it should be mixed with pickled beets and celery, and should be seasoned and finished the same as other salads.

Article CLXVIII.

RAPE.

Colza.
Rübsamen.

No. 1262.—This plant is cultivated for its seed, from which Rape seed oil is obtained. The seed is also used as food for canary birds, and the leaves for salad, when mixed with cress or lettuce.

CULTURE.

No. 1263.—Sow the seeds broadcast or in drills, in May, the same as mustard seeds are sown. The soil should be rich and moist to obtain a rapid growth, and tender, succulent leaves. The plants should be cut to the ground before the second leaves develop.

ANNUAL ROUGH-LEAVED SUMMER RAPE.

No. 1264.—The radical leaves are lyrate and of a vivid green color.

COMMON OR WINTER RAPE

No. 1265.—This variety is biennial and is better adapted to a Southern climate than to the North. The leaves are smooth, thick, fleshy, and resemble the annual summer variety in shape.

GERMAN RAPE.

No. 1266.—This variety resembles the Winter Rape, and is sown in May, the same way as corn.

SUMMER RAPE.

No. 1267.—A biennial variety with rough, radical leaves, that are fleshy and dark green in color. The best quality of oil is obtained from this variety.

ARTICLE CLXIX.

French **RED CABBAGE.** **German**
Choux Rouge. *Rothkohl or Blaukraut.*

No. 1268.—The Red Cabbage is similar to the white variety in shape, but its color is red or bluish-red. It is preferred by some to the white cabbage. For its cultivation and preparation, see Cabbage, Article XXX.

ARTICLE CLXX.

RHUBARB.
Rhubarbe. *Rhabarber.*

No. 1269.—Rhubarb is a perennial plant, and is cultivated almost exclusively for its leaf stalks. The root leaves are large, round, heart-shaped, and deep green in color, being more or less blistered.

The leaf stalks are large, furrowed, succulent, and of a pale green color, often stained or finely spotted with red, and varying from two to three inches in diameter at the broadest part, and from one to three feet in length. The stalks are used for pies, tarts, jellies, and for various medicinal purposes. The juice makes a tolerably palatable wine.

CULTURE.

No. 1270.—Rhubarb succeeds best in deep, and somewhat retentive soil; the richer its condition, and the deeper it is stirred, the better. Sow the seeds in drills, cover them with one inch of soil, and thin out the plants to six inches apart. Trench a piece of ground in the fall, manure it well, and transplant the young plants in the trench, three feet apart each way. Cover them with leaves during the first winter, and give them a dressing of coarse manure every fall. The stalks should not be plucked until the third year and the plant should never be allowed to run to seed. Seeds can never be relied upon to produce the same variety. The varieties are quite numerous, but those of good quality are limited in number.

DOWNING'S COLOSSAL.

No. 1271.—This is one of the best and largest varieties, having a fine, rich, aromatic flavor. Stalks of medium size are the best for family use. They turn red when cooking. When stewed it resembles currant jelly in color.

ELFORD.

No. 1272.—An early sort with slender stalks that are covered with a thin bright scarlet colored skin. The flesh is of a reddish color, which is retained when cooked, if the skin is not peeled off, a process which is unnecessary.

HAWK'S CHAMPAGNE.

No. 1273.—A variety as early as the Prince Albert, of a deeper and finer color, but more productive and larger.

WYATT'S LINNEOUS.

No. 1274.—A medium sized, very early and productive variety, that is highly flavored and but slightly aciduous. The skin is thin and the flesh tender.

WYATT'S VICTORIA.

No. 1275.—A productive variety, with large leaf-stalks, about three inches broad and over two feet long. They are reddish at the base and are often finely spotted with red to the nerves of the leaves. The skin is thick and the flesh is not very highly flavored.

CAHOON.

No. 1276.—The stalks are short and thick, the skin being thick and green. The texture is coarse and the flavor harsh and strong. It is seldom cultivated for culinary purposes, being used principally in the manufacture of wine. The juice is pressed from the stalks, and to each gallon three and a half pounds of sugar is added. The wine is quite palatable, but lacks the fine aroma of grape wine. Any of the other varieties may be used for wine, sugar being added according to their sweetness.

RHUBARB WINE.

No. 1277.—Cut half a pound of Rhubarb roots into small pieces, put them in an earthen jar, and moisten them with one quart of wine spirits (alcohol). Six days later add one gallon of dry white wine to it and cover the jar tightly. Ten days later filter it and put it into bottles. A wine-glassful taken every morning before breakfast is said to be very healthful.

RHUBARB WATER.

No. 1278.—Cut six ounces of Rhubarb roots into small pieces, put them in a quart bottle, fill the bottle with water, and set it aside for three days. The water diminishes phlegm, strengthens the stomach, and facilitates digestion. Take a wine-glassful at dinner time and mix it with wine. Re-fill the bottle when any is taken out and renew the quantity of Rhubarb roots every two weeks.

STEWED RHUBARB.

No. 1279.—Stewed Rhubarb is used as a relish and for pies and tarts. Peel and cut two pounds of Rhubarb into pieces about an inch long, parboil them for two minutes, then drain and put them into a saucepan, with four spoonfuls of cold water, and set it on a brisk fire, occasionally stirring it with a wooden spoon. When nearly cooked, sweeten it to taste, and let it cook until tender.

NOTE.—When cooked to be served as a relish, the pieces should be kept whole, and in order to do this it is only necessary to be a little more careful in cooking them and not stir them too much. Rhubarb, after being cooked, must always be kept in an earthen bowl or jar and covered with paper.

ARTICLE CLXXI.

French RICE. **German**
Riz.   *Reis*

No. 1280.—Rice is a native of the Orient, where it is a staple food. The best and finest quality is now grown in South Carolina. After bread it is the most healthful nourishment known. It is prepared for food in many different ways as a vegetable, and is extensively used, when ground into a flour, by pastry cooks for puddings, creams, cakes, etc., which will be described in the Book on Pastry. In China an intoxicating wine is made from it. In selecting Rice care should be taken to see that the grains are whole, for when they are broken, or the Rice is of inferior quality, it cannot be prepared properly. When it is properly cooked the grains should remain entire, and should not stick together. There is but one species. The plant is cultivated in warm climates in America, and grows best in low, moist soil, which can be overflowed. It is a light, nutritious food, and is easily digested.

BOILED RICE, PLAIN.

No. 1281.—Wash one pound of Rice in cold water, and then put it in a saucepan with some lightly salted water. Stir it until it boils, so it will not become attached to the bottom of the pan. Then cover the saucepan and let it cook slowly for twenty minutes. After this set it on the side of the fire to allow the moisture to become dry. It may be served as a vegetable or a garniture, and in soups where Rice is required.

BOILED RICE (ANOTHER WAY).

No. 1282.—Wash one pound of Rice in cold water, then drain it and put it into a saucepan. Pour over it twice as much cold water as there is Rice, season with salt and add a piece of butter. After it has boiled six minutes, cover the pan and let it cook slowly for twenty minutes. The Rice should then be cooked dry. When cooked in this manner it is used as a vegetable, and for garnitures or borders.

STEAMED RICE.

No. 1283.—Rice is the same, either steamed or boiled, differing only in the mode of cooking. Wash and drain the Rice and put it in a saucepan or a can. Pour over it twice as much cold water as there is Rice and season it with salt. Place the pan or can into the steam boiler, cover the boiler, turn on the steam and let it remain there about thirty minutes, when it should be sufficiently cooked. Have the pan or can perfectly clean or the Rice will have a rusty color when cooked.

RICE BOILED WITH BROTH.

No. 1284.—Wash one pound of Rice in cold water, then drain it and put it into a saucepan with plenty of cold water. Set it on a brisk fire to boil for two minutes (occasionally stirring it). Then immerse it in cold water and drain it dry. Then put it into a saucepan and moisten it with broth enough to cover the Rice one and a half times its depth. Season with salt, cover the saucepan and set it on the fire. As soon as it boils set it on the side of the fire, let it boil slowly for twenty minutes, and then the Rice will be cooked dry. Then add six ounces of butter, divided into small pieces, and a pinch of nutmeg, and mix them gently with a wooden spoon. Rice cooked in this way is used for garnitures, borders, Timbals, soups, etc.

RICE BORDERS.

No. 1285.—Cook the Rice as in Nos. 1282 and 1284. Then butter a border mould with clarified butter, press the Rice into it around the sides and bottom tightly, leaving a space in the center. Smooth it nicely on top, cover it with a buttered paper cover, and set the mould in a moderate oven for fifteen minutes. Then take it out, set it on the dish it is to be served on, and in five minutes lift off the mould carefully. Then fill the center of the border with the preparation intended for it.

NOTE.—When Rice is used for garnishing side dishes, it may be moulded in a Charlotte mould, or in a deep kitchen spoon. For the latter style dip the spoon in warm water, fill it with Rice, then gently press the Rice into an oval shape in the spoon. Then place the Rice on the dish that is to be garnished.

RICE FOR PUREES OR BISQUE SOUPS.

No. 1286.—Rice is used in thickening Purees and Bisque or Cream soups, to which it imparts a delicacy for which these soups should always be distinguished. Wash the Rice in cold water, drain it, and put it into a saucepan. Pour over it four times as much chicken or veal broth as there is Rice, season with salt and add a piece of butter, one carrot and one onion, having four cloves stuck into it. Cover the saucepan and let the Rice cook until it is thoroughly done. Then take out the onion and carrot, put the Rice into a mortar and pound it into a fine paste. It may then be used as directed in the Book on Soups.

RICE, FAMILY STYLE.

No. 1287.—Wash and drain one pound of Rice in cold water and put it into a saucepan with some water. Set it on the fire and let it boil for five minutes, occasionally stirring it. Then immerse it in cold water and drain it. Parboil half a pound of lean salt pork, trim it and cut it into pieces about an inch long. Put into a saucepan, fry it lightly and then add a pint of white broth and the Rice. Season with salt and pepper and let it cook slowly, occasionally stirring it up. When the Rice is cooked, add three spoonfuls of reduced Tomato sauce. Mix the whole gently with a spoon, without mashing the Rice, and serve it with fried sausages around the dish.

RICE WITH CURRY.

No. 1288.—Chop one onion finely, put it into a saucepan with a piece of butter, and fry it lightly. Then add two soup-spoonfuls of Curry powder and a pint of broth, and when it boils add half a pound of Rice (previously washed in cold water). Let it boil for five minutes, season with salt, cover the saucepan and let it cook slowly for twenty minutes. Serve as needed.

RICE, CREOLE STYLE.

No. 1289.—Chop one white onion finely, put it into a saucepan with a piece of butter and fry it lightly. Then add two ounces of finely cut lean ham and let it cook for two minutes while stirring it. Then add half a pound of Rice (previously washed in cold water), and four peeled tomatoes cut into small pieces. Season with salt and a pinch of red pepper and moisten it with a pint of hot broth. Then put on the cover and let it cook for twenty minutes.

RICE, MEXICAN STYLE.

No. 1290.—Cut one onion in half, trim off the ends and slice it finely. Put it into a saucepan with two spoonfuls of grated fresh fat pork, fry it lightly and then add two finely sliced green peppers, two peeled finely sliced tomatoes, and half a pound of Rice (previously washed in cold water). Moisten with a pint of chicken broth, season with salt and pepper, cover the saucepan and let it cook for twenty minutes, occasionally stirring it gently from the bottom.

RICE, MILANAISE STYLE.

No. 1291.—Chop one large white onion finely, put it into a saucepan with a piece of butter, and fry it lightly. Add to this, one pound of Rice (previously washed in cold water), a slice of raw ham, and a little Spanish saffron, tied up in a piece of cloth. Then moisten it with broth to cover, stir it occasionally until the broth is reduced, then moisten again, and let it cook until done. Then take it off of the fire, take out the ham and the saffron, and add four ounces of butter, and a handful of grated Parmesan cheese. Mix it gently, dish it up in a nice shape, and pour over it a nut brown Butter sauce, or a reduced Madeira wine sauce, with some tomatoes and essence of mushrooms.

RICE, SPANISH STYLE.

No. 1292.—Chop one white onion finely, put it into a saucepan with a piece of butter, and fry it lightly. Then add half a pound of washed Rice, and let it get thoroughly warmed while stirring it, after which moisten it with a pint of chicken broth. Cut a young and tender roasted chicken into small joints, and add it to the Rice, with a little Spanish saffron, and season with salt and pepper. Cover the saucepan and let it cook slowly for twenty-five minutes.

RICE WITH CABBAGE, RISTORI STYLE.

No. 1293.—Grate four ounces of fresh fat pork and put it into a saucepan with a small head of cabbage, cut into fine shreds, and season with salt, pepper, and a few fennel seeds. Cover the saucepan, and set it on a slow fire. When the cabbage is cooked, add half a pound of Rice, which has been parboiled for five minutes and drained dry. Moisten with a pint of broth, cover the saucepan, and let it cook slowly until the Rice is done. Serve it in nice shape and sprinkle Parmesan cheese over it.

RICE, PARISIAN STYLE.

No. 1294.—Wash one pound of Rice in cold water, and drain it. Then put it into a saucepan with three quarts of boiling water, and add a little salt and the juice of three lemons. Cover the saucepan and set it on the fire to boil. When the grains are soft (so they will not crack), drain it in a sieve, and put it into a medium sized saucepan with six ounces of warm clarified butter. Cover the Rice with a napkin moistened in hot water, and put the cover tightly on the saucepan. Set it in a moderate oven, and in twenty minutes the Rice will be cooked. In dishing it up use only a fork.

RICE WITH CURCUMA, OR TUMERIC.

No. 1295.—Wash half a pound of Rice in cold water and then drain it. Put two quarts of broth in a saucepan, season with salt, and when it boils add the Rice. In ten minutes add four soup-spoonfuls of curcuma diluted in a cup of water, and let it boil briskly until the Rice is cooked. Then drain it on a sieve, return it to the saucepan, add a piece of butter, and keep it warm until wanted.

NOTE.—Rice in this style is used for garnishing deviled chops and curried meats.

RICE, VALENCIENNE STYLE.

No. 1296.—Wash one pound of Rice in cold water, and drain it on a sieve. Chop one large white onion finely, put it in a saucepan with three spoonfuls of olive oil and fry it lightly. Then add the Rice and two ounces of ham cut in small pieces. Let it cook for four minutes, stirring it well with a wooden spoon, and then pour over it three times as much chicken broth as there is Rice. Add a faggot of parsley garnished, one dozen sausages "chipolata," and season with salt and a pinch of red pepper. Set it on the fire to boil for ten minutes, then cover the saucepan tightly and set it on the side of the fire to cook slowly for twenty minutes, when the rice will be cooked. Take out the faggot and add six ounces of butter divided into small pieces, and a garniture of mushrooms and artichoke bottoms scolloped. Mix the whole gently together.

NOTE.—When Rice is prepared in this style on Fast days, use fish broth; omit the sausages and ham, and replace them with oysters, mussels and eels cut in small pieces.

RICE, TURKISH STYLE.

No. 1297.—To prepare Rice in this style, it is necessary, first, to make a chicken or mutton broth, seasoned with salt, and garnished with a faggot of parsley, to which you have added some fine herbs, a few grains of pepper-corn and some cloves. When the broth is cooked strain it through a napkin.

Put one pound of Rice in a saucepan and pour over it twice as much of the above broth as there is Rice. Set it on a brisk fire, and in fifteen minutes the moisture will be nearly absorbed. Then set it on the side of the fire, and when the Rice is dry add four ounces of clarified nut-brown butter. Cover the saucepan tightly and set it in a moderate oven for ten or fifteen minutes. In dishing up the Rice use a fork, and when properly cooked with the best quality of Rice, the grains will be found to be separate from each other. Serve a soup tureen of the broth with the Rice.

RISOTTI, FLORENTINE STYLE.

No. 1298.—Chop one white onion finely, and put it into a saucepan with a piece of butter and four ounces of marrow cut into small pieces. Fry it lightly and then add one pound of Rice, letting it cook slowly for four minutes, while stirring it with a wooden spoon. Then moisten it with twice as much broth as there is Rice. Let it boil for ten minutes, then cover the saucepan and set it on the side of the fire to cook until done. Then add six ounces of butter, divided into small pieces, four ounces of grated Parmesan cheese, some truffles cut into small Juliennes, and four spoonfuls of beef gravy reduced with some Tomato sauce. Serve with this a plate of grated Parmesan cheese and a soup-tureen of Consomme.

RISOTTI, PIEMONTAISE STYLE.

No. 1299.—Chop one white onion finely, put it into a saucepan with a piece of butter and fry it lightly. Then add one pound of Rice, letting it cook for a few minutes, while stirring it with a wooden spoon. Then pour over it twice as much chicken broth as there is Rice. Let it boil for ten minutes, then cover the saucepan and set it on the side of the fire to cook until done, adding a little broth if necessary, without disturbing the Rice. When the Rice is cooked, take it off of the fire and add six ounces of butter divided into small pieces, four ounces of grated Parmesan cheese and three spoonfuls of rich gravy. Mix the whole gently. Serve with a tureen of chicken Consomme and a plate of Parmesan cheese.

RICE FOR GARNITURES.

No. 1300.—Rice prepared in the following styles may be used for garnitures; viz.: Rice Crusts, Timbals and Borders.

RICE CUSTARD FOR SOUP GARNITURE, LANGTRY STYLE.

No. 1301.—Wash and parboil six ounces of Rice for three minutes, then drain it, put it into a saucepan and pour over it twice as much milk as there is rice. Season with salt and a pinch of sugar and nutmeg. Cover the saucepan and let it cook slowly until thoroughly done, then rub it through a fine sieve and add the yolks of sixteen raw eggs diluted in half a pint of cream and half a pint of almond milk. Season to taste with salt, pepper and nutmeg, and strain the whole through a napkin. Then put the custard into small buttered round charlotte moulds and set them in a flat sauce-pan with water to poach. When cooked take them out to get cold, and when ready to use, slice them and put them into the soup.

RICE FOR CONSOMME.

No. 1302.—Wash and parboil the Rice for five minutes, then immerse it in cold water and drain it on a sieve. Then put it in some broth to cook, and when cooked, drain off the broth and put the Rice in the boiling Consomme. Let it boil up once, then skim it and serve.

RICE SOUP.

No. 1303.—Wash four ounces of Rice with plenty of water, drain it and set it on the fire with two quarts of cold water. Stir it occasionally, and as soon as it boils immerse it in cold water and drain it dry. Then put it into a saucepan with three quarts of boiling broth, season to taste and add a faggot of parsley garnished with two leeks. Cover half of the top of the saucepan and let it boil slowly until the Rice is cooked. Then skim it, take out the faggot and serve it, adding a little finely chopped parsley or chives.

NOTE.—Pearl barley, or any Italian paste may be prepared in the same way.

RICE SOUP, INDIAN STYLE.

No. 1304.—Prepare four quarts of thickened chicken broth as described in the Book on Soups, set it on the side of the fire to boil slowly for half an hour and skim it well. Cut two young chickens into pieces about an inch long and trim them nicely. Then put them into a saucepan with a piece of butter and fry them lightly. Add three soup-spoonfuls of curry powder diluted with a quart of broth. Let it cook slowly until the chicken is three-quarters done, then strain the thickened chicken broth through a fine sieve, and into this add a faggot of parsley garnished with celery and a leek. Season to taste, let the soup boil slowly until the chicken is done, then skim off the grease and remove the faggot. Before serving add half a pint of cream, into which dilute the yolks of four raw eggs. Serve with a garniture of plain boiled Rice.

RICE SOUP, WITH MILK.

No. 1305.—Wash four ounces of Rice in cold water, then drain it and put it in a saucepan with two quarts of cold water. When it boils immerse it in cold water. Boil two quarts of milk in a saucepan and then add the Rice, stirring it until it boils. Season with salt and a pinch of sugar and let it boil slowly on the side of the fire until the Rice is cooked.

NOTE.—Soups made with milk, to which vermicelli, farina, semoule, or other pastes are added, are prepared in the same way. A cup of cream, in which the yolks of two raw eggs are diluted, with a piece of butter and a little finely chopped parsley, will make it more nourishing.

RICE SOUP, WITH ALMOND MILK.

No. 1306.—Wash and parboil six ounces of Rice, then immerse it in cold water and drain it. Then put it in a saucepan with three pints of boiled milk and let it cook slowly until the Rice is done. Peel half a pound of sweet almonds and six bitter almonds, put them in a mortar and pound them into a fine paste, occasionally adding a little milk to prevent them from turning oily. Dilute the paste with one quart of milk and press it through a napkin. Then add this to the soup, season to taste, and, when thoroughly warmed, serve it, being very careful not to let it boil after mixing the almond milk with the soup.

RICE SOUP, ITALIAN STYLE.

No. 1307.—Wash and parboil six ounces of Rice, then immerse it in cold water and drain it. Put into a saucepan one finely sliced white onion with four ounces of scraped fat pork and fry it lightly (not letting it get browned). Then add the Rice and season with salt and a pinch of red pepper. Let it cook for two minutes, while stirring it with a wooden spoon. Then add two quarts of chicken Consomme, and when it boils set it on the side of the fire to boil slowly for twenty minutes. Skim it and then serve it with a plate of grated Parmesan cheese.

CREAM OF RICE, RACHEL STYLE.

No. 1308.—Wash one pound of Rice and put it in a saucepan with four quarts of cold water. Set it on the fire to boil for two minutes, stirring it occasionally. Then immerse it in cold water and drain it dry. Return the Rice to a saucepan with three pints of chicken broth, season with salt, a little nutmeg and red pepper, and add a faggot of parsley garnished with two leeks, one carrot and one onion, into which stick four cloves. Cover the saucepan and let it cook thoroughly on a slow fire. Then take out the faggot, carrot, and onion, and rub the Rice through a fine sieve. Dilute this puree with two quarts of chicken broth and one quart of Cream sauce. Set it on the fire and stir it until it boils, then let it simmer slowly for twenty minutes. Then skim it well and strain it through a fine sieve into another saucepan, and keep it warm in a hot water bath until ready to use it. Before serving add eight ounces of butter, divided into small pieces, and a pint of cream, in which dilute the yolks of eight raw eggs. Stir it well until the butter is melted, and serve it with a garniture of green asparagus tops.

CREAM OF RICE, LANGTRY STYLE.

No. 1309.—Wash one pound of Rice and put it in a saucepan with four quarts of cold water. Set it on the fire to boil for two minutes, stirring it occasionally. Then immerse it in cold water and drain it dry. Return the Rice to a saucepan with three quarts of chicken broth, season with salt, a little nutmeg and pepper, and add a faggot of parsley garnished with two leeks, one carrot and one onion, in which stick four cloves. Then add one chicken, cover the saucepan and let it cook thoroughly on a slow fire. Then take out the chicken, faggot, carrot and onion and add two quarts of Cream sauce to the Rice. Rub the whole through a fine sieve, and dilute the puree with chicken broth to its proper consistency. Then strain the soup through a fine sieve and keep it warm in a hot water bath until ready to use. With the breast of the chicken, make the following preparation: Pound the breast of two braised chickens in a mortar, into a fine paste, then add eight ounces of butter and the yolks of eight raw eggs and rub the whole through a fine sieve. When ready to serve the soup, put this in a saucepan with half a pint of cream and add the soup slowly while stirring it briskly with a wire whisk. Care must be taken not to let it boil or it will curdle. Serve with a garniture of small green asparagus tops or pearl barley.

CREAM OF RICE WITH RICE FLOUR, ASTOR STYLE.

No. 1310.—Put one gallon of chicken Consomme in a saucepan, and when it boils add slowly, while stirring it, half a pound of Rice flour diluted with cold broth. (If it gets lumpy it must be strained through a fine sieve and returned to the saucepan, stirring it until it boils.) When it boils season with salt, pepper, and a pinch of nutmeg, and add one chicken and a faggot of parsley, garnished with two leeks and two green onions. Let it boil slowly for three quarters of an hour, then skim it well, take out the chicken and faggot, and strain the soup through a fine sieve. Put it back in a saucepan to keep warm in a hot water bath. When ready to serve, add half a pound of butter, divided into small pieces, and a pint of almond milk, diluted with the yolks of six raw eggs. Stir it well until the butter is melted, and serve it with a garniture of green peas, or pearl barley, cooked in Consomme.

RICE WATER.

No. 1311.—Wash six ounces of Rice, put it in a saucepan with two quarts of cold water, set it on the fire and stir it until it boils. Then set it on the side of the fire to boil slowly until the Rice is thoroughly cooked. Then rub it through a fine strainer and put it back in the saucepan. If found too thick add a little more water, and let it warm thoroughly. Sweeten with sugar or honey.

NOTE.—Rice Water is a good nutritive drink for fevers and inflammatory affections of the bowels, as well as for diarrhœa. Care must be taken to see that the Rice is cooked soft. It may be used hot or cold.

RICE GRUEL.

No. 1312.—Wash four ounces of Rice and put it in a saucepan with one quart of boiling milk. Stir it until it boils, then set it on the side of the fire to cook slowly for half an hour. Sweeten with sugar and a pinch of nutmeg. This may be used hot or cold, and can also be made of Rice flour.

SMALL CRUSTS (OR CROUSTADES) OF RICE.

No. 1313.—Wash two pounds of Rice, put it in a saucepan and pour over it twice as much chicken broth as there is Rice. Then season with salt, add a piece of butter, cover the saucepan and let it cook slowly for twenty-five minutes, when the Rice will be cooked dry. Then take it off of the fire and add four ounces of butter, six ounces of grated Parmesan cheese, and a pinch of nutmeg, and mix the whole well together. After this put enough Rice in a buttered square tin pan to cover the bottom two inches deep. Smooth the surface of the Rice and cover it with a buttered paper cover, on top of which set another pan, so as to slightly press the Rice, and set it aside to get cold. When the Rice is cold turn it on the table, and with a round cutter, the size of a dollar, cut out as many crusts as possible (dip the cutter in lukewarm water after each cut). Roll the crusts in fresh bread crumbs, then dip them in beaten eggs and bread them again. Shape them nicely, and with a small cutter the size of a twenty-five cent piece, make on the top of each one a slight impression. Then fry them in hot lard, and when they are nicely browned, drain them. Take off the covers, scoop out the centers, and be careful not to break the shell.

CRUSTS (CROUSTADES) OF RICE, VICTORIA STYLE.

No. 1314.—Prepare the crusts as in No. 1313, and fill them with a garniture of mushrooms and shrimps, to which add a reduced Cream sauce. Garnish the tops of the crusts with a border of shrimps arranged in crescent shape.

CRUSTS (CROUSTADES) OF RICE, WITH EGGS AND CHEESE.

No. 1315.—Prepare a Risotti, Piemontaise style, as in No. 1299, having the Rice somewhat firmer, and then proceed to make the crusts as in No. 1313, filling them with eggs scrambled with cheese.

CRUSTS (CROUSTADES) OF RICE, WITH CURRIED LOBSTER.

No. 1316.—Prepare a Risotti, Florentine style, as in No. 1298, having the Rice somewhat firmer, and then proceed to make the crusts, as in No. 1313, filling them with a garniture of lobster, cut in small square pieces, to which add a reduced Curry sauce. Garnish the top of each crust with a piece of scalloped lobster and a slice of truffles, nicely glazed.

CRUSTS (CROUSTADES) OF RICE, WITH PUREE OF CHICKEN.

No. 1317.—Prepare the crusts as in No. 1313, and then fill them with a puree of chicken. Garnish the top of each crust with a small lamb sweet bread nicely glazed.

CASSEROLES OF RICE.

No. 1318.—The Rice, when cooked, is put in a buttered mould of any shape desired, and is pressed hard so as to have it in a solid mass. When it is cold turn it out of the mould, and cut it in any vase-like shape. Then scoop out the center so as to leave the shell half an inch thick.

HOW TO COOK RICE FOR CASSEROLES.

No. 1319.—Wash two pounds of Rice in several waters, and drain it dry. Then put it in a medium sized saucepan, and pour over it twice as much water or white broth as there is Rice. Season it with salt, add a small piece of butter, and set it on a brisk fire to boil, stirring it occasionally. Five minutes after it boils, cover the saucepan tightly, and set it in a moderate oven for forty minutes, when the rice will be thoroughly cooked. Then add two ounces of butter (six ounces of cheese if desired), and a pinch of nutmeg; mix the whole briskly with a wooden spoon, and press it tightly into the plain or fluted buttered moulds. Cover the moulds with a buttered paper cover, on top of which put a wooden cover that fits into the mould, and on this cover a weight to press the Rice down. When the Rice is perfectly cold, turn it out, and cut it into any vase-like shape. Then scoop out the center, and leave the shell about half an inch thick. Dilute the yolks of two raw eggs in a spoonful of water, and baste the Casserole inside and outside; then set it in a moderate oven until nicely colored.

NOTE.—Casseroles may be filled with any kind of meat garniture, fish or purees, and must always be nicely garnished over the top. They take their name from the garniture with which they are filled.

TIMBALS OF RICE.

No. 1320.—Cook three pounds of Rice as in Nos. 1298 or 1299, having it somewhat firmer. Butter the Timbal or Charlotte moulds with clarified butter, and place them in a cool place to allow the butter to harden. (They may also be decorated with truffles, beef tongue or raspings of bread.) When the Rice is cool and the moulds are ready, line the moulds carefully with it, pressing it tightly together around the sides and bottom, but being careful not to disturb the decorations. Fill the centres with a garniture of meats or purees. (The Timbal is named after the garniture it is filled with.) Then cover the Timbals with a layer of Rice, smooth it evenly, and cover it with a buttered paper cover. Then set them in the oven to keep warm until ready for use. When ready to serve them, pass a knife between the mould and the Timbal to loosen it, and then turn it on to the dish it is to be served on.

NOTE.—When making large Timbals, the Rice should be from one-half to three-quarters of an inch thick in the mould; for small garnitures, from one-quarter to one-half of an inch will be sufficient.

PANADE OF RICE FLOUR FOR FORCED MEATS.

No. 1321.—Put one pint of white broth in a saucepan, and when it boils add one pint of Rice flour and a small piece of butter. Stir briskly with a wooden spoon while adding the flour, and continue stirring for five minutes, being careful to have the paste clear and smooth so it will not stick to either the saucepan or spoon. Then take it off of the fire, put it in a plate or earthen bowl, cover it with a buttered paper cover to prevent it from crusting, and let it get cold until needed.

NOTE.—This Panade is superior to the others for any kind of forced meats, but it must always be used fresh. For other Panades, see Book on Sauces and Preparations for Forced Meats.

RICE CROQUETTES, CREOLE STYLE.

No. 1322.—Cook two pounds of Rice as in No. 1289, having it somewhat firmer and drier. When cooked, take it off of the fire, and add a small piece of butter, six ounces of grated Parmesan cheese, and a small garniture of mushrooms, beef tongue, truffles, and the breast of a roasted partridge, quail or chicken, all cut into small square pieces. Mix the whole thoroughly, and put it in a buttered square tin pan, having the Rice about an inch deep. Smooth the top evenly, cover it with a buttered paper cover, and set it aside to get cold. When cold, cut out some pieces with a round cutter (the size of half a dollar), and roll them in grated Parmesan cheese. Dip them in beaten eggs, then roll them in fresh bread crumbs, and form them nicely. Fry them in hot lard until nicely colored, then drain them, and serve them on a napkin, with fried parsley to garnish the base.

NOTE.—When these Croquettes are used for garnitures, add the yolks of six raw eggs. When putting the above mixture to the Rice, roll them in any shape desired while the Rice is warm; then bread them, etc.

RICE FRITTERS (SUBRICS).

No. 1323.—Wash one pound of Rice in cold water, parboil it for two minutes, immerse it in cold water, and drain it in a sieve. Then put it in a saucepan, and pour twice as much boiling milk over it as there is Rice. Cover the saucepan and let it cook slowly until the Rice is cooked dry. Then take it off of the fire to get cool; after which add two ounces of butter, three ounces of grated Parmesan cheese, the yolks of six raw eggs, a pinch of salt and one of nutmeg. Mix the whole well together. Put some clarified butter in a frying-pan, and drop into it a tablespoonful of Rice in a lump. Repeat this until the bottom of the pan is well covered, not allowing the lumps to touch each other. Fry them on both sides over a brisk fire, and when nicely browned, drain them and then serve them hot.

RICE CROQUETTES.

No. 1324.—Wash one pound of Rice in cold water and drain it. Then put it in a saucepan with two quarts of boiled milk, the peelings of one lemon and one stick of cinnamon. Cover the saucepan, set it on a slow fire to cook gently, and when the Rice is nearly done add six ounces of powdered sugar and two ounces of butter and let it cook until thoroughly done. Should the Rice get too dry while cooking add a little more milk to it. Take it off of the fire, take out the lemon peelings and the stick of cinnamon, mix the Rice well together, and when it is somewhat cool, add to it the yolks of six raw eggs, a little essence of lemon or orange-flower water, (whichever may be desired). Mix it well together and put it into a buttered pan. Cover it with a buttered paper cover and let it get cold. Then roll the Rice in any croquette shapes desired, dip them in beaten eggs, then in fresh bread crumbs, arrange them in proper shape, fry them in hot lard, drain them, roll them in powdered sugar into which add a little ground cinnamon, and then dish them up on a napkin.

NOTE.—Either a Hard sauce or a Wine sauce flavored with Maraschino or rum can be served with this.

RICE FRITTERS.

No. 1325.—Cook the Rice as in No. 1324. Then add some stoned raisins and currants that are perfectly clean, or some small square pieces of citron. Mix them all thoroughly, and, when the Rice is cold, roll it into balls about the size of a walnut. Dip them in frying batter, then fry them in hot lard, and drain them. After this, dip them in powdered sugar, and serve them on a napkin.

NOTE.—The Fritters may be flavored with lemon or orange flower water, as they are considered the best flavors for Rice. The Fritters are always named after the ingredients that are put into them.

RICE CAKE, SOUFFLÉ.

No. 1326.—Prepare the Rice as in No. 1324, and when it is cooked, put it in a pan to get cold. Then flavor it with lemon or orange, add the yolks of six raw eggs, and mix the whole thoroughly. Then beat the whites of four eggs to a stiff froth, and mix it gently with the rice. Butter some Charlotte moulds, and dust them with bread crumbs; then fill them three-quarters full with the Rice, and set them in a moderate oven to bake. When baked, turn it on a dish and let it stand a few minutes; then remove the mould, sprinkle it with powdered sugar, and serve it with a bowl of lemon sauce separate.

NOTE.—Raisins, currants or any kind of crystallized fruit may be added.

RICE CAKE, GLAZED.

No. 1327.—Prepare the Rice as in No. 1324, and, when it is cooked, put it in a pan to cool. Then add four whole raw eggs, the yolks of four more raw eggs, and six ounces of stoned raisins, currants, or citron cut in small pieces. Mix the whole thoroughly, and flavor with lemon or vanilla. Butter a square pan, in the bottom of which lay a buttered paper. Sprinkle it with flour, and put the Rice in the pan to the thickness of an inch. Set the pan into a larger pan containing some water, being careful not to let any of the water touch the Rice. Then set it in the oven to bake. When baked set the Rice out to cool. Then turn it out on a board or the bottom of another pan, remove the paper, and glaze the cake with a glaze made with rum or maraschino. Then set it in a moderate oven to dry, after which cut it in any shape desired, and serve with a Lemon or Rum sauce.

RICE FOR COMPOTES OF FRUIT.

No. 1328.—Wash one pound of Rice in cold water, and drain it. Then put it in a saucepan with three quarts of boiled milk, stirring it until it boils. Then add the peelings of one lemon and a stick of cinnamon. Cover the saucepan and let it cook slowly. When the Rice is three-quarters cooked, sweeten it to taste, and, should it be too thick, add a little more milk. When it is done keep it warm for use. When the fruit is cooked as for Compotes, dish up the Rice, and garnish it with the fruit intended to be served with it.

NOTE.—For full description of Compotes, see the Book on Pastry.

RICE WITH MILK, FOR INVALIDS.

No. 1329.—Wash half a pound of Rice in cold water, drain it dry and put it in a saucepan with six ounces of powdered sugar, two ounces of fresh butter, three soup-spoonfuls of white honey and half a teaspoonful of ground cinnamon. Then add three pints of fresh milk, cover the saucepan tight and set it in a hot oven to cook for forty-five minutes.

NOTE.—Care must be taken to have the saucepan high enough to prevent the milk from running over, as when the milk rises it should fall back to the Rice. This is light, agreeable, nourishing and healthful for persons having inflammation of the chest or stomach.

RICE CRUSTS, OR STANDS FOR HOT OR COLD SIDE DISHES.

No. 1330.—Crusts upon which side dishes are dressed, are generally cut from bread and are formed in various shapes, but those of Rice will be found much better and more secure, as they are very firm and will not soften like the bread, especially when the dish to be served must remain on the table for some time. Besides this, the whiteness of the Rice, when the crust is well made, presents a much more pleasing effect than the bread. This will be found to be the case, especially in cold dishes, owing to the fact that the Rice can be cut or carved into any shape after it has been moulded, but it requires experience and practice to shape them nicely.

HOW TO COOK RICE FOR CRUSTS OR STANDS.

No. 1331.—Wash four pounds of Rice in plenty of cold water and drain it. Then put it in a saucepan and pour over it three times as much water as there is Rice. Add a little salt and a small piece of butter and set it on the fire to boil, stirring it well. Six minutes after this, put the cover on the pan tightly, and set in a moderate oven for one hour, when the rice will be cooked dry. (If any of the Rice on top has become browned, remove it.) Then take the Rice from the saucepan with a spoon, being careful not to remove any that adheres to the side or bottom of the pan. Put it in a mortar, pound it to a fine paste and put it on a clean table board. Then dip your hands in cold water and work the Rice well together. Then butter a mould of the desired shape, fill it with the Rice, and smooth the surface evenly. Put a buttered paper cover on top, and on this place a wooden cover that will fit inside of the mould. A heavy weight must be put on the board to press the Rice down solid. Then set it aside for ten hours to get cold, and, when ready to use it, dip the mould in hot water and turn the Rice out on a dish. Then cut the Rice into any shape desired with a small sharp knife, and keep it covered with a damp napkin until wanted.

ARTICLE CLXXII.

ROCAMBOLE.

Rocambole. *Rocambole.*

No. 1332. Rocambole is a half-hardy perennial plant, and is a native of Denmark. They partake of the character of the shallot and garlic, and should always be dipped in boiling water for a few minutes before using, as they have a bitter taste. They are used in the same manner as shallots or garlic.

CULTURE.

No. 1333.—It is propagated by planting either the underground bulbs or the small cloves or bulbs that are produced upon the stem of the plant. Plant them in April, five inches apart, in drills that are ten inches apart. They will attain their full size in August, and may then be used for cooking, or may be spread out to dry, then tied in bunches and kept in a dry place for future use.

ARTICLE CLXXIII.

ROCKET.

French **German**
Roquette. *Winterkresse.*

No. 1334.—Rocket is a hardy, annual plant, a native of the south of Europe. The leaves are long, lobed, smooth, glossy, succulent and tender, and are eaten when young as a salad.

CULTURE.

No. 1335.—The seeds are sown thickly in shallow drills one foot apart, as early in spring as the ground will admit. If they are sown in a dry season, or in poor soil, the leaves are liable to be rough and acrid; therefore, be careful to use rich loam, and to water the plants well. If they grow rapid and vigorous, the foliage will be succulent and mildly flavored.

ARTICLE CLXXIV.

French   ROSEMARY.   **German**
Romarin.   *Rosmarin.*

No. 1336.—Rosemary is a half-hardy, shrubby plant, with a fragrant odor, and a warm, aromatic, bitter taste. The leaves vary in form and color in the different varieties. It is used for flavoring meats and soups, and also in the manufacture of cologne. Its flowers and calyxes form one of the principal ingredients in the distillation of Hungary water. Drinks are made by an infusion of the leaves.

CULTURE.

No. 1337.—Rosemary requires a light, dry soil, in a sheltered situation. The seeds are sown in April, in small nursery beds, and the seedlings, when two inches high, are transplanted in rows two feet apart, and sixteen inches apart in the rows. When propagated by cuttings, they should be taken off in May or June, when six inches long, and set two-thirds of their length in the earth, in a moist and shady situation. When well rooted, transplant as for seedlings.

GOLD STRIPED.

No. 1338.—A variety of the common green-leaved. The foliage is striped, variegated with yellow.

SILVER STRIPED.

No. 1339.—A sub-variety of the common green-leaved, and the most tender of all sorts. The leaves are striped, variegated with white. Both the gold and silver striped varieties are cultivated for ornamental plants.

NARROW LEAVED.

No. 1340.—A smaller variety, with less branches, and not as much esteemed as the others.

COMMON OR GREEN LEAVED.

No. 1341.—This is the best variety for cultivation. It is of a spreading habit, and is more aromatic than the others. The leaves are green and narrow, being rounded at the ends.

Article CLXXV.

French
Rue.

RUE.

German
Raute.

No. 1342.—This is a hardy, perennial plant, having a peculiar odor. The leaves are bitter and so acrid as to blister the skin. It is a stimulant and anti-spasmodic, but must be used with great caution, for unless this is done its use may result in serious injury. It must not be allowed to run to seed, and does best in poor soil. The plant is rarely used in this country for other than medicinal purposes. In the Eastern countries it is used in soups, and the leaves are boiled and pickled in vinegar.

BROAD-LEAVED RUE.

No. 1343.—The stem is shrubby and the compound leaves are of a grayish-green color, having a strong odor. The flowers are yellow, in terminal, spreading clusters. The fruit is a roundish capsule, and contains four rough, black seeds.

NARROW-LEAVED RUE.

No. 1344. This variety is hardier than the broad-leaved. The flowers are produced in longer and looser clusters.

Article CLXXVI.

RUTA-BAGA—RUSSIAN OR SWEEDISH TURNIP.

Navet Rave. *Stechrübe.*

No. 1345.—The Ruta-baga, or Russian Turnip, is extensively grown for a farm crop. The roots are closely grained and very hard, and will endure a considerable degree of cold without injury. They are preserved best in a pit or cellar during the winter, and are excellent for the table early in spring. Sow them from the end of June to the middle of July, in drills two feet apart, and thin them out to eight inches in the rows.

AMERICAN PURPLE TOP.

No. 1346.—This is the leading variety. It is very hardy and productive, being equally good for stock or table use. The flesh is yellow, solid, sweet and finely flavored.

SKIRVING'S PURPLE TOP.

No. 1347.—This is a good large variety that keeps well. The flesh is firm, solid and sweet.

SHAMROCK.

No. 1348.—One of the finest purple top varieties in cultivation, and keeps well. It forms a handsome bulb, with small tops, and but a few leaves.

LARGE WHITE FRENCH.

No. 1349.—This is a superior and popular variety. The flesh, which is white, firm and solid, has a rich sweet flavor and attains a large size.

ARTICLE CLXXVII.

French **RYE.** **German**
Seigle. *Korn-Roggen.*

No. 1350.—Rye is a hardy (secale cereal) plant and is closely allied to wheat. The grain is ground into flour and constitutes a large portion of breadstuff. The Rye flour is the best for making a cake called congloffs, which is of Polish origin. The various recipes will be found in the Book on Pastry.

CULTURE.

No. 1351.—The time for sowing is from the middle of August to the first of September, and it succeeds best in sandy soil. One ploughing is given, and the seed is sown broadcast. If cut before it is fully ripe, the grain makes better flour and produces a larger quantity. If intended for seed, the grain should be fully ripe.

ARTICLE CLXXVIII.

French
Safran.

SAFFRON.

German
Saffran.

No. 1352.—The common cultivated Saffron is a perennial plant. It is cultivated for its flowers, which are large, of a beautiful lilac color, and are used in dyeing, and to make the cosmetic called Rouge. The Saffron has been known for ages in Greece and Asia Minor. There are several different varieties. The French Saffron is much superior in color, and the Spanish is the best in flavor. The Saffron is cultivated in the United States as a garden flower only. The flowers are gathered after they show themselves, as their period of flowering is very short. The stigmas, or summits of the petals, with a portion of the style, are separated from the remainder of the flower, and are carefully dried by artificial heat, or in the sun. During this process they are made into the form of a cake, by pressure; but the finest Spanish Saffron is dried loosely. They are distinguished by the name of cake, or hay-Saffron. It must be kept in a dry place, in well-stopped vessels. Saffron has a peculiar aromatic odor, a warm, pungent, bitter taste, and a rich, deep orange color. When soaked in water it colors the liquid an orange-yellow color. It is much used in the Spanish and Southern countries for culinary purposes, for flavoring soups and rice dishes, and also by confectioners, and for medicinal purposes. From the seed a fixed oil is obtained somewhat similar to that of the sunflower. On account of the high price of the Spanish Saffron it is adulterated frequently. The flowers of other plants, such as safflower, marigold and arnica, are mixed with the genuine stigmas. They may be detected by their shape, which is rendered obvious by putting a portion of the so-called Saffron in hot water, which will cause them to expand. Much of this is to be found in the United States, and is sold under the name of African Saffron. Other adulterations are made with yellow-colored chalk, or sulphate of barrium, made into a thin paste, probably with honey, and attached to stigmas. The pure Saffron will always be clear when diluted with water, assuming a fine pure yellow tint, and the Saffron its red color. Less than the ordinary brightness of color in the Saffron should lead to the suspicion of adulteration. Saffron should not be very moist nor dry. The freshest is the best and should not be over a year old. When it is put in acidulated water it should color it bright yellow.

YELLOW COLORING FOR CULINARY PURPOSES.

No. 1353.—To a quarter of a pound of Saffron add a pint of water and one ounce of alum. Let it boil for fifteen minutes, then strain it through a towel and put it into bottles. When it is cold, cork the bottles tightly.

ARTICLE CLXXIX.

French   SAGE.   **German**
Sauge.   *Salbei.*

No. 1354.—This is a hardy, perennial plant, possessing some medicinal properties. It is cultivated principally for use as a condiment, and is used more extensively than any other herb, both green and in a dried state, for seasoning stuffings, meats, stews and soups. It is also used for flavoring cheese, and, in the form of a decoction, is sometimes employed for medicinal purposes. It should be gathered for drying before the development of the flowering shoots; and when cultivated for its leaves, the shoots should be cut off as they make their appearance. The product will be largely increased, as the leaves are put forth in much greater numbers and attain larger size.

CULTURE.

No. 1355.—Sow it early in spring, in very rich ground. Cultivate it often and thin the plants to sixteen inches apart. The plants will survive the winter, and, if divided, will give a second crop superior to the first in quality.

BROAD-LEAVED GREEN SAGE.

No. 1356.—The stem is shrubby, and the leaves are large, broad and heart-shaped, woolly, toothed on the margin, and produced on long foot-stalks. It is rarely employed for cooking purposes, but for medicinal purposes it is considered better than any other sort.

COMMON OR RED-LEAVED.

No. 1357.—This is the common Sage leaf of the garden, and, with the green-leaved—which is but a sub-variety, is the most esteemed for culinary purposes. The young stalk, the leaf-stems, the ribs and the nerves of the leaves are purple. The young leaves are sometimes tinged with the same color, but generally change by age to clear green. The red-leaved is generally regarded as possessing a higher flavor than the green-leaved, and is preferred for cultivation.

GREEN-LEAVED.

No. 1358.—A variety of the red-leaved. The young shoots, the leaf-stalks, the ribs and the nerves of the leaves are green.

NARROW-LEAVED GREEN SAGE.

No. 1359.—This variety is mildly flavored and is the most esteemed of all the sorts for use in a crude state. It is also one of the best for decoctions.

DRIED SAGE.

No. 1360.—Sage, when used for culinary purposes, is best in its dry state, whole or ground; but like all other herbs, it should be used moderately.

ARTICLE CLXXX.

French
Sayou.

SAGO.

German
Sago.

No. 1361.—Sago is a dry, granulated starch that is imported from the East Indies. It is the prepared pith of the Sago and other palms. Numerous trees in the East Indies and on the coast of the Indian Ocean, contain a farinaceous pith which is prepared for nutriment by the natives. The Sago Palm is one of the smallest, its height seldom exceeding thirty feet. The trunk is thick, erect and cylindrical, and is covered with a beautiful crown of foliage, of large, pinniate leaves, extending in all directions from the summit and curving gracefully downwards. The medullary matter contains most of the starch. When the large leaves have fallen off and the flowers commence to take their place, the tree is felled and the trunk is cut into billets about six feet long, which are then split to facilitate the extraction of the pith, which is obtained in the state of a coarse powder. This is mixed with water in a trough having a strainer at the end. The water, loaded with farina, passes through the strainer and is received in convenient vessels, where it is allowed to stand until it has settled. It is then drained off and the farina is dried and formed into cakes by the natives. The Sago as sold here is prepared by forming the meal into a paste with water, and rubbing it into grains. This is produced in the greatest abundance in the Moluccas, but the finest quality comes from the Eastern coast of Sumatra, in Malacca and Singapore. It is refined so as to give the grains a fine pearly lustre. This is what is called Pearl Sago, which is the kind generally used. It is a small grain about the size of a pin-head. The common Sago is larger, and the grains are of a more unequal size and of a duller aspect, being mixed with more or less dirty looking powder. Sago is used as an article of diet, being nutritive and digestible, and wholly destitute of irritating properties.

SAGO FOR INVALIDS.

No. 1362.—In its preparation care must be taken to boil it long in water or broth. Drop it into boiling water or broth while stirring it, so the grains will dissolve thoroughly and not form in lumps. Should any portion not be dissolved it must be strained, as it might offend a delicate stomach. A table-spoonful of Sago to a pint of water is sufficient for ordinary purposes. It may be seasoned with sugar, nutmeg or other spices, and wine may be added if advisable.

SAGO GRUEL.

No. 1363.—Boil one quart of water in a saucepan and then drop in three spoonfuls of Sago slowly, while stirring it with a wooden spoon. When it boils steadily, set it on the side of the fire to boil slowly and add a pinch of salt. In three-quarters of an hour add a wine-glassful of good white wine, the juice of one lemon, a soup-spoonful of powdered sugar and a pinch of nutmeg. Serve it hot or put it in an earthen bowl and serve it when cold.

SAGO FOR SOUPS.

No. 1364.—Drop the amount of Sago necessary in boiling broth, or consomme, stirring it until it boils steadily. Sago is added to many purees and cream soups as a garniture. Sago or tapioca with chicken or veal broth, is partaken of in the morning by prima donnas to a considerable extent.

SAGO SOUP WITH CREAM.

No. 1365.—Wash the Sago in cold water, then drop it in a saucepan containing one quart of chicken broth, and let it boil slowly until well cooked. Then season it lightly and add half a pint of cream diluted with the yolks of two raw eggs, which will render it more nourishing.

ARTICLE CLXXXI.

French   **SALAD GARNITURES.**   **German**
Fourniture de Salade.   *Salat Kräuter.*

No. 1366.—Salad garnitures comprise the many pungent and aromatic herbs that are mixed with, or added to, green salads in small quantities. The following is a list of the herbs that are used, all of which are described under their respective headings: Anise, Bell-Peppers, Borage, Burnet, Bugloss, Basil Sweet, Costmary, Coriander, Chives, Chervil, Garlic, Green Onion, Mustard leaves, Nasturtium, Oxalis, Picridium, Pepper Cress, Parsley, Tarragon, Welsh Onion, Wood Sorrel.

ARTICLE CLXXXII.

SALSIFY, OR OYSTER PLANT.

Salsifis.   *Haferwurz l.*

No. 1367.—Salsify is a hardy biennial plant, and is principally cultivated for its roots, the flavor of which resembles that of oysters. The leaves are long and grass-like. The roots are long and tapering, like the parsnip, and when grown in good soil measure about ten inches in length and an inch in diameter. Their flavor is sweet and delicate, and they are said to contain medicinal properties which have a tendency to alleviate consumption.

CULTURE.

No. 1368.—Salsify succeeds best in a light and well enriched soil, which should be worked to a depth of twelve inches. The manure should be well rotted, for when fresh and coarse the roots will grow irregular and ill-shaped. Sow early and quite deep, and give the same general culture as for parsnips. The roots are hardy and may remain out all winter, but should be dug early in the spring as they deteriorate rapidly after growth commences. For winter use store them in the sand.

HOW TO PREPARE IT FOR COOKING.

No. 1369.—Scrape the skin off carefully and cut them in halves. Then slice them in sticks about two inches long, and throw them into a pan of acidulated cold water to keep them white.

SALSIFY, WITH BUTTER SAUCE.

No. 1370.—Prepare the Salsify as in No. 1369. Put a saucepan on the fire with some water in it, and when it boils add a piece of butter, a little salt, two spoonfuls of vinegar and the Salsify. Let them cook until tender, then drain them in a colander and put them in a saucepan. Add five spoonfuls of Butter sauce and season with salt, pepper and a few drops of lemon juice. Then toss them well together and serve them.

NOTE.—When Salsify is to be cooked and kept for future use, add to the water when it boils, two spoonfuls of flour, diluted with cold water. When they are cooked put them, with the broth, in an earthen bowl or jar, cover it with a paper cover, and keep it in a cool place.

SALSIFY, WITH CREAM SAUCE.

No. 1371.—Prepare the Salsify as in No. 1370, and when they are drained put them in a saucepan with a glassful of cream. When the moisture is reduced add three spoonfuls of Cream sauce and let it simmer for five minutes. Serve hot.

SALSIFY, FRENCH STYLE.

No. 1372.—Prepare and cook the Salsify as in No. 1370; then drain them and put them in a flat saucepan with a small piece of butter. Season with salt and pepper and toss them over the fire until the moisture is reduced. Then add four spoonfuls of Allemande sauce and toss them well together. Before serving, add the juice of half a lemon and a little finely chopped parsley.

SALSIFY WITH BROWN SAUCE, SPANISH STYLE.

No. 1373.—Prepare and cook the Salsify as in No. 1370; then drain them and put them in a flat saucepan with a small piece of butter. Toss them over the fire, and when lightly browned, add some thickened veal gravy, to which add a few drops of essence of ham. Toss them over the fire again for a few minutes; then add a little finely chopped parsley and serve hot.

NOTE.—Four spoonfuls of Espagnole sauce may be used instead of the veal gravy.

SALSIFY FRIED IN BATTER.

No. 1374.—Prepare and cook the Salsify as in No. 1370; then drain them, and put them in an earthen bowl. Season with salt, pepper and the juice of a lemon, and in one hour they will be ready for use. Then take them out, dip them in a batter and fry them in hot lard. Then drain them on a napkin, season them lightly with salt, and dress them on a napkin, with fried parsley as a garniture.

FRIED SALSIFY, VILLEROI.

No. 1375.—Prepare and cook the Salsify as in No. 1370; then drain them, and put them in an earthen bowl. Season with salt and pepper, and when they are cold, take them out and dip them in a well-reduced Allemande or Cream sauce. Then arrange them in a pan, and set them in a cool place so the sauce will adhere well. After this, dip them gently in a light batter, and fry them in hot lard.

SALSIFY FRIED IN BUTTER.

No. 1376.—Prepare and cook the Salsify as in No. 1370; then drain them. When they are cold, season them with salt and pepper, roll them in flour. Put a frying pan, with a piece of butter in it, on the fire. When the butter is warm, add the Salsify, and fry them nicely on both sides. Serve them on a napkin.

SALSIFY SALAD.

No. 1377.—Prepare and cook the Salsify as in No. 1370; then drain them, and when they are cold, slice them into small stems about two inches long. Put them in a salad bowl, season with salt, pepper, sweet oil and vinegar, and add a few finely-sliced gherkins. Mix them all well together, dress them nicely, and sprinkle a little finely chopped parsley over the salad.

Article CLXXXIII.

SALEP.

French
Salep or Saloop.

German
Salep.

No. 1378.—Salep is a small, oval, irregular or oblong tuber of a yellowish color, a feeble odor and a mild mucilaginous taste. It is one of the numerous species of the genus *Orchis*. It is prepared principally in the Levant and in Germany, and is highly nutritious, being used in the same manner as sago, tapioca and other fecula for invalids.

SALEP SOUP FOR INVALIDS.

No. 1379.—Put a pint of chicken or veal broth in a saucepan, and when it boils add in slowly a teaspoonful of the Salep while stirring it briskly. Let it boil about twenty minutes, season it lightly and then serve it.

ARTICLE CLXXXIV.

French *Sel.* **SALT.** German *Salz.*

No. 1380.—This mineral production, so necessary to mankind, is universally distributed over the globe. Most animals have an instinctive relish for it, and from its frequent presence in the solids and fluids of the animal economy, it may be supposed to perform an important part in assimilation and nutrition. It is used to some extent in medicine, but its principal use is in cookery, where it is employed in seasoning certain kinds of food and for the preservation of meat.

ARTICLE CLXXXV.

SALT-PETRE.

Salpêtre. *Salpeter.*

No. 1381.—Salt-petre, or nitre, is both a natural and an artificial product. Its quality varies considerably. That which comes in yellow crystals is called crude salt-petre; while the finer lots, in small, comparatively clear crystals, approaching to white, are called East India refined. It is considered refrigerant, diuretic, and diaphoretic, and is known to be a powerful antiseptic. In cookery it is employed for the purpose of retaining the red color in meat, such as beef, tongue or ham, when they are put in brine.

ARTICLE CLXXXVI.

SAMPHIRE, OR SEA-FENNEL.

Crête marine. *Meerfenchel.*

No. 1382.—This is a half-hardy perennial plant that is common to rocky localities on the sea-coast. The stalk, which is from one to two feet in height, is tender and succulent. The leaves are half an inch long, green in color and fleshy. They have a warm, pleasant, aromatic flavor, and when pickled in vinegar, are used in salads and for seasoning.

GOLDEN SAMPHIRE.

No. 1383.—This is a hardy perennial that grows naturally on the sea-coast. The stalk is from one to two feet high, standing erect, with clusters of small fleshy leaves. This plant is used for the same purposes, but lacks the pleasant flavor of the true Samphire, though it is often sold as the genuine variety and used as a substitute.

CULTURE.

No. 1384.—Either kind can be cultivated, but with the best of care and attention it is impossible to secure a cultivated variety possessing the flavor of the wild kinds. It is best to put them in large pots in the garden, filled with earth and sand. They must be watered well in dry weather.

ARTICLE CLXXXVII.

French   SAVORY.   **German**
Sarriette.   *Saturei.*

No. 1385.—Savory is a perennial plant, with a rigid, angular, branching stem, about one foot and a half high. The leaves, when bruised, emit a strong, pleasant, mint-like odor. They are used for culinary and medicinal purposes.

CULTURE.

No. 1386.—Summer Savory is always raised from seed that is sown in April or May, in shallow drills fourteen inches apart. When they are three inches high, thin them out to six inches apart in the rows. It thrives best in light, mellow soil.

Winter Savory is also raised from seed, or may be increased by a division of the roots. The seeds are sown in May in shallow drills fifteen inches apart. The roots may be divided in spring or autumn.

SUMMER SAVORY.

No. 1387.—This is an annual species of Savory, and a native of the southern part of Europe. It is about one foot high, erect but slender, and produces its branches in pairs. The leaves, which are narrow and rigid, have a pleasant odor and a warm, aromatic taste.

When the plants have commenced to flower, they should be cut to the ground, tied in small bunches and dried in an airy, shady situation.

WINTER SAVORY.

No. 1388.—This is a hardy evergreen shrub, about a foot in height, with a low, branching stem. The leaves are like those of Summer Savory.

USE OF SAVORY.

No. 1389.—The green or dried aromatic tops of the plant are used to mix in stuffing for meat or fowl, in faggots for stews, in salads and with peas and beans. When dried it is sometimes pulverized, and should then be kept in well-stopped vessels. The dried tops are preferred to the green ones for flavoring.

ARTICLE CLXXXVIII.

French   **SAVOY CABBAGE.**   **German**
Chou Savoy.   *Savoyer or Mailänder.*

No. 1390.—This variety of Cabbage is a native of Italy. They are distinguished from the common head Cabbage by their peculiarly wrinkled or blistered leaves. They resemble the cauliflower somewhat in texture and flavor, having but little of the musky odor and taste of the large varieties of Cabbage. They are hardier and more easily cultivated than the other varieties, but will seldom survive through the winter in open ground. A little frosty weather is considered necessary for the complete perfection of their texture and flavor. Their treatment during winter is the same as that of common Cabbages. For varieties and preparation, see Cabbage, Article XXX.

ARTICLE CLXXXIX.

SCORZONARA, OR BLACK SALSIFY.
Scorsonère.   *Haferwurzel.*

No. 1391.—This is a hardy, perennial plant. The root is tapering, slender and about one foot in length and an inch in diameter across the crown; the skin is grayish-black in color, and coarse. It is cultivated exclusively for the roots, the flesh of which is white, tender, sugary and well flavored. Before they are cooked the coarse outer rind should be scraped off and the roots soaked for a few hours in cold water to extract their bitter flavor. Prepare them for table use, the same as parsnips or as oyster plant are prepared.

CULTURE.

No. 1392.—It is cultivated in the same way as carrots or turnips, being sown in April in the Southern States, or in July or August in the North, as the plants are liable to flower and run to seed, which impairs the value of the roots. Sow them fifteen inches apart in drills and half an inch deep. The roots will be ready for use in October. If required for use during winter, store them away the same as oyster plant.

ARTICLE CXC.

French   **SCURVY GRASS.**   **German**
Cochlearia.   *Löffelkraut.*

No. 1393.—This is a hardy, annual, maritime plant, common to the sea-coast. The root-leaves, which spread regularly from a common center, are heart-shaped, fleshy, smooth and glossy. The stem leaves are oblong and toothed on the margin. The radical leaves are used as a salad, and are sometimes mixed with cress. When bruised they emit an unpleasant odor, and have an acrid, bitter taste when eaten. The plant is used more for medicinal purposes than for cookery.

ARTICLE CXCI.

SEA BEET.

Bette.   *Mangold.*

No. 1394.—This is a hardy, perennial plant. It is cultivated exclusively for its leaves, which are the only part of the plant eaten. They are an excellent substitute for spinach, and by some are preferred to it. If planted in good soil it will supply excellent leaves for years. The leaves that are produced earliest are the best, and are fit for use from May until when the plant begins to run to flower. However, they may be continued in perfection through the whole summer and autumn by cutting off the flower stems as they arise.

CULTURE.

No. 1395.—Sow them in April, in rows sixteen inches apart, and one inch under the soil. Thin them out to twelve inches apart in the rows. The leaves should not be cut from the seedling plants during the first season. There are two varieties. The English Sea Beet is a dwarf variety, with ovate leaves about four inches in length, of a thick, fleshy texture, and a dark-green color. The Irish Sea Beet is about the same, but has larger leaves, and is generally considered superior to the English variety.

ARTICLE CXCII.

SEA-KALE.

French — *Choux Marins ou Crambe Maritime.*
German — *Seekohl, or Meerkohl.*

No. 1396.—Sea-Kale is a favorite vegetable in the Southern States. The young shoots that appear in spring are the parts eaten, but they are not good until blanched. Their flavor is somewhat like that of asparagus. As the plant is perennial, the young shoots do not appear until the second spring, and are then blanched. The sprouts are cut for use when from three to six inches high and continue in season about six weeks. They are prepared the same as asparagus. The roots are injured by excessive cutting, and some of the shoots should be allowed to make their natural growth, so that strength may be secured for the next spring crop.

CULTURE.

No. 1397.—The ground should be trenched one or two feet deep, according to the soil, and should be well enriched throughout. When the plants are to remain, sow the seeds in April. Keep the plants clear from weeds, nip off the shoots of those that tend to run to flower and, in autumn, when the leaves have decayed, add a liberal dressing of compost manure. Early in spring stir a rake over the bed, being careful not to injure the crowns of the roots, and cover them from eight to ten inches deep with the material intended for blanching. A bed, with good culture and moderate use, will produce well for five or six years.

SEA-KALE, WITH BUTTER SAUCE.

No. 1398.—Remove the leaves, wash and peel the stems carefully, and tie them in bunches the same as asparagus is tied. Then boil them in lightly salted water and, when cooked, drain them. Serve them on a napkin or on a piece of toast, with Butter sauce or Cream sauce in a separate dish.

SEA-KALE, HOLLANDAISE STYLE.

No. 1399.—Prepare the Sea-Kale as in No. 1398, and when it is cooked, serve it on a dish with some Hollandaise sauce poured over it.

SEA-KALE WITH BROWN SAUCE.

No. 1400.—Prepare and cook the Sea-Kale as in No. 1398. Then drain it, and put it in a saucepan with a piece of butter. Toss it over a brisk fire, season with salt and pepper, and add a little Espagnole sauce, the juice of one lemon and a little finely chopped parsley.

PUREE OF SEA-KALE.

No. 1401.—Cut the Sea-Kale in small pieces and boil them in lightly salted water. When done, drain them on a napkin, and put them in a saucepan with a small piece of butter. Season with salt, pepper, nutmeg and a pinch of sugar; then toss them over a brisk fire for a few minutes, and moisten them with some white broth. When the moisture is reduced, add some Allemande or Cream sauce, rub it through a fine sieve, put it in a flat saucepan and add a glass of cream to reduce the puree to its proper consistency. Add a piece of butter before serving.

ARTICLE CXCIII.

SEMOULE.

Semoule. *Semoule.*

No. 1402.—Semoule is a paste similar to vermicelli, but comes in small hard grains. It is made from the whitest part of wheat flour, and in America is largely sold under the name of farina (see Farina, Article LXXXVIII). The White Semoule is made from rice flour, and the yellow kind from wheat flour, to which a saffron dye is added, with some coriander and the yolks of eggs. The yellow Semoule is considered best and is much relished when boiled in milk and sweetened. Semoule is used for soups and a variety of culinary preparations, and is a good food for invalids.

CONSOMME, WITH SEMOULE.

No. 1403.—Put four quarts of Consomme in a saucepan, and when it boils add in slowly half a pound of Semoule, stirring it well so it will not get lumpy. Let it boil slowly for twenty minutes, season to taste, then skim it and serve.

NOTE.—A Consomme with farina, manioca, sago, tapioca, vermicelli, or any kind of paste may be made the same as the above and, by adding a little cream diluted with the yolks of eggs, it will be more nourishing.

SMALL CRUSTS OF SEMOULE, PALERMITAINE.

No. 1404.—Put three quarts of clear white broth in a saucepan, add a small piece of butter, season with salt and, when it boils, add in slowly two pounds of Semoule, stirring it gently, so it will not get lumpy. Then set it on the side of the fire to cook slowly until thoroughly cooked, keeping it firm. When done take it off of the fire and add two ounces of butter and six ounces of grated Parmesan cheese. Mix it well together and put it in a buttered square tin pan, having the mixture about one and a half inches deep. Smooth the surface evenly, cover it with a buttered paper cover and set it aside to get cold. Then turn it out on a table and, with a round cutter the size of a dollar, cut out as many pieces as possible. Roll them in fresh bread crumbs, dip them in beaten eggs, and then bread them again. Form them nicely in shape and, with a cutter the size of a twenty-five cent piece, make a slight impression on the top of each to mark the cover. Then fry them in hot lard and, when nicely browned, drain them and in a few minutes take off the cover and scoop out the center, being careful not to injure the crust. Keep them warm until ready for use. Then make a garniture of small boiled macaroni (spaghetti), cut in pieces a quarter of an inch long, mixed with the same quantity of small pieces of the breast of roasted quails or partridges, and an equal quantity of lean boiled ham and artichoke bottoms cut in small pieces. Put the garniture in a reduced Madeira wine sauce, add a few drops of lemon juice and mix it gently together. Then fill the crusts with the garniture and serve hot.

BALLS OF SEMOULE (QUENELLES,) VILLEROI.

No. 1405.—Put one quart of milk in a saucepan and, when it boils, add in slowly three-quarters of a pound of Semoule, stirring it gently, so it will not get lumpy. Then set it on the side of the fire to cook slowly until it is thoroughly cooked, keeping it firm. Take it off of the fire, let it cool a little, then add a handful of grated Parmesan cheese and the yolks of ten raw eggs, mixing it well, and season with salt and a pinch of nutmeg. Then let it get cool.

Now cut some truffles, mushrooms and the breast of a roasted fowl, in a short Julienne, and add them to a succulent and well reduced Madeira wine or Allemande sauce, and set it aside to get cold.

Prepare some small, oblong granulated Tartlet moulds and butter them with clarified butter. Put in each mould a thin layer of Semoule and smooth it neatly with a knife, leaving the centre hollow. Then fill them with the above garniture, cover the top with Semoule, allowing it to form on top in a semi-oval shape, and smooth it off neatly. Set them aside to get cold and firm. Then take them out of the moulds and dip them in a cool Villeroi sauce, place them in a pan side by side, and set the pan on the ice so the sauce will adhere to them. Then trim them nicely, roll them in fresh bread crumbs, dip them in beaten eggs and bread them again. (Handle them very carefully.) Now fry them in hot lard and, when nicely colored, drain them and serve them on a napkin.

Article CXCIV.

| French | SHALLOT, OR ESCHALOT. | German |
| Echalote. | | Schalotte. |

No. 1406.—The Shallot is a native of Palestine, and is used in the same manner as the onion, or garlic. The root of the plant is composed of several small bulbs united at the base, the whole being enclosed in a thin skin, varying in color in the different varieties. The ripening will be indicated by the decay of the leaves. After the bulbs are dried they should be stored in a light, dry situation. When exposed to frost or put in a damp cellar they rapidly decay. In flavor it is mild and pleasant, resembling the leek. They are prepared and cooked in the same manner as onions or garlic.

CULTURE.

No. 1407.—The Shallot will thrive in any soil that is adapted to the onion. The bulbous roots are readily increased by off sets, but seldom attain a large size. Plant them in April in drills one foot apart, and cover them lightly with soil.

COMMON SMALL SHALLOT.

No. 1408.—This is an excellent early variety, and keeps well. The bulbs are about three-fourths of an inch in diameter and have a reddish yellow skin.

JERSEY.

No. 1409.—A very early variety, quite tender, but decays early. The large bulbs are enclosed in a light-brown skin as fine in texture as the onion skin.

LONG KEEPING.

No. 1410.—This variety resembles the common Shallot, but is considered superior to it on account of its keeping qualities, and as it is less subject to the attacks of the maggot. It will keep from twelve to eighteen months.

ESSENCE OF SHALLOTS.

No. 1411.—Chop one dozen Shallots finely, put them in a saucepan with a piece of butter, and fry them lightly. Then add one pint of veal gravy and let it reduce to one-third of its quantity. Then season with salt and pepper and strain it through a towel.

ARTICLE CXCV.

French   SHEPHERD'S PURSE.   **German**
Capselle.   *Täschelkraut.*

No. 1412.—This is a hardy annual plant that grows naturally in gardens. The root leaves spread out from a common centre, and in good soil attain a length of about eight inches. The stem leaves rest closely upon the stalk, being oval at the base. Under high cultivation the plants will attain a diameter of twenty inches. It is prepared in the same manner as spinach, or is served like endives, making an excellent salad.

CULTURE.

No. 1413.—Sow them in May in shallow drills fourteen inches apart and thin the young shoots to four inches apart. Cover the beds with coarse stable litter late in Autumn, and remove it in the latter part of February. The plants will be ready for use in March or April.

ARTICLE CXCVI.

French   **SIEVA, OR SMALL LIMA BEAN.**   **German**
Siève (Petite Fève).   *Bohne.*

No. 1414.—The Sieva is a variety of the Lima Bean, the plant attaining a height of ten feet. The pods are small and uniform in size, generally about three inches long and seven inches wide. When young they are green and wrinkled, but when ripe they turn to a pale yellowish-brown. They are a little earlier than the Lima Bean, but require the whole season for their complete maturity. The seeds are white, or of a dull yellowish-white, broad and flattened. They are similar to the Lima Beans, and are almost as delicate and richly flavored. The young pods are hard and tough, and are never eaten. This is the most productive of all varieties.

MOTTLED SIEVA.

No. 1415.—A sub-variety of the Sieva, the only difference between them being in the variegated character of the seeds, which are of a dull white color, spotted and streaked with purple.

ARTICLE CXCVII.

SKIRRET.

Berle Chervi.   *Zuckerwurzel.*

No. 1416.—Skirret is a hardy perennial plant that is cultivated for its roots, which are produced in bunches at the crown or neck of the plant. They are oblong and fleshy, with a russet-brown skin, the flesh being white and sugary. When well grown they measure from six to eight inches in length and almost an inch in diameter. They are the whitest and sweetest of esculent roots and are very nourishing. They are prepared for the table in the same manner as the oyster plant.

Article CXCVIII.

SNAKE OR SERPENT CUCUMBER.

French *Concombre Serpentine.* **German** *Schlangengurke.*

No. 1417.—This resembles the musk-melon in its manner of growth and in the color and taste of the ripe fruit, which is slender and flexuous. It is about three feet long and is often gracefully coiled in a serpent-like form. The skin is green, and its flesh is white when young and yellow at maturity. It is grown principally on account of its peculiar shape for a garden vegetable, but is seldom used in cookery. The fruit may be pickled in the same manner as common cucumbers.

CULTURE.

No. 1418.—Sow the seeds in May in hills six feet apart, and cover them with half an inch of soil. Give them the same attention that cucumbers or melons require.

Article CXCIX.

SORREL.

Oseille. *Sauerampfer.*

No. 1419.—Sorrel is a hardy perennial plant. The species as well as the varieties differ to a considerable extent in height and general habit, yet their usage is nearly the same. The finest roots are obtained from seedlings. These varieties are propagated by dividing the roots. This method must be adopted in the propagation of the divicious kinds when the male plants are required. All of the varieties will send up a flower-stalk in summer, and it is necessary to cut the stalk when it first develops in order to render the leaves larger and more tender. Sorrel is used for soups and purees, and is preserved for winter use. It is one of the most wholesome vegetables, and would be particularly beneficial to that class of the community that live much upon salt provisions.

CULTURE.

No. 1420.—Sorrel is cultivated easily, and may be grown in almost any soil or situation, but thrives best in rich, moist soil. Sow it in April in drills fifteen inches apart, and cover it with half an inch of soil. Thin them out to ten inches apart.

BELLEVILLE SORREL.

No. 1421.—The leaves are about ten inches long, by six inches in diameter, and are larger and less acid than the common garden Sorrel. The leaf stems are red at the base.

BLISTERED-LEAF SORREL.

No. 1422.—This is similar to the common variety except that the foliage is blistered. It develops slowly and consequently remains longer in season.

FERVENT'S LARGE SORREL.

No. 1423.—This is a hardy and excellent variety that produces abundantly. The leaves are large, of a yellowish-green color, and are put forth very early.

SARSCELLE BLOND SORREL.

No. 1424.—This is a sub-variety of the Belleville, with larger and narrower leaves, and pale leaf-stems. It puts forth the leaves earlier than the common Sorrel and is of excellent quality.

FRENCH, OR ROUND-LEAVED SORREL.

No. 1425.—The leaves vary in form, being roundish and heart-shaped, smooth, glaucous and entire on the borders. The leaves are more acidnous than any of the other varieties, and for this reason are preferred by many.

SORREL WITH CREAM.

No. 1426.—Pick the stems off of the Sorrel, wash the leaves in plenty of cold water, then drain them, and chop them finely with a head of lettuce, the same quantity of young beet leaves, and a little chervil. Mix them well together; then put them in a saucepan with a small piece of butter, and stir them slowly until the butter is melted. Then season with salt and pepper and, when well cooked, add a pint of cream diluted with the yolks of five raw eggs. Serve hot.

SORREL WITH GRAVY.

No. 1427.—Prepare and cook the Sorrel as in No. 1426, and, when cooked, drain off some of the moisture, and add a good gravy instead of the cream.

SORREL PUREE, FOR GARNITURES.

No. 1428.—Prepare and wash the Sorrel as in No. 1426; then put it in a saucepan with a pint of water, and season it with salt and pepper. Set it on a brisk fire, and stir it with a wooden spoon until it is well cooked. Then drain it in a colander, and in twenty minutes rub it through a fine sieve. Then put four ounces of butter and two spoonfuls of flour in a saucepan, and let it cook for five minutes, stirring it well. Add the Sorrel, moisten it with a pint of broth and let it cook for ten minutes. Then add a cup of milk diluted with the yolks of three raw eggs, and stir the whole well until thoroughly mixed.

SORREL PUREE, WITH SAUCE, FOR GARNITURES.

No. 1429.—Prepare and cook the Sorrel as in No. 1426, and when it is rubbed through the sieve, put it in a saucepan with four spoonfuls of Allemande sauce. When it is reduced to its proper consistency, season it with salt, pepper and nutmeg. Before serving, add a piece of butter, mixing it all well.

SORREL SOUP.

No. 1430.—Wash and trim two pounds of Sorrel, two heads of lettuce and a little chervil, and then cut them in fine shreds. Put them in a saucepan with six ounces of butter, and stir the whole over the fire for twenty-five minutes with a wooden spoon until it is melted. Then add four spoonfuls of flour, and let it cook for ten minutes, stirring it well. (Dilute the flour so there will be no lumps.) Then add in slowly two quarts of boiling water, and as soon as it boils up, set it to one side to boil slowly, and season with salt and pepper. Twenty minutes later add one quart of broth.

When it is ready to serve, prepare the following: Dilute a pint of cream with the yolks of four raw eggs; beat it up well, and strain it through a sieve. Add this to the soup with six ounces of butter stirring it well until the butter is melted. Cut two French rolls in fine slices, brown them nicely in the oven, and put them in a soup tureen. Then pour the soup over them and serve.

SORREL SOUP FOR FAST DAYS.

No. 1431.—Prepare the soup as in No. 1430, but instead of broth add one quart of milk diluted with six raw eggs.

SORREL SOUP WITH CREAM.

No. 1432.—Prepare the soup as in No. 1430, and, when the flour is cooked, moisten it with three quarts of chicken or veal broth, stirring it until it boils. Then set it on the side of the fire to boil slowly for twenty-five minutes, and season with salt and pepper.

When ready to serve, prepare the following: Dilute a pint of milk with the yolks of eight raw eggs and six ounces of butter. Add this to the soup, stirring it well until the butter is melted. Cut two French rolls in fine slices, brown them in the oven, and put them in a soup tureen. Then pour the soup over them and serve.

PRESERVED SORREL.

No. 1433.—Wash and trim the Sorrel and put it in a saucepan with one quart of water. Then set it on a brisk fire, stirring it until it is melted. Then drain it in a colander and let it stand for one hour. After this rub it through a fine sieve and put it in quart tin cans or in jars. Close them hermetically, and boil them in a hot water bath for one hour and a half. When ready to use, finish it the same as in Nos. 1426 and 1427.

ARTICLE CC.

French   **SOUTHERWOOD, OR BALM-MINT.**   **German**
Aurome Citronnelle.   *Stabwurz.*

No. 1434.—This is a hardy shrubby plant, which is propagated by dividing the roots. The leaves, which are pale-green in color, are divided into narrow, thread-like segments, and have a strong, resinous, aromatic and pleasant odor, but are bitter to the taste. The root is seldom used, but the leaves and young branches are employed in the same manner and for the same purposes as common wormwood.

ARTICLE CCI.

French   **SPANISH OYSTER PLANT.**   **German**
Salsifis.   *Haferwurz.*

No. 1435.—This is generally treated as an annual plant when cultivated. The roots are almost white, fleshy, long and tapering in their general form. When they are bruised, a thick, viscous fluid exudes, which is almost flavorless, and of a milky-white color. It is cultivated exclusively for its roots, which are taken up in September or October, and are served during the winter. They have a pleasant, delicate flavor, and are healthful and nutritious. They are prepared the same as Salsify or Oyster Plant. See Article CLXXXII.

CULTURE.

No. 1436.—Sow the seeds in April, in drills fourteen inches apart, and cover them with one inch of soil. Thin the young plants out to five inches apart, and during the summer treat the growing crops as you would parsnips or carrots.

ARTICLE CCII.

SPEARMINT.
Menthe Verte.   *Frauenmünze.*

No. 1437.—Spearmint is a hardy perennial plant, and is generally cultivated in gardens, but grows naturally about springs of water, and in rich, wet localities. It may be grown from seed, but is propagated best by a division of the roots, which are long and creeping, and readily establish themselves wherever they are planted. The roots may be set either in autumn or spring. Spearmint is used mixed in salads and boiled with green peas, and with the addition of sugar and vinegar forms a much esteemed relish for roasted lamb. The common Mint is superior to Spearmint for every purpose.

ARTICLE CCIII.

French
Epice.

SPICES.

German
Würze.

No. 1438.—Spices are used to season, aromatize and enrich numerous culinary preparations. They are all vegetable substances with the exception of salt. Their importance cannot be overestimated as they are used constantly, yet often wrongfully. The art of spicing or seasoning properly is one that must be acquired, and experience is the best teacher. Many preparations would be indigestible and almost tasteless without the use of spices. Salt is probably used most, and after it comes the onions, shallots, chives, and garlic. The onion is used principally as an alimentary substance, while the others may be considered energetic stimulants to the appetite. High seasoning is more in vogue in the Southern States and in all warm climates, than in the North. The French, as a rule, use less strong spices in cooking than any other nation, preferring aromatic herbs instead, which answer the same purpose and are less exciting. India furnishes the major portion of strong spices, such as mulligatawny, chutney, curry, etc.

SPICES FOR SALTED BEEF.

No. 1439.—Home-made spices are far superior to many of those bought from dealers, as the latter kinds are generally adulterated, and if not kept tightly corked lose their aromatic flavor by evaporation. The following is the best recipe for making Spices for salted beef: Procure the following quantities of dried herbs: Two ounces each of thyme, sage, nutmeg, cloves, mace, and bay leaves; three ounces of white pepper, and one ounce each of marjoram and rosemary. Then pound each kind separately in a mortar and sift them through a fine sieve. Put the mixture in bottles and keep them tightly corked. When ready to use it add one ounce of the Spice to one pound of salt.

SPICED SALT, FOR STUFFINGS.

No. 1440.—Procure the following quantities of dried herbs: One-half of an ounce each of powdered thyme, cloves, nutmeg, white or black pepper, and one-quarter of an ounce each of powdered bay leaves, marjoram, and red pepper. Mix them with one and a half pounds of fine salt, then put them in bottles and keep them tightly corked. Use it for stuffing.

INFUSION OF SPICES FOR TURTLE SOUP.

No. 1441.—Put a few fresh marjoram leaves in a saucepan and add equal quantities of thyme, basil, savory and parsley, with two bay leaves, three chopped shallots, and some trimmings of fresh mushrooms. (Dried mushrooms can be used if desired.) Then boil one pint of good Maderia wine and pour it over the herbs, etc. Cover the saucepan tightly, and in half an hour strain the infusion through a napkin and add it to a clear turtle soup.

NOTE.—Should the turtle soup be thick instead of clear, use powdered spices instead of leaves and add them to the stock.

MIXED SPICES.

No. 1442.—The following mixture of Spices will always be found useful in the kitchen. Procure the following quantities of ground Spices: Eight ounces of thyme, one ounce of bay leaves, half an ounce of marjoram, half an ounce of rosemary, one and a half ounces of nutmeg, one and a half ounces of cloves, one ounce of white pepper, and half an ounce of red pepper. Mix them well together, put them in bottles and keep them tightly corked. These Spices may be used as they are, or may be mixed with salt. Three ounces of Spice is the proper quantity for three-quarters of a pound of salt.

SPICED SAUCE.

No. 1443.—Put in a bowl a teaspoonful of ground cloves, one ounce of Anchovy paste, half a teaspoonful of cayenne pepper, and a wine-glassful each of walnut and tomato catchup (strained). Add to this one and a half quarts of white wine vinegar, and mix it well together. Then put it in an earthen jar, cover it, and set it in a saucepan containing water. Let it boil for two hours; then take out the jar, set it aside for a week, and then filter the sauce. Put it in bottles and cork them tightly.

SPICES, HERBS AND FLAVORS.

No. 1444.—The following Spices, Herbs and Flavors should always be kept in every family kitchen: Fine and coarse salt, whole and ground red, white and black pepper, cloves, allspice, nutmeg, mace, dried thyme, sage, marjoram, bay leaves, and the mixed spices; garlic, shallots, English mustard, powdered and stick cinnamon. The flavors are vanilla, lemon, orange, orange-flower water, olive oil, wine, tarragon and Chili pepper vinegar; granulated, powdered and cube white sugar and brown sugar.

ARTICLE CCIV.

French
Epinard.

SPINACH OR SPINAGE.

German
Spinat.

No. 1445.—Spinach is a hardy annual plant, and is said to be of Asiatic origin. The leaves and young stems are the only parts of the plant that are used, being extremely wholesome and palatable, and retaining their bright green color after being cooked. The leaves are smooth and oval-oblong shaped, though varying in the different varieties. Spinach is prepared in various ways and is eaten with almost every kind of meat. The expressed juice is used to impart a greenish color to certain dishes. It affords but little nourishment, but when eaten freely, is mildly laxative, diuretic and cooling.

CULTURE.

No. 1446.—It should be planted in very rich ground. Sow it a foot apart, in drills, and commence thinning out the plants when the leaves are an inch wide. When they are two or three inches wide, they will be fit to gather. This is done by cutting them up with a knife entirely to the bottom, or by only cropping the large outer leaves. The root and heart should remain to shoot out again according to the season.

FLANDERS SPINACH.

No. 1447.—This is a winter variety, and is considered superior to the Prickly Spinach which is in general cultivation during the winter season. The seeds are sown about the last of August, in drills one foot apart and nearly an inch deep. The Prickly-seeded Spinach is cultivated and used the same way as this variety.

LETTUCE-LEAVED SPINACH.

No. 1448.—This is a fine productive variety, having short stems and large leaves that are rounded and of a deep green color tinged with blue.

SORREL-LEAVED SPINACH.

No. 1449.—The leaves are pointed, of medium size, deep green, thick and fleshy.

SUMMER ROUND-LEAVED SPINACH.

No. 1450.—This variety should be sown early in spring, but it soon runs to seed, particularly in warm, dry weather. The leaves are large, round, thick and fleshy.

WINTER COMMON PRICKLY SPINACH.

No. 1451.—This is a hardy perennial plant that is prepared in the same way as the common Spinach. The leaves are arrow-shaped, smooth, deep green, undulated on the borders, and mealy on the under surface.

HOW TO PREPARE SPINACH FOR BOILING.

No. 1452.—Remove the large stems, wash the leaves in plenty of cold water, and drain them in a colander. Then put them in a saucepan containing some lightly salted boiling water and, with a wooden spoon, keep the Spinach under the water, letting it boil over a brisk fire until cooked. Then immerse it in cold water, drain it, and press out all of the water.

SPINACH, ENGLISH STYLE.

No. 1453.—Prepare and cook the Spinach as in No. 1452. Let it remain entire, or, if desired, chop it coarsely and put it in a saucepan with a piece of butter. Season with salt and pepper and, when it is thoroughly warmed, serve it plain, or garnish it with slices of boiled bacon.

SPINACH, AMERICAN STYLE.

No. 1454.—Prepare and cook the Spinach as in No. 1452; then chop it finely and put it in a saucepan with a piece of butter. Season with salt, pepper and a pinch of nutmeg; stir it well with a wooden spoon, and when it is thoroughly warmed, add a few spoonfuls of veal gravy. Then serve it, having the dish garnished with hard-boiled eggs cut in quarters, or small pieces of buttered toast cut in fancy shapes.

SPINACH WITH GRAVY, FRENCH STYLE.

No. 1455.—Prepare and cook the Spinach as in No. 1452, and chop it finely. Then put four ounces of butter in a saucepan and, when it is melted, add two soup-spoonfuls of flour and let it cook to a light-brown. Then add three large handfuls of the chopped Spinach, stir it in well with a wooden spoon, then add some veal broth, and season with salt, pepper, and a pinch of nutmeg. Before serving add a piece of butter and garnish the dish with poached eggs, or small pieces of toasted bread.

SPINACH WITH MILK, AMERICAN STYLE.

No. 1456.—Prepare and cook the Spinach as in No. 1445, using boiled milk instead of meat gravy.

SPINACH WITH CREAM SAUCE.

No. 1457.—Prepare and cook the Spinach as in No. 1445, then press out all of the water and chop it finely. Put four ounces of butter in a saucepan, and when it is lightly browned add three handfuls of the chopped Spinach. Stir it well with a wooden spoon, while adding a cup of cream, and season with salt, pepper, and nutmeg. (Two spoonfuls of Cream or Allemande sauce may also be added, if desired.) Serve with hard boiled eggs, cut in halves, and arranged around the dish.

SPINACH, PIEMONTAISE.

No. 1458.—Prepare and cook the Spinach as in No. 1452, and chop it finely. Then put a piece of butter in a saucepan, and when it is melted add a little finely chopped garlic, and shortly after, add three handfuls of the chopped Spinach and a spoonful of Anchovy paste. Mix them well together, season with salt and pepper and add two spoonfuls of light Espagnole sauce. Before serving garnish the dish with poached eggs, or small pieces of toasted bread.

SPINACH FOR GARNITURES.

No. 1459.—Spinach prepared as in No. 1453, is used as a garniture for boiled bacon, pigs' jowl, or any large joints when Spinach is served with them.

Spinach prepared as in Nos. 1455, 1456 and 1457, is served as a garniture for braised meats, entrees, or any kind of broiled or fried meat, especially veal and lamb.

SPINACH FRITTERS (SUBRICS).

No. 1460.—Chop one quart of boiled Spinach finely and put it in a flat saucepan with four spoonfuls of Cream or Allemande sauce. Reduce it on a brisk fire and then set it on the side of the fire,

Season with salt, pepper and nutmeg, and add a small piece of butter and the yolks of eight raw eggs. Mix the whole well together and set it aside to get cold. Then put some clarified butter in a frying pan, and drop the Spinach into it, one spoonful at a time, and manage it so that they will not touch each other. Fry them nicely on both sides; then serve them on a napkin and garnish with fried parsley.

GREEN COLOR OF SPINACH.

No. 1461.—Pick, wash and drain five large handfuls of Spinach. Then put it in a mortar, pound it finely and add six glassfuls of cold water. After this, strain it through a towel, pressing it well to extract all of the moisture. Then put it in a saucepan on the fire, and just before it boils, set it on the side of the fire, keeping it at the boiling heat, but not allowing it to boil. Then drain it in a fine hair sieve. That which remains in the sieve is used for coloring.

Another way of making the green color is as follows: Throw three handfuls of Spinach in some boiling water, with a little parsley and chives. Let it remain there one minute; then immerse it in cold water, drain it, and press it dry. Then put it in a mortar, pound it finely, and rub it through a fine sieve. After this moisten it with a little cold white broth.

CREAM OF SPINACH.

No. 1462.—Put four soup-spoonfuls of finely-chopped cooked Spinach and one dozen sweet almonds in a mortar, and pound them into a fine paste. Then add four macaroons made with bitter almonds, and sweeten with sugar to taste. Pound the whole well, and then add a quart of cream and the yolks of ten raw eggs. Mix them well together and strain the mixture through a sieve. Put it in a small mould and cook it the same as a custard.

ARTICLE CCV.

French	SQUASH.	German
Courge.		*Kuerbis.*

No. 1463.—The Squash is one of the most nutritious and valuable of all garden vegetables. The summer varieties appear early, and are very palatable, while the winter sorts can be had in perfection in August. All of the varieties are tender annuals and thrive best in a warm temperature.

CULTURE.

No. 1464.—Plant them in warm weather, and cultivate them generally as you would cucumbers or melons, being particular about the soil. The summer varieties should be planted six feet apart each way, and the winter varieties at a distance of eight feet. Three plants are sufficient for one hill. Care should be taken not to injure or break the stems of those intended for winter use, as the slightest injury increases their liability to decay.

SUMMER VARIETIES.

APPLE SQUASH.

No. 1465.—This variety is healthy and vigorous, but not stocky. The skin is thin, tender and yellowish-white in color when young. It is hard and shell-like when ripe. When green and small, the flesh is dry and well flavored.

CROOKED NECK SUMMER BUSH SQUASH.

No. 1466.—This is a dwarf variety about two and a half feet high. The fruit is largest at the blossom end and tapers gradually to the neck, which is solid and more or less curved. The skin is tender, warty and easily broken. When young, the flesh is of a greenish-yellow color, dry and well flavored. It is one of the finest summer varieties, but is used only when young and tender and when the skin can be pierced easily. When the skin hardens the flesh becomes watery, strongly flavored and unfit for table use.

EARLY YELLOW SCALLOPED BUSH SQUASH.

No. 1467.—This is an erect, dwarf variety. The fruit is hemispherical in form, and expanded at the edge, which is deeply and regularly scalloped. It is yellow in color, and the skin, while young, is thin and easily pierced. When it matures the skin is hard and shell-like. The flesh is pale-yellow in color, finely grained and well flavored. It is not as dry as the summer crooked neck variety.

EGG SQUASH.

No. 1468.—This is an ornamental variety and is generally cultivated for its peculiar egg-like fruit, being seldom used for the table.

GREEN STRIPED BERGEN SQUASH.

No. 1469.—This variety, which is largely cultivated in the Eastern States, is early, but not very productive. It is eaten either when green or when fully ripe. It is a small and vigorous plant, with bell-shaped fruit of a dark green color, striped with white.

LARGE WARTED, CROOKED NECK SUMMER SQUASH.

No. 1470.—It is similar to the dwarf variety but much larger in size. The skin is of a clear, bright yellow color, with wart-like excrescences over the surface. The flesh is of a greenish-yellow color and is coarse in texture. It is hardy and productive.

ORANGE SQUASH.

No. 1471.—This variety is cultivated more as an ornament than for table use. The fruit is of the size, form and color of an orange.

AUTUMN AND WINTER VARIETIES.

AUTUMNAL MARROW SQUASH.

No. 1472.—The fruit is pointed at the extremities, and the stem is large and fleshy. The skin is thin and easily bruised or broken, having a creamy-yellow color when first ripened, which changes to red when the fruit remains on the plants after maturity. The flesh is of a salmon-yellow color, being dry, finely grained, sweet and excellent in flavor. If kept free from cold and dampness they may be preserved until March.

BUSH OR DWARF VEGETABLE, MARROW SQUASH.

No. 1473.—This is a small, early, hardy and productive variety. It will keep through the winter, but is not particularly excellent for table use. It is a good Squash for pie.

CANADA CROOKED NECK SQUASH.

No. 1474.—This variety is the smallest and best of its class, and will keep well all of the year. The skin is of moderate thickness, and of a creamy-yellow color when ripe, becoming darker, however, after maturity. The flesh is of a salmon-red color, closely grained, sweet and finely flavored.

CASHAW.

No. 1475.—There are two kinds of this variety. The first is nearly round and the other somewhat curved. The latter is the most desirable.

COCOA-NUT SQUASH.

No. 1476.—The fruit is oval, almost twenty inches long and ten inches in diameter. The thin skin is of an ashy-gray color, spotted with light drab. The flesh, which is of a deep orange-yellow color, is of medium thickness. The quality varies. Sometimes the flesh is finely grained, dry, sweet and of a rich nut-like flavor, but often some that are well matured are coarse, fibrous, watery and unfit for the table.

CUSTARD SQUASH.

No. 1477.—The fruit is oblong, and gathered in deep folds near the stem, having a creamy-white skin. The flesh is pale-yellow in color, but not particularly fine in texture, having, however, a good flavor.

EGG SHAPED SQUASH.

No. 1478.—The fruit is large, with a reddish skin. The flesh is red, firm, and excellent in flavor, being a good table Squash.

HONOLULU SQUASH.

No. 1479.—This variety has thick flesh, of a reddish-orange color, and good flavor. It keeps well, and is excellent for pies and table use.

HUBBARD SQUASH.

No. 1480.—The flesh is thick, finely grained, sweet, dry and of excellent flavor, which resembles that of roasted or boiled chestnuts.

MAMMOTH SQUASH.

No. 1481.—This is the largest fruited variety known, weighing from one hundred to two hundred pounds, if grown under favorable conditions. The fruit is round, and sometimes a little flattened on the under side. It is used only when full grown, but will keep through the winter, if kept in a warm situation. The flesh is sweet, though generally coarsely grained and deep yellow in color. It is used for pies and soups.

TURBAN SQUASH.

No. 1482.—This is classed as one of the best varieties, although its keeping qualities are not good. It is fit for use early in autumn.

VEGETABLE MARROW SQUASH.

No. 1483.—The skin is hard, and of a pale yellow color when perfectly ripe. The flesh is white, tender and succulent, even until the seeds are ripe, and may be used in any stage of its growth. It will keep through the winter, when perfectly ripe, if stored in a dry place out of the reach of frost.

WILDER SQUASH.

No. 1484.—This kind is superior to many of the other varieties for pies and culinary purposes.

WINTER CROOKED-NECK SQUASH.

No. 1485.—This is a hardy productive variety, that ripens with great certainty, and suffers less from insects than the other sorts. It keeps well.

WINTER, STRIPED, CROOKED-NECK SQUASH.

No. 1486.—This variety is hardy, prolific and large, and keeps well.

YOKOHAMA SQUASH.

No. 1487.—A roundish, somewhat flattened, Japanese variety, strongly ribbed. The skin is warted, and deep green in color when young, changing to a dull yellow. The flesh is of an orange-yellow color, finely grained, dry and sweet.

MASHED SQUASH.

No. 1488.—Peel the Squash, cut it in scallops, and put them in a saucepan containing sufficient water to cover them. Add a little salt, cover the pan, and set it on a brisk fire to boil. When they are cooked, drain them, and then rub them through a colander. Then put them back in the saucepan, season with salt and pepper, add a piece of butter, mix them well and let them get thoroughly warmed. The Squash may also be steamed the same as potatoes.

NOTE.—All varieties of Squash are prepared in the same manner.

STUFFED SQUASH, ROMAN STYLE.

No. 1489.—Select two dozen small, young, and tender Squash. Cut off the top of each and scoop out the center, leaving the shell half an inch stick. Parboil them for three minutes, then drain them on a napkin with the open side at the bottom.

Now chop two white onions finely, put them in a saucepan with a small piece of butter, and fry them lightly. Cut the Squash that was scooped out in small pieces, put them in the saucepan with a little broth, and let them cook until the broth is reduced to a glaze. Then add one quarter of a pound of roast lamb cut in small pieces, one quarter of a pound of rice that has been cooked in broth, and a little finely chopped parsley. Season with salt and pepper and add four spoonfuls of reduced Espagnole sauce. Mix the whole well together over the fire. Fill the Squash with this stuffing, put them in a flat saucepan lined with thin slices of fat pork, and moisten them with broth. Set them in the oven to cook slowly and, when nicely browned, dish them up. Pour a teaspoonful of reduced plain Tomato sauce over each Squash and serve separately a bowl of Tomato sauce.

STUFFED SQUASH, STANFORD STYLE.

No. 1490.—Prepare the Squash as in No. 1489. Chop two large onions finely, put them in a saucepan with a piece of butter or sweet oil and fry them lightly. Then add the Squash and, when the moisture is reduced, add two handfuls of fresh bread crumbs. Season with salt, pepper and nutmeg, add a little finely chopped parsley and the yolks of four raw eggs and mix the whole well together. Stuff the Squash with this preparation, sprinkle bread crumbs over them and put a piece of butter on top of each one. Put them in a buttered baking pan, bake them slowly in the oven until nicely browned, and serve them with a reduced Madeira wine sauce.

FRIED STUFFED SQUASH, AMERICAN STYLE.

No. 1491.—Prepare, stuff and bake the Squash as in No. 1490. Then let them get cold. Now peel them and cut them in halves. Roll them in fresh bread crumbs, dip them in beaten eggs and bread them again. Then fry them in hot lard and serve them on a napkin with a brown Italian sauce separate.

FRIED SQUASH, BOSTON STYLE.

No. 1492.—Peel half a dozen Squash, cut them in scallops half an inch thick, throw them into boiling water for three minutes, and then drain them. Put them into an earthen bowl, season with salt and pepper, and let them remain there for one hour, tossing them over occasionally. Then dry them on a napkin, roll them in flour, fry them in hot lard, and serve them on a napkin.

SQUASH, SPANISH STYLE.

No. 1493.—Peel one dozen Squash, cut them in quarters, trim them, and parboil them for three minutes. Then drain them dry, arrange them in a flat saucepan lined with thin slices of fat pork, and moisten them with broth to cover. Season with salt and pepper, add a faggot of parsley garnished with a sprig of thyme and one bay leaf, and cook them on a brisk fire. When the broth is reduced to one-quarter, the Squash will be cooked. Then take them out, strain the broth into another saucepan, skim off the grease, and add two spoonfuls of reduced Espagnole sauce. Then add the Squash with a little finely-chopped parsley, and serve.

SCALLOPED SQUASH, ASTOR STYLE.

No. 1494.—Peel half a dozen small, young and tender Squash. Cut them in quarters, trim the edges, and parboil them for three minutes. Then drain and dry them, and put them into a flat saucepan with some clarified butter. Season with salt and pepper. Cover the saucepan and let them cook slowly until nicely glazed. Dish them up, and add to the gravy in the saucepan a small piece of butter, the juice of half a lemon and some finely-chopped parsley. Stir it well, off of the fire, until the butter is melted; then pour it over the scallops, and serve them hot.

Article CCVI.

STRAWBERRY TOMATO, OR ALKEKENGI.

French — *Tomate (fraise.)*   German — *Lieberapfel Erdbeere.*

No. 1495.—This is a hardy annual plant common to the Southern States. They are prolific and will thrive in almost any kind of soil. The fruit has a juicy pulp, and when first tasted has a pleasant, strawberry-like flavor with a certain degree of sweetness and acidity combined. The after taste, however, is much less agreeable, being similar to that of the common Tomato. The fruit is served raw with the addition of lemon juice, and is also preserved like plums and stewed and served like cranberries. Sow and cultivate them the same as the common Tomatoes.

PURPLE ALKEKENGI.

No. 1496.—The fruit is roundish and of a deep purple color, being more acidulous, less perfumed, and not as palatable. In its raw state it is a superior variety for preserving.

SCARLET ALKEKENGI.

No. 1497.—The fruit is of a brilliant scarlet color at maturity. The plant is highly ornamental. The Fall and Common Yellow Alkekengi are similar to it, except in color.

ARTICLE CCVII.

<small>French
Patate.</small>   **SWEET POTATOES.**   <small>German
B.taten.</small>

No. 1498.—The Sweet Potato is a native of the East and West Indies, where it grows natural as a perennial plant, but when cultivated it is always treated as an annual. They thrive well in the Southern States, but those grown in the North are much inferior, as the plants seldom blossom and the tubers never ripen perfectly. Though numerous varieties are cultivated, none can compare with those grown in the South.

CULTURE.

No. 1499.—The Sweet Potato is cultivated much in the same manner as our common potato, and succeeds best in light warm soil, which should be deeply stirred and well enriched. The slips or sprouts are planted twelve inches apart in ridges that are four feet wide. Give the plants ordinary culture in the summer, and early in October the tubers will have attained their growth and will be ready for harvesting. The slips or sprouts are generally obtained by setting the tubers in a hot-bed in March and breaking off the sprouts from them when they are five inches high. For transplanting in a favorable season the plucking may be repeated about four times. In setting out the slips the lower part should be sunk one-half of their depth, and when dry weather occurs water should be applied moderately. Dryness and a warm and even temperature are essential for the preservation of Sweet Potatoes, for if these conditions are not supplied the tubers will decay rapidly. They may be preserved until spring by packing them in dry sand and storing them in a warm dry room.

NANSEMOND.

No. 1500.—This is an early variety that matures in short seasons. It is very productive and succeeds well in almost any tillable soil. It does particularly well in the Northern States. The tubers are large, yellow, dry, unctuous, sweet, and well flavored.

LARGE WHITE.

No. 1501.—This variety requires a long season for its full development, and will succeed well in the Middle States. The tubers are large, the skin of a dusky white color, and the flesh is nearly white, with a shade of yellow, being farinaceous and well flavored, but not finely grained.

KENTUCKY EARLY RED.

No. 1502.—The tubers are of medium size, with a red or purplish-red skin, the flesh being yellow, dry, sweet and of good quality.

PURPLE SKINNED.

No. 1503.—The skin is smooth and of a reddish-purple color, and the flesh is finely grained, sugary and of excellent quality. This variety is early and does not keep well.

AMERICAN RED.

No. 1504.—The tubers are long, slender, and of a purplish-red color. The flesh is yellow, finely grained, unctuous, sugary and farinaceous. It is hardy, and an abundant bearer, but does not keep well.

ROSE-COLORED.

No. 1505.—This variety is hardy, productive, and keeps well. The tubers are large, egg-shaped, and often grooved or furrowed. The skin is of a rose color, shaded with yellow, while the flesh is sweet, and has a pleasant nut-like flavor.

YELLOW SKINNED, OR YELLOW CAROLINA.

No. 1506.—This is a favorite variety in North and South Carolina. The tubers are from six to ten inches long, smooth, and of a yellowish color. The flesh is yellow, finely grained, and very sugary.

BAKED SWEET POTATOES.

No. 1507.—Wash the Potatoes in cold water, and dry them. Then put them in the oven, turning them occasionally to have them cooked evenly, and, when done, serve them on a napkin.

NOTE.—In the Southern States they are served in cups that are similar to egg cups. Cut off the top end, scoop out a teaspoonful of the Potato, and put in its place a piece of fresh butter.

BOILED SWEET POTATOES.

No. 1508.—Sweet Potatoes are boiled or steamed in the same manner as common potatoes. When cold they are peeled, sliced and fried in butter.

FRIED SWEET POTATOES.

No. 1509.—When raw, the Sweet Potatoes are fried in the same manner as common potatoes. When they have been boiled, the large Potatoes should be sliced lengthwise, and the small ones left entire, before being fried.

FRIED SWEET POTATOES, PUFFED (SOUFFLÉ).

No. 1510.—Peel some medium-sized Sweet Potatoes, and slice them lengthwise in pieces one-quarter of an inch thick. Fry them in lard that is not too hot, and when soft, drain them. Then let the lard get hot again, after which throw the Potatoes in, turning them with the skimmer for a few minutes. When they get puffed and browned, drain them on a napkin. Season with salt and pepper, and serve them on a napkin.

SWEET POTATO FRITTERS.

No. 1511.—Peel half a dozen boiled Sweet Potatoes, cut off both ends, and then slice them in pieces half an inch thick and one inch wide. Put them in an earthen bowl, moisten them with a wineglassful of brandy, add the peeling of one lemon, and allow them to macerate for half an hour. Then drain them, dip them in a batter, fry them in hot lard until nicely browned, and drain them. Serve them on a napkin and sprinkle powdered sugar over them.

CREAM OF SWEET POTATOES, FOR PIES.

No. 1512.—Boil or steam one dozen Sweet Potatoes. When they are three-quarters done, put them on a pan in the oven to bake.

When they are cooked, peel them and pound them through a colander. Then add two eggs and the yolks of four raw eggs, six ounces of butter, a pinch of salt, and half a pound of macaroons ground into crumbs. Flavor it with lemon flavor, or one wine-glassful of rum, and sweeten with sugar. Then mix the whole well together.

CAROLINA CAKE, WITH SABAYON SAUCE.

No. 1513.—Prepare two dozen Sweet Potatoes as in No. 1512, and pound them through a fine colander. Have a cream ready made of three pints of milk with one pound of corn-starch. Add it to the Potatoes, mix them well together and, when cold, add half a pound of citron cut in small square pieces, half a pound of stoned raisins, one-quarter of a pound of currants, and half a pint of rum. While mixing them well together, add in slowly four raw eggs and the yolks of one dozen raw eggs, and sweeten it to taste. Now prepare some small pudding moulds, butter and flour them and fill them with the above preparation. Put the moulds in a pan containing an inch of water, and set in a moderate oven to bake. Serve them with Sabayon sauce.

NOTE.—A square pan with an inch border may be used instead of the moulds. Butter a paper on both sides, place it in the bottom of the pan and also butter the sides of the pan. Then flour it and put in the preparation, cooking it the same as above. When ready for use turn it out on a board, cut in pieces and serve with a Saboyan sauce. When the Cake is cold, it can be cut in pieces three inches long and half an inch thick, which should be dipped in beaten eggs, then rolled in bread crumbs and shaped nicely. Then fry them in hot lard and serve them as croquettes.

CAROLINA FRITTERS, NELLIE GRANT STYLE.

No. 1514.—Prepare the Potatoes as in No. 1513, and bake the cake in a square pan. When it is cold, cut it in round pieces with a round cutter about the size of half a dollar. Then dip them in a batter considerably thinner than you would use for queen fritters, and made of the same ingredients. Serve them with a Madeira wine or Hard sauce.

SWEET POTATO PUDDING.

No. 1515.—Steam half a dozen medium sized Sweet Potatoes, and when they are cooked peel them and pound them through a fine colander. Add four ounces of butter, sweeten with sugar to taste, flavor with lemon flavor, and add the yolks of six raw eggs. Mix them well together, and then add half a pound of mixed fruit cut in small pieces and cooked in a syrup. When the mixture is cold, add the whites of six eggs beaten to a froth, and mix it gently. Then put the mixture in small pudding moulds, which have been buttered and floured, and steam them, or bake them, as you would Carolina cake in No. 1513.

SWEET POTATOES, SPANISH STYLE.

No. 1516.—Boil one dozen Sweet Potatoes and, when they are cold, peel them and then cut them in slices one-quarter of an inch thick. Put some clarified butter in a frying pan and, when it is warm, add a layer of potatoes and fry them on both sides. Then drain them and serve them on a napkin.

ARTICLE CCVIII.

SWISS CHARD, OR SEA KALE BEET.

French
Carde Poirée.

German
Yunge Mangoldpflanze.

No. 1517.—The Swiss Chard, Silver or Sea Kale Beet, is a distinct vegetable, and is much superior to the common beet for greens. If sown at the same time, it will be fit to use before them. Later, the plants form broad, flat, beautiful white wax-like stems to the leaves, which are very delicious. For preparation, see Sea Kale, Nos. 1398, 1399, 1400 and 1401.

ARTICLE CCIX.

TANSY.

Tanaisie. *Wurmkraut.*

No. 1518.—Tansy is a hardy, herbaceous, perennial plant. The stem is about three feet high. The leaves are finely toothed and divided on the margin, and of a rich, deep green color. When it is cultivated for its leaves, the flowering shoots should be cut off as they make their appearance. The leaves have a strong aromatic odor and a bitter taste. It possesses the tonic and stomachic properties common to bitter herbs, but is seldom used for culinary purposes. There are three varieties. The curled leaved Tansy differs from the common variety in its curled or frilled leaves. The large leaved variety is less fragrant, and the variegated-leaved variety has a peculiar color. Tansy is propagated by dividing the roots, as the variegated character of the foliage is not produced from seeds.

ARTICLE CCX.

French *Tapioca, or Manioca.*   **TAPIOCA, OR MANIOCA.**   **German** *Tapioca.*

No. 1519.—Tapioca is a coarsely granular substance obtained by heating, and thus partly changing the moistened starch obtained from the roots of the *Janipha manihot*, a plant which is a native of Brazil. There are two chief varieties, and about thirty sub-varieties. The root of the sweet cassavas may be eaten with impunity; that of the bitter, which is the most extensively cultivated, abounds in an acrid, milky juice, which renders it highly poisonous if eaten in the recent state. The root is prepared for use by washing, scraping and grating or grinding it into a pulp, which, in the bitter variety, is submitted to pressure so as to separate the deleterious juice. It is now in the state of meal or powder, which is made into bread, cakes or puddings. As the poisonous principle is volatile, the portion which may have remained in the meal is entirely dissipated by the heat employed in cooking. Being nutritious, and at the same time easy of digestion, and destitute of irritating properties, Tapioca forms an excellent diet for the sick and convalescent. It is prepared for use by boiling it in water, and is used, like sago, in soups and puddings. A factitious Tapioca, known as Pearl Tapioca, is made from potato starch, and is sometimes sold as the genuine article.

NOTE.—The Tapioca obtained from grocers in the United States, is in the form of hard, white, irregular, rough grains. That which is sold under the name of Manioca, is smaller and finer, being preferred to the large Tapioca.

TAPIOCA SOUP, WITH BROTH OR CONSOMME.

No. 1520.—Put four quarts of consomme or broth in a saucepan, and when it boils, drop in it eight ounces of Tapioca or Manioca slowly while stirring it. Let it boil up once, and then set it on the side of the fire to boil slowly until cooked. Then skim it and serve.

ARTICLE CCXI.

French
Estragon.

TARRAGON.

German
Dragun.

No. 1521.—Tarragon is a hardy perennial plant, originally from Siberia. It is cultivated for its young shoots and leaves, the latter being long-pointed, smooth and aromatic. Both are used as ingredients in salads, pickles, soups, etc.

CULTURE.

No. 1522.—Tarragon is propagated annually by dividing the roots. Select a warm, dry situation in April, and set the shoots in rows, fifteen inches apart, and cover them with three inches of soil. It is sometimes improved by cutting, when they are set three inches apart in moist earth. When not allowed to run to flower, the plants will be more healthy, and of finer quality, and will yield more abundantly.

TARRAGON VINEGAR, PLAIN.

No. 1523.—This is made by an infusion of the leaves in wine vinegar, and is greatly esteemed with salads.

TARRAGON VINEGAR, FRENCH STYLE.

No. 1524.—Put in a demijohn two gallons of wine vinegar, four green bell-peppers cut in quarters, and one dozen shallots. Cork it tightly and set it in the cellar for four weeks. Then strain it through a flannel, put it in bottles, cork them tightly, and keep them in a cool place.

ARTICLE CCXII.

Thé.

TEA.

Thee.

No. 1525.—The Tea plant is a native of China and Japan, being cultivated extensively in both countries. In Japan it forms hedgerows around the rice and cornfields; in China, whence immense quantities of Tea are exported, whole fields are devoted to its culture. It is propagated from seeds, and in three years the plant yields leaves for collection, and in six years attains a height of five or six feet. After the leaves are gathered they are dried by artificial heat, and while hot are rolled in the palms of the hands, so as to be brought into the form in which they are found in commerce. The odor of the Tea leaves themselves is very slight, and it is customary to mix with them the flowers of certain aromatic plants, as those of the orange, jasmine, rose, etc., in order to render them pleasant to the smell. The flowers are afterwards separated by sifting. There are two principal varieties— the green and the black—which differ considerably in flavor and strength. By chemical tests it has been ascertained that green Tea is colored by sulphate of calcium and Prussian blue. Tea is astringent and gently excitant, and in its finer varieties exerts a decided influence over the nervous system, producing exhilaration and wakefulness. When taken moderately it is perfectly harmless, but in large quantities it produces nervousness, dyspepsia, and excites the brain and stomach. Green Tea is more injurious than black Tea, and should not be used by those who are dyspeptic.

TO MAKE TEA.

No. 1526.—Tea is made in several different ways.

The Chinese, who are supposed to know something about it, put a few Tea leaves in a cup, then pour boiling water over the leaves, and let them steep for a few minutes, having placed a saucer over the cup to keep the essence from evaporating. The liquid is then strained into another cup, previously warmed with hot water, and is ready for use. They use neither milk nor sugar, claiming that they injure the delicate aroma of the Tea, which is true.

The general method of making Tea in America is as follows: Use an earthen tea-pot in preference to one of metal. Scald the pot well; then put in the quantity of Tea desired, set the pot on the stove, pour over the Tea sufficient boiling water to cover it, and let it stand ten minutes to draw. Keep the cover on the pot, and do not let the Tea boil. Then pour in as much boiling water as is desired, and the Tea is ready for use. Do not pour water over Tea unless it is boiling hot, as unboiled water will not extract the flavor from the Tea leaves, and will spoil the Tea. Never let Tea boil after it is made. Use the tea-pot only for making Tea. Use cold cream in Tea.

TEA, RUSSIAN STYLE.

No. 1527.—An agreeable beverage is made as follows: Peel some fresh, juicy lemons, and slice them in thin pieces. Put one piece in the bottom of each cup, sprinkle it with white sugar, and then pour in the hot Tea. Sometimes the lemon peel is not removed, which imparts a slightly bitter taste to the Tea.

ICED TEA.

No. 1528.—A delicious cold beverage for summer is made by making some mixed Tea (black and green), putting it in bottles, and setting them on the ice to cool. When ready to serve, pour the Tea in goblets, that contain some cracked ice, and sweeten it with sugar. A little champagne or rum may be added to each glass, if desired, but never add milk.

AFTER-DINNER TEA.

No. 1529.—Tea may be served after dinner the same as coffee. Serve with some double cream or brandy or rum, whichever may be desired. Sandwiches or small cakes usually accompany it.

TEA FOR INVALIDS.

No. 1530.—Put the yolk of one raw egg and a teaspoonful of sugar in a bowl and mix them well together. Dilute it with four soup-spoonfuls of cold milk, then add a cup of hot Tea slowly while stirring it briskly. Serve immediately.

TEA CUSTARD, IN CUPS.

No. 1531.—Make a cupful of the best strong Tea and set it aside to cool. Then put the yolks of twelve raw eggs in a saucepan and add half a pound of powdered sugar. Mix them well together with a wooden spoon and then dilute it with the cold Tea. Add in slowly one quart of cooled boiled milk, stirring it gently. Then strain the mixture through a fine sieve and put it in custard cups. Set the cups in a flat saucepan containing hot water, which must reach up to the middle of the cups. Put the pan in a moderate oven, and as soon as the custard becomes firm take it out. Cover it if desired, while cooking. Do not let the water boil, or the custard will be full of little holes, instead of being solid throughout.

NOTE.—Coffee custard may be made in the same way by using a cupful of strong, black coffee, instead of Tea.

ARTICLE CCXIII.

THYME.

French — *Thym.*
German — *Thymian.*

No. 1532.—There are two species of Thyme cultivated for culinary purposes: the Common Garden, and the Lemon or Evergreen Thyme, both of which are hardy perennial plants, having a shrubby character and a comparatively long growth. The leaves have an agreeable, aromatic taste, and are used for flavoring soups, stuffings and sauces. They should be used with moderation, as too much imparts a bitter taste to the substance.

CULTURE.

No. 1533.—They are propagated from seeds, or by dividing the roots; but the finest plants are produced from seeds. Sow them in April, in shallow drills twelve inches apart. They should be thinned out to eight inches apart, and all weeds should be carefully removed. They may be cut for use as soon as they have made sufficient growth; but for drying, the stalks are gathered as they come into flower.

BROAD-LEAVED THYME.

No. 1534.—This is the favorite variety. The stem is shrubby, of a brownish color, and much branched. The leaves are small, green above and whitish beneath.

NARROW-LEAVED THYME.

No. 1535.—The leaves are long, narrow and sharply pointed.

LEMON THYME.

No. 1536.—This is a low green shrub, with a somewhat trailing stem. It is distinguished from the other varieties by the soft, pleasant, lemon-like odor of the young shoots and leaves.

ARTICLE CCXIV.

TOMATO.

Tomate. *Liebesapfel.*

No. 1537.—The Tomato is a half-hardy annual plant, originally from South America. It is very extensively used in the United

States, being served on the table the entire year in different forms, and is one of the most healthful and best of all garden vegetables. The plant, when full grown, is about eight feet high, with a branching irregular recumbent stem and dense foliage. The fruit is red, white or yellow, and is exceedingly variable in size as well as form. The varieties are numerous, few of them appearing to be distinct or permanent. Much depends on the cultivation and the temperature of the soil.

CULTURE.

No. 1538.—The Tomato is raised from seed and succeeds best in light warm and not over rich soil. Success depends on securing a rapid, vigorous, unchecked growth during the early part of the season. Sow it in hot beds during March, or from six to eight weeks before they can be set out of doors. When the plants have four leaves transplant them into shallow boxes, setting them five inches apart. Give them plenty of air and endeavor to secure a vigorous but steady and healthful growth, so that, at the time of setting them in the open ground, they will be strong and stocky and about as broad as they are high. A slight check, while the plants are young, will materially diminish their productiveness. Set them out of doors as soon as danger from severe frost is over, but before doing so harden off the plants by gradually exposing them to the night air and by the withdrawal of water until the wood becomes hard and the leaves thick and of a dark green color. Transplant them carefully and cultivate well as long as the vines will permit. The fruit is improved in quality if the vines are tied to a trellis or to stakes. Sufficient plants for the garden of a small family may be started with little trouble by sowing a few seeds about the middle of March in a garden box or large flower pot and placing it in a sunny window of the kitchen. Transplant them in the open ground as soon as the weather will permit and the plant is strong enough.

To have an extra large and beautiful Tomato, as soon as a cluster of flowers is visible top the stems down to the cluster, so that the flowers terminate the stem. The effect is that the sap is immediately impelled into the two buds next below the cluster, which soon push strongly and produce another cluster of flowers each. When these are visible the branch on which they belong is also topped down to their level, and this is done five times successively. By this means the plants become stout dwarf bushes about eighteen inches high. In order to prevent their falling over, sticks or strings are stretched horizontally along the rows so as to keep the plants erect. In addition to this all laterals whatsoever are nipped off. In this way the ripe sap is directed into the fruit, which acquires a beauty, size and excellence that is unattainable by other means.

THE CARDINAL.

No. 1539.—In color it is remarkable, coloring right up to the calyx; and every specimen is of one color, and that is the most brilliant cardinal red, very glossy, and looking, when ripe, almost as if varnished. The flesh appears to have the same brilliant color, being but very little lighter in shade. They make the handsomest sliced Tomato, and have no green core. Its type is perfect, being uniformly smooth and free from any ridges. It is as early as any good Tomato, and is much larger in size than the average. It is exceedingly solid and firm, and of a vigorous growth, and comparatively compact in habit, with strong stalks, which bear abundantly throughout the season.

LIVINGSTON FAVORITE.

No. 15,0.—One of the largest and most perfect shaped varieties in cultivation. It ripens evenly and early, and keeps its size to the end of the season. It is very prolific, with but few seeds and has solid flesh.

MAYFLOWER.

No. 1541.—This is one of the earliest large Tomatoes grown. Its shape is perfectly globular, slightly flattened and smooth, of a glossy red color, and ripens evenly and well, close up to the stem.

PERFECTION.

No. 1542.—It is as early as the Canadian Victor; is almost round in shape, perfectly smooth, very firm, and of the best quality, bearing all through the season until frost. It ripens all over at the same time, and is blood-red in color.

ACME.

No. 1543.—This is one of the earliest and handsomest varieties. The fruit is of medium size, perfectly smooth and regular in shape, very firm, and a great bearer. Its color is quite distinct, being crimson with a pinkish tinge.

PARAGON.

No. 1544.—Same as the Acme in all respects, with the exception that the color is of a bright, glossy crimson, entirely free from the pinkish tinge.

THE TROPHY.

No. 1545.—This, when well grown is, without doubt, one of the best Tomatoes in cultivation. It is unsurpassed for flavor, productiveness and every other desired quality.

CHAMPION CLUSTER.

No. 1546.—A distinct and valuable variety, growing in clusters, from ten to twenty large sized, smooth and well shaped Tomatoes on one bunch. They are very smooth, and free from inequalities. The color is a rich dark crimson, and the flesh is very solid.

APPLE-SHAPED.

No. 1547.—The fruit is somewhat flattened, inclining towards a globular shape, deepened about the stem, but smooth and regular in its general outline. The skin is of a deep rich crimson color, and the flesh a bright rose color; the rind being thick and hard, and not readily reduced to a pulp when cooked. It is early and hardy, keeps well, and for salad is much esteemed.

THE CONQUEROR.

No. 1548.—One of the earliest varieties, with fruit of a good size and very uniform in shape.

BERMUDA.

No. 1549.—Extensively grown in the Southern States, and is of little value or merit when grown in the North. Its color is rose-red, and it varies considerable in size.

FEJEE.

No. 1550.—The fruit is either a bright red or pinkish color, very firm, well flavored, and is a good late Tomato.

ARLINGTON.

No. 1551.—This is one of the earliest varieties. The fruit is of a good size, and is very uniform in shape.

GENERAL GRANT.

No. 1552.—This is of a superior quality. The fruit is large and ripens rapidly and thoroughly.

FIG, OR RED PEAR.

No. 1553.—A small red pear-shaped species. The flesh is either pale-red or pink, and very firm. It is very little used except for preserving and for making Tomato figs.

YELLOW PLUM.

No. 1554.—A beautiful variety, used principally for pickling.

RED CHERRY.

No. 1555.—A small early variety of the size and shape of a cherry, and is used for pickling.

STRAWBERRY, OR WINTER CHERRY.

No. 1556.—The fruit has a pleasant strawberry-like flavor, and is much esteemed.

GREEN GAGE.

No. 1557.—Resembles a yellow plum in shape and color, and is excellent for preserving.

YELLOW CHERRY TOMATO.

No. 1558.—This is a yellow variety of the Red Cherry Tomato, differing only in color.

YELLOW PEAR, OR FIG SHAPED.

No. 1559.—A sub-variety of the red pear-shaped Tomato, with a clear, semi-transparent yellow skin and yellow flesh. It is used for pickling and preserving.

QUEEN.

No. 1560.—A variety speedily grown for canning. The fruit somewhat resembles the Trophy in appearance.

CANADA VICTOR.

No. 1561.—This is one of the earliest, of a medium size, and is very symmetrical in shape.

HATHAWAY'S EXCELSIOR.

No. 1562.—This is an early Tomato, medium sized, smooth, firm, and of excellent quality.

GOLDEN TROPHY.

No. 1563.—Identical in form and size with the Trophy, but its color is a beautiful canary-yellow, being sometimes streaked lightly with red. It is well suited for preserving, as well as for table use.

ISLAND BEAUTY.

No. 1564.—The fruit is large and medium early, resembling the Trophy in appearance, and is produced in clusters of about ten finely formed Tomatoes in a bunch. It is deep crimson in color, and of the best quality.

TOMATOES FOR RELISH.

No. 1565.—Select ripe and firm Tomatoes of equal size, wipe them clean and slice them an eighth of an inch thick. Serve them on relish dishes the same as cucumbers, with some finely sliced green onions around the edge of the dish. Or dip them into boiling water for one minute, then peel and slice them, sprinkle them with salt, and serve them plain or mixed with cucumbers, with some finely sliced green peppers on each end of the dish. Serve with them a mustard and oil sauce, into which add some finely chopped chives and parsley.

TOMATO SALAD, PLAIN.

No. 1566.—Peel and slice the Tomatoes as in No. 1565. Season them with salt, pepper, olive oil and vinegar, and garnish with finely sliced celery.

NOTE.—Raw Tomatoes may be used to garnish green salads.

TOMATO SALAD WITH CUCUMBERS.

No. 1567.—Peel and slice the Tomatoes as in No. 1565, and season them with salt and pepper. Then slice the same quantity of cucumbers, sprinkle them with salt and set them aside for twenty minutes. Then press out the water, and put them in a salad bowl with the Tomatoes. Add a little finely chopped parsley, a little oil and vinegar, and mix the whole well together without breaking the Tomatoes.

The Tomatoes can be put in a salad bowl with the cucumbers, and a light Mayonnaise sauce poured over them, with a little mustard and cream added to the sauce. Garnish with the hearts of lettuce.

TOMATO SALAD, SPANISH STYLE.

No. 1568.—Prepare the Tomatoes as in No. 1567, add some sliced green peppers, and season highly.

TOMATO SALAD, GERMAN STYLE.

No. 1569.—Prepare the Tomatoes as in No. 1567, add some sliced green onions and a little anise seed.

TOMATO SALAD, HESKETH STYLE.

No. 1570.—Peel the Tomatoes and slice them a quarter of an inch thick. Put a layer of them in a plate or dish and season them with salt and pepper. Then on these put another layer and season as before. Set them in a cool place for half an hour before using, in a slanting position, and, with a spoon, gather up the juice occasionally and pour it over the Tomatoes. When ready, dress them carefully in a salad bowl, with some finely chopped parsley over them. Mash the yolk of a hard boiled egg, and dilute it with oil, vinegar and cream. Season it with salt and pepper and pour this dressing over the Tomatoes when serving them.

FRIED TOMATOES.

No. 1571.—Slice the Tomatoes half an inch thick and season them with salt and pepper. Then sprinkle them with flour, and fry them in clarified butter. Serve them with fried parsley to garnish.

STEWED TOMATOES.

No. 1572.—Pour boiling water over the Tomatoes and peel them. Then cut them in quarters, put them in a saucepan, set it on the fire, and when they are cooked pound them through a colander into a saucepan, and set them on the fire again. When they boil add some fresh bread crumbs to thicken them, and season with salt, pepper, and a little sugar. Let them simmer for twenty minutes, and before serving add a piece of butter.

BAKED STEWED TOMATOES.

No. 1573.—Prepare them as in No. 1572, and put them in a buttered baking dish. Sprinkle bread crumbs over the tops, add a piece of butter, and bake them in a slow oven.

HOW TO PREPARE TOMATOES FOR STUFFING.

No. 1574.—Take Tomatoes of even size that are not too ripe. Slice off the end of the Tomato that adheres to the stalk, scoop out the centre without breaking the sides and set them in a pan upside down, so as to drain off all of the moisture. Save the parts scooped out and chop them finely, adding some finely chopped peeled Tomatoes with them, if necessary, and also to the stuffing intended for the Tomatoes.

STUFFED TOMATOES, PROVINCIAL STYLE.

No. 1575.—Prepare two dozen Tomatoes as in No. 1574. Chop half a dozen shallots finely and put them in a saucepan with a piece of butter or a little sweet oil, and fry them lightly. Then add half a pound of finely chopped mushrooms and the finely chopped Tomatoes. Let them cook until the moisture is almost reduced. Then add a handful of fresh bread crumbs, a little finely chopped parsley and cooked ham, and season with salt, pepper, and nutmeg. Mix the whole well together, stirring it with a wooden spoon for five minutes. Then add the yolks of three raw eggs, and set it aside to get cold. Stuff the Tomatoes with this preparation and sprinkle fresh bread crumbs over them. Put a few drops of sweet oil on each one, arrange them in a pan and put them in the oven to bake. Serve them with a brown Italian sauce.

STUFFED TOMATOES, MACKAY STYLE.

No. 1576.—Prepare two dozen Tomatoes as in No. 1574. Then chop a quarter of a pound of lean pork, a quarter of a pound of veal, and six ounces of marrow finely, and season with salt, pepper and nutmeg, adding a little finely chopped parsley, chives, garlic and tarragon. Mix the whole well together and stuff the Tomatoes with it. Arrange them in a buttered flat saucepan with a thin slice of fat pork over each one and bake them in an oven. Before serving press the juice of a lemon over them and serve them with a half glaze or a plain reduced purée of Tomatoes.

STUFFED TOMATOES, TURKISH STYLE.

No. 1577.—Prepare two dozen Tomatoes as in No. 1574. Cook a quarter of a pound of rice in chicken broth dry. Chop an onion finely and fry it lightly in butter. Then add the chopped Tomatoes, and when the moisture is reduced, add two spoonfuls of Tomato sauce and the rice. Season with salt and pepper and add a little finely chopped chives or parsley. Mix the whole well together and stuff the Tomatoes with it. Sprinkle some fresh bread crumbs over them, put a piece of butter on each and arrange them in a buttered baking pan. Then bake them in an oven and serve Tomato sauce with them.

STUFFED TOMATOES, AMERICAN STYLE.

No. 1578.—Prepare two dozen Tomatoes as in No. 1574. Chop two white onions finely and put them in a saucepan with a piece of butter. Fry them lightly and add four finely chopped Tomatoes and the flesh that was scooped out of the Tomatoes to be stuffed. When the moisture is nearly reduced, add a handful of finely chopped fresh mushrooms. Cover the saucepan, and when the moisture is reduced, add two handfuls of fresh bread crumbs and season with salt and pepper. Stir it over the fire for ten minutes and add the yolks of four raw eggs and a little finely chopped parsley. When it is well mixed put it on a plate and cover it with a buttered paper. When this preparation is cold, stuff the Tomatoes with it, sprinkle some fresh bread crumbs over them, put a piece of butter on each, and arrange them in a buttered baking pan. Then bake them in a moderate oven and serve them with a Tomato sauce.

STUFFED TOMATOES, CARDINAL STYLE.

No. 1579.—Prepare two dozen Tomatoes as in No. 1574. Chop half a dozen shallots finely and put them in a saucepan with four ounces of butter. Cover the saucepan and let them cook on a slow fire (not letting them get browned). Then add the finely chopped Tomatoes and two handfuls of finely chopped fresh mushrooms. When the moisture is reduced, add six spoonfuls of reduced Allemande sauce and a handful of fresh bread crumbs and season with salt and pepper. When it is well mixed add the yolks of three raw eggs. Stuff the Tomatoes with this preparation, sprinkle them with fresh bread crumbs, arrange them in a flat saucepan and put a few drops of sweet oil on each. Bake them in a quick oven. When they are browned dish them up, put a few drops of glaze on each and serve with a puree of Tomatoes around the dish.

BAKED TOMATOES.

No. 1580.—Cut the ends off of half a dozen Tomatoes, and slice them in halves. Season with salt and pepper. Put two spoonfuls of clarified butter in a frying pan and, when it is warm, add the Tomatoes, and fry them lightly on both sides. Sprinkle them with fresh bread crumbs and a little finely chopped parsley. Then arrange them in a baking dish, sprinkle bread crumbs and parsley over them, put a piece of butter on top of each, and bake them in the oven.

NOTE.—Finely chopped garlic or shallots may be added with the parsley, if desired.

TOMATOES FOR GARNITURE.

No. 1581.—Any of the different varieties of stuffed Tomatoes may be used as a garniture for large entrees or relevés; and, when alternated with green peppers, artichokes, mushrooms or cauliflower, make a very pretty effect—caused by the different colors of the vegetables.

PLAIN TOMATO SAUCE.

No. 1582.—Select four dozen nice ripe Tomatoes, cut them in quarters, and put them in a saucepan with a small faggot of parsley garnished with two green onions, one leek, one bay leaf, a few cloves and some pepper-corns. Cover the saucepan, and cook them on a brisk fire until the Tomatoes are thoroughly done. Then take out the faggot, and rub the Tomatoes through a fine sieve. Put the puree in a flat saucepan, reduce it on a brisk fire to the proper consistency, season with salt and pepper, and before serving, add a piece of butter. This sauce is much admired for its beautiful red color and fine flavor when served with broiled meats.

TOMATO SAUCE.

No. 1583.—Put four ounces of butter in a saucepan, to which add two sliced onions, two carrots, and half a pound of lean raw ham. Fry them until nicely browned; then add four dozen ripe Tomatoes (which have been washed and cut in quarters), a faggot of parsley garnished with a sprig of thyme, a few grains of pepper, and two bay leaves, and season with salt. Cover the saucepan and let them cook slowly. When done, thicken them with flour diluted with cold broth to the proper consistency. Stir well with a wooden spoon until it boils; letting it cook slowly for half an hour, after which take out the ham and faggot, and rub it through a fine sieve.

PUREE OF TOMATOES.

No. 1584.—Prepare the Tomatoes as in No. 1583, but instead of thickening with flour, add a loaf of square bread (after removing the crust), cut in slices, and let it cook with the Tomatoes for twenty-five minutes. Then rub the puree through a fine sieve and put it in a flat saucepan. Reduce it on a brisk fire to its proper consistency while stirring it with a wooden spoon, after which add a piece of butter and a pinch of sugar.

SOUP—PUREE OF TOMATOES, AMERICAN STYLE.

No. 1585.—Prepare the Tomatoes as in No. 1583, and when they are strained add one quart of good broth, a piece of butter and a pinch of sugar. Serve with fried bread crumbs.

SOUP—PUREE OF TOMATOES, FRENCH STYLE.

No. 1586.—Wash and trim three dozen Tomatoes and cut them in quarters. Put in a saucepan a piece of butter, two finely sliced carrots, two finely sliced onions and some trimmings of lean ham. Fry them lightly. Then add four spoonfuls of flour, stirring it with a wooden spoon while it is cooking until it is nicely browned. Then add the Tomatoes, two quarts of broth, a faggot of parsley garnished with one celery, one leek, a sprig of thyme, two bay leaves, and a few grains of pepper, and season with salt and a pinch of red pepper. Keep stirring until it boils, then set it on the side of the fire to cook slowly for three quarters of an hour. Then take out the faggot, strain the puree through a fine sieve, and put it back in the saucepan to keep it warm. Before serving add a pinch of sugar and four ounces of butter. Stir it well until the butter is melted and serve with fried bread crumbs.

NOTE.—This may also be used as a sauce.

TOMATO SOUP, WITH RICE.

No. 1587.—Prepare the Tomatoes as in Nos. 1583 or 1586. Boil four ounces of rice in broth and have it dry when it is boiled. Serve it with the Tomatoes in a soup tureen.

TOMATO SOUP, FLORIDA STYLE.

No. 1588.—Prepare one gallon of Tomato soup as in Nos. 1583 or 1586. Boil one-quarter of a pound of sago in some white broth, and when it is cooked put it in the soup. Let it boil for a few minutes and then serve.

TOMATO CATSUP, NO. 1.

No. 1589.—Cut four dozen ripe Tomatoes in quarters and put them in a saucepan to cook. When they are thoroughly cooked rub them through a fine sieve. Then put the puree in a saucepan with one pint of wine vinegar, one ounce of ground cloves, allspice, cinnamon and ground pepper, and a little salt, and reduce it to its proper consistency. When it is cold put it in bottles, cork them tightly, and then boil them in a hot water bath for half an hour.

TOMATO CATSUP, NO. 2.

No. 1590.—Cut six dozen ripe Tomatoes in quarters, put them in a saucepan and, when they are thoroughly cooked, rub them through a fine sieve. Put them back in the saucepan and add one ounce of mustard flour, a teaspoonful of ground mace, one of cloves, one of black pepper, a little salt, a pinch of Cayenne pepper, and one ounce of celery seed tied up in a bag. Let it boil slowly until reduced to one-third of its original quantity. Then add one pint of wine vinegar and pour it into an earthen jar. When cold take out the celery seed, bottle the catsup, cork them tightly, and boil them in a hot water bath for twenty minutes.

TOMATO CATSUP, NO. 3.

No. 1591.—Peel six dozen nice ripe Tomatoes, cut them in quarters, put them in a saucepan and add four finely sliced onions, six sliced bell peppers, two ounces of brown sugar, an ounce of cinnamon, a little ginger, salt and a grated nutmeg. Moisten with two quarts of wine vinegar, and when the Tomatoes are thoroughly cooked, strain them through a fine sieve. Put the catsup in bottles, cork them tightly and boil them in a hot water bath for twenty minutes.

TOMATO CATSUP, EPICUREAN STYLE.

No. 1592.—Select six dozen nice ripe Tomatoes, cut them in halves, put them in a saucepan and boil them for fifteen minutes. Then drain them on a cloth, which you place in a colander. When dry rub them through a fine sieve. Put this puree in a flat saucepan, season it with salt and red pepper, and add a pint of Worcestershire sauce and a glassful of wine vinegar. Then reduce the catsup to its proper consistency, take it from the fire, and when cold bottle it. Cork them tightly and boil them in a hot water bath for twenty-five minutes. Keep the bottles tightly corked at all times.

TOMATOES, YUM-YUM.

No. 1593.—Wash and clean six dozen green Tomatoes, slice them finely and add to them about the same quantity of finely sliced green peppers. Put them in an earthen jar with one pound of salt, mix the whole well together, and on the following day drain off the moisture and add one ounce of ground allspice, half an ounce of cloves, four ounces of grated horse-radish and six ounces of mustard seed. Mix the whole well together and pour over them some boiled wine vinegar to cover. Cover the jar tightly and keep it in a cool place.

PRESERVED TOMATOES.

No. 1594.—Use only ripe Tomatoes, wash them in cold water and trim off the stems. Pour boiling water over them, peel them, cut them in quarters and lay them in a wooden tub until all are finished. Then put them in a quart or gallon can, solder on the cover and boil it in a hot water bath. The quarts require forty-five minutes and the gallons an hour and a half to boil.

PRESERVED TOMATO SAUCE.

No. 1595.—Select nice red ripe Tomatoes, trim them, wash them in cold water, cut them in quarters and put them in a saucepan on a brisk fire. Let them boil for fifteen minutes. Spread a cloth over a basket or strainer and put the Tomatoes on this cloth to drain for one hour. Then rub them through a fine sieve and put the sauce in champagne bottles. Cork them tightly, tie the corks down and boil the bottles in a hot water bath for thirty minutes. All preserves should be put on to boil with cold water. When bottles are used they should be packed in straw, and when boiled let them stand until the water, in which they have been boiled, is cool before removing them. When ready for use this sauce may be prepared the same as fresh Tomatoes, and for this purpose it is only necessary to thicken the sauce, season it to taste and strain it again.

WHOLE TOMATOES, PRESERVED IN SAUCE.

No. 1596.—Select small, red, ripe, firm Tomatoes, dip them in boiling water and peel them. Put them into large-mouthed bottles, without injuring the Tomatoes, and do not have the bottles too full. Fill the bottles with sauce made as in No. 1595 to cover. Cork the bottles tightly and tie the corks down. Then boil them in a hot water bath for three-quarters of an hour. Before using these Tomatoes they should always be warmed in their own sauce.

TOMATO FIGS PRESERVED.

No. 1597.—The Fig or Red Pear Tomato, as described in No. 1553, is one of the very best varieties for preserving. Dip them in boiling water and peel them, being careful not to injure them. Put five pounds of the Tomatoes in an earthen jar with five pounds of crushed cube sugar, then cover them and set them in a cool dry place for two or three days. Then drain the juice into a copper basin, set it on the fire to boil, skim it well and, when clear of all the scum, let the syrup cool and then pour it over the Tomatoes. Repeat this operation three times in one week. After this, when the weather is favorable, take the Tomatoes out of the jar and place them on dishes or plates in the sun to dry for about six or seven days, occasionally turning them over, and when they are dried put them in boxes lined with white paper. Sprinkle some powdered sugar over them, then put another layer of Tomatoes (not too close together), then powdered sugar again, then Tomatoes, and continue this until the box is full. Cover them and keep them in a dry place.

ARTICLE CCXV.

French
Tonka (Feve).

TONKA BEAN.

German
Tonkabohne.

No. 1598.—The Tonka Bean is the seed of a large tree that grows in Guiana, Mexico and the Southern part of America. The seed or bean is inclosed in an oblong, ovate pod, and is about one inch long and one-eighth of an inch wide. It has a dark brown, wrinkled, shining, thin and brittle skin, and a light brown oily kernel. It has a strong, agreeable aromatic odor and a bitterish taste. It is used for culinary purposes as a substitute for vanilla, which it resembles in flavor. Tobacconists use it largely to flavor tobacco and to mix with snuff when ground or powdered.

ARTICLE CCXVI.

Truffles.

TRUFFLES.

Trüffle.

No. 1599.—Truffles are a species of fungi that are subterranean in their habit and are mostly found in the neighborhood of oak and chestnut trees, but do not thrive well in thick woods. They are found from two inches to one foot below the soil. They have neither roots nor stems, and vary in color from white to light brown and black. They are somewhat globular in form and vary in size. Their surface is knotty or warty, and is covered with a skin or network which resembles veins. When they have attained their full growth they diffuse an agreeable odor which is quite peculiar. The flesh is solid and has a delicious taste, but when the Truffles are exposed for a few days they begin to decay and become bitter and disagreeable. They are put up in cans and bottles and can be obtained from all first-class grocers. But when canned they have little of the fine flavor and good qualities of the Truffle in its fresh state. They are used principally for stuffing turkeys, capons, and with goose-liver patés, etc. They have always been held in high esteem by epicures, and, owing to their rarity, have always commanded a high price. French Truffles can occasionally be obtained in New York from the stewards on Atlantic steamers, but the majority of those used in the United States are preserved, and the best brands can only be obtained from responsible importers. The district of Perigord in France furnishes the best flavored Truffles, which are of a black color. In the other parts of France they are grayish in color. The Italian Truffles from Piedmont are of a whitish color and have an excellent flavor. Truffles have not yet been found in the United States, although tubers that resemble them have been discovered in California, but it has not been accurately determined whether they are genuine Truffles or not. The following recipes are for canned Truffles.

TRUFFLES (SERVED WHOLE), WITH CHAMPAGNE SAUCE.

No. 1600.— Open a can of Truffles and put the juice of the Truffles in a small saucepan. Add a faggot of parsley garnished with a few grains of pepper and two cloves, a small slice of lean raw ham and a large glass of dry champagne. Cover the saucepan and set it on the fire, and when this is reduced to one-quarter of its original quantity, add the Truffles and season with salt and pepper. When the Truffles are thoroughly warmed take out the faggot and dish them up. Pour the gravy over them and serve them with a dish of fresh butter.

NOTE.—When Truffles are allowed to boil in their sauce, or to remain too long on the fire, they become shrivelled and hard.

TRUFFLES, ITALIAN STYLE.

No. 1601.—Chop two shallots finely and put them in a saucepan with one spoonful of sweet oil. Warm it thoroughly and be careful not to let it get browned. Then add a wine-glassful of Madeira wine and reduce the whole to one-quarter of its original quantity. Then add two spoonfuls of Espagnole sauce and a small clove of garlic chopped finely, and let it boil for five minutes. Then add the Truffles, cut in thick slices, and toss them over when thoroughly warmed. Add a piece of butter, to which add a little anchovy paste, toss them well over until the butter is melted, and then serve.

TRUFFLES, PIEMONTAISE STYLE.

No. 1602.—Reduce half a pint of Madeira wine sauce and add the Truffles with their juice. When they are thoroughly warmed dish them up, and again warm the gravy and add to it half a tea-spoonful of Anchovy butter and a piece of fresh butter. Mix it well off of the fire until the butter is melted, then pour it over the Truffles and serve them hot.

NOTE.—If the Truffles are large slice them, and if small leave them whole.

BAKED TRUFFLES, WITH CREAM SAUCE.

No. 1603.—Put a wine-glassful of white wine in a saucepan, and when it is reduced to one-quarter of its original quantity add one spoonful of meat glaze with four spoonfuls of Cream sauce and a small can of sliced Truffles. Season with a little salt and nutmeg, then put them in a buttered baking dish and sprinkle some grated Parmesan cheese over the top. Wipe the border and bake it in a moderate oven.

TRUFFLES BAKED IN SHELLS.

No. 1604.—Cut the Truffles in small pieces or slice them and then put them in a reduced Madeira wine sauce. Butter the shells, fill them with the Truffles, sprinkle some fresh bread crumbs over them, put a piece of butter on the top of each, and bake them in an oven. Serve them on a napkin.

NOTE.—They may also be made with Cream sauce, using a reduced Cream sauce in place of the Madeira wine sauce.

TRUFFLES, WITH MADEIRA WINE SAUCE.

No. 1605.—Reduce a Madeira wine sauce with the juice of the Truffles, and when ready to serve, add the Truffles (sliced), and a piece of butter. Toss them over well. They may be served on toast or gratinated crusts.

ESSENCE OF TRUFFLES.

No. 1606.—As we have no fresh Truffles in this country, the juice of the canned article must be used. Put the juice in a saucepan, add a little Madeira wine, cover the saucepan, and reduce it to half of its quantity. Use it in the sauce with the Truffles, or in any sauce where an essence of Truffles is needed.

TRUFFLES FOR GARNITURE.

No. 1607.—For large garnitures, peel the Truffles and warm them thoroughly in champagne or Madeira wine. The black ones are preferred, and are dressed in bunches with other garnitures. To garnish entrees they are served with a white or brown sauce. The small ones are glazed, and may be used baked in shells, or cut in the shape of olives and used with other garnitures.

TRUFFLES, FOR COLD GARNITURES.

No. 1608.—The Truffles may be used whole, or can be peeled and sliced. Cook them in champagne or Madeira wine, as for a hot garniture. Then let them get cool, and glaze them with Aspic jelly, or mask them with a cold Champagne sauce. Dress them in bunches with Aspic jelly, or in crusts cut in fancy shapes, or pepper boxes. Garnish it with Aspic jelly.

PUREE OF TRUFFLES, FOR GARNITURES.

No. 1609.—Pound half a pound of Truffles and six ounces of butter in a mortar into a fine paste, and rub it through a fine sieve. Prepare a pint of Madeira wine sauce reduced with the juice of the Truffles. When ready to serve, add the paste to the sauce, stirring it off of the fire until melted.

TRUFFLE SALAD, WITH ARTICHOKES, LUNING STYLE.

No. 1610.—Peel half a dozen young, tender artichokes. Cut the bottoms in thin slices, and sprinkle them with a little salt. Let them macerate for twenty minutes, then drain them on a napkin. Now slice finely one-quarter of its quantity of Truffles, and put them in a salad bowl with the artichokes, having previously rubbed the bottom of the bowl with some garlic. Season with salt and pepper. Rub the yolks of two hard boiled eggs through a fine sieve, and put them in a bowl with half a teaspoonful of English mustard diluted with oil and tarragon vinegar. Pour this dressing over the Truffles and artichokes, cover the bowl and, when ready to serve, mix the whole well together, and arrange it properly.

TRUFFLE SALAD, WITH POTATOES, RUSSIAN STYLE.

No. 1611.—Slice one dozen boiled new potatoes, and put them in a salad bowl with the same quantity of sliced Truffles. Season with salt, pepper, oil and vinegar, and cover the bowl. In twenty minutes add a little finely-chopped parsley, tarragon and chives, and mix them well together. Arrange the salad properly, and mask it with a Mayonnaise dressing mixed with a little mustard.

SMALL TRUFFLE PATÉS, BENNETT STYLE.

No. 1612.—Prepare two dozen patés with puff paste. Cut the Truffles in small pieces, and put them in a saucepan with a glassful of dry champagne. When the moisture is reduced add the Truffles, four spoonfuls of Madeira wine sauce, and one spoonful of game puree. Fill the patés with this mixture, put on the covers, and serve them hot.

STUFFED TRUFFLES.

No. 1613.—Scoop out the centres of two dozen large Truffles, without injuring the sides, and chop the parts scooped out finely. Chop two shallots finely, put them in a saucepan with a piece of butter, and cook them without letting them get browned. Then add a small glass of Madeira wine and the chopped Truffles. Let them cook until the moisture is reduced, after which allow them to get cold. Then add a forced meat of chicken or game. Stuff the Truffles with this mixture, arrange them in a flat saucepan, and set them in the oven for a few minutes until they are glazed. Serve them with a reduced Madeira wine sauce around the dish.

ARTICLE CCXVII.

TUBEROUS-ROOTED CHICKLING WETCH, or TUBEROUS-ROOTED PEA.

French
Gesse.

German
Knotig Gess.

No. 1614.—This is a perennial plant, having spreading roots that are furnished with numerous black irregular-shaped tubers, which weigh from one to three ounces each. The roots are farinaceous, and when cooked have a rich taste, somewhat like roasted chestnuts.

ARTICLE CCXVIII.

French   **TURMERIC, OR CURCUMA.**   **German**
Curcuma, or Turmeric.   *Curcumei.*

No. 1615.—The root of this plant is perennial, tuberous, palmate and internally of a deep yellow color. It is a native of the East Indies and China, the latter furnishing the best kind. The odor is peculiar; the taste warm, bitterish, and feebly aromatic. It tinges the saliva yellow. The root is a stimulant aromatic, bearing some resemblance to ginger in its operation, and is much used in India as a condiment. It is used in cookery to impart a yellow color to rice and foreign soups.

ARTICLE CCXIX.

TURNIP.
Navet.   *Rübe.*

No. 1616.—The Turnip is a hardy biennial plant, and has been cultivated from time immemorial. The roots of all the varieties attain their full size during the first year. It is most easily affected in its form and flavor by soil, climate, and mode of culture. There are a great many varieties. It is a wholesome and agreeable vegetable.

CULTURE.

No. 1617.—Sow in drills fourteen inches apart, and half an inch deep. Keep them perfectly free from weeds and, when the bottoms begin to enlarge brush away the earth from about the roots to the depth of half an inch or more, and give them a light dressing of wood ashes. It is the surest mode of obtaining fair and smooth turnips in old gardens, where they are almost certain to grow wormy if the earth is allowed to remain in contact with the roots. For the spring and summer crops it is important to get them started very early, so that they may have time to grow to a sufficient size before hot weather, when they will soon become tough and strong.

For the fall crop sow in the Middle and Western States in the latter part of July and August, as directed for the spring sowing.

WHITE FLESH VARIETIES.

EARLY PURPLE TOP MUNICH.

No. 1618.—A very early handsome Turnip of a white color, with a bright purplish-red top. It is of good quality when young, but bitter when old. It is one of the best for first crop.

WHITE EGG.

No. 1619.—A quick growing egg-shaped, perfectly smooth, pure white variety, growing half out of the ground, with a small top and rough leaves. The flesh is very sweet and mild, never having the rank strong taste of some varieties.

EARLY WHITE STONE.

No. 1620.—This is round, of firm texture and quick growth; medium size, and much cultivated.

JERSEY TURNIP.

No. 1621.—An exceedingly delicate, sweet, white Turnip for table use. It is very popular, and is esteemed as one of the best. It grows long, and is somewhat like a parsnip in form.

EARLY WHITE DUTCH.

No. 1622.—A medium sized, white flat Turnip, of quick growth, juicy and of excellent quality when young. Sow it in the spring or fall.

EARLY WHITE FLAT DUTCH STRAP-LEAVED.

No. 1623.—A most excellent garden variety, that is much used in the Southern States. It is very early, erect and tender, and one of the best for table use.

EARLY PURPLE TOP STRAP-LEAVED.

No. 1624.—Similar to the preceding variety, except in color, being purple or dark red on the top. It is of good quality.

COW HORN, OR LONG WHITE.

No. 1625.—Carrot-like in form, growing nearly half out of the ground, and is generally slightly crooked. It is pure white, except a little shade of green near the top. It is delicate and well flavored, of very rapid growth, and is a favorite for fall and winter use.

PURPLE TOP MAMMOTH.

No. 1626.—Globe-shaped and large, firm in texture, juicy, of exceedingly quick growth, and very hardy.

LARGE WHITE FLAT NORFOLK.

No. 1627.—A variety universally grown. It is round and flat, being white in color. The tops of this variety are used for greens,

POMERANEAN WHITE GLOBE.

No. 1628.—One of the most productive kinds, and is of the most perfect globe-shape, the skin being white and smooth.

PURPLE-TOP WHITE GLOBE.

No. 1629.—A variety of the purple-top flat Turnip that is globular in form, beautiful in appearance, of most excellent quality, and a good keeper.

SWEET GERMAN.

No. 1630.—A popular variety in the New England States. The flesh is white, hard, firm and sweet. It keeps well, and is one of the best for winter use.

SEVEN TOP.

No. 1631.—Cultivated extensively in the South for the tops, which are used for greens. It is very hardy, and will grow all winter, but does not produce a good bulb, and is only recommended for the tops.

YELLOW-FLESHED SORTS.

EARLY YELLOW MONTMAGNY.

No. 1632.—The most beautiful of the yellow-fleshed varieties, and very early. The bulb is oval, medium sized, and clear yellow, stained with bright purple at the top. The flesh is yellow, finely grained, sweet and tender.

LARGE AMBER GLOBE.

No. 1633. — One of the best varieties. Flesh yellow, finely grained and sweet. The skin is yellow, with a green top. It grows to large size, and is a good keeper.

ORANGE JELLY, OR GOLDEN BALL.

No. 1634.—One of the most delicate and sweetest of yellow-fleshed Turnips. It is not of large size, but is firm, hard and of most excellent flavor. It keeps well, and is a superior table variety.

PURPLE-TOP YELLOW ABERDEEN.

No. 1635.—The roots are medium in size and round in form. The flesh is pale-yellow, tender and sugary. It is hardy and productive, and keeps well.

EARLY YELLOW FINLAND.

No. 1636.—An early yellow-fleshed variety, beautiful in form and medium sized. The flesh is remarkably fine, closely grained and of a rich, sugary flavor. An excellent early variety.

EARLY YELLOW MALTA.

No. 1637.—This is a beautiful, symmetrical, early variety, of medium size. The skin is very smooth, and of a bright orange-yellow color. It is sweet and tender, and one of the best yellow summer Turnips.

MASHED TURNIPS.

No. 1638.—Pare the Turnips and cut them in slices (when they are old parboil them for five minutes), put them in a saucepan, cover them with boiling water, season with salt, cover the saucepan and boil them until tender. Then drain them in a colander, and when dry, pound them through a fine colander, return them to the saucepan, season with salt and pepper, add a piece of butter, mix the whole well together and warm them thoroughly.

PUREE OF TURNIPS, WITH CREAM.

No. 1639.—Prepare the Turnips as in No. 1638, and, when they are dry, rub them through a fine colander. Then put them in a flat saucepan, season with salt, pepper, and a little nutmeg, add one glassful of cream, and reduce the puree to its proper consistency while stirring it with a wooden spoon. Before serving add a piece of butter.

NOTE.—When they are to be used as a garniture they should be rubbed through a fine sieve.

PUREE OF TURNIPS, WITH CREAM, FRENCH STYLE.

No. 1640.—Pare two dozen young white Turnips, slice them and parboil them until they are nearly tender. Then drain them and put them in a saucepan with a piece of butter. Season them with salt, pepper, a little nutmeg and a pinch of sugar, cover the saucepan and let them cook until the moisture is nearly reduced (not letting them get browned). Then add four spoonfuls of Cream sauce, mix them well together, and rub them through a fine sieve. Put the puree in a flat saucepan and reduce it to the proper consistency while slowly adding a cupful of cream. Before serving add a piece of butter.

GLAZED TURNIPS (BROWN) FOR GARNITURE.

No. 1641.—Pare one dozen Turnips and cut them in four or six pieces, according to their size. Trim them in a clove-like shape, and parboil them for five minutes. Then drain them and put them in a small saucepan. Moisten them with broth and add a piece of butter, a pinch of sugar and a little salt. Cook them on a brisk fire, and when the broth is reduced and the Turnips nicely glazed, dish them up without breaking them. This may be served with brown gravy or with stewed ducks, or any kind of braised meats, using the gravy the meats were braised in.

GLAZED TURNIPS (WHITE) FOR GARNITURE.

No. 1642.—Prepare the Turnips as in No. 1641, but be careful not to let them get too brown in color. Serve them with a Butter, Cream or Allemande sauce, with a boiled leg of mutton or any meat where a white vegetable garniture is required.

STEWED TURNIPS, SPANISH STYLE.

No. 1643.—Use only small young Turnips. Peel and round them all of equal size, parboil them for three minutes, then drain them and put them in a saucepan with a piece of butter. Fry them lightly and season with salt, pepper and a pinch of sugar, then moisten them with white broth and finish cooking them. When they are done dish them up. Reduce the broth to a light glaze and add two spoonfuls of Espagnole sauce. In two or three minutes take it off of the fire, add a piece of butter and stir the same well until the butter is melted. Then add a little finely chopped parsley and pour it over the Turnips.

STEWED TURNIPS WITH ONIONS.

No. 1644.—Pare one dozen Turnips, cut them in four or six parts and trim the edges. Peel one and a half dozen small white onions and put them in a saucepan with the Turnips. Add water or broth to cover them, a piece of butter and a little salt. Cover the saucepan and let them cook until done, then drain off the broth and dish them up in a deep vegetable dish. Make a Butter sauce, into which add a teaspoonful of mustard flour and a pinch of nutmeg and, when ready to serve, pour it over the Turnips.

STEWED TURNIPS, CONVENT STYLE.

No. 1645.—Pare and cut one dozen Turnips in quarters, trim the edges, parboil them for five minutes and then drain them. Put them in a saucepan with a pint of chicken broth, a little salt, a pinch of sugar and four ounces of marrow cut in small squares, cover the saucepan and let them cook until thoroughly done when the broth should be three-quarters reduced. Then set them on the side of the fire and add two ounces of butter and a cup of cream, into which dilute the yolks of four raw eggs. Toss the whole well over until the butter is melted. Serve them immediately as they must not be allowed to remain on the fire after the eggs are mixed.

BOILED TURNIPS, PLAIN.

No. 1646.—Pare the Turnips and cut them in four or six pieces. Then trim the edges and parboil them for three minutes. Put them in a saucepan, cover them with water or broth, add a piece of butter, a little salt and a pinch of sugar, cover the saucepan and let them boil until thoroughly done. Then drain and serve them with a little butter over them.

BOILED TURNIPS WITH WHITE SAUCE.

No. 1647.—Prepare and cook the Turnips as in No. 1646 and, when they are done, drain them, and put them in a saucepan with a piece of butter. Toss them over the fire a few minutes and add a few spoonfuls of Allemande sauce. Before serving sprinkle a little finely chopped parsley over them.

NOTE.—The above is known as Turnips, Poulette style. A very nice sauce may be made of the broth in which the Turnips were cooked that is somewhat similar to a Butter sauce.

SOUP—PUREE OF TURNIPS.

No. 1648.—Pare and slice two dozen white Turnips, parboil them for five minutes, drain them and put them in a saucepan with a piece of butter and a little sugar. Set them on the fire and, when the moisture is reduced, let them get lightly colored. Then add two quarts of white broth and a faggot of parsley, garnished with two leeks. Cover the saucepan and let them get well cooked. Then add two quarts of lightly thickened chicken or veal broth. Fifteen minutes after this skim it well, take out the faggot, and rub the soup through a fine sieve. Put it back in a saucepan to keep warm, and season to taste. Before serving add six ounces of butter and a pint of cream, in which dilute the yolks of eight raw eggs. Stir it well until the butter is melted, and serve it with boiled rice or small pieces of toasted bread.

SOUP—PUREE OF TURNIPS, WITH CREAM.

No. 1649.—Prepare the Turnips as in No. 1648, and, when reducing the moisture, keep the Turnips white. When they are cooked add three quarts of Cream sauce, rub it through a fine sieve, and put the puree in a saucepan to keep warm in a hot water bath. Season to taste, and before serving add six ounces of butter divided into small pieces, and a pint of cream, in which dilute the yolks of eight raw eggs. Stir it briskly until the butter is melted, and serve with pearl barley, previously cooked in broth.

SOUP—PUREE OF TURNIPS, WITH FARINA.

No. 1650.—Prepare a puree of Turnips as in Nos. 1648 or 1649, with white or yellow Turnips. When the soup is done add some farina, which must be cooked separately in broth. This soup must not be too thick.

PECTORAL BROTH, WITH TURNIPS.

No. 1651.—Put in a saucepan one gallon of cold water, with four pounds of veal shin, cut in small pieces, two pounds of lights, and one ounce of shelled almonds. Set it on the fire to boil slowly until the broth is reduced to half its original quantity. While the broth is being reduced prepare one dozen Turnips. Pare them, then wrap them in cooking paper and bake them. When they are done remove the papers and put the Turnips in the broth. Then reduce the broth to one quarter of its original quantity. Then strain the broth, return it to the saucepan, and add two ounces of rock-candy and one of white powdered gum. Keep the broth warm and serve it as required.

ARTICLE CCXX.

French — *Chou rave.* TURNIP-CABBAGE, OR KOHL-RABI. **German** — *Kohlrübe.*

No. 1652.—The Turnip-Cabbage, or Kohl-rabi, is a vegetable that is intermediate between the cabbage and the turnip, combining the flavor of both. The edible part is a turnip-shaped bulb that is formed by the swelling of the stem. For table use it should be cut when small, as it is then tender and delicate. When it attains its full size it becomes tough and stringy.

CULTURE.

No. 1653.—It is cultivated best by sowing the seeds in rows, from May to July. It is difficult to transplant, hence it is best to sow the entire crop from seed, and thin it out as it stands.

EARLY WHITE VIENNA.

No. 1654.—An early, small and handsome variety, with a white bulb.

EARLY PURPLE VIENNA.

No. 1655.—This is similar to the White Vienna, except in color.

STUFFED TURNIP CABBAGE.

No. 1656.—Peel and wash one dozen Turnip-Cabbages of equal size, parboil them until they are nearly cooked, and then immerse them in cold water and drain them. Cut the top parts off, and scoop out half of the centre of each, which you will chop finely. Add to it some raw forced meat of veal with fine herbs, season with salt, pepper, nutmeg and some finely-chopped chives, and mix them well together. Then stuff the scooped Cabbages with this preparation and arrange them in a buttered flat saucepan. Moisten them with a little veal gravy, then let them boil up once, after which set them on the side of the fire to cook slowly until tender, basting them occasionally with the gravy. When done dish them up. Strain the gravy into another saucepan, skim off the grease, and add two spoonfuls of Espagnole sauce. Reduce it to its proper consistency and pour it over the Turnip-Cabbages.

TURNIP-CABBAGE, WITH CREAM SAUCE.

No. 1657.—Peel one dozen Turnip-Cabbages, cut them in scallops and boil them in lightly salted water, in which a piece of butter has been put. When they are tender drain off the water, add four spoonfuls of Cream sauce and a piece of butter, and season with salt and pepper. Toss them well together in the pan, and then serve.

TURNIP-CABBAGE, WITH BUTTER SAUCE.

No. 1658.—Prepare them as in No. 1657, using Butter sauce instead of Cream sauce.

TURNIP-CABBAGE, GERMAN STYLE.

No. 1659.—Peel and slice one dozen Turnip-Cabbages, parboil them for five minutes and then drain them. Slice two onions finely and put them in a saucepan with a piece of butter. Fry them lightly and then add the Cabbages. Season with salt, pepper, and nutmeg, and moisten them with a good broth. Cover the saucepan and let them cook until tender, when the broth will be nearly reduced. Then add three spoonfuls of Butter or Allemande sauce, and a little veal gravy, allowing it to simmer for fifteen minutes. Before serving add a little finely-chopped parsley.

TURNIP-CABBAGE, SMOTHERED AND GLAZED.

No. 1660.—Peel one dozen Turnip-Cabbages of even size, parboil them until they are half cooked, then immerse them in cold water and drain them on a napkin. Then cut out the center of each with a round cutter, without breaking them. Arrange them in a deep flat saucepan lined with thin slices of fat pork. Then chop one handful of fresh mushrooms finely and put them in another saucepan with one chopped shallot and a piece of butter. Cover the saucepan and let them cook until the moisture is reduced. While doing this chop the portion of the Cabbage that you scooped out finely, and add it to the mushrooms when the moisture is reduced. Season them with salt, pepper and nutmeg, add four spoonfuls of reduced Allemande sauce and mix the whole together while adding the yolks of four raw eggs. Now put this preparation in an earthen bowl and when it is cold, add to it four spoonfuls of forced meat of chicken. Then fill the centres of the Cabbages with this mixture, moisten them lightly with veal broth, put the cover on the pan and set it in a moderate oven. When they are nicely glazed dish them up and serve with them a reduced Allemande sauce flavored with essence of mushrooms.

TURNIP CABBAGE, FOR GARNITURES.

No. 1661.—For garnishing joints prepare it as in No. 1656, and alternate with stuffed tomatoes or mushrooms. For entrées of chops, etc., prepare them as in No. 1657 and 1658. Pour a light sauce over them and arrange the chops around them, on the dish, in a circle.

ARTICLE CCXXI.

TURNIP-ROOTED CHERVIL.

Cerfeuil (enraciné). *Knolig Gartenkerbel.*

No. 1662.—This is a hardy biennial plant that is cultivated for its root, which is a valuable esculent. The roots are of fusiform, about four or five inches long, and nearly one and a half inches in diameter. The skin is grayish-black in color, and the flesh is white and farinaceous. It is boiled and prepared in the same manner as the oyster plant.

CULTURE.

No. 1663.—Sow it in drills, in rich, mellow soil, either in April or October, and treat it as you would carrots.

ARTICLE CCXXII.

UNICORN ROOT.

Unicorn. *Einhornwurzel.*

No. 1664.—This is a hardy annual plant with peculiarly shaped seed-pods, which, when young and tender, are highly prized for pickling, and by many are considered superior to cucumbers. The pods are produced in large numbers and should be gathered when about half grown, as they are worthless when the flesh hardens.

CULTURE.

No. 1665.—Sow them in April or May, in open ground, about three feet apart in each direction, as the plants spread considerably when growing. They are cultivated easily.

ARTICLE CCXXIII.

French   **VALERIAN.**   **German**
Valeriane.   *Baldrian.*

No. 1666.—This is an annual plant, the roots of which are used for medicinal purposes. When in blossom the plant presents a beautiful appearance. The stem is smooth and branching, and the leaves are oblong, thick, fleshy and of a glossy-green color. The young leaves are used as a salad.

CULTURE.

No. 1667.—It succeeds best in warm light soil. Sow the seeds during the latter part of April in drills that are fourteen inches apart. Continue sowing every fortnight until July for a succession of crops.

ARTICLE CCXXIV.

VANILLA.

Vanille.   *Vanille.*

No. 1668.—This is a genus of orchidaceous plants that are natives of South America, the West Indies, and Mexico. It is a fleshy, dark green perennial, climbing plant, with a long, smooth, dark green stem, much branched, and finished at the nodes with aerial roots, which cling to and obtain nourishment from the tree supporting the plant. The dark green tough leaves are oval, sessile, fleshy and veinless. The pale, greenish-yellow flowers are about two inches in diameter. The fruit is a slender pod about eight inches long, filled with an oily mass containing numerous small, black, shining seeds. The pods are collected before they are quite ripe, dried in the shade, covered with a coating of fixed oil, and then tied in bundles which are surrounded with sheet lead, or enclosed in small metallic boxes, and sent to market. Several varieties of Vanilla exist in commerce. The most valuable is the Manza Vanilla. It has a peculiar, strong, agreeable odor, and a warm aromatic, sweetish taste. The interior pulpy portion is the most aromatic. The Simarona Vanilla is smaller, of a lighter color, and less aromatic. The pods are dry, and contain no Vanilla. The Pompona or Babo Vanilla has pods that are from five to seven inches long, of a dark brown color, and possessing a strong odor something like anise. Vanilla is used in medicine, in perfumery, and for flavoring in cookery.

VANILLA FLAVOR.

No. 1669.—Cut four Vanilla beans in pieces one inch long; then split them, and put them in a quart bottle. Pour over them some wine spirits or white whiskey, and cork the bottle tightly. Shake it well every day for a week, and then it will be ready for use. Keep the bottle tightly corked always.

VANILLA BEANS.

No. 1670.—A Vanilla Bean may be boiled in the milk when making custards or creams. When it is boiled, remove the Bean, and put it back in the bottle, as it may be used several times. After repeated usage when almost all of the flavor has been extracted from the Bean, put it in a mortar with some powdered sugar and pound them to a fine powder. Then sift it through a fine sieve, put it in a bottle, keep it tightly corked, and use it for flavoring cakes, etc.

ARTICLE CCXXV.

French
Legume (variée).

VEGETABLES.

German
Gemüse.

No. 1671.—All kinds and varieties of plants that are cultivated for culinary purposes are classed as vegetables. Of some kinds merely the seeds or roots are eaten; of others, the leaves or the fruit alone is partaken of, while others are used only for seasoning.

They are classified as follows:

Alliaceous plants, such as garlic, leeks, onions and shallots.

Asparaginous plants, such as asparagus, hops, cardoons and artichokes.

Brassicaceous plants, such as cabbage, cauliflower, kale and Brussels sprouts.

Cucurbitaceous plants, such as melons, cucumbers and squash.

Esculent roots, such as carrots, potatoes, turnips, oyster plant and parsnips.

Esculent fungi, such as mushrooms and truffles.

Leguminous plants, such as beans, lentils and peas.

Oleraceous plants, such as aromatic and pot herbs, as described in Article XIII.

Salad plants, such as celery, endives, lettuce, cress, corn-salad and dandelion.

Spinaceous plants, such as spinach, sorrel, sea-beet, nettle and orach.

VEGETABLE BALLS, TURKISH STYLE.

No. 1672.—Select a good head of cabbage, trim off the white, tender leaves, and parboil them for five minutes. Then immerse them in cold water, dry them on a napkin, and remove the hard ribs. Chop one pound of mutton fillet finely. Put it in a bowl, and add one finely-sliced onion, one handful of lightly-parboiled rice, a little finely-chopped parsley, three spoonfuls of reduced Allemande sauce, and season it highly. Mix the stuffing well together, and roll it into balls about the size of a walnut. Cover them carefully with the parts of the cabbage leaves, arrange them in a flat saucepan close together, in from four to six layers, seasoning each layer, and then moisten with broth to cover. Put a cover on them to keep them down in the pan. Then let them boil until the broth is half reduced. After this set them on the side of the fire to cook slowly. When they are cooked the broth should be almost entirely reduced. Put the balls on the dish they are to be served on, and make a sauce of the strained broth, diluted with the yolks of six raw eggs. Add the juice of one lemon to it, pour it over the balls and then serve them hot.

TIMBAL OF VEGETABLE BALLS, MILANAISE STYLE.

No. 1673.—Prepare the cabbage leaves as in No. 1672. Chop one pound of mutton fillet finely, and put it in a bowl. Add half a pound of grated fresh fat pork, one handful of fresh bread crumbs, one finely-chopped onion, two spoonfuls of finely-chopped fresh mushrooms, and a little finely-chopped parsley. Then season with salt and pepper, add two raw eggs, and mix the whole together. Roll this stuffing into small balls about the size of a walnut. Cover them carefully with the parts of the cabbage leaves, arrange them in a flat saucepan close together, in from four to six layers, seasoning each layer, and then moisten them with broth to cover. Put a cover on them to keep them down in the pan. Then put them on the fire and let them cook until the broth is reduced, and they will be thoroughly cooked.

Prepare separately a Rice Rissoti, as in No. 1299, keeping it firmer, and add to it six ounces of butter and grated Parmesan cheese.

Butter a Timbal mould, line it with the cabbage leaves, and put a layer of the rice around the sides and bottom about one-quarter of an inch thick. Now put in a layer of the balls and sprinkle them with some grated Parmesan cheese, and a little reduced Tomato sauce. Continue doing this until the mould is full. Cover it with a layer of rice, with cabbage leaves over it, and place some thin slices of fat pork on top of the leaves. Set the mould in a moderate oven to bake for half an hour. Take out the mould, remove the pork, and turn the mould over on a saucepan cover to let the moisture drain off. Then put the mould on the dish it is to be served on, remove the mould and pour over the Timbal a reduced Madeira wine sauce, flavored with essence of mushrooms.

VEGETABLE BORDERS.

No. 1674.—To make vegetable borders the larger vegetables must first be cut with a spoon or column cutter, in any desired shape. Those generally used are Carrots, Turnips, Artichoke bottoms, Green Peas, String Beans, Brussels Sprouts, Flageolet Beans, and the flower buds of Cauliflower. The Carrots, Turnips and Artichokes are first parboiled, then cooked in broth seasoned with salt and a pinch of sugar. The other vegetables are boiled in plain water lightly salted, then immersed in cold water, so they will retain their color. Then drain and dry them on a napkin. Care must be taken when cooking vegetables for borders not to have them underdone.

Butter the mould lightly with clarified butter, and set it in a pan in which you have some broken ice. Dip the vegetables desired for the border in clarified butter, and place them against the mould in whatever design you like, alternating them in color. When the butter gets cold the vegetables will adhere to the side of the mould. When the border is finished cover it with a layer of forced meat of chicken, being careful not to disarrange the design, and to have the layers of equal thickness. Then fill the mould with a vegetable garniture, to which add a reduced Allemande or Cream sauce. Cover it with a forced meat of chicken, and smooth it nicely. On this put a buttered paper cover, and poach it for twenty minutes.

When it is ready to serve place a napkin on a saucepan cover, and turn the mould on to this napkin. Let it set for a little while to drain off the moisture. Then turn the mould on to the dish the border is intended to be served on, and carefully remove the mould.

NOTE.—This border may be filled with potatoes, or any kind of vegetable puree. Other Borders can be prepared with a puree of vegetables, such as celery, green peas, spinach, and chestnuts, reducing the purees well. When they get a little cooled add the yolks of raw eggs, mix them well together, and then fill the moulds with the puree. Then poach them and proceed as explained above.

CHARTREUSE.

No. 1675.—Chartreuse is one of the finest and most elaborate of all vegetable entrees. Young vegetables should be obtained, if possible; and they must be prepared with care, and in a tasteful manner. Those that are used to ornament the mould should consist only of such as will not lose their color in cooking, as their fresh and bright appearance is what gives the fine effect to the entree.

Wash and scrape some nice young red carrots, and cut them in pieces two inches long. With a column cutter cut out as many red pieces as possible, having them one-quarter of an inch in diameter. Put them in a basin of cold water as you cut them.

Now prepare an equal quantity of turnips in the same manner. When they are both ready, parboil them separately in lightly-salted water; then immerse them in cold water, and drain them. Put them in separate saucepans, cover each with sufficient white broth to cook them; add a pinch of sugar, and let them cook slowly until tender, when the broth will be reduced. Put napkins on two plates; place the carrots on one plate and the turnips on the other; cover each with a napkin, and set them aside to get cold. (Some of the carrots may be cut in squares or in diamond shape if desired.)

While these are cooking, make a vegetable essence of the carrot trimmings, a few turnips, a head of celery cut in small pieces, a few parsley roots, and two onions, in each of which stick four cloves. Put them in a saucepan with three pints of white broth, and as soon as it commences to boil, skim it well, and then let it boil slowly until the vegetables are thoroughly cooked. Strain the broth through a napkin, and reduce it with four spoonfuls of Espagnole sauce to its proper consistency.

While these are cooking, prepare the following: Cut one head of cabbage in quarters; remove the stalk and hard ribs, and parboil the cabbage for four minutes. Then drain it, and tie each piece together. Put the pieces in a saucepan lined with thin slices of fat pork, and in the centre put a piece of trimmed and parboiled bacon and two sausages, on top of which lay one dressed partridge or four larded quails. Season with salt, pepper and a little nutmeg, and add a faggot of parsley garnished. Cover it with thin slices of fat pork, and moisten it with sufficient broth to cover it. Now put on the cover, let it cook slowly until thoroughly cooked, and then drain it in a colander.

While the above is cooking, butter a large Timbal mould, and decorate the sides and bottom with the pieces of turnips and carrots, placing them side by side, alternating the colors, and arranging them in some nice design. Put the mould in a cool place to allow the butter to harden and keep the vegetables in their proper positions. When the mould is prepared, put the drained cabbage in a napkin, and press out all of the moisture; cut the bacon and sausage in slices, and carve the partridge or quails. Put a layer of the cabbage on the bottom and around the sides. Now put a layer of bacon on top of the cabbage, then a layer of sausage, and then a layer of partridge or quail, and continue doing this until the mould is full, having a layer of cabbage on the top. Put a buttered paper cover over it. Now place the mould in a saucepan in which there is sufficient water to come half way up to the top of the mould. (Be careful not to get any water in the mould.) Set it in a moderate oven to cook for three-quarters of an hour.

Ten minutes before serving, put a napkin on a saucepan-cover and place the mould on it with the top down so that the moisture will drain off. When ready to serve place the mould on a dish and carefully remove the mould that surrounds the vegetables. Then pour over it the sauce with the essence of vegetables.

NOTE.—This Chartreuse can be prepared in various ways as will be explained under the proper headings. Squabs, breast of veal, wild ducks, larks, teal ducks, tenderloins of veal and fish can be used instead of partridges or quails. It is customary by many to put the birds in the moulds whole, but it is best to cut them up beforehand as they can then be served properly. The cabbage can be replaced by braised lettuce and the birds can be roasted, then cut in pieces and arranged accordingly. Chartreuse is sometimes ornamented with green peas, asparagus tops and string beans by inexperienced cooks. But this should not be done, as the steam will change the color of these vegetables and when they are removed from the mould they will be unrecognizable and their beautiful effect will be spoilt.

TIMBALS OF EGG PLANT, MACKAY STYLE.

No. 1676.—Peel half a dozen small Egg plants and cut them lengthwise in six pieces. Trim each piece so as to have them all alike, put them in a bowl and season them with salt. Then cover them and one hour later drain off the water and dry them on a napkin. Put a piece of butter in a flat saucepan, and when it is melted add the Egg plant, fry it lightly and then drain it on a napkin. When it is cold arrange it in a buttered Timbal mould so as to cover the sides and bottom of the mould. Have the following preparation ready to put with this: Peel two Egg plants, cut them in slices, flour them and fry them lightly in clarified butter on both sides; then drain them on a napkin. Cut two braised fillets of mutton in very small pieces, put them in a saucepan and add four spoonfuls of cooked fine herbs and two of fresh bread crumbs. Season with salt and pepper and add the yolks of two raw eggs. Mix the whole well together, then put a layer of this stuffing in the mould and then a layer of the fried Egg plant, continuing in this way until the mould is filled. Cover it with a buttered paper cover and bake it in a moderate oven for half an hour. When ready for use turn the mould on to the dish, remove it carefully and glaze the Timbal with a reduced Madeira wine sauce. Serve a brown Italian sauce separate.

TIMBAL OF SAUERKRAUT, GERMAN STYLE.

No. 1677.—Cook one pound of sauerkraut with half a pound of parboiled lean salt pork and, when they are three-quarters done, drain them in a colander and allow them to get cold.

Prepare a Timbal mould and line it with a paté paste. Put a layer of sausage meat mixed with fine herbs, in the bottom; then put a layer of sauerkraut on that with a few thin slices of the above pork and some slices of fresh fillet of pork over it. Continue doing this until the mould is full. Over this put a layer of paté paste to close the top tightly and place a buttered paper cover over it. Set the mould in a moderate oven to bake slowly for one hour and a half. Then remove the paper cover, turn the Timbal over on a dish and remove the mould. Make a hole in the centre of the Timbal and put in a few spoonfuls of Madeira wine sauce.

SMALL VEGETABLE PATÉS, FRENCH STYLE.

No. 1678.—Cut one onion in small pieces one quarter of an inch square, and put it in a saucepan with a piece of butter. Fry it lightly, and then add one carrot and one turnip cut in small square pieces, the white part of a stalk of celery, half of a parsnip, and a little cabbage cut in fine shreds. Fry this mixture lightly for a few minutes, not letting it get browned. Then season it with salt, pepper, and a pinch of sugar, and moisten it with just enough broth to cook it. Let it cook until the moisture is reduced to a glaze, and then add a soup-spoonful of reduced Allemande or Cream sauce, and some finely-chopped parsley. Then set it aside to get cold.

Now roll out some puff paste on the table as you would do when making pies, and with a three-inch round granulated cutter cut out some pieces. Wet the border of each, put some of the above stuffing in the center, and then place one of the round pieces of puff paste on top to cover each one. Press the edges close together, and put them on a buttered and floured pan. Now baste them with the yolks of eggs, diluted with water, and bake them in a hot oven. Serve them on a napkin.

SMALL VEGETABLE PATÉS, AMERICAN STYLE.

No. 1679.—Cut equal quantities of onions, carrots, celery and cabbage, in small square pieces. Put them in a saucepan with a piece of butter, and fry them lightly. Then moisten them with enough broth to cook them, and let them cook until the broth is reduced to a glaze. Now season with salt, pepper, nutmeg and a pinch of sugar, and add some reduced Allemande or Cream sauce, and some cooked asparagus tops, or green peas, that have been cooked separately (or any kind of vegetable that is in season). Mix the whole well together, add a little finely-chopped parsley, and then set it aside to get cold.

Make a paté paste, or use the trimmings of some puff paste. Roll out the paste, and with a three-inch oblong granulated cutter cut out some pieces. Wet the border of each and put some of the above stuffing in the center, and then place one of the oblong pieces of paste on top to cover each one. Press the edges close together and put them on a buttered and floured pan. Now baste them with the yolks of eggs diluted with water, and bake them in a hot oven. Serve them hot on a napkin.

SMALL VEGETABLE CRUSTS, MACEDOINE STYLE.

No. 1680.—Butter and flour one dozen small Timbal moulds that are a little larger at the top than at the bottom. Now roll out a paté paste, line the moulds with it, and fill them with flour. Cover them with a layer of paste, make a nice border around the top of each, and baste them with the yolk of an egg diluted with a few drops of water. Now bake them in an oven and, when they are cooked, cut out the covers without injuring the borders. Remove the flour, and baste the inside and outside of the crusts with the yolks of eggs. Then set them in a moderate oven to dry. Garnish the crusts with a Macedoine of Vegetables, such as peas, beans, asparagus-tops and carrots, each being cooked separately. The crusts can be filled with these vegetables, mixed or singly. Add to them, before filling, a reduced Allemande or Cream sauce.

VEGETABLE BREAD.

No. 1681.—This is made with any kind of vegetable purees. When the puree is cooked, it should be made firmer than when used as a garniture. The yolks of raw eggs must be added when the puree is cold. Purees that are thin will require more eggs than those that are thick; and a reduced Cream sauce may also be added to make them of the required consistency.

Put the puree in small buttered moulds, poach them, and serve with either Cream, Allemande or Espagnole sauce.

NOTE.—After they are cooked and become cold, they may be cut into a variety of shapes, and used as a garniture for soups. They may also be cut in slices one-quarter of an inch thick, then breaded, and fried, to be used as a garniture.

MACEDOINE OF VEGETABLES, SPANISH STYLE.

No. 1682.—Put two finely sliced white onions in a saucepan with four spoonfuls of sweet oil and fry them lightly. Then add four sliced bell peppers and, after they have simmered for a few minutes, add six red tomatoes that have been peeled and cut in quarters, and one egg plant that has been peeled and cut in small slices. Let them cook until the moisture is reduced and then add one handful of boiled string beans cut in small pieces. Season with salt, pepper and a pinch of red pepper. Now dish them up in a vegetable border and garnish them with plain boiled okra.

MACEDOINE OF VEGETABLES, MEXICAN STYLE.

No. 1683.—Prepare the following vegetables, viz.: Two dozen artichoke bottoms cut in quarters and an equal quantity each of green peas, shelled beans, string beans and asparagus tops, four bell-peppers cut in small pieces, and four heads of lettuce that have been trimmed and parboiled for two minutes.

Put one large onion, chopped finely, in a saucepan with a piece of butter. Fry it lightly and then add six ounces of finely-chopped lean raw ham. Let it cook for ten minutes and then sprinkle over it two soup-spoonfuls of flour. Let it cook for a few minutes, then add three pints of broth. Stir it well until it boils and then add a faggot of parsley garnished with a sprig of thyme and one bay leaf. When it boils slowly add the above vegetables, season with salt and pepper, cover the saucepan and let them cook until tender. Then remove the faggot and dish up the vegetables, being careful not to break or mash them. Reduce the sauce with some essence of truffles, pour it over the vegetables and garnish with small pieces of toasted bread.

NOTE.—This garniture makes a nice effect when dished up in a vegetable border.

MACEDOINE OF VEGETABLES, GERMAN STYLE.

No. 1684.—Wash and scrape two dozen young carrots and cut them in quarters. Parboil them for five minutes, then drain them and put them in a saucepan with a piece of butter. Toss them over the fire a few minutes, then moisten them with broth, and when nearly cooked, add one quart of green peas, and a faggot of parsley garnished with a sprig of thyme. Season with salt, pepper and a pinch of sugar, and cover the pan. When the peas are cooked take out the faggot, add a piece of butter and a glassful of cream, and toss it well over, off of the fire, until the butter is melted. Then serve it in a vegetable border.

MACEDOINE OF VEGETABLES, AMERICAN STYLE.

No. 1685.—Chop one onion finely, put it in a saucepan with a piece of butter, and fry it lightly. Now prepare two dozen young red carrots, cut them in halves, and prepare the same quantity of mixed beets, parsnips, celeriac, and turnips cut in halves and nicely trimmed. Parboil each kind separately for a few minutes, drain them and then put them in the saucepan with just enough broth to cook them. Season with salt and pepper, and let them cook slowly. When done, dish them up carefully.

Prepare separately, one dozen small white glazed onions, and add them to the above. Now reduce the gravy, add to it a teaspoonful of mustard, and pour it over the vegetables.

LARGE MACEDOINE GARNITURE.

No. 1686.—This garniture can be made of almost any kinds of vegetables that are young and tender. Five or six kinds should be used, having them of varied colors if possible. The kinds principally used are carrots, artichoke-bottoms, turnips, green peas, string beans, lima beans, cucumbers, Brussels sprouts, cauliflower, brocoli, small onions and mushrooms. The carrots and turnips are cut in any kind of fancy shapes, parboiled and then glazed. The cucumbers are scalloped and tossed in butter. The string beans are cut in diamond shape, about an inch long, and boiled in lightly salted water and then immersed in cold water, so they will retain their green color. Brussels sprouts and peas must be boiled and treated in the same manner. The flower buds only of cauliflowers and brocoli are used and must be kept in small bunches. The onions are parboiled and glazed. The mushrooms must be kept white and the tops cut in crescent shapes to give them a nice appearance. The artichoke-bottoms, when cooked, are cut in quarters. These vegetables are cooked separately. Then put them together in a flat saucepan, season with salt and pepper and add a little Cream sauce. Toss them gently over the fire.

NOTE.—This can be served as a vegetable if put in a vegetable border.

COLD MACEDOINE GARNITURE.

No. 1687.—This garniture is composed of the same ingredients as in No. 1686. The carrots and turnips are cut with spoon cutters and are cooked in broth and glazed. The green vegetables are boiled plain and kept green. The white vegetables are cooked and kept white. They must all be cooked separately and then drained on a napkin. Season with salt, pepper, oil and vinegar. When they are dry, dip them in Aspic jelly. When cold trim them nicely. Capers and gherkins may be added, and they are then dressed neatly, in bunches, alternating the colors, and garnished with Aspic jelly

SMALL MACEDOINE GARNITURE.

No. 1688.—This can be made with all kinds of vegetables. Use about five kinds at a time, varying them according to their color.

Prepare equal quantities of the following vegetables: Green peas, string beans, cut in diamond shape, artichoke bottoms cut in small pieces, asparagus tops, and flageolet beans. Cook each kind separately, and keep them as green as possible. Also prepare equal quantities of carrots and turnips, cut with a spoon cutter, celery, flower-buds of cauliflower, and glazed cucumbers. Cook each of these separately, and then mix them all together in a saucepan, adding some sliced mushrooms. Then add some Cream sauce.

LARGE GARNITURE, PEASANT STYLE.

No. 1689.—For this Garniture use young carrots cut in halves and nicely trimmed, or if old ones are used, slice them in pieces one quarter of an inch thick. Parboil them, and then cook them in broth to glaze them. Add some cucumbers cut in scollops and glazed, and some broiled sausages cut in pieces about three-quarters of an inch long. Dress the Garniture in bunches.

LARGE GARNITURE, FARMER STYLE.

No. 1690.—This Garniture is composed of carrots, potatoes, cabbage, lettuce, and artichokes. The carrots and potatoes are scooped out with a spoon-cutter. The carrots are boiled and glazed, while the potatoes are boiled and then tossed in butter. The cabbage is braised, and the lettuce stuffed. The artichoke bottoms are cut in halves. The Garniture is dressed in bunches, with the colors alternating.

LARGE GARNITURE, JARDINIERE.

No. 1691.—This Garniture consists of carrots, turnips, turnip-rooted celery, cucumbers, small onions, and artichoke bottoms, each kind being cooked separately and glazed; also the flower buds of cauliflower, or brocoli parboiled in lightly salted water; also green peas, string beans and Brussels sprouts, which must be boiled in lightly salted water, and then immersed in cold water, so the green color will be retained. They must then be tossed in a pan over the fire with a piece of butter until thoroughly warmed. Then dress them in bands, alternating the colors.

SMALL GARNITURE, JARDINIERE.

No. 1692.—This Garniture consists of carrots, turnips, string beans, flageolet beans, and asparagus tops. The carrots and turnips are cut in pieces about one-quarter of an inch long, with a column cutter. They are boiled and then cooked in broth and glazed. The other vegetables are boiled plain, then drained and mixed together in equal quantities. Then add some Allemande or Espagnole sauce, and season with salt, pepper, nutmeg, and a pinch of sugar.

NOTE.—This Garniture can be varied according to the season of the vegetables, one kind being substituted for another.

COLD GARNITURE, JARDINIERE.

No. 1693.—This Garniture is composed of the flower buds of cauliflower, artichoke bottoms, mushrooms, large asparagus tops, string-beans, and young carrots. They are all cooked separately, and then drained. Season them with salt, pepper, oil and vinegar, and then glaze them with Aspic jelly. Dress them in bunches, alternating the colors. The tops of the mushrooms should be grooved in crescent shapes to give them a nice appearance.

COLD GARNITURE, FLORAL STYLE.

No. 1694.—This garniture consists of nice large asparagus tops, mushrooms, truffles, artichoke-bottoms, young carrots and tomatoes. The asparagus tops are cut in pieces about two inches long and kept in bunches. The mushroom heads are cut in crescent shapes. The artichoke-bottoms are left whole. The carrots are nicely trimmed. All of these vegetables are cooked separately, then seasoned with salt, pepper, oil and vinegar, and kept separate. Then drain them and mask them with a Chaufroix sauce, changing the color of the sauce for each vegetable as it makes a finer effect. Dress them in bunches, alternating the colors.

LARGE GARNITURE, PROVINCIAL STYLE.

No. 1695.—This garniture consists of stuffed tomatoes and stuffed green peppers, stuffed artichokes and stuffed mushrooms. Dress them and glaze them with a Madeira wine sauce.

ESSENCE OF VEGETABLES.

No. 1696.—Put the following in a saucepan: One shin of beef, one of veal, one hen, six carrots, six onions and two turnips. Pour two gallons of cold water over them and, when it boils, skim it well. Then add two heads of celery, a faggot of parsley garnished with two heads of lettuce, two leeks, some whole peppers and a few cloves. Now let it cook slowly for four hours, then strain it through a towel and reduce it on the fire to half of its quantity.

FRYING BATTER FOR VEGETABLES.

No. 1697.—Put two pounds of sifted flour in an earthen bowl, make a hollow in the centre, and add four ounces of melted butter and water enough to make a light batter. Mix it well and see that no lumps form, having it nice and smooth, and add a little salt. This batter should be made one hour before it is used. When ready to use it, beat the whites of four eggs into a stiff froth, and add them to the batter, mixing the whole gently.

VEGETABLE SALADS.

No. 1698.—All vegetables that can be eaten raw or cooked can be used in salads. They are seasoned with salt, pepper, oil and vinegar, and are generally eaten cold. Various salad dressings and herbs are sometimes used in their preparation. Salads should vary according to the season of the vegetables. Care should be taken not to bruise any of the vegetables used in a salad. Green salads make a refreshing breakfast dish. Endives and dandelion should be dressed with a plain dressing and a piece of bread rubbed with garlic should always be added. The corn-salad or lamb-lettuce makes a delicious salad, dressed with pickled beets. A mustard dressing should be added to celery, and a few drops of Worcestershire sauce also, to heighten the flavor if desired. Water-cress should be served fresh and plain. It is excellent with roasted or broiled fowl. Lettuce and cos lettuce are two popular salads. Do not dress it until ready to serve. Fine herbs may be added, and also a garniture of hard-boiled eggs. Mixed vegetable salads are best in spring, when the vegetables are young and tender. In mixing them see that they harmonize in taste and color. The best vegetables for salads are green and white beans, new or pickled beets, potatoes, small onions, carrots, artichoke bottoms, asparagus tops, green peas, and gherkins. Occasionally some anchovies, pickled herrings, capers, olives, truffles, and yolks of eggs may be added. Be very careful in seasoning salads. Always season with the oil first, because if too much vinegar is used it will settle in the bottom of the salad bowl, instead of mixing with the oil properly. Never try to mix the salt with the vinegar. It is best to sprinkle it over the salad with the pepper, or it can be mixed with the oil. Green salads are used at breakfast or dinner, while the salads that are made of fowl or fish are best at a luncheon, supper, or collation. Cucumbers and tomatoes can be served with the fish.

Recipes for making the various kinds of sauces for salads will be found in the "Book on Sauces."

COMPOUND VEGETABLE SALAD.

No. 1699.—This salad is composed of cooked green peas, string beans, cut in pieces one inch long, sliced potatoes and white beans. Each kind is dressed separate and seasoned with pepper, salt, oil and vinegar. Make a dressing for it of six spoonfuls of oil and four of wine vinegar, mixed thoroughly, with the addition of a little salt and pepper. Then add a little finely-chopped parsley and burnet, and pour it over the salad. Garnish it with some hearts of lettuce, hard boiled eggs and fillet of anchovies.

VEGETABLE SALAD, AMERICAN STYLE.

No. 1700.—Slice finely equal quantities of cooked artichoke bottoms, celery, celeriac, potatoes, carrots and beets, and have the pieces about equal in size. Put them in a salad bowl and add some shelled beans—white or green. Season with salt, pepper, oil and vinegar, mix them gently together, then cover the bowl and set it in a cool place to allow the salad to macerate for one hour. When it is ready to serve add a little more oil and vinegar, and dress it in a salad bowl. Garnish properly.

MACEDOINE VEGETABLE SALAD.

No. 1701.—Cook the vegetables as described in Macedoine Garniture, No. 1688, and cut them in any shapes desired, with fancy cutters. When they are cooked, keep each kind separate, drain them and season with salt, pepper, oil and vinegar. When ready to serve the salad, the vegetables are mixed and nicely dressed in a salad bowl with a Ravigote or Mayonnaise sauce. For a large salad it is best to dress each vegatable in bunches, alternating them, and, when they are nicely decorated, the effect is pleasing. This salad is generally composed of the following vegetables in equal quantities, but they can be varied, according to the season: Green peas, asparagus-tops, beans, beets, carrots, turnips, artichoke-bottoms, and turnip-rooted celery.

NOTE.—The carrots and turnips should be parboiled, then immersed in cold water and cooked. Use only young and sweetly flavored turnips; if they are old or strongly flavored, they will spoil the salad.

DIPLOMATIC SALAD.

No. 1702.—Cut the tender parts of two stalks of celery in small strips about two inches long. Put them in a bowl, add three or four truffles cut in short Juliennes, and season with salt, pepper, oil and vinegar. Then cover the bowl and set it in a cool place for half an hour. Rub the yolks of three hard-boiled eggs through a fine sieve, and put them in a bowl that has been rubbed with a clove of garlic. Add a teaspoonful of French mustard, work them well together with a wooden spoon, dilute it with oil and vinegar, and season with salt and pepper. Now drain the celery and truffles and put them in a salad bowl. Add the above dressing and a little finely-chopped chives and parsley, mix the whole well together, and then arrange it properly.

VEGETABLE SALAD, ITALIAN STYLE.

No. 1703.—Prepare some turnips and carrots, and with a column cutter the size of a twenty-five cent piece, cut out as many pieces as are desired. Cook them in some lightly salted water, and when they are cold slice them finely in pieces of even size. Add to them equal quantities of boiled potatoes and pickled beets, cut in the same manner. Put them in a bowl, season with salt, pepper, oil and vinegar, and add a little Ravigote sauce. Mix them gently together, arrange them in a salad bowl, and garnish with hard-boiled eggs cut in quarters.

VEGETABLE SALAD, PARISIAN STYLE.

No. 1704.—Rub the yolks of four hard-boiled eggs through a fine sieve, put them in a bowl, and add one teaspoonful of Anchovy paste, and one of French mustard. Mix them well together with a wooden spoon while diluting it slowly with oil and vinegar.

Slice the following vegetables nicely, and put them in a bowl: One beet, one celeriac root, two potatoes, and two pickles. Season with salt and pepper, and add the above dressing with a little finely-cut tarragon and rampion. Mix the whole well together, put it in a salad bowl, arrange it properly, and garnish with the whites and yolks of hard-boiled eggs cut separately in small pieces, and some capers and stuffed olives.

VEGETABLE SALAD, RUSSIAN STYLE.

No. 1705.—Cook some celery, or celeriac, and some potatoes. When they are cold, trim them nicely, slice them finely, and put them in a bowl with some raw sliced gherkins, a raw sliced apple, a few capers, and a few boned Anchovies. Season with pepper, salt, oil and vinegar, add a little grated horse-radish and mustard, and mix the whole gently together. Set it aside for half an hour, and then drain off the moisture and dress it in a salad bowl with a Mayonnaise dressing.

SAUERKRAUT SALAD, GERMAN STYLE.

No. 1706.—Parboil half a pound of Sauerkraut for twenty minutes; then drain it in a colander, and pour some cold water over it to refresh it. Then drain it in a napkin. Prepare an equal quantity of red cabbage, cut it in fine shreds, and put it in a saucepan with a piece of butter. Add three spoonfuls of vinegar, let it cook over a brisk fire for five minutes, and then drain it. Cut one large white onion in small pieces (chopped). Throw them in boiling water for one minute; then immerse them in cold water, and drain them on a napkin.

Now put the sauerkraut, red cabbage and onion into a bowl, add a soup-spoonful of grated horse-radish, and a little finely-chopped chervil. Season with salt, pepper and vinegar. Mix the whole well together, arrange it properly in a salad bowl, and garnish with olives and beets.

VEGETABLE SALAD, CALIFORNIA STYLE.

No. 1707.—Slice one white sweet onion finely. Peel two cucumbers, cut them in halves lengthwise, scoop out the seeds, and then cut them in fine slices. Peel four tomatoes, and cut them in slices one-quarter of an inch thick. Put a layer of the onion in a salad bowl, then a layer of the tomato, and a layer of cucumbers on top, sprinkling each layer with bread crumbs, and seasoning with salt, pepper, oil and vinegar. On top of these three layers put three more layers exactly the same as the first three. Cover the bowl, and set it in a cool place. Always make this salad two hours before serving it. Sprinkle a little finely-chopped parsley and chives over it, and serve it as it is.

MIXED VEGETABLE SALAD, SWEDISH STYLE.

No. 1708.—Select equal quantities of the following cooked vegetables, and cut them nicely with a fancy cutter: young carrots, beets and potatoes. Put them in a bowl, and add some smoked beef-tongue cut in small thin slices, a boned and skinned pickled herring cut in small pieces, and one apple, peeled and finely sliced. Season with salt, pepper, oil and vinegar, and add a little finely-chopped parsley and chervil, and a few spoonfuls of mustard dressing. Mix them well together, arrange them properly in a salad bowl, and garnish with stoned olives and boned anchovies.

HOW TO PREPARE MOULDS WITH ASPIC JELLY, FOR SALADS.

No. 1709.—The salads following this recipe are different from the foregoing, being made in moulds, and dressed on stands or borders, or on bread masked with butter for a relief and as a convenience in garnishing. They are used principally at balls and banquets, and when nicely executed they form a handsome ornament to a table. Much depends upon the proficiency of the party making them; and special care should be taken to have the Aspic jelly clear, and not too firm. In cold weather it need not be as solid as when the weather is warm. They may be made in Charlotte or Timbal moulds, if desired; but it is best to use the regular Salad moulds that are made expressly for this purpose. They contain a false mould, which is inserted after the mould is ornamented. The space around this false mould is filled with jelly, and allowed to become firm. Warm water is then put in the centre of the mould, so it can be removed easily, which leaves the center vacant, to be filled with the salad. Then smooth off the top evenly, and set the mould aside to get cold until ready for use. Then dip the mould in warm water, wipe it dry, and then turn it out on the dish it is to be served on.

The mould is prepared, arranged and decorated as follows: Put the mould in a pan containing some cracked ice, and let it get cold. Put some cool Aspic jelly in the mould, and turn the mould around constantly until it is thinly and evenly coated with the jelly on the sides and bottom. (It takes considerable practice to do this perfectly.) Drain your vegetables, and dry them well on a napkin. Dip each piece separately in a cool Aspic jelly, and arrange them in the bottom and around the sides of the mould in the design that you prefer, alternating the colors. When this is done, line it with another coating of jelly, set it aside to get cold, and then fill the centre with the prepared salad. Truffles, capers, olives and the whites of eggs can be used to decorate the mould, instead of vegetables, if desired.

VEGETABLE SALAD WITH ASPIC JELLY, MACEDOINE.

No. 1710.—This salad is composed of cooked asparagus tops, carrots, beets, celeriac, cauliflower, green peas and flageolet beans.

Cook each kind separately, and when cold season with pepper, salt. oil and vinegar. Decorate the mould with Aspic jelly and the above vegetables, as in No. 1709. Put the remainder of the vegetables in a bowl with a few spoonfuls of Mayonnaise dressing made with Aspic jelly. Put the salad in the centre of the mould to fill it. Smooth the top, and set the mould aside to get firm. When ready to serve, dip the mould in warm water, then turn the salad out on the stand on which it is to be served. Garnish the base with asparagus tops, as in No. 85, and artichoke-bottoms, as in No. 46, with some hard boiled eggs cut in halves, and finely-chopped Aspic jelly.

VEGETABLE SALAD WITH ASPIC JELLY, JARDINIERE.

No. 1711.—Prepare and cook the vegetables as directed in No. 1692. Drain them, keep each kind separate, season with pepper, salt, oil and vinegar, decorate the mould with Aspic jelly and the vegetables, as in No. 1709. Then proceed as in No. 1710, and garnish with a cold Jardiniere as in No. 1693.

VEGETABLE SALAD WITH ASPIC JELLY, ITALIAN STYLE.

No. 1712.—Cut out one dozen potatoes with a round cutter about the size of a twenty-five cent piece, and slice them finely. Then take two pickled beets and cut and slice them the same way. Put them in separate bowls and season with pepper, salt, oil and vinegar. Prepare the fillet of one or two flounders, scrape off the skin, and put them in a buttered flat saucepan. Season with salt and pepper and add a little white wine. Then cook them, keeping them white, and when done put them on a platter and lay them aside to get cold. When cold cut them in scallops, add the same quantity of fillet of boned Anchovies, and season with pepper, salt, oil and vinegar. Decorate the mould with Aspic jelly, capers, olives, anchovies and the whites of hard boiled eggs, as in No. 1709. Put the flounders and anchovies in a bowl and add to them double their quantity of potatoes and beets, after they are drained. Also add some capers and a few spoonfuls of Mayonnaise dressing made with Aspic jelly. Mix them gently together and then fill the centre of the mould. Smooth off the top evenly and set it in a cool place until ready for use. When dressing it garnish with hard boiled eggs and chopped Aspic jelly.

BEAN SALAD, WITH ASPIC JELLY, GERMAN STYLE.

No. 1713.—Boil two pounds of dry white beans, keep them whole and let them get cold in their broth. Select enough of the most perfect beans to decorate a Charlotte mould, splitting half of them in halves to give a variety to the decoration. Drain the remaining beans in a colander, then put them in a bowl, season with pepper, salt, oil and vinegar, and add a little finely-chopped parsley or chives. Also add a few spoonfuls of Mayonnaise dressing, made with Aspic jelly, mix the whole well together, and then fill up the centre of the mould. Smooth off the top and set it aside to get firm. Finish it the same as the other moulds are finished.

Article CCXXVI.

French — *Vesce.*
VETCH, OR TARE.
German — *Wicke.*

No. 1714.—This is a leguminous plant having several varieties, all of which, in properties and habits, resemble the common pea, the seeds being used for food. It is not cultivated to any extent, as it is not prolific. It is cultivated like green peas, and is prepared for the table in the same manner as peas. It is also ground, mixed with corn or rye, and made into bread.

Article CCXXVII.

WATER-MELON.

Melon d'Eau.   *Wasser Melone.*

No. 1715.—The Water-melon is a tropical fruit that is largely and extensively cultivated in the United States. The fruit is roundish or oblong, and in color it is green or of variegated green shades. It is much more vigorous than the musk-melon, though inferior to the cantaloupe. Its abundant and cooling juice renders it very refreshing during summer. It is less liable to injury from insects than any other variety of melon.

CULTURE.

No. 1716.—Water-melons require a rich, though rather sandy soil for their best development, and thrive best in warm latitudes, growing best in the Southern and Southwestern States. Cultivate exactly the same as for musk-melons, except that the hills should be just double the distances apart, namely, eight and ten feet.

GEORGIA RATTLESNAKE.

No. 1717.—One of the largest varieties, and stands shipment long distances better than any other. It is the sort used at the South for northern shipments. It is a beautifully striped variety, of very large size, with red flesh of the finest flavor.

CUBAN QUEEN.

No. 1718.—One of the largest melons known, often attaining upwards of eighty pounds in weight. The vine is vigorous, and the skin striped, light and dark green. The flesh is bright red, solid, very crisp and sugary.

CALIFORNIA OR IMPROVED ODELLA.

No. 1719.—One of the best sorts for shipping purposes, as it has a tough, thin rind, which enables it to stand an amount of handling that would crack open other varieties. The flavor is excellent and quite distinct.

ORANGE.

No. 1720.—So called from its peculiar rind, which separates from the flesh when fully ripe. The flesh is red, tender and sweet.

CITRON AND CALIFORNIA PIE MELON.

No. 1721.—These melons are used in making sweetmeats and preserves by removing the rind and seeds, cutting the flesh in pieces of equal size, then boiling them in syrup which has been flavored with ginger, and then proceeding the same as with musk-melons in Nos. 922 and 923. They ripen late in season and will keep until December. The flesh is white, solid, tough, seedy, very squashy, and unpalatable in its crude state.

BLACK SPANISH.

No. 1722.—Their small vines enables them to be grown closer than any other sorts. They are round in form, and dark-green in color. The flesh is scarlet, rich and sugary in flavor.

SCALY BARK.

No. 1723.—A very popular variety in the South, which will keep in good condition after pickling longer than any other sort. The vines are large, with coarse foliage, the fruit large and oblong, and the flesh red and very tender.

MOUNTAIN SWEET.

No. 1724.—A large, long oval variety. The flesh is scarlet and quite solid to the center, very sweet and delicious.

ICE CREAM.

No. 1725.—This is medium-sized. The flesh is scarlet and very sweet. A good variety for general culture.

FERRY'S PEERLESS.

No. 1726.—The best melon for general use, particularly in the North. The vine is vigorous, hardy and productive. The fruit is medium, oval, and finely mottled with light and dark-green, somewhat in stripes. The rind is thin, and the flesh bright scarlet, solid to the centre, crisp, nutty, and sweet.

EARLY JERSEY.

No. 1727.—One of the earliest varieties, above the medium size, oval round, and light-green in color. The flesh is scarlet, solid, finely grained, very sweet and juicy.

HOW TO SERVE MELONS.

No. 1728.—Water-melons are served as a relish, or for dessert, and should be kept in a cool place for some time before serving. Cut a piece from each end, and then cut the melon in a zig-zag shape in the centre, which will divide the melon in half, and set each half on a dish with a napkin. Place them on the table, and when ready to use, cut them in slices.

NOTE.—Cut a plug out of the melon, pour a glass of brandy inside, replace the plug, keep the melon in a cool place, and occasionally turn it. In twenty-four hours the brandy will be absorbed, and the melon ready to serve. This makes a delicious change from the ordinary way of eating melons.

ARTICLE CCXXVIII.

French **WHEAT.** **German**
Froment. *Weitzen.*

No. 1729.—Wheat is a plant of the genus Triticum. The seed of this plant furnishes a white flour for bread and, next to rice, is the grain most generally used by the human race. The varieties are numerous, comprising the Summer and Winter Wheat, the Bearded Wheat, the White Wheat and the Bald Wheat. The Summer and Winter Wheat furnishes most of the grain that is used for food.

WINTER WHEAT.

MICHIGAN BRONZE OR MEDITERRANEAN HYBRID.

No. 1730.—This is a cross between the old Diehl and the Red Mediterranean, having the fine flavoring quality and bearded head of the latter and the close compact head of the former. It is a vigorous grower and is well adapted to light soil. The heads are somewhat club-shaped, short, but very compact, and are squarely filled out at both ends, containing about sixteen breasts of from three to four kernels each. The berry is of a bright amber color, of medium size and very handsome.

VALLEY.

No. 1731.—This variety originated in Ohio and yields enormously, but needs rich ground and good cultivation. The heads are bearded, long and loose, and have a peculiarly rough and ragged appearance. They contain from sixteen to twenty breasts, having three or four kernels each. The berry is long and hard, and of an amber color.

MARTIN'S AMBER.

No. 1732.—A hybrid variety that originated in the eastern part of Pennsylvania. While young, the plants lie spread out over the ground, affording a good protection to their own roots. The straw is tall and very stiff, standing up better than most varieties. The leaves are dark green and quite free from rust. It has a large, bald, smooth, well-filled head, containing from sixteen to eighteen breasts, and is rather late in ripening. The berry is of a light amber color, good size and very plump and handsome. It has a very thin hull and makes but little bran; however it yields a large return of flour of the very best quality.

DEMOCRAT.

No. 1733.—A variety that originated in Pennsylvania and is becoming very popular in Canada. It is very early. The heads are bearded and compact, with white chaff. The berry is of a very light amber color and is superior for milling qualities.

FULTZ.

No. 1734.—Although not as showy in the field as the Clawson, the Fultz will generally yield quite as much grain—that is of a better milling quality. It is much esteemed in Pennsylvania and Ohio, and is becoming popular elsewhere. The straw stands up well. The leaves are large, of a dark green color and free from rust. It has smooth, medium-sized, compact heads, containing from sixteen to eighteen breasts of two and three kernels each. The berry is of a dull amber color, medium in size and long.

CLAWSON.

No. 1735.—A smooth white Wheat, with red chaff. It is a superior variety.

RED MEDITERRANEAN.

No. 1736.—This is the imported variety fully acclimated. The heads are bearded and well filled. It succeeds well in nearly all localities, and ripens early.

WINTER PEARL.

No. 1737.—The heads are beardless, regular and very handsome, about five and a half inches long, with from eighteen to twenty breasts of four grains each. The kernels are about the size of the Clawson, hard, plump, and of a light amber color. It produces abundantly in good wheat fields.

SPRING WHEAT.

THE INVINCIBLE.

No. 1738.—This is a beardless variety of remarkably robust and vigorous growth. The straw is strong, stiff, well glazed and healthy. The heads are from four to five inches long, compact and well filled. The berry is of a light amber color, plump, hard and very heavy. It is wonderfully prolific. The grains ripen quickly and evenly.

Care should therefore be taken not to let it get over-ripe before harvesting.

ADAMANT WHEAT.

No. 1739.—This is one of the hardiest and most flinty varieties in cultivation, and is very productive and vigorous. It is a beardless, white-chaff variety, with long narrow heads, closely set with medium sized amber-colored kernels, which produce flour of a very superior quality. It is one of the most desirable sorts for cultivation in the Northwest, Colorado and the Pacific Coast, where hard wheat is the favorite sort.

GREEN MOUNTAIN WHEAT.

No. 1740.—A beardless variety much cultivated in Vermont. The straw is of a light yellow color, very strong, and free from rust. The heads average five inches in length, and are somewhat tapering. The kernels are white, large, plump, very hardy and productive.

NOTE.—For any other Wheat or cereal, see the Articles on Barley, Buckwheat, Corn, etc.

WHEAT BROTH.

No. 1741.—Soak six ounces of Wheat in water over night. Then drain and parboil it for two minutes, after which drain it again, and put it in a saucepan with a quart of veal broth. Let it boil slowly for an hour, and season it lightly.

SOUP—CREAM OF GREEN FARINA WHEAT.

No. 1742.—Green wheat can be procured in grains or in the same way as Farina (Semoule). The latter is preferred, as it cooks much quicker. It is greatly relished by Germans.

Put four quarts of broth in a saucepan, and when it boils drop in slowly one pound and a half of the green Farina Wheat, stirring it gently until it boils. Then set it on the side of the fire to boil slowly, and add a faggot of parsley garnished with leeks and green onions. Let it cook for one hour, then skim it, take out the faggot, and strain the soup through a fine sieve. Then put the soup in a saucepan, set it on the fire, and stir it until it boils. Season with salt, pepper, and a pinch of sugar. Let it boil slowly for fifteen minutes, then set it on the side of the fire to keep warm. Before serving add six ounces of butter, and half a pint of cream, diluted with the yolks of eight raw eggs. Mix it well until the butter is melted.

ARTICLE CCXXIX.

French
Pois Ramé.

WINGED PEA.

German
Die Spargelerbse.

No. 1743.—A hardy creeping annual plant. The pods are three inches long, with four longitudinal leafy membranes. The seeds are globular, slightly compressed, and yellowish-white in color. The ripened seeds are used as a substitute for coffee, and the pods, while young and tender, are prepared the same as string beans.

Sow it in double drills an inch and a half deep and two feet apart, the single rows being made twelve inches from each other.

ARTICLE CCXXX.

WITLOEF.

Romaine blanche. *Weisser Endivien.*

No. 1744.—This is a distinct and comparatively new vegetable, somewhat resembling chicory in habit. It produces a moderate sized and beautiful white heart, similar in shape to a cos lettuce, and when prepared as the latter is, or as a salad, it will be found a valuable acquisition to the winter vegetables.

ARTICLE CCXXXI.

WOOD SORREL.

Oseille Oxalide. *Sourklee.*

No. 1745.—Wood sorrel is a hardy perennial plant, growing naturally in woods, in cool and shaded situations. The leaves are radical, inversely heart-shaped, and produce three together at the extremity of quite a long stem. The leaves possess a pleasant acid taste and are mixed with salads, to which they impart an agreeably refreshing flavor. The plant is considered one of the most valuable of all vegetables that are cultivated for their acid properties.

CULTURE.

No. 1746.—It may be propagated either by seeds or by dividing the roots. The soil should be rich and moist. Sow it in April, in shallow drills, twelve inches apart.

Article CCXXXII.

French
Armoise ou Absinthe.

WORMWOOD.

German
Vermouth.

No. 1747.—A hardy perennial, shrubby plant, three feet in height. The leaves are deeply cut or divided, pale-green above, and hoary beneath. The leaves when bruised have a strong, somewhat pungent yet aromatic odor, and are proverbial for their intense bitterness.

An infusion of the leaves and tops of the common Wormwood is used as a vermifuge tonic and stomachic. The leaves are also beneficial to poultry.

ROMAN WORMWOOD.

No. 1748.—Resembles the common Wormwood, but the leaves are smaller and more finely cut; pale-green above and hoary on the under surface. It is preferred to the common for medicinal purposes, as the taste is more agreeable and its odor less pungent.

SEA WORMWOOD.

No. 1749.—The leaves are numerous, long, narrow and hoary, and bitter to the taste. When bruised they emit a strong, pleasant aromatic flavor.

CULTURE.

No. 1750.—They develop best in warm, dry, light soil. They are propagated the same as other hardy shrubs. If sown by seeds, sow them in April in drills. Transplant the seedlings in rows, two feet apart, and a foot between the seedlings.

GENERAL INDEX.

	NO.
ALEXANDER	1
Culture	2
Perfoliate	3
AMBROSIA	4
ANGELICA	5
Culture	6
Syrup	7
Preserved or Candied	8
ANISE	9
Culture	12
Anisette Cordial	10
Pumpernickel	11
AROMATIC, Medicinal and Pot Herbs	13
Culture	14
Varieties	15
ALLSPICE, or Aromatic Nigelle	16
Culture	17
ARTICHOKE	18
Culture	19
Green Large Globe	20
How to Prepare for Cooking	21
With Hollandaise Sauce	22
With Butter Sauce	23
With Mayonnaise or Vinaigrette	24
With Oil or Poivrade Sauce	25
With Oil and Vinegar Sauce	26
Barigoule	27
Barigoule	28
Italian Style	29
Fried, Italian Style	30
Lyonnaise	31
Stuffed, Bordelaise	32
Stuffed, American Style	33
Tossed (sauté) in Butter	34
Puree for Garniture	47
Croquettes	48
Soup, Puree	49
Soup, Cream	50
Pickled	51
How to Cook Pickled Artichokes	52
Preserved Whole	53
Preserved in Quarters	54
Puree Preserved	56
Jerusalem	57

	NO
ARTICHOKE BOTTOMS	35
How to Prepare	35
Stuffed, Clara Louise Kellogg Style	36
Stuffed, Pioneer Style	37
Stuffed, Italian Style	38
Fricassee	39
Fried, Villeroi Style	40
Spanish Style	41
Macedoine	42
Provençale	43
With Fine Herbs	44
Stewed for Garniture	45
For large Cold Garniture	46
Preserved in Cans	55
ASPARAGUS	65
Culture	66
Colossal	67
Giant	68
Crossbred	69
Small Defiance	70
How to Prepare for Cooking	71
With Butter Sauce	72
With Hollandaise Sauce	73
Piemontaise	74
Pompadour	75
Spanish Style	76
With Oil and Vinegar	77
Puree for Garniture	84
Soup—Puree, Conde	89
" Puree, Royal	90
" Puree, St. George	91
" Cream, Countess	92
Preserved in Salt	93
Preserved in Cans	94
Syrup	96
ASPARAGUS TOPS	78
How to Prepare	78
With Sauce	79
Colbert	80
With Truffles, Imperial	81
With Mutton Gravy	82
For Garniture	83
For Large, Cold Garniture	85
Salad, Plain	86
Salad, with Shrimps	87

ASPARAGUS TOPS—Continued.	NO.	BEANS—Continued.	NO.
Salad, with Truffles, Royal.......	88	Dreer's Improved Lima.......	137
Preserved........................	95	Dutch Case Knife	138
ASPARAGUS BEAN....	97	Speckled Cranberry...............	139
		Scarlet Runner...................	140
BALLS..............................	1188	Giant Wax.......................	141
Potatoes, American style	1183	German Wax Pole...............	142
Margot style.....................	1189	English or Broad................	143
(Quenelles) of Corn Meal......	715	Early Mazagan...................	144
" of Potatoes	1204	Broad Windsor...................	145
" of Semoule, Vill·roi...	1405	Sword Long Pod.................	146
Vegetables, Turkish style........	1672	How to Prepare String Beans for	
BALM..............................	98	Cooking........................	147
Culture...........................	99	(String) English Style............	148
BALM-MINT........	100	" Maitre d'Hotel.............	149
BARLEY	101	" With Fine Herbs..... ...	150
Common..........................	102	" Lyonnaise.....	151
Mansury....	103	" Poulette....................	152
Naked, or Hulless.............	104	" Bretonne...................	153
Soup Cream, Neilson style........	105	" German Style........ ...	154
Soup Cream, Marie Louise style..	106	" With Cream	155
Soup Cream, Farragut style......	107	" Country Style...... ...	156
Broth, for Invalids................	108	" Preserved in Salt.	157
Water, for Invalids...............	109	" " " Brine	158
Water, for Gargling........ ...	111	" " " Cans.....	159
Cream, for Invalids	110	" Salted, How to Prepare for	
BASIL SWEET	112	Cooking........................	160
Culture....	113	" Salad	161
		" " German Style.......	162
BATTER for Frying Vegetables	1697	" For Garniture.............	163
BAY, OR LAUREL LEAVES		(Wax) Maitre d'Hotel	164
(Common)...................	114	(White, or Kidney). With Puree of	
" " " " (Larustine)	115	Onion, Soubise.......	165
BEANS.............................	116	" Country Style.............	166
Culture of the Dwarf or Bush Bean	117	White or Kidney Soup Puree, Newton	
Early Feegee.....................	118	Style...............................	198
Early Red Valentine..............	119	(Dry White) Maitre d'Hotel.......	173
White Valentine.................	120	" " German Style.........	174
Gallega, or Large Refugee.....	121	" " With Cream Sauce...	175
Early Mohawk......	122	" " Bretonne.............	176
Black Wax or Butter..............	123	" " Robert................	177
White Wax	124	" " With Bacon..........	178
Ivory Pot Wax....	125	" " " Marrow........	179
Canadian Wonder	126	" " Salad.................	181
Golden Refugee..................	127	" " For Garniture........	182
Crystal White Wax..............	128	" " Puree—White........	183
Golden Wax	129	" " " Brown	184
Refugee..........................	130	" " " With Celery.	185
Large White Kidney...............	131	" " Soup Puree, Pioneer	
White Marrowfat.....	132	Style...	201
Dwarf Soisson	133	" " " " St.George	202
Pole Running.....................	134	Green Flageolet, Maitre d'Hotel...	167
Large White Lima......	135	" " German Style.....	168
Small Lima or Sieva	136	" " With String Beans	169
		" " Puree for Garni-	
		ture...........	171

GENERAL INDEX.

	NO.
BEANS—Continued.	
Green Flageolet, Preserved in Cans	172
" " Soup, Puree, St. Germain	196
" " Soup, Puree, Soubise	197
" " Soup, Cream, Leland Style	200
Red, Bourguignonne	186
" Cardinal, for Fast Days	187
" Donohoe Style, for Fast Days	188
Dry Red, Soup, Puree, Conde	203
Black, With Butter	189
" Soup Puree, Faubonne	199
Soup, Puree for Fast Days	204
For Garniture	170
Broad	190
" With Cream, Poulette	191
Lima	192
" With Butter Sauce	193
" French Style	194
" Macedoine	195
Baked in Pots	180
Notes	205
BEETS	206
Culture	207
Egyptian Turnip	208
Bastian's Blood Turnip	209
Deming's Blood	210
Early Flat Bassano	211
Long Smooth Blood Red	212
Early Yellow	213
Pine Apple	214
Brazilian Variegated	215
Swiss Chard or Sea Kale	216
How to Prepare for Cooking	217
Boiled Beets Stewed	218
Stewed, Hanoverain Style	219
" with Cream Sauce	220
" " Butter "	221
" St Ignatius	222
Roasted	223
For Garniture	224
Fritters, Chartreusse	225
Sugar	226
Juice for Soups	227
Salad with Vegetables	228
Pickled	229
" for Relishes, German Style	230
" " " American "	231
BENE	232
Culture	233
Bi-formed Leaved	234
Oval Leaved	235
Tri-fide Leaved	236

	NO.
BOLETUS (Esculent)	237
BORAGE	238
Culture	239
BORDERS—Potatoes	1207
Rice	1285
Vegetables	1074
BREAD OF VEGETABLES.	1081
BRIAR LEAVES	240
BROCOLI	241
Culture	242
White Cape	243
Purple Cape	244
Italian Style	245
With Hollandaise Sauce	246
For Garniture	247
Soup Cream	248
BROOKLINE OR SPEEDWELL	249
BROTH—Barley for Invalids	108
Celery	473
Dandelion	651
Pectoral with Turnips	1651
Wheat	1741
BRUSSELS SPROUTS	250
Culture	251
Tall French	252
Dwarf Improved	253
How to Prepare for Cooking	254
With Fine Herbs	255
With Sauce	256
Spanish Style	257
For Garniture	258
" " with Broiled Meats	259
Puree for Garniture	260
BUCK'S-HORN OR COCK'S-HEAD PLANTAIN	261
Culture	262
BUCKWHEAT	263
Common	264
Silver Hulled	265
Cakes with Yeast	266
" " Baking Powder	267
Baking of Cakes	268
BUGLOSS	269
Culture	270
BURNET	271
Culture	272
BUTTER—Garlic	730
Horse-radish	761
CABBAGE.	273
Culture	274
Early Jersey Wakefield	275
Early Etampes	276

CABBAGE—Continued.

	NO.
Early York	277
" Large York	278
" Sugar Loaf	279
Little Dixie	280
Henderson's Early Summer	281
Early Flat Dutch	282
" Dwarf Flat Dutch	283
" Winningstadt	284
" Bleichfield Giant	285
Filder Kraut	286
Drumhead Short Stem	287
Early Large Schweinfurt	288
Imperial French Ox Heart	289
Red Dutch, for Pickling	290
Fine Blood Red	291
Marblehead	292
Late Flat Dutch	293
Large Drumhead	294
Marblehead Mammoth Drumhead	295
Green Glazed	296
Early Dwarf Ulm Savoy	297
Green Globe Savoy	298
American Savoy	299
Drumhead Savoy	300
Boiled	301
With Potatoes, Flamande	302
Braised, French Style	303
German Style	304
With Bacon, Family Style	305
Stuffed	306
" Hunter's Style	307
Bismarck Style	308
With Cream	309
Stewed, Spanish Style	310
With Quails or Partridges	311
Hot Slaw	312
Cold Slaw	313
Salad	314
Salad, Boston Style	315
Salad, with Cream, American Style	316
For Garniture	321
Soup	322
Soup, Served with Broth, Garbure	323
Pickled	324
Red Cabbage Salad	317
Red Cabbage, German Style	318
Red Cabbage, Hollandaise Style	319
Red Cabbage, Valencienne Style	320
Red Cabbage, Pickled, English	325
Sauer Kraut	326
Sauer Kraut, How to Make	327
Sauer Kraut, How to Prepare for Cooking	328
Sauer Kraut, German Style	329
Sauer Kraut, French Style	330

CABBAGE—Continued.

	NO.
Sauer Kraut, Bavarian Style	331
Sauer Kraut, Flemish Style	332
Sauer Kraut, Baked, Dufour	333
Sauer Kraut, Baked, with Fillet of Soles	334
Sauer Kraut, with Partridges or Quails	335

CAKES

Batter	595
Buckwheat, with Yeast	266
Buckwheat, with Baking Powder	267
How to Bake Buckwheat Cakes	268
Carolina, with Sabayon Sauce	1513
Corn	594
Flannel	596
Flap Jacks, or Trimmed Lace	597
Graham Griddle	739
Green Corn	576
Corn Griddle	594
Potato	1201
Rice Glazed	1327
Rice Souffle	1326

CALABASH, OR COMMON GOURDS ... 336

CALAMINT ... 337

CANDIED ANGELICA ... 8

CANTALOUPE, or Persian Melons. 338

Germek	339
Geree	340
Darce	341
Green Hoosaine	342
Green Valencia	343
Ispahan	344
Melon of Keisiug	345
Melon of Seen	346
How to Serve	347
Preserved in Cans	348
Preserved in Syrup	349

CAPERS. ... 350

Pickled in Vinegar	351
Sauce	352

CAPILLARY, OR VENUS HAIR ... 353

Syrup	354

CARAWAY ... 355

Culture	356

CARDOON ... 357

Culture	358
Large Spanish	359
The Ordinary	360
Artichoke-leaved	361
Large Tours Solid	362
With Marrow	363
With Parmesan Cheese	364

GENERAL INDEX.

	NO.
CARDOON—Continued.	
With Cream Sauce	365
With Essence of Ham	366
Fricassee	367
For Garniture	368
Puree	369
Salad, Spanish Style	370
Preserved	371
Puree Preserved	372
CARROT	373
Culture	374
Early French Forcing	375
Early Scarlet Horn	376
Half Long Red (Stunted Roots)	377
Half Long Red Scarlet (Pointed Roots)	378
Early Half Long Scarlet Carenton	379
Long Orange	380
Danvers	381
Altringham	382
Long White Belgian	383
Yellow Belgian	384
How to Prepare for Cooking	385
Maitre d'Hotel	386
Stewed, German Style	387
With Butter Sauce	388
With Green Peas, Strasbourgeoise	389
Stewed, Indian Style	390
Stewed, for Garniture	391
For large Garniture Flament	392
For small Garniture, Olive-shaped	393
Garniture, Nivernaise	394
Puree for Garniture	395
Soup Puree, Aurore	396
" " Stanley	397
" " German Style	398
" " Crecy	399
" " " for Fast days	400
Pickled	401
Preserved for Garniture	402
Puree Preserved for Soups or Garniture	403
CASSEROLES of Rice	1318
CATERPILLAR	404
Culture	405
CATNIP	406
Culture	407
CATSUP	408
Elderberry	692
Mushrooms	896
Tomato No. 1	1589
" No. 2	1590
" No. 3	1591
" Epicurean	1592

	NO.
CAULIFLOWER	409
Culture	410
Early Snowball	411
" Dwarf Erfurt	412
" Paris	413
Nonpareil	414
Early London	415
Lenormand Short-stemmed	416
Walcheren	417
Algiers	418
Weith's Autumn Giant	419
How to Prepare for Cooking	420
With Butter Sauce	421
Hollandaise	422
Baked, au Gratin	423
Fried, Villeroi	424
Fried in Batter	425
Italian Style	426
For Garniture	427
Puree for Garniture	428
Salad	429
Soup—Cream	430
Soup Puree	431
Pickled	432
Preserved in Brine	433
CELERIAC, or Turnip Rooted Celery	434
Culture	435
Large Erfurt	436
Apple Shaped	437
Fried, Villeroi	438
Puree for Garniture	439
Stewed, Spanish Style	440
Stewed with Allemande or Cream Sauce	441
Use of Celeriac Tops	442
With Gravy (Half-Glaze)	443
For Soups	444
Preserved	445
Pickled	446
Preserved in Brine	447
CELERY	448
Culture	449
Dwarf White	450
Sandringham Dwarf White	451
Giant White Solid	452
White Walnut	453
Half Dwarf	454
Golden Dwarf	455
London Red	456
Major Clark Pink	457
Hood's Dwarf Red	458
How to Prepare for General Use	459
Plain for Relishes	460
Dressed	461
With Gravy (Half-Glaze)	462

	NO.
CELERY—Continued.	
Stewed, Spanish Style	463
Stewed with Allemande Sauce	464
Stewed with Cream Sauce	465
Sauce	466
Fried Villeroi	467
With Parmesan Cheese	468
For Garniture	469
Puree For Garniture	470
With White or Brown Sauce	471
Salad	472
Broth	473
Soup, Puree, Spanish Style	474
Cream Soup	475
Puree, Preserved	476
Preserved	477
Preserved in Brine	478
Vinegar	479
Flavor	480
CENTAURY	481
CEPES	897
Bordelaise	897
Provincial	898
Polonaise	899
With Cream	900
Preserved	997
CHAMOMILE	482
Culture	483
CHAPON, FOR SALAD DRESSING	731
CHARTREUSSE	1675
CHERVIL	484
Culture	485
Tuberous-Rooted	486
CHESTNUT	487
Soup, Puree	488
" Cream, Hunter's Style	489
" Garbure, Polignac	490
Puree	491
Glazed	492
CHICK OR EGYPTIAN PEA	493
Culture	494
Red	495
White	496
Yellow	497
CHICKLING WETCH, OR SPANISH LENTIL	498
CHICCORY, OR SUCCORY	499
Culture	500
CHINESE SPINACH	501
CHINESE YAM, OR POTATO	502
CHOCA	519

	NO.
CHOCOLATE, PLAIN	520
Pot	521
With Eggs or Cream	522
Adulterated	523
CHIVES, OR WELSH ONION	503
Common, or Red Welsh Onion	504
White Welsh Onion	505
CHUFA, OR EARTH NUT	508
Culture	509
CICELY SWEET, OR SWEET SCENTED CHERVIL	510
CINNAMON	511
CLARY	512
CLAVARIA	513
CLOVES	514
COCOA	515
Ground	516
Shell	517
Broma	518
Choca	519
Plain Chocolate	520
Pot Chocolate	521
Chocolate, with Eggs or Cream	522
Adulterated Chocolate	523
COFFEE	524
Remarks on Mixing	525
For Family Use	526
Boiled	527
Boiled	528
German Style	529
Essence, for Cream	530
Ice	531
COLT'S-FOOT, Common	532
Culture	533
COLORS for Culinary Purposes, Green	1461
For Culinary Purposes, Yellow	1353
COMMON CHIVES	506
Culture	507
CORIANDER	534
Culture	535
CORN	542
Culture	543
Early Marblehead	544
Dolly Dutton	545
Extra Early Adams	546
Early Minnesoth	547
Early Red Narragansett	548
Crosby's Extra Early	549
Russell's Early Prolific Sugar	550
Early Sweet Sugar	551
Moore's Early Concord Sweet	552
Black Mexican	553

	NO.
CORN—Continued.	
Excelsior	554
Amber Cream	555
Triumph	556
Egyptian Sweet	557
Mammoth Sweet	558
Stowell's Evergreen Sweet	559
Burlington Early Adams	560
Early Canada	561
Lackawaxen	562
Early White Flint	563
Large Red Blazed	564
Early Golden Dent	565
Chester County Mammoth	566
Blunt's Prolific	567
Rice Corn for Parching	568
Boiled Green	569
With Milk or Cream	570
Stewed Green	571
With Beans	572
Succotash	573
With Tomatoes	574
Fritters	575
Cakes	576
How to Prepare Canned Corn	577
Roasted	578
Soup—Cream	579
Chowder	580
Hulled	581
Boiled Coarse Hominy	582
Fine Hominy	583
Fried Hominy	584
Hominy Croquettes	585
Baked Hominy	586
Corn Meal	587
Boiled Mush	588
Fried Mush	589
Corn Meal Gruel	590
Polainta of Corn Meal with Cheese	591
" With Game	592
Crusts of Polainta, Milanaise Style	593
Griddle Cakes	594
Batter Cakes	595
Flannel Cakes	596
Flap Jacks or Trimmed Lace	597
Corn Starch	598
CORN POPPY, or Coquelicot	536
CORN SALAD, or Lamb Lettuce	537
Culture	538
Salad	539
With Beets	540
With Celery	541
COUCH GRASS	599
COS LETTUCE, OR ROMAINE	600

	NO.
COSTMARY, OR ALECOST	601
Culture	602
CRANBERRY	603
Culture	604
Sauce	605
CREAM. Barley for Invalids	110
Oat Meal	954
Spinach	1462
Sweet Potatoes for Pies	1512
CRESS, OR PEPPER GRASS	606
Culture	607
CRESS, GARDEN	608
CRESS, WATER	609
Culture	610
Its Use	611
CROQUETTES, Artichokes	48
Hominy	585
Potatoes	1185
Rice	1322
Rice, Creole Style	1325
CRUSTS. Morels	863
Mushrooms	890
Potatoes	1208
Polainta, Milanaise Style	593
Polainta, Italian Style	712
Rice, small	1313
" " Victoria Style	1314
" " With Eggs and Cheese	1315
" " " Curried Lobster	1316
" " " Puree of Chicken	1317
Semoule, small, Palermitaine	1404
Vegetables, Macedoine Style	1608
CUCUMBER	612
Culture	613
Early White Spine	614
Extra Large White Spine	615
Boston Pickling	616
Early Frame	617
Early Cluster	618
Green Prolific	619
Early Russian	620
Long Green	621
English Frame or Forcing	6.2
With Cream Sauce	623
Poulette	624
Duchesse	625
Spanish Style	626
Stuffed, Spanish Style	627
Stuffed, Italian Style	628
Stuffed, Turkish Style	629
Scalloped for Garniture	630
" " " with Sauce	631
Puree	632

	NO.
CUCUMBER—Continued.	
Soup—Cream, Queen Style	633
Soup Puree, Patti Style	634
With Soup Puree of Chicken	635
For Relish	636
Salad, French Style	637
" Spanish "	638
" German "	639
Preserved	640
Pickled	641
Pickled (Pickles or Gherkins)	642
" Mixed Pickles	643
CUCKOO-FLOWER CRESS	644
CUMIN	645
CURRY	646
CUSTARD—Coffee in Cups	1531
For Soup Garniture, Langtry Style	1301
Onion, for Soup Garniture	1014
Tea in Cups	1531
DANDELION	647
Culture	648
Large Leaved	649
Salad	650
Broth	651
DILL	652
Culture	653
DIET-DRINKS (Tisanes)	654
Decoction of Malt	655
Herb Juice	656
Iceland Moss or Lichen	657
Coltsfoot	658
Anti-bilious	659
Emollient	660
Pectoral	661
Apozems	662
" Diuretic or Aperient	663
" Vermifuge	664
" Anti-Scorbutic	665
" Astringent	666
" Stomachic	667
" Purgative	668
" German or White Decoction	669
DUXELLE	744
EGG-PLANT	670
Culture	671
Early long Purple	672
Black Pekin	673
Large New York Purple	674
Improved Large Purple	675
Guadaloupe Striped	676
Ornamental Varieties	677
Fried, French Style	678

	NO.
EGG-PLANT—Continued.	
Breaded and Fried, American Style	679
Lyonnaise	680
With Cheese, Neapolitan Style	681
With Cream and Cheese	682
Puree	683
Stuffed, American Style	684
" Brazilian "	685
" Turkish "	686
" Parisian "	687
For Garniture	688
Salad	689
EGYPTIAN CUCUMBER	690
ELDERBERRIES	691
Catsup	692
ELECAMPANE	693
ENDIVE OR CHICOREE	694
Culture	695
French Moss	696
Broad Leaved Batavian	697
Green Curled	698
With Cream Sauce	699
German Style	700
With Poached Eggs	701
With Veal Gravy	702
Puree	703
Salad, French Style	704
" German "	705
" American "	706
Soup—Cream with Poached Eggs	707
Preserved in Cans	708
ESSENCE	530
Coffee, for Creams	530
Mushroom	894
Shallots	1411
Truffles	1606
Vegetables	724
"	1696
FAGGOT OF PARSLEY	1039
FARINA	709
Polainta of Corn Meal Piemontaise	710
" " " on Skivers	711
Crusts (Polainta) of Corn Meal, Italian Style	712
Crusts, or Stands of Corn Meal, for Hot or Cold Side Dishes	713
Tartlets of Corn Meal	714
Balls, or Quenelles of Corn Meal	715
Fried Farina (Polainta) of Corn Meal, Ramequin	716
Polainta for Garnitures	717
Gruel	718
FECULA	719

	NO.
FENNEL (SWEET)	720
Culture	721
Stewed	722
FINE HERBS	742
Cooked	742
Raw	743
In Sauce	745
FLAVORS—ESSENCES AND EXTRACTS	723
Essence of Vegetables	724
Flavor of Celery	480
" " Vanilla	1669
FLOUR	725
Repére	726
FRICASEE	
Artichoke Bottoms	39
Cardoons	307
Lentils	795
FRIED Artichokes, Italian Style	30
" Bottoms, Villeroi	40
Cauliflower, Villeroi	424
" In Batter	425
Celeriac, Villeroi	438
Celery, Villeroi	467
Egg Plant, French Style	678
" " Breaded, American Style	679
Farina, Ramequin	716
Hominy	584
Hops	752
Lettuce, Stuffed	820
Morels	862
Mushrooms	589
Onions	991
Parsnips	1050
Potatoes, Saratoga Style	1192
" Long Branch Style	1193
" French Style	1194
" Julienne Style	1195
" Parisian Style	1196
" Puffed (Soufflé)	1199
Salsify, in Batter	1374
" Villeroi	1375
" in Butter	1376
Squash, Stuffed, American Style	1491
" Boston Style	1492
Sweet Potatoes	1509
" " Puffed (Soufflé)	1510
Tomatoes	1571
FRITTERS	
Beets, Chartreusse	225
Carolina Cake, Nellie Grant Style	1514
Corn	575
Parsnip	1052

	NO.
FRITTERS—Continued.	
Rice	1325
" (Subrics)	1323
Spinach (Subrics)	1460
Sweet Potatoes	1511
GARBURE	727
GARNITURES	
Artichoke Bottoms, Stewed	45
" " Large Cold	46
Asparagus Tops	83
" " Large Cold	85
Beans, Dry White	182
" String	163
Beets	224
Brocoli	247
Brussel's Sprouts	258
" " for Broiled Meats	259
Cabbage	321
Cardoons	368
Carrots Stewed for	391
" Flamant, Large	392
" Olive-shaped, Small	393
" Nivernaise	394
Cauliflower	427
Celery	469
Cucumbers, Scolloped	630
" with Sauce	631
Egg Plant	688
Farina Polenta	717
Farmer's Style, Large	1690
Floral Style, Large	1694
Jardiniere, Large	1691
" Small	1692
" Cold	1693
Jerusalem Artichokes	63
Lettuce	822
Macedoine, Large	1686
" Small	1688
" Cold	1687
Morels	864
Mushrooms	889
Okra	964
Onions	1001
" Small Baked	1002
Onion Custard for Soups	1014
Parsley, Fried	1041
" Plain	1042
Peas, Green	1087
Peasant Style, Large	1689
Peppers, Green	1118
Potatoes	1202
Provincial, Large	1695
Radishes	1256
Rice	1300
" Custard for Soup	1301

GENERAL INDEX.

	NO.
GARNITURES—Continued.	
Spinach	1459
Tomatoes	1581
Truffles	1607
" Cold	1608
Turnips, Brown	1641
" White	1642
Turnip Cabbage	1661
GARLIC	728
Culture	729
Butter or Gascony Butter	730
Chapon for Salad Dressing	731
Puree	732
GHERKIN	733
GINGER	734
GLOBE CUCUMBER	735
GOOSE-FOOT, or White Quinoa	736
Culture	737
GRAHAM FLOUR	738
Griddle Cakes	739
GRUEL	
Corn Meal	590
Farina	718
Oat Meal	951
" " Scotch	952
Oats	951
Rice	1312
Sago	1363
HERBS	740
Culture	741
Cooked	742
Raw..;	743
Duxelle	744
Sauce	745
Dry	746
HOLLYHOCK, OR ROSE MALLOW	747
HOOSUNG OR OOSUNG	748
HOPS	749
Boiled with Sauce	750
Stewed " "	751
Fried	752
HOARHOUND	753
Culture	754
HORSE-RADISH	755
Culture	756
For Relish	757
Sauce	758
" with Apples	759
" " Cream	760
Butter	761
Vinegar	762

	NO.
HYSSOP	763
Culture	764
INDIAN STAR ANISE SEED	765
INFUSION FOR TURTLE SOUP	1441
JAPAN PEA	766
Culture	767
JASMINE	768
JERUSALEM ARTICHOKE	57
Culture	58
With Butter Sauce	59
Italian Style	60
Cracovienne	61
Puree for Garniture	62
For Garniture	63
Soup Puree, Palestine	64
JUNIPER	769
KALE OR BORECOLE	770
Culture	771
Tall Green Curled Scotch	772
German Dwarf Purple	773
" " Green	774
Dwarf Erfurt	775
Cottagers	776
With Cream	777
For Greens, with Salt Pork or Bacon	778
LAVENDER	779
LEEK	780
Culture	781
London Flag	782
Little Montague	783
Proliferous	784
Yellow Poiton	785
Large Rouen	786
Soup, Puree Viennoise	787
LENTIL OR LENS	788
Culture	789
Common	790
Green	791
Large	792
Small	793
Maitre d' Hotel	794
Fricassee	795
Puree, for Garnitures, Conde	796
Soup, Puree	797
" " Conde	798
" " Hunter's Style	799
LETTUCE	800
Culture	801
Early Tennis Ball	802
Black seeded Simpson	803
Simpson Early Curled	804
Early Boston Curled	805
" Prize Head (Ferry's)	806

GENERAL INDEX.

	NO.
LETTUCE—Continued.	
Hanson	807
Deacon	808
Early Curled Silesia	809
Frankfort Head	810
Large Drumhead	811
Philadelphia Butter	812
Brown Dutch	813
Green Fringed	814
White Paris Cos	815
Salamander	816
Braised, Spanish Style	817
" German Style	818
Stuffed	819
" and Fried	820
With Cream	821
" Gravy	822
For Garniture	823
Salads	824
With Consomme, Garbure	825
Water for Invalids	826
Preserved Whole	827
" in Cans	828
When Used in Vegetable Soups	829
LICORICE	830
Culture	831
LIMA BEANS	832
Culture	833
Green	834
Mottled	835
LIME OR LINDEN TREE	836
LOVAGE	837
Culture	838
LUPINE	839
MACE	840
MACEDOINE Garniture, Large	1686
Garniture, Small	1688
Garniture, Cold	1687
Vegetables, American Style	1685
" German Style	1684
" Mexican Style	1683
" Spanish Style	1682
MADRAS RADISH	841
MALLOW—CURLED LEAVED	842
MARANTA, OR ARROWROOT PLANT	843
Preparation of its Flour	844
Its Use	845
MARJORAM	846
Culture	847
Sweet	848
Common	849
Pot	850
Winter Sweet	851

	NO.
MARSH MALLOW	852
MELILOT	853
MINT	854
Culture	855
Sauce, American Style	856
Sauce, French Style	857
MOREL	858
Poulette	859
Spanish Style	860
On Skivers	861
Fried	862
With Gratinated Crusts	863
For Garniture	864
Stuffed	865
MULLEN OR MULLEIN	866
MUSHROOMS	867
Culture	868
Common	869
Agaricus Comatus	870
Sweet, or Delicious	871
St. George	872
Blewitt's Blue Hats	873
Agaricus Primulas	874
Fairy King	875
How to Clean and Prepare	876
Cooked for General Purposes	877
With Allemande Sauce	878
With Espagnole Sauce	879
On Toast (Sauté)	880
Puree	881
Broiled on Toast, Maitre d'Hotel	882
Broiled, Bordelaise	883
Provincial	884
Piemontaise	885
Use of Trimmings and Peelings	886
Stuffed with Fine Herbs	887
Stuffed, Italian Style	888
For Garniture	889
With Gratinated Crusts	890
Baked in Shells	891
Poulette	892
With Cream Sauce, American Style	893
Essence of Fresh	894
Soya Sauce	895
Catsup	896
Cepes, Bordelaise	897
" Provincial	898
" Polonaise	899
" with Cream	900
" Preserved	907
Tartlets with Cream	901
In Shells, Russian Style	902
Dry	903
Preserved in Cans	904
" in Jars	905

GENERAL INDEX.

MUSHROOMS—Continued.
Preserved Trimmings, for Fine Herbs 906
MUSKMELON 908
  Culture 909
  Beechwood 910
  Christiana 911
  Citron 912
  Hardy Ridge 913
  Large Ribbed, Netted 914
  Nutmeg 915
  Pineapple 916
  Skillman's Fine Netted 917
  Victory of Bath 918
  White Japan 919
  For Relishes 920
  Pickled (Mangoes) 921
  Preserved, Spiced 922
    "   in Syrup 923
MUSTARD 924
  Culture 925
  White 926
  Chinese, or Pékin 927
  Curled 928
  Cut Leaved 929
  Black 930
  Charlock 931
  Mixed, for Table Use 932
  Anchovy 933
  Ravigote 934
  Sauce, for Deviled Meats 935
NASTURTIUM 936
  Culture 937
  Small 938
  Tall 939
  Dark Flowering 940
  Seed Buds, Pickled 941
NETTLE 942
NEW ZEALAND SPINACH 943
NUTMEG 944
OAK (Common Wall Germander) ... 945
OATS 946
  Black Champion 947
  American Triumph 948
  Russian White 949
  Gruel 950
    " 951
    " (Scotch) 952
  Porridge 953
  Cream of 954
OKRA 955
  Culture 956
  Dwarf Green 957

OKRA—Continued.
Long Green 958
Fall, or Giant 959
Stewed, Plain 960
  " with Tomatoes 961
  "   " Fine Herbs 962
Salad 963
For Garniture 964
For Soup 965
Dry—Its Use 966
Soup, with Chicken 967
ONIONS 968
Preparation of the Soil 969
Culture 970
How to Keep Through Winter 971
Remarks on Small 972
Early Red Globe 973
Extra Early Red 974
Large Red Wetherfield 975
Large Yellow Dutch 976
Yellow Danvers 977
White Portugal, Silver Skin 978
White Silver Skin, for Pickling.. 979
White Globe 980
Large Mexican 981
Early Neopolitan Marzajola 982
Giant Rocca 983
  " White Italian Tripoli 984
New Queen 985
Red, Yellow or White Bottom Sets 986
English Multiplier 987
Potato 988
Boiled, Plain 989
  " with Butter or Cream Sauce 990
Fried 991
Smothered 992
Glazed 993
Stuffed 994
  " American Style 995
Puree (Brown Soubise) 996
  " (White ") 997
Sauce, Brown 998
  " White 999
  " Brown Piquant 1000
For Garniture 1001
Small, Baked for Garniture, Spanish Style 1002
Gravy 1003
  " with Sage 1004
Juice 1005
Chopped for Fine Herbs, etc 1006
Green, for Relish 1007
Peelings, their Use 1008
Soup 1009
  " Stanislaus Style 1010

GENERAL INDEX.

ONIONS—Continued.
  Soup with Milk.................1011
    " Puree, Bavarian Style.......1012
    " " Bretonne " 1013
  Custard for Garniture of Soups...1014
  Soup, Garbure....................1015
  Pickled..........................1016
  " 1017
  Vinegar..........................1018

ORACH, OR MOUNTAIN SPINACH 1019
  Green............................1020
  Lurid 1021
  Purple 1022
  Red..............................1023
  Red Stalked Green................1024
  " " White........................1025
  White............................1026

ORRIS, OR IRIS ROOT...........1027

OXALIS, OR TUBEROUS ROOTED WOOD SORREL........1028
  Culture..........................1029

PAK-CHOI......................1030

PALMATE-LEAVED RHUBARB.1031

PALM CABBAGE.................1032

PANADE OF RICE FLOUR, for Forced Meats..................1321

PARSLEY......................1033
  Culture..........................1034
  Fine Tripled Curled..............1035
  Carter's Fern Leaved.............1036
  Plain 1037
  Hamburg or Turnip Rooted.........1038
  Faggot of........................1039
  Chopped..........................1040
  Fried for Garnishing.............1041
  For Garnishing 1042

PARSNIPS.....................1043
  Culture..........................1044
  Long Smooth Yellow.............. 1045
  " White Dutch....................1046
  The Student.....................1047
  Short Round French...............1048
  With Butter Sauce................1049
  Fried............................1050
  Mashed...........................1051
  Fritters.........................1052

PATES........................
  Truffles, Bennett Style..........1612
  Vegetables, Small, American Style.1679
  " " French Style...1678

PATIENCE.....................1053

PEA-NUT......................1054
  Culture..........................1055
  African..........................1056
  Wilmington.......................1057
  Tennessee 1058

PEAS.........................1059
  Culture..........................1060
  American Wonder..................1061
  Kentish Invicta..................1062
  Laxton's Alpha...................1063
  Early Tom Thumb..................1064
  Blue Peter.......................1065
  Extra Early......................1066
  Little Gem.......................1067
  Premium Green....................1068
  McLean Advancer..................1069
  Carter's Little Wonder...........1070
  Early Philadelphia...............1071
  Dwarf Champion...................1072
  Champion of England..............1073
  Large Blue Imperial..............1074
  " White Marrowfat................1075
  Dwarf Marrowfat..................1076
  Large Black-eyed Marrowfat.......1077
  Yorkshire Hero...................1078
  Dwarf Gray Sugar.................1079
  Tall Sugar.......................1080
  Field Sorts......................1081
  English Style....................1082
  Parisian Style...................1083
  Family Style.....................1084
  With Cream, Sharon Style.........1085
  With Bacon.......................1086
  For Garniture....................1087
  Puree for Garniture..............1088
  Soup Puree.......................1089
  " " St. Germain 1090
  " " of Split Peas................1091
  " " " " with Julienne, Conde.....1092
  " " " Dried Green Peas, German Style....1093
  Preserved Green..................1094

PENNYROYAL...................1095

PEPPER 1096
  Culture 1097
  Chili............................1098
  Long Red Cayenne.................1099
  Large Squash.....................1100
  Golden Dawn......................1101
  Large Bell.......................1102
  Sweet Mountain 1103
  Cranberry........................1104
  Grossum..........................1105

	NO.
PEPPER—Continued.	
Cherry or Little Gem	1106
Chili Peppers preserved in Vinegar	1107
Chili Pepper Vinegar	1108
Vinegar	1109
Preserved Pickled Bell Peppers	1110
Preserved Stuffed Pickled Bell Peppers	1111
Pickled Stuffed Bell Peppers, Sharon Style	1112
How to make Red Pepper	1113
How to make White Pepper	1120
Broiled Bell Peppers	1114
Stuffed Bell Peppers, American Style	1115
Stuffed Bell Peppers, French style	1116
Stuffed Bell Peppers, Brazilian Style	1117
Green Peppers, for Garniture	1118
For Relishes	1119
PEPPERMINT	1121
PICKLED	
Artichokes	51
Artichokes, how to Cook	52
Beets	229
Beets for Relish, German Style	230
Cabbage	324
Cabbage, Red, English Style	322
Capers	311
Carrots	401
Cauliflower	432
Celeriac	446
Cucumbers	462
Cucumbers, Mixed Pickles	643
Melons (Mangoes)	921
Nasturtium Seed Buds	941
Onions	1016
"	1017
Peppers, Bell, Sharon Style	1112
PICKLES	1123
Mixed	1124
Chow-Chow	1125
PICRIDIUM	1126
PI-TSAI	1122
POKE, OR PIGEON BERRY	1127
Stalks, with Butter Sauce	1128
POPPY	1129
Culture	1130
PORRIDGE, Oat Meal	953
PORTUGAL CABBAGE	1131
POTATOES	1132
Culture	1133
Early Mayflower	1134

	NO.
POTATOES—Continued.	
Wall's Orange	1135
Jumbo	1136
Champion of America	1137
Rochester Favorite	1138
Saint Patrick	1139
Beauty of Hebron	1140
Early Rose	1141
White Rose	1142
Late Rose	1143
Peerless	1144
Snowflake	1145
Early Telephone	1146
Vermont Champion	1147
Peach Blow	1148
Mammoth Pearl	1149
Early Gem	1150
Carter	1151
Buckeye	1152
California Red	1153
Boiled	1154
" Peeled	1155
" New	1156
" German Style	1157
Steamed	1158
Stewed, American Style	1159
" Maitre d'Hotel	1160
" Epicurean Style	1161
Baked Stewed, with Cream, Chadwick Style	1162
Stewed, Bretonne Style	1163
" Hanoverian Style	1164
" with Mustard Sauce	1165
" " Bacon	1166
Hashed, " Cream	1167
Hashed, Browned	1168
Baked Hashed with Cream	1169
" with Salt Herrings, Berlin Style	1170
Baked, Carlsruhe Style	1171
Baked, with Anchovies	1172
Boiled, Italian Style	1173
Tossed in Butter (Sauté)	1174
Lyonnaise	1175
Tossed, Italian Style (Sauté)	1176
Sauté, Hollandaise	1177
Broiled	1178
Baked	1179
Baked, New	1180
Mashed	1181
Baked Mashed	1182
Baked Mashed with Spinach, Frankfort Style	1183
Baked Mashed with Ham, Buckeye Style	1184

GENERAL INDEX.   423

POTATOES—Continued.	NO.
Croquettes	1185
Duchesse	1186
Stuffed, Surprise	1187
Balls, American Style	1188
Balls, Margot Style	1189
Couvent or Pelerine Style	1190
Dauphine	1191
Fried, Saratoga Chips	1192
" Long Branch Style	1193
" French Style	1194
" Julienne Style	1195
" Parisian Style	1196
Brabant Style	1197
Chateaubriand	1198
Soufflé (Puffed)	1199
Puree, Jackson Style	1200
Cake	1201
For Garniture	1202
Flour (Fécule)	1203
Balls for Soups (Quenelles)	1204
Soup-Puree, with Cream, Parmentier	1205
Soup Puree, Jackson Style	1206
For Borders	1207
Crusts	1208
Salad	1209
" with Anchovies or Herrings	1210
" with Truffles	1211
" Bennett Style	1212
" with Aspic Jelly, Chartreusse	1213
PRESERVED	
Artichokes, Whole	53
" in Quarters	54
Artichoke Bottoms, in Cans	55
Artichoke Puree	56
Asparagus in Salt	93
" in Cans	94
" Tops	95
Beans, String in Salt	157
" " in Brine	158
" " in Cans	159
" Flageolet, in Cans	172
Cardoons	371
Cardoon Puree	372
Carrots for Garniture	402
" Puree, for Garniture and Soups	403
Cauliflower in Brine	433
Celeriac	445
" in Brine	447
Celery	477
" in Brine	478
" Puree	476
Endives in Cans	708

PRESERVED—Continued.	NO.
Lettuce, Whole	827
" in Cans	828
Melons in Cans	348
" in Syrup	349
" Spiced	922
" " in Syrup	923
Mushrooms in Cans	904
" in Jars	905
Mushroom Trimmings, for Fine Herbs	906
Mushrooms (Cepes)	907
Peas	1094
Peppers, Chili	1107
" Bell	1111
Sorrel	1433
Tomatoes	1594
Tomato Sauce	1595
Tomatoes, Whole, in Sauce	1596
Tomato Figs	1597
PUDDING OF SWEET POTATOES	1515
PUMPKIN	1214
Culture	1215
Large Yellow	1216
Cushaw	1217
Sweet Sugar	1218
Nantucket	1219
Diet Drink (Tisane)	1220
Baked, Vermont Style	1221
Mashed	1222
Soup—Cream of	1223
PUREE	
Artichoke	47
" Preserved	56
Asparagus	84
Beans, New	170
" Green Flageolet	171
" Dry White—White	183
" " —Brown	184
" " with Celery	185
Brussels Sprouts	260
Cardoons	369
Carrots	395
" Preserved, for Garnitures and Soups	403
Cauliflower	438
Celeriac	439
Celery	470
Chestnuts	491
Cucumbers	632
Egg Plant	683
Endive	703
Garlic	732

PUREE—Continued.

	NO.
Lentil, Conde	796
Mushrooms	881
Onions, Brown Soubise	996
" White "	997
Peas, Green	1088
Potatoes, Jackson Style	1200
Sea Kale	1401
Sorrel	1428
" with Sauce	1429
Tomato	1584
Truffles	1609
Turnip, with Cream	1639
" " French Style	1640

PURSLAIN 1224
Common	1225

RADISH 1226
Culture	1227
Spring and Summer	1228
Oblong Brown	1229
Olive Shaped Scarlet	1230
Scarlet Turnip-rooted	1231
Long Scarlet	1232
Long White	1233
Long White, purple top	1234
Small Yellow Turnip-rooted	1235
White Crooked	1236
Yellow Turn p-rooted	1237
Long Salmon	1238
Long Purple	1239
Early Black	1240
" Long Purple	1241
" Scarlet Turnip-rooted	1242
" White Turnip-rooted	1243
Gray Olive-shaped	1244
Gray Turnip-rooted	1245
Autumn and Winter	1246
Large Purple Winter	1247
Black Spanish	1248
Long Black Winter	1249
Long-leaved White Chinese	1250
Rose-colored Chinese	1251
Winter Spanish	1252
California Mammoth White Winter	1253
Red for Relishes	1254
Black for Relishes	1255
For Garnitures	1256
The Oil	1257

RAMPION 1258
Culture	1259

RAMPION, or German or Evening
Primrose	1260
Salad	1261

RAPE 1262
Culture	1263
Annual Rough-leaved Summer	1264
Common or Winter	1265
German	1266
Summer	1267

RED CABBAGE 1268

REPERE 726

RHUBARB 1269
Culture	1270
Downing's Colossal	1271
Elfort	1272
Hawk's Champagne	1273
Wyatt's Linneous	1274
Wyatt's Victoria	1275
Cahoon	1276
Wine	1277
Water	1278
Stewed	1279

RICE 1280
Boiled Plain	1281
Boiled	1282
Steamed	1283
Boiled with Broth	1284
Borders	1285
For Purees or Bisque Soups	1286
Family Style	1287
With Curry	1288
Creole Style	1289
Mexican Style	1290
Milanaise Style	1291
Spanish Style	1292
With Cabbage, Ristori Style	1293
Parisian Style	1294
With Curcuma or Turmeric	1295
Valencienne Style	1296
Turkish Style	1297
Risotti—Florentine Style	1298
Risotti—Piemontaise Style	1299
For Garniture	1300
Custard for Soup Garniture, Langtry Style	1301
For Consomme	1302
Soup	1303
" Indian Style	1304
" with Milk	1305
" " Almond Milk	1306
" Italian Style	1307
" Cream, Rachel Style	1308
" " Langtry Style	1309
" " of Rice Flour, Astor Style	1310
Water	1311
Gruel	1312

GENERAL INDEX.

	NO.
RICE—Continued.	
Crusts	1313
" Victoria Style	1314
" With Eggs and Cheese	1315
" " Curried Lobster	1316
" " Puree of Chicken	1317
Casseroles	1318
How to Cook Rice for Casseroles	1319
Timbals	1320
Panade of Rice Flour for Forced Meats	1321
Croquettes, Creole Style	1322
Fritters (Subrics)	1323
Croquettes	1324
Fritters (Sweet)	1325
Cake (Souffle)	1326
" Glazed	1327
For Compotes of Fruit	1328
With Milk for Invalids	1329
Crusts or Stands for Hot or Cold Side Dishes	1330
How to Cook it for Crusts or Stands	1331
RISOTTI	
Florentine Style	1298
Piemontaise Style	1299
ROCAMBOLE	1332
Culture	1333
ROCKET	1334
Culture	1335
ROSEMARY	1336
Culture	1337
Gold Striped	1338
Silver Striped	1339
Narrow Leaved	1340
Common or Green Leaved	1341
RYE	1342
Broad Leaved	1343
Narrow Leaved	1344
RUTA-BAGA, Russian or Swedish Turnip	1345
American Purple Top	1346
Skirving's Purple Top	1347
Shamrock	1348
Large White French	1349
RYE	1350
Culture	1351
SAFFRON	1352
Yellow Coloring for Culinary Purposes	1353
SAGE	1354
Culture	1355
Broad Leaved Green	1356
Common or Red Leaved	1357

	NO.
SAGE—Continued.	
Green Leaved	1358
Narrow Leaved Green	1359
Dried	1360
SAGO	1361
For Invalids	1362
Gruel	1363
For Soups	1364
Soup with Cream	1365
SALAD	
Asparagus, Plain	86
" with Shrimps	87
" " Truffles, Royal	88
Beans, String	161
" German Style	162
" Dry White, with Aspic Jelly, German Style	1713
" Dry White	181
Cabbage	314
" Boston Style	315
" with Cream, American Style	316
" Red	317
" " German Style	318
Cardoons, Spanish Style	370
Cauliflower	429
Celery	472
Corn-Salad	539
" " with Beets	540
" " " Celery	541
Dandelion	650
Diplomatic	1702
Egg Plant	689
Endive, French Style	704
" German Style	705
" American Style	706
Lettuce	824
Okra	963
Potato	1209
" with Anchovies and Herrings	1210
" " Truffles	1211
" Bennett Style	1212
" with Aspic Jelly, Chartreuse	1213
Salsify	1377
Tomato, Plain	1566
" with Cucumbers	1567
" Spanish Style	1568
" German Style	1569
" Hesketh Style	1570
Truffle, with Artichokes, Luning Style	1610
" " Potatoes, Russian Style	1611

GENERAL INDEX.

SALAD—Continued.   NO.
  Vegetable 1698
    " California Style. 1707
    " Swedish Style 1708
    " Compound. 1699
    " American Style 1700
    " Macedoine 1701
    " Italian Style 1703
    " Parisian Style 1704
    " Russian Style 1705
    " Sauerkraut, German Style 1706
    " with Aspic Jelly, Macedoine. 1710
    " " " " Jardiniere. 1711
    " " " " Italian Style. 1712
SALAD GARNITURES 1366
SALSIFY OR OYSTER PLANT .. 1367
  Culture 1368
  How to Prepare it for Cooking 1369
  With Butter Sauce 1370
  " Cream Sauce.. 1371
  French Style. 1372
  With Brown Sauce, Spanish Style.. 1373
  Fried in Batter..... 1374
  " Villeroi 1375
  " in Butter 1376
  Salad 1377
SALEP 1378
  Soup for Invalids 1379
SALT 1380
SALTPETER 1381
SAMPHIRE, OR SEA FENNEL .. 1382
  Golden 1383
  Culture 1384
SAUCE, Caper 352
  Celery 406
  Cranberry 605
  Fine Herbs 745
  Horseradish 758
  Horseradish with Apples 759
  Horseradish with Cream 760
  Mint, American Style 856
  Mint, French Style 857
  Mustard for Deviled Meats 935
  Onion, Brown 998
  Onion, White 999
  Onion, Piquant 1000
  Soya 895
  Spiced 1443
  Tomato, Plain 1582
  Tomato 1583
  Tomato, Preserved 1595

SAUERKRAUT. 326
  How to Make it 327
  How to Prepare for Cooking 328
  German Style 329
  French Style 330
  Bavarian Style 331
  Flemish Style 332
  Baked, Dufour 333
  Baked, with Fillet of Soles 334
  Baked, with Partridges or Quails.. 335
  Salad, German Style 1706
  Timbal, German Style 1677
SAVORY. 1385
  Culture 1386
  Summer 1387
  Winter 1388
  Use of 1389
SAVOY CABBAGE 1390
SCORZONARA, or Black Salsify ... 1391
  Culture 1392
SCURVY GRASS 1393
SEA BEET 1394
  Culture 1395
SEA KALE 1396
  Culture 1397
  With Butter Sauce 1398
  Hollandaise Style 1399
  With Brown Sauce 1400
  Puree 1401
SEMOULE 1402
  Consomme with 1403
  Crusts of, Palermitaine 1404
  Balls (Quenelles) Villeroi 1405
SHALLOTS, OR ESCHALOTS 1406
  Culture 1407
  Common Small 1408
  Jersey 1409
  Long-keeping 1410
  Essence 1411
SHEPHERD'S PURSE 1412
  Culture 1413
SIEVA OR SMALL LIMA BEAN . 1414
  Mottled 1415
SKIRRET 1416
SNAKE OR SERPENT CUCUMBER 1417
  Culture 1418
SORREL 1419
  Culture 1420
  Belle Ville 1421
  Blistered Leaf 1422
  Fervent's Large 1423

GENERAL INDEX.

	NO.
SORREL—Continued.	
Sarscelle Blunt	1424
French or Round-leaved	1425
With Cream	1426
With Gravy	1427
Puree for Garnitures	1428
Puree with Sauce for Garniture	1429
Soup	1430
" for Fast Days	1431
" with Cream	1432
Preserved	1433
SOUP	
Cabbage	322
Cabbage, Garbure	323
Celeriac	444
Corn Chowder	580
Chestnut Garbure	490
Gumbo	867
Lettuce	825
Okra, with Chicken	867
Onion	1009
" Stanislaus Style	1010
" with Milk	1011
" Garbure	1015
Rice	1303
" Indian Style	1304
" with Milk	1305
" with Almond Milk	1306
" Italian Style	1307
Sago with Cream	1365
Salep for Invalids	1379
Semoule	1403
Sorrel	1430
" for Fast Days	1431
" with Cream	1432
Tapioca	1520
SOUP—PUREE	
Artichoke	49
Asparagus, Conde	80
" Royal	90
" St. George	91
Bean, Green Flageolet, St. Germain	196
Bean, Green Flageolet, Soubise	197
" Fresh White, Newton Style	198
" Black, Faubonne	199
" Dry White, Pioneer	201
" " St. George	202
" " Conde	203
" For Fast Days	204
Carrots, Aurore	396
" Stanley	397
" German Style	398
" Crecy	399
" " for Fast Days	400

	NO.
SOUP—PUREE—Continued.	
Cauliflower	431
Celery, Spanish Style	474
Chestnut	478
Jerusalem Artichoke, Palestine	64
Leek, Viennoise	787
Lentil, Conde	798
" Hunter's Style	799
Onion, Bavarian Style	1012
" Bretonne Style	1013
Peas, Green	1080
" " St. Germain	1090
" Split	1091
" " with Julienne, Conde	1092
" Dried Green, German Style	1093
Potato, with Cream, Parmentier	1205
" Jackson Style	1206
Tomato, American Style	1585
" French "	1586
" with Rice	1587
" Florida	1588
Turnip with Cream	1649
" " Farina	1650
SOUP—CREAM	
Artichoke	50
Asparagus, Countess	92
Barley, Nelson Style	105
" Marie Louise Style	106
" Farragut Style	107
Bean, Green Flageolet, Leland Style	200
Broccoli	248
Cauliflower	430
Celery	475
Chestnut, Hunter's Style	489
Corn	579
Cucumber, Queen Style	633
Endive, with Poached Eggs	707
Pumpkin	1223
Rice, Rachel Style	1308
" Langtry Style	1309
" with Flour, Astor Style	1310
Wheat, Green Farina	1742
SOUTHERNWOOD, OR BALM-MINT	1434
SPANISH OYSTER PLANT	1435
Culture	1436
SPEAR-MINT	1437
SPICES	1438
For Salted Beef	1439
Salt for Stuffings	1440
Infusion for Turtle Soup	1441
Mixed	1442
Sauce	1443
Herbs and Flavors	1444

GENERAL INDEX.

	NO.
SPINACH, OR SPINNAGE	1445
Culture	1446
Flanders	1447
Lettuce-leaved	1448
Sorrel-leaved	1449
Summer round-leaved	1450
Winter Common Prickly	1451
How to Prepare for Boiling	1452
English Style	1453
American Style	1454
With Gravy, French Style	1455
" Milk, American Style	1456
" Cream Sauce	1457
Piemontaise	1458
For Garniture	1459
Fritters (Subrics)	1460
Green Color	1461
Cream of	1462
SQUASH	1463
Culture	1464
Apple	1465
Crooked Neck Summer Bush	1466
Early Yellow Scalloped Bush	1467
Egg	1468
Green Striped Bergen	1469
Large Warted Crooked Neck Summer	1470
Orange	1471
Autumnal Marrow	1472
Bush or Dwarf Vegetable Marrow	1473
Canada Crooked Neck	1474
Cashaw	1475
Cocoa-nut	1476
Custard	1477
Egg-shaped	1478
Honolulu	1479
Hubbard	1480
Mammoth	1481
Turban	1482
Vegetable Marrow	1483
Wilder	1484
Winter Crooked Neck	1485
Winter Striped Crooked Neck	1486
Yokohama	1487
Mashed	1488
Stuffed, Roman Style	1489
" Stanford Style	1490
Fried Stuffed, American Style	1491
" Boston Style	1492
Spanish Style	1493
Scolloped, Astor Style	1494
STRAWBERRY TOMATO, or Alkekengi	1495
Purple	1496
Scarlet	1497

	NO.
STUFFED	
Artichokes, Bordelaise	32
" American Style	32
Artichoke Bottoms, Clara Louise Kellogg Style	36
" " Pioneer Style	37
" " Italian Style	38
Cabbage	306
" Hunter's Style	307
Egg Plant, American Style	684
" " Brazilian Style	685
" " Turkish Style	686
" " Parisian Style	687
Lettuce	819
" Fried	820
Morels	865
Mushrooms, with Fine Herbs	887
" Italian Style	888
Onions	994
" American Style	995
Peppers, Bell, American Style	1115
" " French Style	1116
" " Brazilian Style	1117
" " Pickled	1111
" " " Sharon Style	1112
Potatoes, Surprise	1187
Squash, Roman Style	1489
" Stanford Style	1490
" Fried, American Style	1491
Tomatoes, Provincial Style	1575
" Mackay Style	1576
" Turkish Style	1577
" American Style	1578
" Cardinal Style	1579
Truffles	1613
Turnip Cabbage	1656
SUCCOTASH	573
SWEET POTATOES	1498
Culture	1499
Nansemond	1500
Large White	1501
Kentucky Early Red	1502
Purple Skinned	1503
American Red	1504
Rose Colored	1505
Yellow Skinned, or Yellow Carolina	1506
Baked	1507
Boiled	1508
Fried	1509
" Puffed (Soufflé)	1510
Fritters	1511
Cream of, for Pies	1512
Carolina Cake, with Sabayon Sauce	1513
Carolina Fritters, Nellie Grant Style	1514

SWEET POTATOES—Continued.

	NO.
Pudding	1515
Spanish Style	1516

SWISS CHARD, or Sea Kale Beet ...1517

SYRUP
Angelica	7
Asparagus	96
Capillary	354

TANSY ...1518

TAPIOCA OR MANIOCA ...1519
Soup with Broth or Consomme	1520

TARRAGON ...1521
Culture	1522
Vinegar, plain	1523
" French Style	1524

TARTLETS
Mushrooms with Cream	901
Corn Meal	714

TEA ...1525
To Make Tea	1526
Russian Style	1527
Iced	1528
After Dinner	1529
For Invalids	1530
Custard, in Cups	1531

THYME ...1532
Culture	1533
Broad-leaved	1534
Narrow-leaved	1535
Lemon	1536

TIMBALS
Egg Plant, Mackay Style	1070
Rice	1320
Sauerkraut, German Style	1677
Vegetable Balls, Milanaise Style	1673

TOMATO ...1537
Culture	1538
The Cardinal	1539
Livingston Favorite	1540
Mayflower	1541
Perfection	1542
Acme	1543
Paragon	1544
The Trophy	1545
Champion Cluster	1546
Apple-shaped	1547
The Conqueror	1548
Bermuda	1549
Feojée	1550
Arlington	1551
General Grant	1552
Fig or Red Pear	1553
Yellow Plum	1554

TOMATO—Continued.

	NO.
Red Cherry	1555
Strawberry or Winter Cherry	1556
Green Gage	1557
Yellow Cherry	1558
Yellow Pear	1559
Queen	1560
Canada Victor	1561
Hathaway's Excelsior	1562
Golden Trophy	1563
Island Beauty	1564
For Relish	1565
Salad, plain	1566
" with Cucumbers	1567
" Spanish Style	1568
" German "	1569
" Hesketh "	1570
Fried	1571
Stewed	1572
Baked Stewed	1573
How to Prepare them for Stuffing	1574
Stuffed, Provincial Style	1575
" Mackay "	1576
" Turkish "	1577
" American "	1578
" Cardinal "	1579
Baked	1580
For Garniture	1581
Plain, Sauce	1582
Sauce	1583
Puree	1584
Soup-Puree, American Style	1585
" " French "	1586
Soup, with Rice	1587
" Florida Style	1588
Catsup	1589
"	1590
"	1591
" Epicurean Style	1592
Yum-Yum	1593
Preserved	1594
" Sauce	1595
" Whole in Sauce	1596
Figs, Preserved	1597

TONKA BEAN ...1598

TRUFFLES ...1599
Whole, with Champagne Sauce	1600
Italian Style	1601
Piemontaise Style	1602
Baked, with Cream Sauce	1603
" in Shells	1604
With Maderia Wine Sauce	1605
Essence of	1606
For Garniture	1607
For Cold Garnitures	1608

	NO.
TRUFFLES—Continued.	
Puree, for Garnitures	1609
Salad, with Artichokes, Luning Style	1610
Salad, with Potatoes, Russian Style	1611
Small Patés, Bennett Style	1612
Stuffed	1613
TUBEROUS - ROOTED CHICKLING WETCH, OR PEA	1614
TURMERIC, OR CURCUMA	1615
TURNIP	1616
Culture	1617
Early Purple Top Munich	1618
White Egg	1619
Early White Stone	1620
Jersey	1621
Early White Dutch	1622
Early White Flat Dutch	1623
Early Purple Top	1624
Cowhorn or Long White	1625
Purple Top Mammoth	1626
Large White Flat Norfolk	1627
Pomeranean White Globe	1628
Purple Top White Globe	1629
Sweet German	1630
Seven Top	1631
Early Yellow Montagny	1632
Large Amber Globe	1633
Orange Jelly or Golden Ball	1634
Purple Top Yellow Aberdeen	1635
Early Yellow Finland	1636
Early Yellow Malta	1637
Mashed	1638
Puree with Cream	1639
Puree with Cream, French Style	1640
Glazed (brown) for Garniture	1641
Glazed (white) for Garniture	1642
Stewed, Spanish Style	1643
Stewed with Onions	1644
Stewed, Convent Style	1645
Boiled Plain	1646
Boiled with White Sauce	1647
Soup—Puree	1648
" " with Cream	1649
" " " Farina	1650
Pectoral Broth with Turnips	1651
TURNIP CABBAGE or Kohl-rabi	1652
Culture	1653
Early white Vienna	1654
Early Purple Vienna	1655
Stuffed	1656
With Cream Sauce	1657
" Butter Sauce	1658
German Style	1659
Smothered and Glazed	1660
For Garnitures	1661

	NO.
TURNIP-ROOTED CHERVIL	1662
Culture	1663
UNICORN ROOT	1664
Culture	1665
VALERIAN	1666
Culture	1667
VANILLA	1668
Flavor	1669
Beans	1670
VEGETABLES	1671
Balls, Turkish Style	1672
Timbal of Balls, Milanaise Style	1673
Borders	1674
Chartreusse	1675
Timbals of Egg Plant, Mackay Style	1676
Timbal of Sauerkraut, German Style	1677
Small Patés, French Style	1678
" " American Style	1679
" Crusts, Macedoine Style	1680
Bread	1681
Macedoine, Spanish Style	1682
" Mexican Style	1683
" German Style	1684
" American Style	1685
Large Macedoine Garniture	1686
Cold Macedoine Garniture	1687
Small " "	1688
Large Garniture, Peasant Style	1689
" " Farmer Style	1690
" " Jardiniere	1691
Small " "	1692
Cold " "	1693
Cold " Floral Style	1694
Large Garniture, Provincial Style	1695
Essence of	1696
Frying Batter for	1697
Salads	1698
Compound Salads	1699
Salad, American Style	1700
Macedoine Salad	1701
Diplomatic Salad	1702
Salad, Italian Style	1703
" Parisian Style	1704
" Russian Style	1705
Sauerkraut Salad, German Style	1706
Salad, California Style	1707
Mixed Salad, Swedish Style	1708
How to Prepare Moulds with Aspic Jelly for Salads	1709
Salad with Aspic Jelly, Macedoine	1710
" " " " Jardiniere	1711
" " " " Italian Style	1712
Bean Salad with Aspic Jelly, German Style	1713
VETCH, OR TARE	1714

	NO.
VINEGAR. Celery	479
Horseradish	762
Onion	1018
Pepper, Chili	1108
Pepper	1109
Tarragon	1523
Tarragon, French Style	1524
WATER	
Barley, for Invalids	109
" for Gargling	111
Lettuce, for Invalids	826
Rhubarb	1278
Rice	1311
WATER-MELON	1715
Culture	1716
Georgia Rattlesnake	1717
Cuban Queen	1718
California, or Improved Odella	1719
Orange	1720
Citron and California Pie Melon	1721
Black Spanish	1722
Scaly Bark	1723
Mountain Sweet	1724
Ice-Cream	1725
Ferry's Peerless	1726
Early Jersey	1727
How to Serve	1728

	NO.
WHEAT	1729
Michigan Bronze or Mediterranean Hybrid	1730
Valley	1731
Martin's Amber	1732
Democrat	1733
Fultz	1734
Clawson	1735
Red Mediterranean	1736
Winter Pearl	1737
Invincible	1738
Adamant	1739
Green Mountain	1740
Broth	1741
Soup — Cream of Green Farina Wheat	1742
WINE	
Rhubarb	1277
WINGED PEA	1743
WITLOEF	1744
WOOD SORREL	1745
Culture	1746
WORMWOOD	1747
Roman	1748
Sea	1749
Culture	1750

www.ingramcontent.com/pod-product-compliance
Lightning Source LLC
Chambersburg PA
CBHW030323020526
44117CB00030B/961